THE CHINA-INDIA RIVALRY IN THE GLOBALIZATION ERA

THE CHINA-INDIA RIVALRY IN THE GLOBALIZATION ERA

T.V. PAUL, EDITOR

Georgetown University Press / Washington, DC

Library of Congress Cataloging-in-Publication Data
Names: Paul, T. V., editor.
Title: The China-India rivalry in the globalization era / T.V. Paul, editor.
Other titles: South Asia in world affairs series.
Description: Washington, DC : Georgetown University Press, 2018. | Series:
    South Asia in world affairs series | Includes bibliographical references and index.
Identifiers: LCCN 2017050521| ISBN 9781626165991 (hardcover : alk. paper) |
    ISBN 9781626166004 (pbk. : alk. paper) | ISBN 9781626166011 (eb)
Subjects: LCSH: China—Foreign relations—India. | India—Foreign relations—China.
Classification: LCC DS740.5.I5 C48415 2018 | DDC 327.51054—dc23
LC record available at https://lccn.loc.gov/2017050521

♾ This book is printed on acid-free paper meeting the requirements of the American National Standard for Permanence in Paper for Printed Library Materials.

19 18   9 8 7 6 5 4 3 2   First printing

Printed in the United States of America

Map 2.1 by Chris Robinson.
Cover design by Jeremy John Parker.
Cover image: Chinese soldiers guard the Nathu La mountain pass, between Tibet and the tiny northeastern Indian state of Sikkim, July 6, 2006. Asian giants India and China opened a Himalayan pass to border trade on Thursday, forty-four years after a brutal frontier war shut down the ancient route. REUTERS/Desmond Boylan (INDIA)

CONTENTS

PART III: STRATEGIES

PART IV: MITIGATORS

PART V: CONCLUSIONS

ILLUSTRATIONS

MAPS

FIGURES

TABLES

ACKNOWLEDGMENTS

This volume grew out of a workshop I organized at McGill University on October 8, 2016, as part of a larger project, Globalization and the National Security State. Subsequently contributors modified their papers, taking into account the comments and feedback by the two reviewers of Georgetown University Press and the discussants at the workshop, Calvin Chen, Paul Diehl, Lorenz Luthi, Sarah-Myriam Martin-Brûlé, Vincent Pouliot, and Mahesh Shankar. Able research assistance was provided by Alice Chesse, Jean-François Bélanger, Zhen Han, and Erik Underwood. I thank Donald Jacobs, senior acquisitions editor at Georgetown University Press, for his strong interest in the volume and the South Asia in World Affairs series. I also appreciate the financial support from the Fonds de recherche du Québec–Société et culture and the James McGill Professors program at McGill University.

The rise of both China and India as major actors in international politics has generated a renewed need to understand the complex relationship between them, in particular the multifaceted sources of their six-decades-long rivalry. I believe this volume captures the nuances of many of these dimensions, including the neglected topic of status competition between the two states and the impact of globalization on keeping this a "managed rivalry."

T.V. Paul
Montreal, September 2017

PART I

INTRODUCTION

Chapter 1

Explaining Conflict and Cooperation in the China-India Rivalry

T.V. PAUL

The rivalry between China and India has entered its sixth decade. Although the territorial disputes began in the 1950s, it has become a deep-rooted, enduring rivalry since the 1962 border war between the two states. Despite several rounds of negotiations on settling the territorial dispute, no end to the rivalry is in sight, while it sees intermittent militarized flare-ups, such as the June–September 2017 Doklam standoff involving Indian and Chinese troops in the trijunction area linking Bhutan, Tibet, and India, a territory contested by China and Bhutan. However, unlike the India-Pakistan rivalry, China-India relations are somewhat positive on the economic front. Since the 1990s, the trade volumes between the two largest economies of Asia have been on a steady increase. In 2000, the trade volume was $2.92 billion, which grew to $70.08 billion in 2016, with a trade deficit of $46.56 billion for India.[1] China is indeed India's leading trading partner, although the reverse is not true, which makes it an asymmetrical economic relationship. At international institutions, India and China seem to agree on issues such as global financial reforms, climate change, and elements of trade rules. However, on global governance, an agreement is missing on United Nations (UN) reforms, especially India's entry as a permanent member of the UN Security Council (UNSC) and its membership in the Nuclear Suppliers Group (NSG).

As China expands its reach in the South China Sea and the Indian Ocean by way of increasing its naval presence, reclaiming and constructing islets, and building ports in countries such as Pakistan and Sri Lanka, India has begun to make countermoves, largely through its joint activities with the United States,

3

such as naval exercises and offering refueling and replenishment of American naval vessels. Indian naval ships visit Southeast Asian waters more frequently while India seeks closer strategic relations with Japan, Australia, and Vietnam. The Japan-India efforts include plans to develop an Asia-Africa Growth Corridor parallel to China's Belt and Road Initiative (BRI), the latter originally called the One Belt One Road (OBOR) project.[2] These efforts show the rivalry assuming a new and larger dimension in the economic and strategic contest between the two Asian giants. India is also developing the port of Chabahar in Iran in an effort to circumvent Pakistan, China's closest ally in South Asia, to obtain greater trade and strategic links with Afghanistan and Central Asian countries. The rivalry has entered a new phase, with China's ambition to become a global power increased since the arrival of Xi Jinping as Chinese leader in 2012 and India's desire under Narendra Modi to be recognized as a rising great power beginning to collide in different spheres. It appears the rivalry is unlikely to end anytime soon as it is becoming a systemic contest surrounding many larger strategic issues and territorial areas that were not previously parts of its domain.

What explains the peculiar contours of this rivalry? Why is it different from the India-Pakistan rivalry in terms of intensity and other behavioral characteristics? What influence does accelerated globalization, especially increased trade and investment, have on this rivalry? What impact does the US-China competition and China's expanding reach into the South China Sea and the Indian Ocean have on this rivalry? Under what conditions will it escalate or end?

I argue that in order to understand the dynamics of this conflict, we need to explore its evolution in diverse issue areas and its differences from India's intense rivalry with Pakistan. Fundamental differences and competition over territorial boundaries, status in Asia and beyond, resources (in particular, water), notions of regional and global order, and strategic culture mark adversarial relations between the two giant states. Regional and global balance-of-power competition, divergent strategies on nuclear and conventional deterrence, and engagement with other states in South Asia and increasingly in the Asia-Pacific region have contributed to the perpetuation of this rivalry in a unique fashion. It is important to know how these diverse issues link together in making this conflict protracted and enduring. No single theory can capture the dynamics of this rivalry fully, and hence more of an eclectic approach is preferred in this project.[3]

In the middle of the divergences, however, several factors mitigate the rivalry and reduce the possibility for an open military conflict in the immediate future. Intensified economic globalization and resultant economic interdependence are crucial factors here. Increasing trade between the two states and their insertion into globalization during the past three decades may have reduced the incentives for war. Chinese and Indian companies and trading groups engage each other, offering avenues of cooperation. The periodic meetings among the top leaders and officials in the context of border talks have reduced opportunities for escalation. Even their agreement as rising powers on many issues of global governance has given them an opportunity to reduce their friction points. The interactions of the two through the Group of Twenty (G-20) forum, the BRICS association (Brazil, Russia, India, China, and South Africa), the ASEAN Regional Forum (ARF), the Shanghai Cooperation Organization (SCO), the Asian Infrastructure Investment Bank (AIIB), and the BRICS New Development Bank (NDB) have opened up avenues for diplomatic engagement and cooperation.

The central claim of this volume is that a limited or managed rivalry persists, but it has remained less intense than the India-Pakistan rivalry due to several mitigating variables, ranging from economic factors to diplomatic ones. Among them is growing asymmetrical economic interdependence between India and China. Globalization has increased economic interactions and has helped to soften friction but has not removed it. The relations seem to be going through periodic ups and downs as the contending issues resurface from time to time. India's willingness to forgo its earlier set condition—that until China settles all the territorial disputes, it will not trade with the country—made a big difference in improving economic relations. The adoption of a "broad position" since the period of Rajiv Gandhi's visit to Beijing in December 1988 showed that "India no longer held other areas of interaction hostage to the settlement of the border issue."[4] Thus the weaker party in this asymmetrical relationship took the initiative to sideline the territorial issue for economic interests, whereas Pakistan, the weaker party in the India-Pakistan rivalry, steadfastly opposes any economic concessions or deep interactions with India until the territorial dispute is resolved. Pakistan has managed to bridge the power asymmetry with India through strategy, weaponry (including nuclear arms), and alliance support of the United States in the past and China since the 1960s.[5] The power asymmetry with China makes India reluctant to take a strong posture on issues of territory, water, and imbalance in trade. China, on the other hand, does not want to push India too hard militarily to compel it to join an active military alliance with the US and other like-minded states. Thus there is no vigorous challenger in this dyad, unlike the India-Pakistan one. This case shows that enduring rivalries do not need to be intense and that they can be made less conflictual through mitigating factors and diplomatic choices that the parties make.

This rivalry has attracted a number of studies. Most treat the territorial dispute as the key source of the conflict.[6] Some recent works have broadened the rivalry's other dimensions, in particular the expansion of the rivalry into the Indian and Pacific Oceans.[7] However, it is important to note that the prolongation of this rivalry is not attributable to territorial dispute alone, as China has settled twelve border disputes with its fourteen bordering states, except India and Bhutan.[8] Even the territorial settlement in this case was talked about in negotiations as feasible, with China accepting India's position in its northeastern state of Arunachal Pradesh in exchange for India conceding Chinese claims in the Ladakh area. Despite these conditions, why is the border dispute with India so difficult to settle? It is probably that other factors identified below interact in such a way that the conflict is too multidimensional and intractable. It needs resolution on multiple fronts, especially at the systemic and subsystemic levels, that is unlikely to occur anytime soon. The number of issues in the rivalry is increasing with the rise of China and its efforts to carve out its geostrategic space in the Pacific and the Indian Ocean with possible military confrontation with the United States and its allies and strategic partners, which now include India. Some of these issues have a long time horizon, encouraging both parties not to make sudden strategic choices that aggravate the conflict. In many senses, the China-India conflict remains a "managed rivalry."[9]

First, I explore each of the factors identified here that generate and perpetuate the conflict, making it an enduring rivalry that is characterized by conflict over unresolved issues, strategic interdependence between the parties, psychological enmity, and repeated militarized conflicts.[10] One study contends that for a rivalry to be called "enduring," at least six militarized disputes should occur over a twenty-year period, and defines it according to "spatial consistence, duration, and militarized competition."[11] This rivalry may not have as many militarized territorial crises as it used to have, but nevertheless the dispute exists, and both sides are making constant efforts to strengthen their military forces and infrastructure on the border. There have been a number of face-to-face standoffs between patrols, and mutual incursions on contested territories have been taking place; it seems their number has increased in recent years with frenzied infrastructure development on both sides.[12] A form of deterrence has worked in preventing the limited mutual incursions from escalating to full-blown war. Several rounds of negotiations have not solved the key differences on the territorial issue. The China-India rivalry is nearly six decades old and hence qualifies as an enduring one. The big question is, if it is not a rivalry, why do both sides increase their military buildup in the border, while stridently clinging to their positions?

I place the factors that perpetuate the India-China rivalry under three clusters: territory and resources, status and conceptions of order, and strategic culture and defense/deterrence strategies.

TERRITORY AND RESOURCES

The key source of lingering divergence appears to be on the nature of the *territorial* demarcations. The differing conceptions of the McMahon Line, which separates the 4,056-kilometer-long border, produced a major flare-up in 1962 and limited skirmishes several times since then. A tenuous peace exists on the border. But the border dispute is yet to become part of the national identity narrative of the two sides as much as in the India-Pakistan case. The territory in contention is sparsely populated, and the colonial-era line that is presumed to separate the two countries is contested. This is different from the manner of the postpartition Kashmir, which both India and Pakistan view as essential to complete their national identities—one built on secularism and the other on Islamic statehood.

There are three sectors where the territory is disputed. In the western sector, India claims but China occupies some thirty-eight thousand square kilometers of territory in the Aksai Chin Plateau of the Ladakh region. In the northeastern sector, China claims ninety-six thousand square kilometers of Indian territory in Arunachal Pradesh (formerly known as the North-East Frontier Agency, or NEFA), which Beijing calls "Southern Tibet." In the middle sector, some two thousand square kilometers of territory near India's state of Uttarakhand is also disputed. India is said to be willing to make concessions on the western sector in return for the Arunachal Pradesh territory, but a key border area called Tawang is what China has refused to concede because of its historic and religious significance for the Tibetan Buddhists. Beyond these claims and counterclaims, the Line of Actual Control (LAC), established following the 1962 war between the two countries, is not properly demarcated, and often military patrols transgress each other's claimed border posts.[13] The territorial claim is intrinsically related to China's efforts to deny the Dalai Lama and his followers any place in Tibet. India has given sanctuary to him and thousands of Tibetan refugees since 1959, which China views as an affront to its sovereignty over Tibet, despite the fact that India recognized Beijing's control over the territory in 1954 and more formally in 2003. In 2017, the territorial dispute got another dimension when India blocked the People's Liberation Army from building a road near the trijunction between India, Bhutan, and Tibet and closer to the strategically significant narrow strip of land called the Siliguri Corridor (or "the Chicken's Neck") that links the Indian states in the northeast with the rest of the country. India used a protectorate agreement with Bhutan and defended Bhutan's right to the contested territory, although its own security was paramount in this decision, which led to a seventy-day crisis, generating fears of a wider war breaking out. What is most interesting is the reluctance on both sides to use any lethal arms even in demonstrative form in the immediate theater.[14]

Along with territory, the control and distribution of resources has become a source of contention over the years. Among the sources of resource conflict, *water* assumes a larger role as the key rivers of India, especially the Brahmaputra and the Indus, originate in the Tibetan Plateau. With China putting up several dams over its side of the twenty-eight-thousand-kilometer Brahmaputra (Yarlung Tsangpo in Chinese), the fear of water diversion has increased in India. The Chinese claim is that the hydroelectric projects are run-of-the-river and so will not affect the water flow, although there are concerns about the adverse ecological impact of the dams and China's water-diversion plans.[15] Still, no water war is in sight, as some have feared.[16] Desecuritization of the water issue is a possibility, although it would require concrete steps, especially by China—such as joining multilateral forums on water-sharing, which Beijing has refused to do.[17] A joint water-sharing mechanism similar to the Nile Basin Initiative or the Mekong River Commission is not in sight. Flood control has been a major issue, although China has supplied some data since an accident in 2000 that flooded riparian regions in India and Bangladesh. China also complains about the Indian hydropower development in Arunachal Pradesh, arguing that the state's economic development will attract large-scale migration and complicate border settlement in the future.[18]

While transborder water-sharing is a source of conflict between India and China, competition for *resources* at the larger international level increasingly characterizes the rivalry. Since India liberalized its economy in the 1990s, the competition has broadened to Africa and Central Asia for hydrocarbons. However, surprisingly, there are also instances of cooperation in the joint exploration of oil and natural gas fields in Burma, Iran, Sudan, Syria, Peru, and Colombia.[19]

STATUS COMPETITION AND CONCEPTIONS OF ORDER

The competition between the two nations appears to be for international and regional status. As two of the world's megacivilizations that suffered under Western colonialism, both nations were viewed at birth in the late 1940s as almost status equals in Asia, but this soon changed after India fell behind China on key measures such as economic growth, social development, and military capability. At the global level, China obtained better recognition by assuming a permanent seat on the UNSC, although following the Chinese Civil War the United States refused to recognize the People's Republic of China as its rightful occupant until 1972. China's joining the anti-Soviet coalition led by the United States in the 1970s improved its status in the West, and its opening of its economy a decade earlier than India gave it a bigger share in global trade and larger appreciation in the international arena. The political systems also diverged, with one a parliamentary democracy and the other an authoritarian system controlled by the Communist Party. Still, accruing greater status, especially among Asian countries, has been a driving factor for this competition from the beginning. Status competition was evident at the 1955 Bandung Conference of Asian and African nations organized by India's first prime minister, Jawaharlal Nehru, Egyptian leader Gamal Abdel Nasser, and Indonesia's ruler, Suharto. Nehru worried that India's leadership would be whittled down by China's deeper engagement with the African and Asian states. Mao Zedong's reference to India as a "lackey of the Western imperialists" and China's efforts to place itself as the champion of developing countries, most evident since the 1962 war, also merit attention in this regard.[20]

India's status competition with China remerged somewhat differently in the post–Cold War era. Although India took a decade more than China to liberalize its economy, its deeper insertion into the global economy allowed India to grow at an average rate of 7 to 8 percent annually for over a decade. The international community began to take India more seriously because of its economic progress, as New Delhi showed further assertiveness vis-à-vis Beijing.[21]

Since 2010, the status competition has widened in the security realm, with India displaying interest in China's Pacific theater and the Chinese navy expanding into India's immediate strategic space, the Indian Ocean. China's maritime strategy is driven by the need for gaining greater status as a global power. Robert Ross has pointed out that status quest and nationalism are the most compelling driving forces behind China's maritime strategy.[22] Yong Deng has argued that China has creatively managed to accrue higher status since the end of the Cold War.[23] Despite these successes, China clearly wants to wash away the "hundred years of insult" (*bainian quru*) it claims to have experienced at the hands of Western powers, and the strategy is also a source of the Communist Party's legitimacy.[24] Even though India's coastline (seventy-five hundred kilometers) is shorter than China's (thirty-two thousand kilometers), the geographical proximity makes India claim dominance in the Indian Ocean.[25] China has been attempting to overcome this constraint through its BRI project, which includes a maritime "Silk Road" and creation of ports in Pakistan and Sri Lanka in particular. The BRI, the product of an ambitious policy initiated by the Xi Jinping regime in October 2013, aims at restoring the old Silk Road and maritime silk routes by creating an interconnected web of roads and ocean links that connect Eurasia. In response, India has signed agreements to develop the aforementioned port of Chabahar in Iran, as well as a road to Afghanistan and on to other parts of Central Asia through the Iranian territory, effectively bypassing Pakistan.[26] The China-Pakistan Economic Corridor (CPEC), the most significant competitive element in this equation, passes through the Gilgit area of Pakistan-controlled Kashmir, which is also claimed by India.

India's nuclear tests in May 1998 and the Chinese opposition to them—plus support for economic sanctions and political isolation by Western countries—had all the elements of a status competition. India's search for a minimal nuclear deterrent was not only driven by China's larger nuclear capability but also by the desire to acquire a status attribute for claiming the role of a major power. Beijing's hostile response to the US-India nuclear accord of 2005 once again showed the intensity of China's opposition, and Beijing remains a steadfast opponent of India's full-scale integration as a de facto nuclear weapon state with privileges such as membership in the NSG. Beijing wants to accord to its close ally Pakistan the same privileges that India is seeking, an indication that it formally treats the two in the same status league in the area of nuclear weapons.

The *balance-of-power* strategy each country has adopted also contributes to the persistence of this rivalry. Balance-of-power competitions, including China-India and Pakistan-India, as well as in the past involving the India-USSR quasi-alliance, and in recent years the India-US and India-Japan limited alignments, have played a role in the rivalry maintenance and the manner in which it is evolving. Today the trilateral nature of balance-of-power competition, previously confined to South Asia, has become quadrilateral and complex, with the United States increasingly entering the picture with its deepening security relationship with India as part of its "pivot to Asia policy." The most recent manifestation of the formation of a limited hard-balancing coalition between Washington and New Delhi is the logistics agreement signed in August 2016 making it possible for the US and India to use each other's selected land, air, and naval facilities for purposes of refueling and replenishment, a major step toward greater military cooperation.[27] Three types of balancing are evident in the China-India relationship: hard balancing relying on internal arms buildup and external formal alignment (as in the China-Pakistan alignment against India), soft balancing through institutions and limited ententes (India, Vietnam, and Japan versus China), and limited hard balancing relying on limited arms buildup and strategic agreements short of formal alliance but higher than simple statements on partnerships (as increasingly evident in the India-US versus China case).[28]

The Indian Ocean is touted as the main area of emerging balance-of-power competition largely involving the United States, India, and China along with the smaller littoral states. However, the balancing activity may be a complicated process as the fragmented threat environment involving many unstable littoral states of the Indian Ocean makes it difficult for any of these states to play an intense balance-of-power game. Regional stability is a common good, and all three benefit from it. Thus far the need for the protection of sea-lanes for oil exports and the common threats of terrorism, piracy, and drug trafficking have made the Indian Ocean a shared zone of limited cooperation.[29] The smaller regional states, although trying to reap maximum benefits from the China-India competition, are constrained in the security arena because if they offer base facilities to one, that may generate intense hostility from the other. But these dynamics may slowly change as the material capabilities and power aspirations of both China and India increase.

In addition to status, India and China have somewhat different *conceptions of regional and global order*, although some commonalities can be found, as argued by Manjari Chatterjee Miller in chapter 4 of this volume. Both have a somewhat hegemonic approach toward their immediate neighborhood. India sees South Asia and the larger Indian Ocean region as its exclusive preserve, while China views the Pacific, including the South China Sea, as its backyard region and sphere of influence. As the power capabilities of the two states have increased, the conceptions of order are also changing, with China entering the Indian Ocean region and India foraying into the Pacific (developing strategic relations with the United States and regional states) and making their naval presences felt.

China's conception of order has been evolving along with the increases in its material capabilities. While some Chinese elites believe that the globalization era has benefited China, others contend that the international order led by the United States benefits Washington disproportionately. The latter worry that displacement of US hegemony may not be easy but that the longer the order persists, the greater the chances of China getting enmeshed in it. There is a domestic dimension to the conception of order, as the Chinese elite value Confucian ideas of social harmony and are driven by elements of communist ideology and their own self-interests, especially preserving their power.[30] An unwitting acceptance of the US hegemony for a prolonged period of time does not bode well for regime security.

Despite remaining "estranged democracies" for much of the Cold War era, India and the United States in recent years have become much closer, and New Delhi's vision of world order does not envision the US abandoning its leadership position or conceding it to China anytime soon. The notion of strategic autonomy still runs deep in India's conception of international order. India often attempts to balance its relations with all powers, including the United States and smaller states in the region, with strategic autonomy a key goal. India also exhibits a softer version of the United States' Monroe Doctrine, with the intention of keeping South Asia as a single strategic unit where outside powers do not interfere.[31] The Indian navy now sees itself as a key maritime security player not only in the Indian Ocean but also in the Pacific.

India's evolving maritime strategy shows the increasing attention paid to China, although it is not explicitly mentioned as a threat. The 2007 maritime military strategy was more focused on peacetime crisis resolution and the maintenance of India's standing in the region. It was criticized for not dealing with the activities of extraregional naval powers, especially in view of the increasing presence of the Chinese navy in the Indian Ocean. Some critics of Chinese strategy believe that the Chinese Silk Road projects will make it necessary for China to acquire surveillance posts and military assets in the Indian Ocean. The increasing visits of Chinese submarines in Sri Lankan, Pakistani, Somali, and Djiboutian ports have been argued as examples of enhanced activism.[32] India's revised naval military strategy of 2014 refers to the blurring of traditional and nontraditional threats and the need for a holistic outlook in order to ensure "freedom to use the seas." Cooperation with other navies, including joint exercises, was discussed as part of the strategy. More important, deterrence against potential adversaries and coercion toward India has also been elevated as a major objective of the naval strategy.[33]

The divergent *diplomatic engagement* the parties have pursued also is a source of conflict, not only between the two at the bilateral level but also in the complex diplomacy with other parties such as the United States and Japan (by India) and Pakistan and regional states (by China). China in particular has adopted a strategy of slowly penetrating South Asian neighbors of India and creating "robust, multidimensional, and essentially unlimited relations with all of India's neighbors."[34] China wants India to take a positive view of this policy, which Indians in general view as a "creeping encirclement." The Chinese tactics include "moving incrementally," making "repeated statements of amity and cooperation with India," "insisting on bilateralism and non-linkage of Sino-Indian relations with other regional states," "using U.S. presence as an umbrella for the growth of Chinese influence," and "maintaining a balance of power vis-à-vis India which fixes in Indian minds the possible high costs of India's anti-China actions."[35] Intensified globalization has made India realize that there are limits to its resisting China's economic inroads into South Asia, partly because India alone cannot fulfill the economic needs of smaller regional states that crave for Chinese investment.

STRATEGIC CULTURE AND DEFENSE/DETERRENCE STRATEGIES

Another key area of divergence appears to be on the *strategic cultures* of the two countries. Iain Johnston offers a definition of strategic culture as "ranked grand strategic preferences derived from central paradigmatic assumptions about the nature of conflict and the enemy, and collectively shared by decision makers."[36] The Chinese strategic culture, deriving its roots from the works of Sun Tzu, Confucius, Mao, and in recent years Deng Xiaoping, seems different from India's, which has some Kautilyan roots but in the modern day has been influenced by conceptions of Mahatma Gandhi, Nehru, and to some extent the Bharatiya Janata Party and its muscular-religious approaches. Strategic culture concerns the extent that the "historically and culturally rooted notions about the ends and means of war" impact the foreign policy behavior of states.[37] The notion of concentric circles in which China acts as the "Middle Kingdom," with vassal states paying tribute constituting the next level and barbarians the next, has been one of the central themes of Chinese historical strategic culture identified by scholars. This to some resembles the Mandala Theory in Kautilya's *Arthashastra*.[38] Despite this apparent similarity, Indian empires in most historical eras had shown little interest in expansion beyond the immediate region, while Chinese empires had used force to achieve pacification and settlement in various peripheral areas. The southern Indian Chola Empire's naval offensives in Southeast Asia in AD 1025 is an exception, although much of the Indian influence in the region occurred through the somewhat peaceful spread of Hinduism, Buddhism, and later Islam. It is argued that postrevolutionary China has shown a proclivity toward hard borders while India has been somewhat satisfied with soft borders, although this has changed since the 1960s.[39] More specifically, though, India, not known to have deep thinking on strategy as opposed to China, developed a passive approach toward strategy due to cultural factors.[40] Indian strategy has also been influenced in the early years by Gandhian and Nehruvian ideas of nonviolent resistance and an aversion to using force or acquiring high levels of military power, unlike Mao's revolutionary China, which showed no qualms about using force to achieve its strategic objectives. These attitudes changed in India following the military debacle with China in 1962 and the ongoing conflict with Pakistan, which saw four wars by 1999 and several crises before and after that period. The nuclear tests in 1998 showed a changing perception of the efficacy of nuclear deterrence. However, the perception of passive India in a strategic-cultural sense still persists. An example of how others perceive the passive-versus-somewhat-aggressive strategic cultures of the two countries is the absence of fear among Southeast Asian states of India's growing military power versus their concerns about China's increasing naval capabilities in the region.

The trilateral alignment is mirrored by the *defense and deterrence strategies* of China and India and the role Pakistan plays in them. The increasing nuclear and conventional arms race between the parties brings another element of challenge to the complex relationship. China has a limited deterrent mostly directed toward the United States, with some deterrent elements toward India, Taiwan, and Japan, although none of the three is likely to engage in a first strike on China. Its more than four hundred warheads may be increasing along with a buildup of its DF intercontinental ballistic missiles (ICBMs), previously believed to number twenty-four. China is developing road-mobile DF-41 ICBMs and the third-generation Type 096 (*Tang* class) submarine, meant to increase deterrence power (in Chinese parlance, "strategic reassurance" and "mutual strategic restraint") vis-à-vis the United States, especially in view of Washington's deployment of its Terminal High Altitude Area Defense system in East Asia, largely in response to North Korean nuclear and missile developments.[41] In the Indian context, the 250-plus nuclear weapons China possesses, especially its solid-fueled intermediate-range ballistic missiles, give it an edge over India, with an ability to reach all major Indian cities, while India's Agni missiles (I–III series) can reach only the southern cities of China. With the deployment of the Agni-IV (with a range of three thousand to four thousand kilometers) and Agni-V (five thousand to eight thousand kilometers) missiles by India in the future, its deterrent capacity will increase, although much of it is still in the developmental stage.[42]

Chinese scholars have argued that due to the capability discrepancy and the focus on Pakistan, India's nuclear forces do not pose a substantial threat to China but that this would change if India makes operational alignments with the United States or other allies in East Asia.[43] India, on the other hand, perceives China's nuclear weapons as a major threat and has been making steady improvements in deploying a minimum force, although the ability to reach major Chinese cities with large numbers of missiles or aircraft may be some years away. Meanwhile, China, through the surrogacy of Pakistan, has been able to dissipate Indian nuclear and conventional-threat capabilities by dividing them between the two theaters.

India's defense posture has been reactive: As China has made much improvement in its border infrastructure, India only recently started its buildup and infrastructure improvements. India's conventional defense/deterrent capability vis-à-vis China includes seven divisions consisting largely of mountain strike and armored brigade categories. In addition, India is raising four new divisions (totaling eighty thousand soldiers); has two mountain strike corps, five hundred T-90 tanks, 180 BMP-2 infantry combat vehicles, and two squadrons of Su-30MKI fighters; is upgrading its air force bases; and is deploying its Akash antiaircraft missile system. India's Achilles' heel is the poor road and rail network in the northeastern states, especially near the China border. China's massive improvements in border infrastructure in Tibet give it a major advantage in a possible large-scale military confrontation.[44] Despite these advantages, the ability of China to achieve a quick victory as in 1962 is no longer assured, as India may have better conventional aircraft to engage in counterattacks in case of a border conflict. The raising of additional mountain divisions and deployment of deep-penetration aircraft such as Su-30s on forward bases have added to India's deterrence and defensive postures vis-à-vis China, especially for limited border clashes in key areas of contest. In the medium term, the overall asymmetries will prevent India from undertaking a serious offensive action, but that may not prevent limited border incursions by both sides, as evident in the 2017 Doklam standoff. The no-first-use doctrines of both China and India gives some assurance that nuclear escalation is not automatic even if a conventional conflict occurs between the parties.

SOURCES OF COOPERATION

In the middle of these divergences, several factors mitigate the rivalry and reduce the possibility for open conflict. The presence (or the relative absence) of these factors, unlike in the India-Pakistan dyad, makes this conflict what I would term a "managed enduring rivalry." Globalization and economic interdependence are crucial here. The increasing trade between the two states and their insertion into the globalized world economy may have reduced the incentives for open conflict and violence. The role of foreign trade for both countries' prosperity has been increasing steadily since the 1990s. In 2014, 49.6 percent of India's gross domestic product (GDP) and 41.5 percent of China's depended on trade.[45] Even their agreement on many issues of global governance has given them an opportunity to reduce their friction points. The creation of the BRICS, the ARF, and the SCO and the possibility of China's membership in the South Asian Association for Regional Cooperation (SAARC) may open up avenues for discussion and engagement.

Why did the rapid rise of China, especially in the post–Cold War era, not produce the kind of decline in relations with India? According to Rusko and Sasikumar, "The concerted efforts in both countries to be seen as responsible participants in the global economy" and "general economic prudence, rather than any specific bilateral factor, may be having a positive effect on the India-China relationship."[46] Frequent visits of top leaders to each other's capitals and key cities have also helped to reduce tensions. More important, the border talks and the limited agreements that they have produced helped to keep it a "managed enduring rivalry."

Convergences also exist between the two countries, especially in the domains of the World Trade Organization and other trade regimes and negotiations for liberalizing global trade. Energy security and supply, as well as responses to energy exploration and utilization, also show some parallel behavioral traits.[47] In recent years, Chinese and Indian companies have joined hands in oil exploration in Iran, Sudan, Central Asia, and some other parts of the world, despite their individual efforts to obtain oil and gas supply or exploration contracts.[48]

International institutions are key arenas of cooperation as China and India perceive that Western-controlled financial institutions do not give them much of a role. Somewhat common positions by the two for quota increases in the International Monetary Fund and the World Bank, as well as the reform of financial institutions, have been noticeable. The NDB, which China helped to create among the BRICS countries in 2014, has a major Indian imprint on it, as its first director was Indian (although its headquarters is in Shanghai).[49] India is a founding member of the Chinese-initiated AIIB, which began operations in Beijing in January 2015. China has a 26 percent and India has a 7.5 percent voting share in this institution, which is based on their financial contributions.[50] Meetings of these institutions offer opportunities for the leaders of the two countries to engage a few times a year, which has helped manage the rivalry.

DIFFERENCES WITH
THE INDIA-PAKISTAN RIVALRY

There are substantial differences between the China-India and India-Pakistan rivalries. The latter is more intense, with a history of four wars and multiple militarized crises since 1947. It is more intense because of the nature of the territorial conflict—that is, Kashmir and the attachment of national identity to the territory in question.[51] One of the participants, Pakistan, is an actively revisionist state and seeks to change the territorial status quo through military means, including terrorism. The power asymmetry between the two is compensated by alliance patterns, weaponry (including nuclear arms), and a favorable terrain, making Pakistan a formidable rival to India.[52] The way the rivalry began—the bloody partition of the subcontinent—and the continued competition involving great powers made the India-Pakistan rivalry more intense. In each of the dimensions I have presented above, the intensity and differences are higher for the India-Pakistan rivalry: territory and resources (including Kashmir and water), status and balance-of-power competition, and strategic culture and deterrence.

Further, cooperation is limited because of the absence of deep-rooted economic interactions between the two states. India-Pakistan trade remains very low at around $2.5 billion annually, constituting less than 0.5 percent of India's and 3 percent of Pakistan's total trade volumes.[53] The dyad also lacks institutions like BRICS, which links India and China and is unlike SAARC, in which India and Pakistan engage in competitive outbidding. Violent militarized interactions are much more frequent in this dyad than in the China-India pair. The presence of an active insurgency in Indian Kashmir and the propensity of Pakistan to send in militants across the border for terrorist strikes in India have made the conflict volatile and potentially more prone to violence. Irredentism is very high, as many stakeholders in the divided parts of Kashmir want to unite as an independent state, while Pakistan seeks incorporation or control of the territory and its majority Muslim inhabitants. There are no such irredentist claims in the India-China rivalry context.

The bargaining strategies each state employs appear to capture some divergence and may very well be the function of particular learning the parties have developed over the other's behavior patterns. Russell Leng has argued that the weaker party—that is, Pakistan—often uses coercive bargaining in the India-Pakistan dyad and actively engages in asymmetrical strategies with the use of jihadists.[54] The Pakistani-supported irredentist struggle has been kept alive through constant propaganda and aggressive diplomacy. The border is fenced on the Line of Control (LOC) as India seeks to restrict the Pakistani-inspired incursions. Unlike in the China-India dyad where it is the weaker party, India does not employ such asymmetrical strategies due to a variety of capability, terrain-constraint, and strategic-cultural factors. One other factor for the variation in these two rivalries may well be the kind of political shocks that led to their onset.[55] Partition had a more profound impact on the daily lives and memories of Indians and Pakistanis. On the other hand, only Indians keep a memory of shame in their defeat in 1962. The Chinese in general view the war as a limited policing action. Even for Indians, it was fought in remote corners of the Himalayan border, and considerable skepticism exists on the culpability or mishandling by Nehru and other civilian and military elite in prosecuting the war.[56]

The divergences between the two rivalries call for different research routes in order to explain the protractedness of different types of rivalries, as some are more strategic than others. The intermingling of variables is also different in these rivalries. As a result, the rivalry remains in the class of "managed enduring rivalries," and its transition to an active and intense rivalry may depend on changes in the factors identified in this volume. What does the future hold for the China-India rivalry as it is fast emerging as both a spatial (i.e., territorial) and positional rivalry, the latter as a result of many variables identified in this volume?[57] The two nations' economic relationship and regular diplomatic engagement appear to have mellowed but not removed the key parameters of the rivalry. Further research is needed on what economic interdependence, especially in the globalization era, has done to enduring rivalries of this nature.

THE CHAPTERS

The contributors to this volume address the aforementioned factors in greater detail. While part I consists of the introduction, part II comprises six chapters focusing on different sources of the rivalry. In chapter 2, Mahesh Shankar offers an overview of the territorial dimensions of the rivalry. He discusses some plausible reasons for the escalation of the territorial dispute into conflict and efforts by both sides to find a modus vivendi to sideline the long-term-resolution issue in favor of improvements in other areas of the relationship. This is partially due to the fact that the status quo in their contested territory, northwest by China and northeast by India, is probably what each can agree on given the strategic importance of the territories concerned for both sides. However, the resolution to the territorial dispute is constrained by domestic and reputation-level concerns.

Status dimensions are the focus of chapter 3 by Xiaoyu Pu, who argues that status is a source of rivalry but an asymmetrical one, with India sensing more of a need for China's recognition of India's status quest than vice versa. China perceives India to be less of a status threat, as its material capabilities are greater than India's and its status position is entrenched in global institutions such as the UN. China views status as a club good, preventing India's entry into the UNSC and the NSG while working with it in some jointly developed institutions such as BRICS for its own goal of creating a multipolar order. Status competition in the rivalry is thus mitigated by these complex strategic goals of the two sides. Nevertheless, it still exists as a source of serious contention.

In chapter 4, Manjari Chatterjee Miller locates the conceptions of international order inherent in the strategic visions of the two megastates. While China's conceptions of order are precolonial, those of India's derive from its postcolonial state-building narratives. Using frameworks such as Gandhian, Nehruvian, Hindutva, and global, Miller contends that contemporary India under Modi is more focused on inward development than outward order-building. China, on the other hand, relies on the *tianxia* system of thinking—waiting to recraft international order in its image and seeking to replace Western/American-dominated international order with its suzerainty, a goal that India does not share. This is increasingly becoming a source of this strategic rivalry, with China expanding its economic and naval presence to the Pacific and Indian Oceans.

In chapter 5, Zhen Han and Jean-François Bélanger bring forth the balance-of-power dynamics as an enabler of the rivalry. The initial conflict itself was not the product of balancing strategies of either side, but after the 1962 war the balancing strategies that both sides adopted helped to entrench the rivalry. India's efforts to acquire arms from the United States and the United Kingdom first and then from the Soviet Union, China's embrace of Pakistan, the larger US-China rapprochement, and the India-USSR relationship (the last two in the 1970s) all had a major role in embedding the rivalry. With the end of the Cold War, balance-of-power dynamics changed as India lost the Soviet Union as an ally. However, the US-India rapprochement and the subsequent nuclear deal between Washington and India and the inclusion of India as part of the Barack Obama administration's pivot to Asia strategy all generated many balance-of-power concerns in China. In recent years, these Chinese concerns have included an India-Japan strategic alignment. For India, the strengthening China-Pakistan economic and strategic relationship generates much concern. Today, the balance-of-power competition between the two states has become more complex with the inclusion of soft-balancing and limited hard-balancing approaches by both sides, even though engagement and economic interactions also characterize the relationship.

In chapter 6, Calvin Chen argues that the competition for resources, especially hydrocarbons, has not become zero-sum, as there are diverse suppliers that both states cannot control and there is a determination on their part to cooperate wherever it is possible, especially in the discovery and exploitation of new sources around the world. In addition, both countries now focus on the development of renewable sources such as solar energy, which will even further reduce the chances of conflict over energy resources. In contrast, in chapter 7, Selina Ho contends that water shortages in both countries and the increasing demands for such resources have compounded the conflictual relationship between the two sides due to territorial and political differences. Further, there are hardly any institutionalized mechanisms between the two for the distribution and management of joint water resources, in particular that originating from the Brahmaputra River. Despite these water challenges, violent conflict is avoided partly because of the asymmetrical nature of the power relationship and the interests of the weaker side not to escalate the conflict given its riparian status.

In part III, two chapters discuss the strategic dimensions of the rivalry. Andrew Scobell focuses on the impact of divergent strategic culture lenses through which China and India look at each other and the roles they ascribe to one another in the strategic milieu. Divergent strategic cultures are not the source of the conflict, but they exacerbate and prolong the rivalry into a chronic condition. In chapter 9, Vipin Narang focuses more closely on the microfoundations of deterrence strategy between these two states in this asymmetrical nuclear dyad. He argues that the nuclear deterrence relationship is quite robust as both seek assured retaliation, preventing too much adventurism. A stable nuclear relationship means less pressure to make escalatory moves, but it also entails that both can continue the competition for a long period to come. Implied here is the possibility that nuclear deterrence actually prolongs rivalry in a relationship of this nature.

In part IV, two chapters explore the mitigating factors in this rivalry that prevent it from escalating. In chapter 10, Matthew A. Castle looks at the role of trade and investment and its asymmetrical value on the relations between the two sides. He contends that economic interdependence has a mitigating effect and also increases tensions. This is because the trade links are asymmetrical and China can afford to take India for granted and take confrontational steps toward India. The BRI and the CPEC offer room for more conflict in this rivalry. A deeper institutionalized cooperation and a more balanced trade relationship may be necessary for economic interdependence to have a positive impact on the reduction of the rivalry relationship. In chapter 11, Feng Liu, on the other hand, seeks to explore the role of institutional engagement and its impact on reducing the rivalry as it facilitates limited cooperation. He sees cooperation in multilateral institutions, both at the global and regional levels, as one of the mitigating factors in reducing the rivalry. However, China's opposition to India's membership in the UNSC and the NSG has generated some challenges, as China sees its interests affected by India's membership even when they cooperate in regional institutional structures. Reforming Western-dominated institutions is a common goal, and this has generated some cooperation among the two Asian giants.

The concluding chapter, by Paul F. Diehl, argues that the China-India relationship has become a less intense enduring rivalry, although some rivalry characteristics exist. Although Diehl considers the limited nature of this rivalry (and in that sense sees it as closer to my characterization of a managed rivalry), there is a challenge in coding this relationship as an enduring rivalry partially because of a tendency of this genre to focus on militarized crises as a necessary condition for an enduring rivalry. In the contemporary world order influenced by the twin forces of nuclear deterrence and economic globalization, the number of conflicts among great powers and rising powers with militarized crises is receding. But there is no indication that some of these rivalries, such as the one between China and India, witness any reductions in military competition, arms buildup, and preparations for war, even though the outbreak of crises and wars today is more unlikely than before. The current enduring-rivalry literature needs to expand to capture complex rivalries of this nature, especially those impacted by economic globalization. Much of the rivalry literature was developed during the Cold War era, which was also the period when the initial consolidation of new states occurred. As these nation-states aged, their militarized crisis behavior has come down in some instances, although the territorial and other disputes still linger on. This volume, if nothing else, points toward the new face of the old rivalries and the need to study the dynamic nature of interstate rivalry itself. The China-India case also shows that states can be in a rivalry and at the same time attempt to manage the conflictual relationship and in that process may get further into rivalry spirals as systemic changes among great powers affect the regional dynamics along with their power capabilities and status aspirations.

NOTES

1. Ananth Krishnan, "India's Trade with China Falls but Deficit Widens," *India Today*, January 14, 2017, http://indiatoday.intoday.in/story/india-china-trade-ties indo-china-trade-deficit-export-import/1/857157.html.
2. Wade Shepard, "India and Japan Join Forces to Counter China and Build Their Own New Silk Road," *Forbes*, July 31, 2017, https://www.forbes.com/sites/wadeshepard/2017/07/31/india-and-japan-join-forces-to-counter-china-and-build-their-own-new-silk-road/2. The "Belt" is a network of overland road and rail routes, oil and natural gas pipelines, and other infrastructure projects that will stretch from Xi'an in central China through Central Asia and ultimately reach as far as Moscow, Rotterdam, and Venice. Rather than one route, belt corridors are set to run along the major Eurasian Land Bridges, through China-Mongolia-Russia, China-Central Asia and West Asia, China-Indochina Peninsula, China-Pakistan, and Bangladesh-China-India-Myanmar corridors. The "Road" is its maritime equivalent: a network of planned ports and other coastal infrastructure projects that dot the map from South and Southeast Asia to East Africa and the northern Mediterranean Sea." Bert Hofman, "China's One Belt One Road Initiative: What We Know Thus Far," World Bank, April 12, 2015, http://blogs.worldbank.org/eastasiapacific/china-one-belt-one-road-initiative-what-we-know-thus-far. In this volume, OBOR and BRI are used interchangeably as the latter is the new name for the same initiative.
3. For this approach, see Rudra Sil and Pater J. Katzenstein, eds., *Beyond Paradigms: Analytical Eclecticism in the Study of World Politics* (New York: Palgrave Macmillan, 2010).
4. Shalendra D. Sharma, *China and India in the Age of Globalization* (Cambridge: Cambridge University Press, 2009), 170–71.

5. T.V. Paul, "Why Has the India-Pakistan Rivalry Been So Enduring? Power Asymmetry and an Intractable Conflict," *Security Studies* 15, no. 4 (October–December, 2006): 600–630.

6. Key works include N. Maxwell, *India's China War* (New York: Random House, 2000); A. G. Noorani, *India-China Boundary Problem, 1846–1947: History and Diplomacy* (New Delhi: Oxford University Press, 2011); K. N. Raghavan, *Dividing Lines: Contours of India-China Conflict* (New Delhi: Leadstart, 2012); Steven A. Hoffmann, *India and the China Crisis* (Berkeley: University of California Press, 1990); and John W. Garver, *Protracted Contest: Sino-Indian Rivalry in the Twentieth Century* (Seattle: University of Washington Press, 2001), 91–100.

7. More recent works include Tien-Sze Fang, *Asymmetrical Threat Perceptions in India-China Relations* (New Delhi: Oxford University Press, 2013); Jeff M. Smith, *Cold Peace: China-India Rivalry in the Twenty-First Century* (Lanham, MD: Lexington Books, 2015); Kanti Bajpai, Jing Huang, and Kishore Mahbubani, eds., *China-India Relations: Cooperation and Conflict* (London: Routledge, 2016); Harsh Pant, *China Syndrome: Grappling with an Uneasy Relationship* (New Delhi: HarperCollins, 2010); Bertil Lintner, *Great Game East: India, China, and the Struggle for Asia's Most Volatile Frontier* (New Haven, CT: Yale University Press, 2015); and Chris Ogden, *China and India: Asia's Emergent Great Powers* (Cambridge: Polity Press, 2017).

8. M. Taylor Fravel, *Strong Borders, Secure Nation: Cooperation and Conflict in China's Territorial Disputes* (Princeton, NJ: Princeton University Press, 2008).

9. Some chapters in this volume, including the concluding one by Paul F. Diehl, contend that the China-India relationship is not a rivalry in the traditional sense. The decrease in the number of militarized crises over time is shown as indication of this trend. To me, this not a strong argument, as contemporary rivalries need not show high levels of militarized interstate crises. Theories on rivalries developed during the Cold War era do not adequately capture different types of rivalries, especially ones that show mixed patterns of conflict and cooperation under conditions of economic globalization. The insistence on militarized crises also ignores the role nuclear and conventional deterrence play in stabilizing a rivalry.

10. Zeev Maoz and Ben Dor, *Bound by Struggle: The Strategic Evolution of Enduring International Relations* (Ann Arbor: University of Michigan Press, 2002), 5.

11. Paul F. Diehl and Gary Goertz, *War and Peace in International Rivalry* (Ann Arbor: University of Michigan Press, 2001), 44, 48. On rivalries, see Gary Goertz and Paul F. Diehl, "Enduring Rivalries: Theoretical Constructs and Empirical Patterns," *International Studies Quarterly* 37, no. 2 (June 1993): 147–71.

12. Sudhi Ranjan Sen, "Will Line of Actual Control with China Become like Line of Control with Pakistan?," *India Today*, August 18, 2017, http://indiatoday.intoday.in/story/line-of-actual-control-line-of-control-india-china-pakistan/1/1029138.html.

13. Brig. Gurmeet Kanwal, "Xi Must Rein in the PLA from Running Its Own Foreign Policy," Rediff.com, September 18, 2014; Ajay Shukla, "Sino-Indian Tensions: A Border in Limbo," January 17, 2014, http://ajaishukla.blogspot.ca/2014/01/sinoindian-tensions-border-in-limbo.html.

14. On this, see Oriana Skylar Mastro and Arzan Tarapore, "Countering Chinese Coercion: The Case of Doklam," War on Rocks, August 29, 2017, https://warontherocks.com/2017/08/countering-chinese-coercion-the-case-of-doklam/.

15. Sudha Ramachandran, "Water Wars: China, India and the Great Dam Rush," *The Diplomat*, April 3, 2015.

16. The most alarming of these accounts have been by Indian analyst Brahma Chellaney. See his *Water: Asia's New Battleground* (Washington, DC: Georgetown University Press, 2013).

17. Sebastian Biba, "Desecuritization in China's Behavior towards Its Transboundary Rivers: The Mekong River, the Brahmaputra River, and the Irtysh and Ili Rivers," *Journal of Contemporary China* 23, no. 85 (2014): 21–43; Selina Ho, "River Politics: China's Policies in the Mekong and the Brahmaputra in Comparative Perspective," *Journal of Contemporary China* 23, no. 85 (2014): 1–20; and Uttam Kumar Sinha, "Examining China's Hydro-Behaviour: Peaceful or Assertive?," *Strategic Analysis* 36, no. 1 (January 2012): 41–56.

18. On these challenges, see Joel Wuthnow, "Water War: This River Could Sink China-India Relations," *National Interest*, April 19, 2016.

19. Rosalind Reischer, "China and India Unite on Energy," *The Diplomat*, July 11, 2012, http://thediplomat.com/2012/07/china-and-india-unite-on-energy/.

20. Cited in Richard Sisson and Leo E. Rose, *War and Secession: Pakistan, India and the Creation of Bangladesh* (Berkeley: University of California Press, 1990): 247.

21. On India's status quest, see Rajesh Basrur and Kate Sullivan de Estrada, *Rising India: Status and Power* (London: Routledge, 2017).

22. Robert Ross, "China's Naval Nationalism: Sources, Prospects and the U.S. Response," *International Security* 34, no. 2 (Fall 2009): 46–66. See also Xiaoyu Pu and Randall L. Schweller, "Status Signaling, Multiple Audiences, and China's Blue Water Naval Ambition," in *Status in World Politics*, ed. T.V. Paul, Deborah Welch Larson, and William C. Wohlforth (Cambridge: Cambridge University Press), 141–62.

23. Yong Deng, *China's Struggle for Status: The Realignment of International Relations* (Cambridge: Cambridge University Press, 2008).

24. Tung-Chich Tsai, "China and India: Comparisons of Naval Strategies and Future Competition," in *India and China in the Emerging Dynamics of East Asia*, ed. G. V. C. Naidu et al. (n.p.: Springer India, 2015), 123. See also, Manjari Chatterjee Miller, *Wronged by Empire: Post-Imperial Ideology and Foreign Policy in China and India* (Stanford, CA: Stanford University Press, 2013).

25. Tsai, "China and India," 127.

26. Tarique Ata, "India and Iran Sign 'Historic' Chabahar Port Deal," BBC News, May 23, 2016, http://www.bbc.com/news/world-asia-india-36356163.

27. Yeganeh Torbati and Idrees Ali, "U.S., India Sign Military Logistics Agreement," Reuters, August 29, 2016, http://www.reuters.com/article/us-india-usa-military -idUSKCN114241.

28. For the three types of balancing, see T.V. Paul, *Restraining Great Powers: Soft Balancing from Empires to the Globalization Era* (New Haven, CT: Yale University Press, forthcoming), ch. 6.

29. Chunhao Lou, "US-India-China Relations in the Indian Ocean: A Chinese Perspective," *Strategic Analysis* 36, no. 4 (July/August 2012): 624–39.

30. Thomas Fingar, "China's Vision of World Order," in *Strategic Asia 2012–13*, ed. Ashley J. Tellis (Seattle: National Bureau of Asian Research, 2012), 343–73.

31. David Brewster, "Indian Strategic Thinking about the Indian Ocean: Striving toward Strategic Leadership," *India Review* 14, no. 2 (April 2015): 221–37.

32. Abhijit Singh, "The Indian Maritime Strategy for an Era of Geopolitical Uncertainty," *Journal of Defence Studies* 9, no. 4 (October–December 2015): 7–19.

33. Indian Ministry of Defense (Navy), *Ensuring Secure Seas: Indian Maritime Security Strategy* (New Delhi: Naval Strategic Publications, October 2015), http://indiannavy.nic.in/sites/default/files/Indian_Maritime_Security_Strategy _Document_25Jan16.pdf.

34. John W. Garver, "The Diplomacy of a Rising China in South Asia," *Orbis* 56, no. 3 (Summer 2012): 392.

35. Ibid., 391–409.

36. Alaistair Iain Johnston, *Cultural Realism: Strategic Culture and Grand Strategy in Chinese History* (Princeton, NJ: Princeton University Press, 1998), ix.

37. Alaistair Iain Johnston, "Thinking about Strategic Culture," *International Security* 19, no. 4 (Spring 1995): 43.

38. See Mohan Malik, *China and India: Great Power Rivals* (Boulder, CO: Lynne Rienner, 2011), 18–19.

39. Ibid., 25.

40. George K. Tanham, *Indian Strategic Thought: An Interpretative Essay* (Santa Monica, CA: Rand Corp., 1992).

41. Liping Xia, "China's Nuclear Doctrine: Debates and Evolution," *Regional Insight*, Carnegie Endowment for International Peace, June 30, 2016, http://carnegieendowment.org/2016/06/30/china-s-nuclear-doctrine-debates-and-evolution-pub-63967.

42. Gurmeet Kanwal, "India's Nuclear Force Structure 2025," *Regional Insight*, Carnegie Endowment for International Peace, June 30, 2016, http://carnegieendowment.org/2016/06/30/india-s-nuclear-force-structure-2025-pub-63988.

43. On this see, Xiaoping Yang, "China's Perceptions of India as Nuclear Weapons Power," *Regional Insight*, Carnegie Endowment for International Peace, June 30, 2016.

44. Shukla, "Sino-Indian Tensions."

45. Cited from World Bank, World Development Indicators, 2015. On the importance of trade for India, see Aseema Sinha, *Globalizing India* (Cambridge: Cambridge University Press, 2016), 3.

46. Christopher J. Rusko and Karthika Sasikumar, "India and China: From Trade to Peace?," *Asian Perspective* 31, no. 4 (2007): 109.

47. James Clad, "Convergent Chinese and Indian Perspectives on the Global Order," in *The India-China Relationship: What the United States Needs to Know*, eds., Francine R. Frankel and Harry Harding (New York: Columbia University Press, 2004), 267–72.

48. Karolina Wysoczańska, "Sino-Indian Co-operation in Africa: Joint Efforts in the Oil Sector," *Journal of Contemporary African Studies* 29, no. 2 (2011), 193–201.

49. "Brics Countries Launch New Development Bank in Shanghai," BBC News, July 21, 2015, http://www.bbc.com/news/33605230.

50. "50 Nations In, AIIB Takes Shape," *The Hindu*, June 30, 2015, http://www.thehindu.com/news/national/india-signs-articles-that-determine-each-countrys-share-in-asian-infrastructure-investment-bank/article7368050.ece.

51. On the importance of territory, see John A. Vasquez, "Distinguishing Rivals That Go to War from Those That Do Not: A Quantitative Comparative Case Study of the Two Paths to War," *International Studies Quarterly* 40, no. 4 (December 1996): 531–58.

52. Paul, "Why Has the India-Pakistan Rivalry Been So Enduring?"

53. Mohsin Khan, "Realising the Potential of India-Pakistan Trade," East Asia Forum, March 20, 2016, http://www.eastasiaforum.org/2016/03/20/realising-the-potential-of-india-pakistan-trade/.

54. On the bargaining strategies, see Russell J. Leng, "When Will They Ever Learn? Coercive Bargaining in Recurrent Crises," *Journal of Conflict Resolution* 27 (1983): 379–419; Russell J. Leng, *Bargaining and Learning in Recurrent Crises: The Soviet-American, Egyptian-Israeli, and Indo-Pakistani Rivalries* (Ann Arbor: University of Michigan Press, 2000), ch. 5. On learning in rivalries, see Zeev Maoz and Ben D. Mor, "Enduring Rivalries: The Early Years," *International Political Science Review* 17, no. 2 (1996): 141–60.

55. On the importance of this factor, see Gary Goertz and Paul F. Diehl, "The Initiation and Termination of Enduring Rivalries: The Impact of Political Shocks," *American Journal of Political Science* 39, no. 1 (February 1995): 30–52.
56. For instance, see Noorani, *India-China Boundary Problem*.
57. On these categories of rivalries, see William R. Thompson, "Principal Rivalries," *Journal of Conflict Resolution* 39, no. 2 (June 1995): 195–223.

PART II
SOURCES

Chapter 2

Territory and the China-India Competition

MAHESH SHANKAR

Much of the scholarship on the China-India relationship agrees that the long-standing territorial dispute between the two countries constitutes one of the underlying pillars of their overarching "rivalry."[1] The dispute, revolving around the issue of the delineation of borders between the two countries and the status of Tibet, has its roots in the region's colonial history but broke out into crisis only in the late 1950s. That crisis eventually led to the only war between the two countries, in 1962, and a few more militarized crises since then, most notably in the late 1980s. In recent years, the two countries have fortunately found mechanisms imparting a modicum of stability to the relationship, especially on territorial issues. However, periodic tensions caused by reassertions of territorial claims and mutual accusations of transgressions across the Line of Actual Control (LAC) continue to be an irritant in the relationship, and the resolution of the territorial dispute continues to stubbornly evade the two sides.

Interesting to note in all of this is the fact that while the China-India dispute continues to be intractable, it is also in many ways markedly distinct from India's other territorial rivalry, with Pakistan, in that it is for the most part unburdened by the frequency and intensity of violence that has become an unfortunate aspect of the dispute over Kashmir. This chapter argues that this paradoxical aspect of the conflict—an intractable yet manageable dispute—points to the fact that at the level of the respective governments the dispute lacks (and has lacked) the essential salience, and consequently the zero-sumness and revisionism, that underlies the violence of the India-Pakistan territorial conflict. This in turn has made the dispute, as evidenced from developments in recent decades, more amenable to management. On the other hand, however,

27

the challenges to resolution of the conflict are equally real and point to how factors divorced from any inherent value of the territories under consideration—including rivalry dynamics (however asymmetrical), status concerns, historical memory, and domestic politics—will continue to impede seemingly reasonable paths out of the territorial imbroglio. Indeed, in August 2017, the two countries de-escalated arguably the most consequential of stand-offs between them for decades, in the disputed Doklam area at the trijunction of the borders between India, China, and Bhutan, an area under dispute between China and Bhutan but where Beijing's actions to unilaterally solidify its position through the construction of a road portend ominous intentions in China that pose challenges to both India's border security and its broader strategic interests in the region and beyond.

This chapter begins with a historical overview of the territorial issues that have bedeviled the two countries and how they have contributed to the emergence and persistence of what at least one side (India) considers to be a rivalry that overarches all disagreements between the two sides.[2] Such perceptions of rivalry, I argue, are to a great extent the legacy of the way the territorial dispute evolved in the first two decades after both countries became independent entities in the late 1940s. Building on that background, the core of the chapter focuses on the paradox identified above, that the dispute seems at the same time both intractable and manageable. It identifies factors and trends that have allowed for the dampening of tensions and the absence of major violence and potentially war on the one hand and the broader, more nonterritorial considerations—particularly on the Indian side but also increasingly in China—that seem to hamper the actual resolution of the dispute itself on the other. All of this serves to suggest that crucial as the territorial conflict was to the emergence of a broader competition between the two countries, it is perhaps not as central to its persistence in contemporary times. Rather, while the territorial dispute itself serves as a continuing irritant to bilateral ties, it is the perception on at least one side of a broader competition or rivalry, as well as developments in each country's domestic politics, that imparts a persistent intractability to the territorial dimension of the China-India relationship.

THE TERRITORIES IN QUESTION AND THE ORIGINS OF "RIVALRY"

The origins—and especially the intensity—of the China-India competition are intrinsically linked to the emergence of territorial conflict between the two countries in the years immediately following decolonization in that part of the world. These territorial disagreements in turn were driven by two distinct but interrelated sets of questions: the correct delineation of borders between the two states and issues surrounding the status of the territory of Tibet. While strictly speaking the border issues were and continue to be at the core of the territorial dispute between the two sides, China's troubles in Tibet and perceptions of India's role in it were arguably crucial to Beijing's treatment of the overall conflict.

The Boundary Issue

In 1949, as the communists ascended to power in China—India had become independent in 1947—the potential for a dispute over where the frontiers between the two countries lay was apparent. Much of the expansive border (some four thousand kilometers in length) between the two countries had never been mutually agreed to and demarcated by the British and Chinese authorities in earlier years. This meant that both sides had very different understandings of which parts of the territory in the frontier areas belonged to them and which belonged to the other side.[3] These gaps were particularly stark in the two extremities of this long border, with several more minor disagreements in the more central regions of the frontier areas. In the eastern sector abutting Burma, some eighty-three thousand square kilometers of territory, largely encompassing the India-controlled and -administered North-East Frontier Agency (NEFA)— later the state of Arunachal Pradesh—was under question. India's claim to this territory is based on the contention that in accordance with its inherited maps, the boundary in that sector had been delimited by the British-proposed McMahon Line at the Simla Convention in 1913 and 1914. The Chinese, on the other hand, contested such claims by suggesting that the territory had historically been part of the Tibet region of China. The Chinese, moreover, argued that the McMahon Line was a colonial imposition that New Delhi was perpetuating because China had never agreed to it. While its representative had initialed the agreement in Simla, the Chinese government immediately repudiated the act upon his return and never actually ratified the agreement.[4]

In the western sector, on the other end of the China-India border, some thirty-seven thousand square kilometers of largely barren and inhospitable territory came to be disputed. Here the status of the Aksai Chin Plateau became central to the contestation. Moreover, in contrast to the eastern side, the situation was even more ambiguous in this sector, as reflected by the fact that even the British had left this border undefined on their maps. Colonial policy had wrestled with three different conceptions about where the border ought to lie but had never managed to agree to a mutually acceptable delineation of those borders with the Chinese. Both China and India therefore based their claims on what they contended was traditional and customary in the area. For the Chinese, custom placed Aksai Chin within their territory, or so they claimed. India, on the other hand, settled on something less than the most expansive of the British lines—the Ardagh-Johnson Line—which nevertheless left the plateau within India.[5] By the time conflict broke into the open, India controlled the contested territory in the eastern sector up to the McMahon Line, whereas the Chinese—who had progressively expanded their physical presence in the region

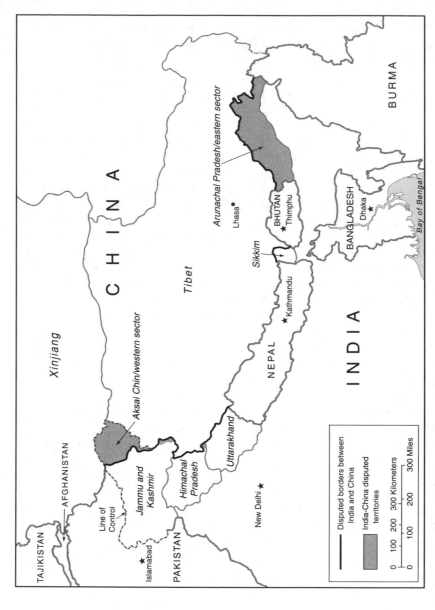

MAP 2.1. China-India Frontier Disputes

over the previous years—held the advantage in the west. By 1957, in fact, in a development that first sparked India's broaching of the subject, the Chinese had, unbeknownst to the Indians, built an all-weather road through Aksai Chin.

Tibet

The issue of Tibet added an additional dimension to territorial disagreements between the two sides, especially in the Chinese view. By 1950, soon after gaining control of the mainland, the new communist regime in China had begun the process of forcibly "liberating" Tibet and integrating it more deeply into the Chinese state. At different points in history, Tibet had enjoyed an immense degree of autonomy from China, to the extent that many considered the region to be more or less independent in 1949. This showed notably in the relationship that the British colonizers of India had established with Tibet, involving numerous special rights, privileges, and responsibilities, including trading posts, military escorts, and control over the postal and telegraph systems. The British even had a special term—"suzerainty"—for the ties they saw as existing between China and Tibet, one that did not amount to full independence for the territory but also fell short of Chinese sovereignty over it.[6]

Independent India was an inheritor of this legacy, and the new government in New Delhi no doubt recognized the great strategic value in the status of Tibet continuing as it was, leaving the large landmass as something of a buffer between India and China.[7] The Chinese leaders, on the other hand, viewed Tibet as an integral part of their territory and India's special status in Tibet as a colonial imposition and one more remnant of the country's century of national humiliation. India and its prime minister, Jawaharlal Nehru, were in turn viewed with suspicion as successors to the imperialists, who would seek to sever Tibet from China.[8] In any case, by the early 1950s, China had pushed on into Tibet, leading Nehru to swiftly recognize—in a concession to reality—that there was little his government could practically do to maintain the status quo ante in Tibet. India simply did not have the capabilities, or an overriding interest for that matter, to forcefully resist China's expansion into Tibet.[9] What he sought instead was, on the one hand, to be able to facilitate some kind of peaceful accommodation between the Chinese state and the Tibetan people that would leave the latter with the maximum extent of autonomy possible. On the other hand, to assuage Chinese fears about his government's intentions and hopefully dampen the potential for China-India conflict, Nehru by 1954 had concluded an agreement with Beijing wherein New Delhi gave up all of its special rights in Tibet and also accepted Chinese sovereignty—not suzerainty—over Tibet.[10] Unfortunately, such concessions did little to allay Chinese fears, which persisted in the following years and reached their peak as rebellion broke out in Tibet in 1959.

Given the existence of such obvious disagreements on territorial issues, the emergence of war and what appears to be in some respects an intractable rivalry between India and China is in some ways unsurprising. This is also in keeping with much of the literature on war and rivalry in international relations, which has identified territorial conflict as being the single most important factor behind why states go to war and why they end up in long-lasting rivalries.[11] Disputes over territory inspire conflict, this scholarship suggests, in part because of the intrinsic territorial bent of human nature. Beyond this more primal attachment to land, however, pieces of territory often acquire more idiosyncratic—what one set of scholars have termed "relational"—value for the contestants in a dispute, depending on the specific characteristics of the territory itself.[12] Consequently, more often than not, states seem to prefer to assume the undoubted costs of conflict and war rather than make the sort of concessions that would lead to the peaceful resolution of such disputes.

Over time, this literature suggests, it is natural that these dyadic relationships settle into the sort of uneasy and dangerous equilibrium that characterizes enduring rivalries as they experience repeated crises and wars that progressively reinforce the hostility between the contestants.[13] In time, these rivalries, which often originate in territorial conflict, become so deeply set in that they gradually encompass an increasing number of issues "relating to survival, identity, and power position [which] become embedded at both interstate and societal levels." Eventually "state elites and the public may perceive the opponent's gains as their own losses and vice versa"—that is, they will view the entire relationship in zero-sum terms.[14]

As detailed below, such rivalry dynamics—even if they are asymmetrical in many ways—are clearly apparent in the China-India case. The existence of a territorial dispute did eventually lead to war in 1962. That war, in turn, engendered the sort of hostility on both sides that provoked future crises and the adoption of more conflictual and zero-sum positions on a range of issues, including ties with third parties, nuclear weapons possession, and the quest for regional and global influence and status. Simultaneously, mistrust and grievance were embedded in the domestic politics of at least one side, India, where humiliation and a sense of Chinese betrayal still animate the public's collective memory of the war.

ROOM FOR MANEUVER

Yet, interestingly, if we look more closely at the stakes involved in the territorial dispute, it is also clear that from the very beginning there was nothing necessarily inevitable about the descent to war. In stark contrast to the Kashmir issue, where the disputed territory holds deep salience for both sides, the China-India case is more puzzling because it seemed (and seems) to be more amenable to a negotiated solution. For one thing, as pointed out above, the Tibet issue had ostensibly been resolved in 1954 with India's acceptance of China's complete sovereignty over the territory. More important, it is clear that on border issues both sides clearly did not hold all the disputed territory to be of equal salience to themselves. In India's case, it was apparent from soon after the Chinese expanded into

Tibet that it was the disputed territory in the eastern sector—territory below the McMahon Line—where New Delhi was most concerned about maintaining physical control. In strategic terms, were the Chinese to control any area south of the McMahon Line, it would have posed a stark strategic threat to the Indian northeast, a region that is connected to the rest of India only by the narrow Siliguri Corridor (or "Chicken's Neck").[15] The new Indian government consequently had reason to view the disputed territory in the east in much the same way as their British predecessors had done, as something of a buffer area vital to maintaining the territorial integrity of the country.[16]

The territory in the western sector, on the other hand, was a different matter altogether. Aksai Chin, an uninhabited high-altitude desert extending west from the Tibetan Plateau, was of little to no ostensible value—in strategic, economic, or symbolic-nationalist terms—to the new Indian government.[17] As late as in 1959, Nehru had referred to the area as a remote and insignificant landmass, where not even a blade of grass grows.[18] India's claims to the region, moreover, were recognized in New Delhi to be far from ironclad. This lack of importance in turn manifested itself most obviously in the notable lack of attention paid to it by the new Indian government in the early years. Internal discussions in India and the country's actions were, in other words, preoccupied with the McMahon Line throughout much of this period. The western sector acquired an unexpected prominence in the Indian government's consciousness only in the latter part of the 1950s, after the Chinese road in Aksai Chin had been discovered.[19]

For India, then, territory in the eastern sector (territory that it physically controlled) was of crucial importance, while its attitude toward disputed territory in the western sector (which it showed little desire to control) was one of almost complete indifference. For the Chinese, in contrast, the territorial stakes were diametrically different. In general, as Taylor Fravel has pointed out, the frontier territories were viewed by Beijing as unimportant, primarily owing to the fact that they did not form part of the ethnic Han homeland, and they moreover possessed little in terms of exploitable resources or a sizeable population.[20] Consequently, it is clear that Beijing from the very beginning had a clear hierarchy of salience as far as territorial issues were concerned. Mainly, border territorial issues were always secondary to the core problem as the Chinese leaders viewed it: Tibet. This was evident, for instance, in early interactions between Zhou Enlai and Nehru's ambassador to China, K. M. Panikkar, following which the latter observed that the Chinese premier had evinced little interest in discussing border issues and seemed focused exclusively on getting India to cooperate with China's struggle to stabilize Tibet.[21] That task seemingly was accomplished with the 1954 agreement over Tibet. But by 1956, the issue had begun to acquire urgency again as signs of trouble began emerging among the Tibetan populace, exploding eventually into a full-fledged rebellion in 1958 and 1959.[22]

The imperative of controlling Tibet, importantly, also shaped how Beijing viewed the disagreements over borders. In contrast to India, Beijing ended up attaching much greater value to the disputed territory in the western sector

(Aksai Chin). The road connecting Xinjiang and Tibet that traversed through Aksai Chin, after all, provided the only all-season road linking Tibet to the rest of China. Without its availability to move troops and supplies to Tibet, China's attempt at controlling the region was certain to suffer. In strategic terms, then, it was crucial for the Chinese leaders that they retain the disputed territory in Aksai Chin and avoid the possibility of a hostile country coming into possession of the area.[23] By contrast, at several junctures since 1954 the Chinese had more or less explicitly suggested a willingness to adhere to the status quo in the eastern sector along the McMahon Line, even though they clearly rejected the colonial antecedents of that frontier.[24]

THE DESCENT TO WAR

Notwithstanding the no doubt substantial territorial disagreements between the two countries, then, there was—and always has been—a potential path to peace in this dispute. Such a resolution could ostensibly involve India's acquiescence to China's control of Tibet and the contestants holding territory in the border areas that was most important to them and that they already physically controlled. In turn, both sides would give up land that was less salient to them and where they lacked physical presence. India, in other words, would retain territory in the eastern sector, while China would do the same in the west. Nevertheless, the two countries swiftly hurtled toward crisis and eventually war in 1962, establishing a legacy that plagues relations between the two sides to this day.

Several factors played into this denouement. In India, on the one hand, Nehru believed (perhaps mistakenly but certainly not unreasonably) that in return for his government's concessions in 1954, Zhou had acquiesced to a gentleman's agreement that all border issues had been more or less settled, barring some minor disagreements here and there.[25] The Chinese premier confirmed as much in the next few years during one-on-one meetings with Nehru where he clarified that barring the issue of the McMahon Line—on which Beijing would take a position favoring the status quo—there were no major disagreements between the two sides.[26] No mention was made by Zhou in these meetings of the western sector, despite the fact that Indian maps after 1954 had clearly shown Aksai Chin as part of India. In this context, the construction of the road in the western sector and China's following assertion that the entire border was under dispute were viewed by Nehru as perfidious acts. They also activated preexisting fears in the Indian administration that if history was any guide, a strong China would potentially be an expansionist country, tendencies that Nehru's early accommodative efforts had in part sought to temper.[27]

The fears thus animated are central to understanding Nehru's more intransigent position on territorial issues during the 1960 talks than one would otherwise have expected. Indeed, there had been plenty of evidence until as late as 1959 that New Delhi was open to some kind of concessions in the western sector, provided it could be done in a context where it was not in response to the acceptance of an act of Chinese unilateralism. However, Beijing's actions—beginning from the invasion of Tibet in the early 1950s but especially the "new" territorial claims and increasing encroachment in the western sector toward the end of that decade—were viewed in New Delhi as evidence of an expansionist China as well as the growing inevitability that India and China were destined to be competitive rivals in Asia. Failure to firmly resist such tendencies, Nehru felt consequently, was sure to only further encourage Beijing's assertiveness.[28] Simultaneously, as these perceived Chinese perfidies became public knowledge in India and the territorial crisis reached increasing intensity, domestic political pressures and audience costs served to reinforce the government's stance of standing firm.[29] The democratic nature of India's political system meant that Nehru became vulnerable to demands from parliamentary opposition and public opinion at large that no compromise be made to Beijing and that New Delhi reverse any Chinese trespassing on Indian territory. The Indian government only further opened the doors to such pressures in 1959 by agreeing in Parliament to release white papers on all correspondence between New Delhi and Beijing since India's initial protest over the road in Aksai Chin.[30] Furthermore, as other scholars of the dispute have often pointed out, an element of nationalism—inspired by a sense of India's historical borders but also by a feeling of historical "victimhood"—contributed to Nehru's intransigence on maintaining the entirety of the country's territorial claims.[31]

A combination of these factors also eventually precipitated New Delhi's perplexing decision in late 1961 to supplement a stance of diplomatic firmness with the pursuit of the militarily provocative Forward Policy, despite the fact that India simply did not have the military capability to resist a Chinese military response, if there were to be one.[32] The Forward Policy had sought to stem the advance of the People's Liberation Army, primarily in the western sector, by setting up posts in areas of the disputed territory where Chinese troops had yet to establish their presence, with frequently outnumbered Indian forces directed to defend the posts if they came under enemy pressure, in order to establish resolve.[33]

In China, on the other hand, Tibet held centrality in the leaders' attitude toward the relationship with India. As rebellion flared up in the region by 1959, deep suspicions—almost certainly misperceptions—of India's intentions had resurfaced. Indeed, the Chinese leaders very quickly convinced themselves that India was complicit in encouraging the dissidents.[34] As Zhou put it, "the center of the Sino-Indian conflict" lies in the fact that the Indian government "had inherited England's old policy of saying Tibet is an independent country."[35] Evidence that the US Central Intelligence Agency had been assisting Tibetan rebels and conducting overflights in Tibet was taken to have been done with the cooperation and knowledge of a hostile India.[36] India's eventual decision to offer asylum to the Dalai Lama and thousands of Tibetans feeling the Chinese assault—justified in New Delhi on purely humanitarian grounds—only confirmed for Beijing that Nehru's commitment to the 1954 agreement had been insincere. The Chinese leaders, moreover, found it curious that the Indian government had become more active on the territorial front at roughly the same time as their problems in Tibet were peaking.[37] Nehru's insistence on Aksai Chin as Indian territory when all this time his government's focus had been on the McMahon Line arguably only reinforced fears in Beijing that India's true intentions were related to Tibet.[38]

Such suspicions, of course, reached a head in the aftermath of the failed April 1960 talks in New Delhi. In those talks, it is now clear from Indian records, Zhou made what has been termed the "package" deal proposing that India keep the disputed territory in the eastern sector in return for allowing China to hold territory in the western sector.[39] For Chinese leaders, Nehru's rejection of the offer was simply confirmation that India was bent on maximal territorial gains with the real aim of fueling Tibetan separatism. New Delhi's initiation in late 1961 of the Forward Policy aggravated these concerns. It was this context that for the Chinese leaders justified the eventual decision to go to war in late October 1962. The war was explained by Beijing as aimed not at the fulfillment of China's territorial claims but rather to put India in its place by punishing it for its transgressions against Beijing's interests and for its refusal to adopt a reasonable path of "give and take" on territorial issues. Nehru's India had been playing the role of the upstart, and Mao and his colleagues had determined that a serious "lesson" was in order.[40]

THE WAR'S AFTERMATH

The initiation of war by China and the humiliating defeat suffered by India in it are central—as much as any other factor—to understanding the roots of the China-India rivalry, at least as the Indians view it, and its persistence over time. In India, the devastating loss and sense of victimhood associated with it concretized the notion of a traitorous China that was implacably hostile to it. As Nehru concluded following the war, it was in China's nature to expand during its periods of strength. India, in this view, was China's only competitor for influence and leadership in the broader Afro-Asian world, and the war was, as much as anything else, an attempt by the Chinese leaders to put India in its place once and for all.[41] For Nehru, "China as constituted today is an aggressive and expansionist country, possibly with vast designs for the future."[42] To the extent that resolving the border issue was central to relaxing any grievances between the two countries, the experience of the war made it a much more complicated enterprise. In keeping with the insights of the rivalry literature, then, the territorial dispute and the consequent war served the function of both deepening hostility on both sides and broadening the scope of the China-India competition.

Such realpolitik concerns were supplemented by a spike in fury and grievance at the level of domestic public opinion, especially in India. The national narrative following the war only reinforced in the public mind that the disputed lands are indisputably a part of India and that the territory in the western sector was lost to the machinations of Chinese leaders who had exploited Indian goodwill by stabbing the country in the back. Consequently, over the years a sense of national honor has become so attached to this territorial issue in sections of public opinion and an often rabidly jingoistic television media, as well as opportunistic opposition political parties, so as to present somewhat of an unsurmountable barrier for any political leaders considering a compromise-based resolution of the territorial conflict with China.[43] The rise in public support over the years for the right-wing Hindu nationalist Bharatiya Janata Party, which has since 2014 found itself in a position of dominating domestic politics under the leadership of Prime Minister Narendra Modi, only reinforces the fact that nationalism is hardly likely to dissipate as a salient pressure on Indian policy on the border issue with China in times to come.

Such domestic political pressures have, of course, never been as salient in the more authoritarian single-party state of communist China. They have nevertheless become far from negligible in recent times, as the regime transitioned in a post-Mao, reformist China from a legitimation strategy based on communism to one based on nationalism.[44] As scholars have pointed out, this move has made for a political leadership simultaneously more reliant on and vulnerable to public opinion in dealing with issues that ostensibly impinge on the country's sovereignty, honor, and pride.[45] While such pressures have naturally focused most intensely in the recent past on emotion-laden issues such as the relationship with Japan and the dispute over the Senkaku/Diaoyu Islands, it would be no stretch to contend that such nationalistic pressures within public opinion and segments of the political-military elite may significantly curtail the concessions Beijing might now be willing to make on the border issue with India. Such tendencies may partly explain China's increasingly firm stance regarding claims to Arunachal Pradesh in recent years. Indeed, in 2006, China's then ambassador to India stated his government's position to be that "the whole of the state of Arunachal Pradesh is Chinese territory. . . . We are claiming all of that."[46] This newly inflexible position may very well be driven by other realpolitik concerns, such as the deepening of India-US ties, but it is still true that a newly nationalistically charged environment in China makes it problematic for the current-day regime to back away from such claims in the future.

The experience of war also directly shifted other aspects of the China-India relationship into more competitive directions, making the territorial issue in turn far more intractable, particularly in India. Immediately following the war, diplomatic ties were broken by New Delhi, and it took another two decades for the two sides to even attempt to reestablish some level of civil normality between themselves. In the meantime, other developments served to build on the territorial sources of the burgeoning rivalry to further deepen mistrust and hostility on both sides. For one, the Indian leaders' immediate priority had become redressing the severe military imbalances that had exposed India's defenses during the war, to which end New Delhi abandoned much of the idealism that had to some extent driven its complacency on defense preparedness in previous years and began pursuing a program of rapid conventional military buildup.[47]

This stretch of time was punctuated by the periodic outbreak of tense crises along the border, the most severe of which occurred in as late as 1986 and 1987. The crisis featured troop mobilization by both sides against the backdrop of Indian accusations that the Chinese had encroached into the Sumdorong Chu Valley in the eastern sector and India's own decision to grant full statehood to the NEFA region as the new state of Arunachal Pradesh.[48] During the same period, both sides were accusing each other of actively assisting dissident and separatist groups within their borders—the Indians accused Beijing of doing so in the country's northeast, while the Chinese accused India of continuing to meddle in Tibet.[49] China's testing of nuclear weapons in 1964 at Lop Nor only added another significant dimension to tensions and fears that now animated the competition between the two countries.[50]

A final, and crucial, development in the immediate aftermath of the war related to the reorientation of the two sides' external ties with third parties, specifically the superpowers. In India, defeat had significantly dampened in Nehru and others the idealistic aspects of their commitment to nonalignment. Nehru admitted as much when he conceded that he had been living in a make-believe world thus far.[51] His immediate reaction to the outbreak of war was to turn to China's ideological foe in the United States, where the John F. Kennedy administration was more than willing to provide India with the assistance it needed to help repel the Chinese invasion.[52] While this latent potential of a significant upswing in US-India ties was frittered away by both sides soon after Kennedy's untimely death in 1963, by 1971 India (now under Nehru's daughter, Indira Gandhi) had turned toward the Soviet Union.[53]

By that time, China-USSR ties had undergone an acrimonious collapse,[54] one serious enough to allow for both sides in the China-US dyad to become open to a mending of their own relationship.[55] Beijing now also quickly turned toward undermining India's influence, not only in the wider Afro-Asian world but also its preeminence in South Asia, by actively cajoling the likes of Nepal, Sri Lanka, and Bangladesh (after 1971) out of New Delhi's "sphere of influence."[56] In later years, such efforts manifested notably in China's undertaking of strategic infrastructure projects in these and other countries surrounding India, leading some in the latter to describe it as a "string of pearls" strategy seeking to eventually choke off India's reach.[57] Most consequentially, of course, the Chinese leaders also quickly turned toward the welcoming arms of Pakistan in these years. Indications of this shift came soon after the 1962 war when China and Pakistan swiftly announced a resolution of their own territorial disagreements, part of which included—to India's consternation—territory in disputed Kashmir.[58] By 1965, China-Pakistan relations had flowered to an extent that leaders in Rawalpindi—which had replaced Karachi as the capital in 1958—were able to boast that the Chinese would intervene on their behalf in the war with India that year, and they seemed to believe the same again later in the 1971 war that led to the creation of Bangladesh.[59] Into the 1980s, so tightly bound were the two countries in an "all-weather friendship" that it was widely suspected that Beijing was actively assisting Pakistan in developing its nuclear weapons program and had even provided the country with bomb-development plans.[60]

Many of these developments, and at least the rapidity with which they were given effect, can be directly attributed to the rivalry dynamics that were precipitated by the descent of territorial disagreements into war. Over the decades, as both countries have risen to harboring global aspirations, these security-, power-, and status-related motivators have arguably assumed even greater prominence in the China-India relationship. India's coming out as a nuclear weapons state in 1998, the path toward which had in a crucial sense originated with the war in 1962 and China's own tests two years later, added a dimension of dangerous complexity to the relationship.[61] Indeed, immediately prior to those tests, the then Indian defense minister George Fernandes had courted controversy by publicly declaring China (not Pakistan) as India's "potential threat no. 1," something that he said necessitated a reassessment of India's stance on nuclear weapons possession.[62]

Consequently, to the extent that the relationship does possess some rivalry-like features—however asymmetrical these perceptions may be—their origins can be attributed to the territorial dispute and war. And insofar as it is this issue (territory) that animates public imagination (particularly in India) about the nature of the relationship, it is by no means an insignificant factor in the persistence of tensions. In this, the China-India case nicely bears out the argument that often emerges from the rivalry literature, that territorial issues are often central to the emergence of enduring rivalries, which then often take on a life of their own over time as other (nonterritorial) issues begin to bear on the competitive aspects of the relationship.

THE EMERGING THAW

What is notable, nevertheless, about the China-India relationship is that as the vectors along which the two sides compete have expanded, the territorial aspect has become ostensibly less important. This does not mean, as discussed above, that the dispute is any more resolvable than it was before. However, it is also true that over the last two decades or so both sides have found means to move toward a dynamic that offers some degree of stability and management on the territorial front while attempts are made to find a final solution to conflict itself. The record on this score has no doubt been far from exemplary, but it is also true that these developments have significantly dampened the prospects of crises and war on the borders.

The path to management began with New Delhi's cautious moves to normalize relations in the late 1970s. In 1977, the Janata Party dethroned Indira Gandhi from power. Shortly after, in 1979, India's then foreign minister and later prime minister Atal Bihari Vajpayee became the first senior Indian official to visit Beijing since the war. An agreement to reestablish diplomatic relations was reached soon after, with the understanding that dialogue over resolving the territorial issue was of paramount importance. Consequently a China-India dialogue on border issues was initiated with eight rounds of vice-ministerial level talks held from 1981 to 1987.[63] The crisis at Sumdorong Chu temporarily put relations back in cold storage, which were resuscitated only with an Indian prime-ministerial visit by Rajiv Gandhi to China in 1988. During this visit, China-India border talks were upgraded to joint working group (JWG) discussions, fourteen of which were held till 2003. The joint communiqué from that 1988 visit stressed the need—especially in the context of the recent backsliding of relations—for restoring tranquility along the border and achieving a "fair and reasonable settlement of the boundary question."[64]

These border-management efforts acquired greater momentum in the early 1990s with the signing of a raft of agreements by the two sides. In 1993, both sides concluded the Agreement on the Maintenance of Peace and Tranquility along the Line of Actual Control in the India-China Border Areas, which yet again reiterated both sides' commitment to resolving the boundary issues "through peaceful and friendly consultations" and their determination to avoid the threat or use of force in the interim.[65] This latter goal (of keeping the border areas calm) was given more concrete expression soon after in the November 1996 Agreement on Confidence Building Measures in the Military Field along the Line of Actual Control in the India-China Border Areas.[66] Through this agreement both sides committed to instituting numerous confidence-building measures (CBMs) along the borders—including more concretely delimiting the exact coordinates of the LAC—in an effort to minimize the possibility of tensions. In 2003, the Declaration on Principles for Relations and Comprehensive Cooperation between India and China replaced the JWG process, with both sides appointing special representatives (SRs) to "explore from the political perspective of the overall bilateral relationship the framework of a boundary settlement."[67] Nineteen rounds of these talks have been held till present, the latest of them in April 2016 between India's national security adviser, Ajit Doval, and Chinese state councilor Yang Jiechi. In April 2005, in an indication that they had reached some basic consensus with regard to the ground rules for ongoing negotiations, both sides signed the Political Parameters and Guiding Principles for the Settlement of the India-China Boundary Question, expressing hope that "an early settlement of the boundary question" could be found.[68] The 2006 joint declaration went further in declaring that the SRs "shall complete at an early date the task of finalizing an appropriate framework for a final package settlement covering all sectors of the India-China boundary."[69]

To what extent have these efforts been successful? The record has been mixed at best, but the positives are nevertheless noteworthy. Through the years, these agreements have had two basic goals in mind: movement toward the resolution of the territorial dispute and the establishment of some degree of tranquility on the borders in the meanwhile. On the first, there is no doubt progress has been "glacial" at best, as one scholar has put it.[70] The sheer number of discussions in various formats since the early 1980s, including most recently SR-level talks, is enough to suggest that the two countries have not really arrived at a place where an ultimate solution to the territorial dispute might be considered as being in the offing. The Shared Vision for the 21st Century of the People's Republic of China and the Republic of India signed by the two countries in 2008 seemed to acknowledge as much—that resolving the territorial dispute was currently far-fetched—in implicitly suggesting that the territorial issues be set aside and not be allowed to impinge on the development of relations between the two countries in other arenas.[71] A broader, final solution to the territorial issue is therefore seemingly out of reach, regardless of the fact that what may be considered to be an ostensibly reasonable model for doing so has existed since the 1960 talks. This is not surprising given the fact that, as discussed above, historical memory and domestic political factors seriously constrain political leaders on both sides from undertaking drastic alterations of their long-standing stances on the areas under dispute. Indeed, both sides seem to be incredibly hesitant to clarify publicly—or even privately—what, in their view, would be a fair and final solution to the border dispute. Nevertheless, the suggestion of former Indian national security adviser Shivshankar Menon in 2014 that the primary barrier toward a solution lies not in the technicalities (which had been more or less dealt with) but the ability—or willingness—on both sides to make the actual political decision points clearly to why the first, more ambitious goal still eludes the leaders of the two countries.[72]

On the second, less ambitious but no less important goal—the establishment of some tranquility on the borders—the record has certainly been more sanguinary. It is worth pointing out right away, however, that this does not mean that there have been no challenges on this front either. Indeed, many of the goals set by the two parties as part of the above-mentioned agreements are far from finding fruition. For instance, while the 1996 agreement sought to clarify the location of the LAC so as to minimize the possibility of inadvertent incursions by troops from either side, officials of the two countries have yet to actually share maps to facilitate this process, except in the more minor middle sector.[73] As both sides have accelerated their physical presence in border areas through military and infrastructure buildup in recent years, the risks of incursions on both sides have grown.[74] Arguably the most severe of the resultant crises—the Daulat Beg Oldi incident—happened as late as April and May 2013 when a platoon of Chinese troops intruded deep (some ten kilometers) into Indian territory in Ladakh and refused to vacate the area for some two weeks. They only did so a few days before Chinese premier Li Keqiang's scheduled visit to India. Curiously, similar incursions were reported in September 2014 in the midst of Chinese president Xi Jinping's first visit to India.[75] Most recently, from June through late August 2017, India and China engaged in a long, tense, but fortunately not violent standoff in the Doklam area at the trijunction of the China-India-Bhutan borders. While not strictly driven by the China-India border dispute, as the territory in question here is contested by China and Bhutan, Beijing's attempt to extend a road onto this patch of land and India's response of having its troops cross into the area in support of Bhutan's claims had both countries staking positions that to most observers were difficult to rescind on both sides without serious loss of face.[76] So severe was this crisis that rhetoric escalated in the Chinese media to the uncharacteristically dangerous level of threatening war and a repeat of 1962 in reaction to the Indian government's seeming determination to maintain its troop presence in the disputed area in a show of resolve.[77] Important to note here is the fact that Indian actions were driven by the strategic importance of the area to its own security—a Chinese presence here brings it in dangerous proximity to India's vulnerable Siliguri Corridor—a desire to deter, and a need for credibility management in the face of Beijing's seeming tendency in recent years to renege on earlier understandings. The actions aimed at extended deterrence in aid of Bhutan, a country with which India has a "special relationship," one that has historically involved Thimpu being "guided" by New Delhi in its foreign and national security policies.[78] Such incidents are naturally far from propitious for stability and point to the continuing challenges of managing the China-India border areas in a context where the rise of both countries risks potentially exacerbating the rivalry dynamics in their relationship.

Nevertheless, it would not be incorrect to claim that in general the CBMs and dialogue processes, as well as the normative environment generated via successive agreements between the two sides, have ensured two things. On the one hand, these agreements have meant—at least until Xi Jinping's ascension to power in China—that such crises have emerged only infrequently, considering especially the length of the border, the large expanses of territory under contention, and the potential for a charged public opinion pushing for adventurist stances in both countries. They have also meant, on the other hand, that when trouble does emerge, both sides have been able to, in most instances, nip it in the bud and arrest escalatory dynamics fairly swiftly. Officials on both sides have also in such cases quickly sought to minimize the import of cross-border transgressions in order to moderate reactions at home. In explaining away reported incursions by Chinese troops in September 2014, for instance, India's defense minister, Manohar Parrikar, underplayed their import by noting in Parliament that there is "no commonly delineated LAC between India and China. There are areas along the border where India and China have differing perceptions of LAC." Transgressions therefore happened on both sides because of each "undertaking patrolling up to their respective perception of LAC."[79] The 2017 Doklam crisis was notable precisely for the facts that the duration of the standoff and the uncharacteristically shrill public rhetoric from the Chinese side suggested that the decades-long mechanisms that had kept the China-India border fairly stable had begun to fray. The fact that the two sides managed to arrive at a de-escalatory arrangement in even this case does, however, suggest that the crisis-management structures in which the two sides have invested over the past few decades are indeed robust.[80]

In other words, even as border incursions, troop and infrastructure buildups, and administrative matters in disputed territories such as Arunachal Pradesh have periodically sparked tensions between the two sides, New Delhi and Beijing have managed to curtail escalation and adhere to the basic understanding that the status quo ought to be maintained. In order to institutionalize this process, both sides concluded a border-defense cooperation agreement in October 2013 aimed, as one observer put it, at developing a "nuts-and-bolts crisis management mechanism, intended to help both sides de-escalate tensions should a border incident take place."[81] The agreement was signed in immediate response to the preceding tensions, pointing to the fact that the two sides have established a modus vivendi that allows them now to respond to burgeoning crises with some level of institutionalized alacrity. This record of relative stability in the border areas and an institutionalized setup to address any tensions that might emerge is particularly noteworthy given the stark contrast it offers with the state of affairs in India's other territorial rivalry, that with Pakistan over Kashmir. In that case, while resolution of the dispute is even more distant, mere attempts at managing it and establishing limited stability have had a disastrous record. The experience rather has been one of constant crises punctuated by rare and brief periods of hope and a tendency for crises that do erupt to escalate quickly, at least at the rhetorical level, and with more unrestrained fervor within domestic politics, media, and public opinion.[82]

Central to understanding why this far-from-perfect thaw has been possible at all is the paradoxical fact that, as discussed in detail earlier, for all the centrality of territory to the emergence and persistence of the rivalry in the first place, the territorial stakes involved have also always been amenable to compromise. In essence, there has been some recognition in both countries—at least at the elite/governmental level—that each side in fact holds territory that was and is most important to them. While the experience of the 1962 war, the historical memories associated with it, and in general the broader (and expanding) contours of a more overarching competition do deeply complicate the potential for a resolution of the territorial dispute, the lower stakes on the territorial issue have ensured that there is little incentive on either side to pursue potentially provocative policies aimed at altering the status quo. Again, the contrast with the India-Pakistan equation is telling, where both sides attach deep salience to the territory being contested and at least one of the sides (Pakistan) has had an abiding agenda of seeking to alter the status quo by any means possible. Indeed, as has been pointed out elsewhere, Pakistan's revisionist goals have led it to actively find ways to overcome the massive asymmetries that in general disadvantage it against India.[83] India, on the other hand, has invested much less effort in truncating the asymmetry with China because it lacks essentially revisionist goals. The China-India territorial dispute has, therefore, paradoxically become more amenable to management and stabilization even as the dimensions of contestation between the two countries have on the whole only further increased and intensified over the years.

ECONOMIC INTERDEPENDENCE

This basic ability to sideline or manage the territorial issue has in turn both allowed for and been encouraged by both countries' recognition and pursuit of the potentially immense mutual benefits promised by sharing the fruits of economic globalization and interdependence. Perhaps not coincidentally, then, efforts at management of the territorial conflict gathered steam simultaneously, with both sides moving firmly toward reforms aimed at integrating their economies closely with global markets. Both countries had been gradually transitioning in this direction in previous years. In India, by the mid- to late 1980s, the Indira Gandhi and Rajiv Gandhi governments had begun to push for more business-friendly economic policies, emulating to some extent a process that the Chinese themselves had chosen to initiate earlier in that decade.[84] Yet real momentum toward economic reforms was only truly found in both countries in the early 1990s. The collapse of the Soviet Union—and the end of the Cold War—had, to put it briefly, dramatically transformed both the strategic and ideological environment at a systemic level, forcing a reassessment of policies in both India and China. In Beijing this resulted in a conscious decision to move from a gradualist process of reform to beginning a major push at opening up the country's economy.[85] Indian leaders in turn, confronted with a severe balance-of-payments crisis at the same time, utilized the new climate and the need for International Monetary Fund (IMF) support to push through a major overhaul of the very ideational foundations of the Indian economy, putting the country on the path to economic liberalization.[86]

As India and China have progressively embraced economic liberalization in the following years, it has become apparent on both sides that there are potentially massive economic returns to be mutually reaped through deepening economic ties. Both countries, after all, enjoy the unique advantage of being two of the largest (and fastest growing) economies and markets in the world, who also fortuitously enjoy the logistical benefits of proximity that comes with being neighbors. Not surprisingly, then, bilateral trade between the two sides has increased substantially as both countries have opened up their economies further. Bilateral trade jumped from being worth under $200 million in the 1980s to over $70 billion in 2015.[87] As the Confederation of Indian Industry has recently noted, trade between the two countries has expanded by 15 percent annually on average every year since 2007.[88] Also over this period, China became India's largest trading partner, while India became a growing but significantly less important partner of China's. Similarly, recent years have seen both sides more seriously explore the potential for foreign direct investment (FDI) in each other's economies. Again, while still low, as Matthew A. Castle points out in chapter 10 in this volume, on both sides this number has more than doubled over the last decade.[89] Indeed, the Modi government in India has been actively courting Chinese FDI in the country to complement its "Make in India" campaign. In accordance with this, Chinese president Xi

Jinping committed to $100 billion worth of investment over five years during his 2014 visit to India.[90]

This is not to say that the story is exclusively positive. As the respective rankings of each country in the other's list of largest trading partners suggests (and is even more apparent if one looks at the actual balance of trade between the two countries), there is a significant asymmetry at play to India's disadvantage. The practical implication is that India is much more dependent for its economic prosperity on trade with China than is the case in the other direction. As Castle notes, "when we break down the bilateral trade to examine the products that are traded, Indian importers may be more vulnerable to a disruption in Chinese exports, while Indian exporters in key products are more reliant on the Chinese export market and therefore more sensitive to decreases in Chinese demand." Even on FDI there is significant asymmetry that characterizes the relationship in that Chinese FDI in India amounts to far more than vice versa.[91] This trend of asymmetry has only become progressively worse over the years, leading to undeniable anxiety in New Delhi that Beijing has been getting the better end of the deal in this economic relationship.[92]

This asymmetry, of course, indicates that economic ties between the two countries are not so robust as to facilitate the kind of peace that liberal scholars suggest. After all, while India may have very little incentive to provoke conflict in this relationship, similar considerations do not constrain Chinese leaders, who are far less dependent on economic ties with India.[93] Nevertheless, it is also true that while a positive peace is unlikely to result as a consequence of the current levels of interdependence, they are—and have so far been—useful in establishing a kind of negative peace, or stability. This can be explained to some extent by the major insight of the discussion above, that the territorial stakes are just not high enough on either side for the pursuit of a revisionist agenda, which in turn has facilitated a conscious expansion of economic ties on both sides. More crucially, cooperation in the economic arena has been incentivized by the fact that economic growth has become crucial to the domestic agendas of leaders in both countries. Legitimacy of governments (especially in China) since reforms began has at least to some extent been understood to be associated with a continuing ability to deliver the fruits of growth and economic prosperity to their people.[94] To the extent that this is true, and to the extent that the potential for China-India economic ties are far from realized, it does put some constraints on even the Chinese to avoid upsetting economic progress by precipitating serious conflict. On the global level, similarly, economic growth is central to the pursuit of the rising international ambitions of both countries for more power, influence, and importantly status. Both China and India—arguably more so the latter—have historically viewed their role in the world as incommensurate to their size and history, and to the extent that higher status requires a substantial material (military and economic) base, sustained economic growth is essential.[95] Indeed, much of what has been achieved by both countries in terms of a greater global institutional role and status accommodation in recent years—be it through a larger say at the IMF or a more tangible say for the BRICS (Brazil, Russia, India, China, and South Africa) through the New Development Bank (NDB)—has been in the economic realm, suggesting that status in the economic arena might be the lower fruits available to be picked for both countries.[96]

To put it another way, as the salience of deeper ties to both sides' economic fortunes has grown, it has become easier and more vital for them to also recognize that the territorial stakes are not so significant as to demand the pursuit of conflictual policies in any kind of sustained manner. Consequently, as China-India economic ties have expanded substantially in recent years, they—in keeping with liberal expectations—have further incentivized both sides to at the least stay the course on maintaining relative stability on territorial issues. While periodic crises are inevitable in this increasingly complex and competitive relationship, and even regarding economic issues such as the terms of trade and FDI there are challenges to be confronted, on the whole the necessity of managing territorial issues has become more important to both countries as the economic stakes of the relationship have grown. Such a dynamic can be encouraged even further by concerted efforts on both sides—but particularly by China—to begin addressing some of the deficiencies in the relationship. The trade imbalance is one of these, and greater access to the Chinese market for Indian goods is likely necessary. The flip side of this is the need for a concerted effort on the Indian side to expand its manufacturing base and efficiency so as to be able to make its exports more attractive in China. The Make in India program seems to at least aspire to that.[97] FDI is another area where again there is much room for progress. While India has been active in inviting Chinese investment in India and Beijing seems willing to make strides in that direction, it would behoove both sides to also make greater efforts to address the asymmetry in the relationship, which has so far seen much greater Chinese FDI entering India than is the case in the other direction. If both sides are able to constructively address these issues, the promise for economic interdependence remains great, with all the positive implications that will have for the continued management, and eventually resolution, of the territorial dispute.

CONCLUSION

The territorial dispute between India and China has been central to the emergence and persistence of the broader competition—an asymmetrical rivalry, some would suggest—between the two countries. While the issues on which the conflictual aspects of the relationship revolve have significantly expanded over the years, the origins of that process can be clearly linked to the mistrust and disagreements over territorial issues (including Tibet) that emerged soon after the independence of India and the rise to power of the communists in China. Indeed, while the portents of rivalry may have always existed—not least in the very structural fact of two large, historically important, and ideologically different states being pitted against each other in the same regional context—that potential was truly triggered only with and through the outbreak of territorial conflict beginning in the late 1950s. The experience of war itself was seminal in cementing that hostility, leading both sides to reorient their foreign and security policies in ways that have only exacerbated the competition since then.

This initial centrality of the territorial dispute in the China-India relationship, the emotional and reputational stakes that have become associated with it over time, and the consequent expansion of issues over which India and China now compete have, in turn, naturally complicated the territorial issue itself to an extent that its final resolution seems unlikely in the foreseeable future. The fact that, despite regular dialogue over the last couple of decades, differences over territorial issues have perceptibly only expanded rather than narrowed—with shifting goalposts and more cases of intrusions in recent years—attests to this unfortunate fact. Despite this, however, this chapter has also argued that the nature of the stakes and disagreements over the disputed territory are (and always have been) such that they paradoxically have allowed the two sides to find a modus vivendi to manage the border and establish some degree of stability and predictability. With both sides in control of territory that has always been of most importance to them, neither has the desire or incentive to alter a status quo that elites in both countries know well enough will likely be the alignment along which a future solution undoubtedly lies. This limited salience of the territory for each country has allowed both sides to consensually pursue a policy of management and confidence-building in the disputed border regions, even as a final solution remains unlikely given the entangling of the issue in a broader competition and the heavy historical baggage that resonates deeply in domestic politics.

It bears to caution, however, that this can by no means be taken to be a permanent state of affairs. The 2017 Doklam standoff, while it did end with successful de-escalation, also presents the troubling possibility that the border-management mechanisms that the two countries have developed in recent decades may be all too fragile. If China's initial assertiveness in the area, in step with its general conduct in other areas such as the South China Sea and the Indian Ocean in recent years, is indeed a manifestation of its desire to stamp its dominance in the region, as many in India and elsewhere fear, then there is little doubt that rivalry dynamics will make such standoffs increasing likely and more severe in the coming years as an India that is ambitious in its own right responds with similar resolve as in Doklam.[98] Indeed, as the two countries increasingly compete and disagree on an increasing range of issues, new and old, related to regional and global governance and security (as in the case most recently of the Chinese Belt and Road Initiative and the China-Pakistan Economic Corridor), it is most likely that such tensions and related signaling will manifest themselves on the ground in the border areas.[99] Needless to say, then, the role of robust management mechanisms to help diplomatically de-escalate such tensions will be indispensable in future crises. In the aftermath of Doklam, it behooves both sides to recognize the fact that the stabilizing measures that they have mutually developed in recent decades are in need of serious nurturing and to pay renewed attention to risks that their simultaneous rise and rising ambitions in the global arena pose for the resuscitation of conflict on their borders.

NOTES

1. For a classic overview of the rivalry, see John W. Garver, *Protracted Contest: Sino-Indian Rivalry in the Twentieth Century* (Seattle: University of Washington Press, 2001). See also Jeff M. Smith, *Cold Peace: China-India Rivalry in the Twenty-First Century* (Lanham, MD: Lexington Books, 2014); C. Raja Mohan, *Samudra Manthan: Sino-Indian Rivalry in the Indo-Pacific* (Washington, DC: Carnegie Endowment for International Peace, 2012); and Francine R. Frankel and Harry Harding, eds., *The India-China Relationship: What the United States Needs to Know* (New York: Columbia University Press, 2004).

2. See chapter 3 by Xiaoyu Pu in this volume for a discussion of the asymmetry in perceptions of rivalry. Also see David Malone and Rohan Mukherjee, "India and China: Conflict and Cooperation," *Survival* 52, no.1 (February/March 2010): 137–58.

3. For detailed discussions of both sides' claims, see Steven A. Hoffmann, *India and the China Crisis* (Berkeley: University of California Press, 1990); Alastair Lamb, *The McMahon Line: A Study in the Relations between India, China, and Tibet, 1904 to 1914* (London: Routledge, 1966); Neville Maxwell, *India's China War* (London: Cape, 1970); A. G. Noorani, *India-China Boundary Problem, 1846–1947: History and Diplomacy* (New Delhi: Oxford University Press, 2011); and Srinath Raghavan, *War and Peace in Modern India* (New York: Palgrave Macmillan, 2010).

4. The Chinese vociferously reiterated these claims during the 1960 talks. See, for one, the record of meeting between Nehru and Zhou (April 22, 1960), P. N. Haksar Papers, subject file 24, Installment I/II, Nehru Memorial Museum and Library (NMML).

5. Hoffmann, *India and the China Crisis*, 15. See also Raghavan, *War and Peace*, 239.

6. For a detailed history, see Tsering Shakya, *The Dragon in the Land of Snows: A History of Modern Tibet since 1947* (New York: Penguin Compass, 2000), 33–130.

7. Garver argues that whether or not this was true, the Chinese certainly believed it to be the case, a central precipitating cause for their initiation of war in 1962. John W. Garver, "China's Decision for War with India in 1962," in *New Directions in the Study of China's Foreign Policy*, ed. Alastair I. Johnston and Robert S. Ross (Stanford, CA: Stanford University Press, 2006), 105.

8. Prithwis Chandra Chakravarti, *India's China Policy* (Bloomington: Indiana University Press, 1962), 11; and Garver, *Protracted Contest*, 18–19.

9. Andrew Bingham Kennedy, *The International Ambitions of Mao and Nehru: National Efficacy Beliefs and the Making of Foreign Policy* (New York: Cambridge University Press, 2012), 221.

10. Relinquishing certain inherited Indian rights in Tibet was, as R. K. Nehru characterized it, "a concession only to realism." Quoted in Raghavan, *War and Peace*, 241. The most the Indian prime minister expected from the agreement was curbing "to some extent undesirable urges in the other country." Jawaharlal Nehru to K. K. Chettur, May 9, 1954, in *Selected Works of Jawaharlal Nehru*, Second Series, ed. Sarvepalli Gopal et al. (New Delhi: Jawaharlal Nehru Memorial Fund and Oxford University Press, 1984), 25:479.

11. See the voluminous literature on this issue: Paul F. Diehl, ed., *A Road Map to War: Territorial Dimensions of International Conflict* (Nashville: Vanderbilt University Press, 1999); Paul K. Huth, *Standing Your Ground: Territorial Disputes and International Conflict* (Ann Arbor: University of Michigan Press, 1996); Paul Domenic Senese and John A. Vasquez, *The Steps to War: An Empirical Study* (Princeton, NJ: Princeton University Press, 2008); John A. Vasquez, *The War Puzzle* (Cambridge: Cambridge University Press, 1993); and John A. Vasquez and Marie T. Henehan, *Territory, War, and Peace* (New York: Routledge, 2010).

12. Gary Goertz and Paul F. Diehl, *Territorial Changes and International Conflict* (London: Routledge, 1992), 132–33.

13. Paul F. Diehl and Gary Goertz, *War and Peace in International Rivalry* (Ann Arbor: University of Michigan Press, 2001), 44, 48.

14. T.V. Paul, "Why Has the India-Pakistan Rivalry Been So Enduring? Power Asymmetry and an Intractable Conflict," *Security Studies* 15, no. 4 (2006): 602.

15. Several groups, particularly the Nagas, have been fighting for their own independent state since independence. Garver, *Protracted Contest*, 91–100. Sardar Patel—India's home minister—had noted in 1950 that the people of the northeast had "no established loyalty or devotion to India." Sardar Patel to Nehru, November 7, 1950, in *Sardar Patel's Correspondence, 1945–50*, ed. Durga Das (Ahmedabad: Navajivan Publishing House, 1971), 10:338.

16. Hoffmann, *India and the China Crisis*, 18–20; and Maxwell, *India's China War*, 74.

17. Hoffmann, *India and the China Crisis*, 9–12; and Garver, *Protracted Contest*, 88.

18. Jawaharlal Nehru, "Speech in Rajya Sabha (August 31, 1959)," in *Prime Minister on Sino-Indian Relations: In Parliament* (New Delhi: External Publicity Division of External Affairs, Government of India, 1962), 98.

19. For details, see Mahesh Shankar, "Showing Character: Nehru, Reputation, and the Sino-Indian Dispute, 1957–1962," *Asian Security* 11, no. 2 (2015): 99–115.

20. M. Taylor Fravel, *Strong Borders, Secure Nation: Cooperation and Conflict in China's Territorial Disputes* (Princeton, NJ: Princeton University Press, 2008), 41–69.

21. Panikkar to Nehru (September 28, 1951), quoted in Sarvepalli Gopal, *Jawaharlal Nehru: A Biography* (Cambridge, MA: Harvard University Press, 1976), 2:177.

22. Shakya, *Dragon in the Land of Snows*, 201–3.

23. Garver, *Protracted Contest*, 80–88.

24. See Nehru's record of talks with Zhou in 1956–1957: "Talks with Zhou Enlai" (December 31, 1956, and January 1, 1957), *Selected Works*, 36:598–600; and Nehru to U Nu, April 22, 1957, *Selected Works*, 36:507–8.

25. Dawa Norbu, "Tibet in Sino-Indian Relations: The Centrality of Marginality," *Asian Survey* 37, no. 11 (1997): 1080–82.

26. Nehru to U Nu, April 22, 1957, *Selected Works*, 36:507–8.

27. B. N. Mullik, *My Years with Nehru: 1948–1964* (Bombay: Allied Publishers, 1972), 78–80. See also B. R. Nanda, "Introduction" in *Indian Foreign Policy: The Nehru Years*, ed. B. R. Nanda (New Delhi: Radiant 1990), 16–17.

28. For a detailed discussion of these perceptions in New Delhi, see Shankar, "Showing Character," 107–10.

29. Judith M. Brown, *Nehru: A Political Life* (New Haven, CT: Yale University Press, 2003), 260–61; Nancy Jetly, *India-China Relations, 1947–1977: A Study of Parliament's Role in the Making of Foreign Policy* (New Delhi: Radiant, 1979); Shashi Tharoor, *Reasons of State: Political Development and India's Foreign Policy under Indira Gandhi, 1966–1977* (New Delhi: Vikas, 1982), 40.

30. Raghavan, *War and Peace*, 253.

31. Hoffmann, *India and the China Crisis*; and Manjari Chatterjee Miller, *Wronged by Empire: Post-Imperial Ideology and Foreign Policy in India and China* (Stanford, CA: Stanford University Press, 2013).
32. As is most apparent in the report by Lt. Gen. T. B. Henderson Brooks and Brig. Premindra Singh Bhagat. Report by Lt. Gen. T. B. Henderson Brooks and Brig. Premindra Singh Bhagat, part I, http://www.indiandefencereview.com/wp-content/uploads/2014/03/TopSecretdocuments2.pdf.
33. Raghavan, *War and Peace*, 284–87.
34. Maxwell, *India's China War*, 104, 263.
35. Garver, "China's Decision," 94–95.
36. See Bruce Riedel, *JFK's Forgotten Crisis: Tibet, the CIA, and the Sino-Indian War* (Washington, DC: Brookings Institution Press, 2015), 100–101.
37. Zhou to Nehru, September 8, 1959, in *Notes, Memoranda and Letters Exchanged and Agreements Signed between the Governments of India and China* (New Delhi: Ministry of External Affairs, Government of India, 1959–68), white paper 2, 27–33.
38. Garver, *Protracted Contest*, 85–87, 90–91.
39. Subimal Dutt to Indian Mission, April 27, 1960, in P. N. Haksar Papers, subject file 25, NMML.
40. Fravel, *Strong Borders*, 190–97; and Garver, "China's Decision," 39.
41. Jawaharlal Nehru, *Pakistan Seeks to Profit from Chinese Aggression* (New Delhi: Government of India, Ministry of Information and Broadcasting, 1963), 4.
42. Quoted in Russell Brines, *The Indo-Pakistani Conflict* (London: Pall Mall, 1968), 196.
43. For discussion of how India remembers the 1962 war, see Dibyesh Anand, "Remembering 1962 Sino-Indian Border War: Politics of Memory," *Journal of Defence Studies* 6, no. 4 (2012): 229–48. See also Shivshankar Menon, "The India-China War of 1962 and Its Political After-Life," *The Wire*, July 17, 2017, https://thewire.in/114314/review-remaking-national-memory-of-the-1962-sino-indian-war/.
44. Yinan He, "History, Chinese Nationalism and the Emerging Sino-Japanese Conflict," *Journal of Contemporary China* 16, no. 50 (2007): 1–24.
45. See Jessica Chin Weiss, *Powerful Patriots: Nationalist Protest in China's Foreign Relations* (Oxford: Oxford University Press, 2014).
46. Nilova Roy Chaudhury, "China Lays Claim to Arunachal," *Hindustan Times*, November 14, 2006, http://www.hindustantimes.com/india/china-lays-claim-to-arunachal/story-QDVTkQ1kDNBBf9QMvsDdBM.html.
47. Vidya Nadkarni, "India: An Aspiring Global Power," in *Emerging Powers in a Comparative Perspective: The Political and Economic Rise of the BRIC Countries*, ed. Vidya Nadkarni and Norma C. Noonan (New York: Bloomsbury, 2013), 138–40.
48. For an account of some the developments in this period, see John W. Garver, "Sino-Indian Rapprochement and the Sino-Pakistan Entente," *Political Science Quarterly* 3, no. 2 (Summer 1996): 323–47.
49. In 1978, the new Chinese regime of Deng Xiaoping announced an end to its support of insurgencies in India's northeast. See Mohan Guruswamy and Zorawar Daulet Singh, *India-China Relations: The Border Issue and Beyond* (New Delhi: Viva Books, 2009), 93.
50. Itty Abraham, *The Making of the Indian Atomic Bomb: Science, Secrecy and the Postcolonial State* (London: Zed Books, 1998), 125.
51. Jawaharlal Nehru, "Changing India," *Foreign Affairs* 41, no. 3 (April 1963), https://www.foreignaffairs.com/articles/asia/1963-04-01/changing-india.

52. See Riedel, *JFK's Forgotten Crisis*, 109–46.

53. Srinath Raghavan, *1971: A Global History of the Creation of Bangladesh* (Cambridge, MA: Harvard University Press, 2013), 108–30.

54. Lorenz M. Luthi, *The Sino-Soviet Split: Cold War in the Communist World* (Princeton, NJ: Princeton University Press, 2008).

55. On the China-US rapprochement, see Evelyn Goh, *Constructing the U.S. Rapprochement with China, 1961–1974: From "Red Menace" to "Tacit Ally"* (Cambridge: Cambridge University Press, 2005).

56. Garver, *Protracted Contest*, 138–215.

57. For the naval dimensions of such perceptions and India's response, see Walter C. Ladwig III, "Delhi's Pacific Ambitions: Naval Power, 'Look East,' and India's Emerging Influence in the Asia-Pacific," *Asian Security* 5, no. 2 (2009): 87–113.

58. For a detailed discussion of the China-Pakistan border agreement, see Rudra Chaudhuri, "The Making of an 'All Weather Friendship': Pakistan, China and the History of a Border Agreement: 1949–1963," *International History Review* (March 2017): 1–24, doi: 10.1080/07075332.2017.1298529.

59. Zulfikar Ali Bhutto, then minister of foreign affairs, boasted in 1965 that such a war would "involve the security and territorial integrity of the largest state in Asia." Quoted in T.V. Paul, *Asymmetric Conflict: War Initiation by Weaker Powers* (Cambridge: Cambridge University Press, 1994), 118.

60. For an overview of this relationship, see Andrew Small, *The China-Pakistan Axis: Asia's New Geopolitics* (Oxford: Oxford University Press, 2015).

61. For the nuclear dimension in this relationship, see chapter 9 by Vipin Narang in this volume.

62. John F. Burns, "India's New Defense Chief Sees Chinese Military Threat," *New York Times*, May 5, 1998, http://www.nytimes.com/1998/05/05/world/india-s -new-defense-chief-sees-chinese-military-threat.html.

63. Malone and Mukherjee, "India and China," 143.

64. Text of the communiqué is available in "India-China Joint Press Communiqué," *Indian Journal of Asian Affairs* 2, no. 1 (June 1989): 53–55.

65. "Agreement on the Maintenance of Peace and Tranquillity along the Line of Actual Control in the India-China Border Areas," in *India-China Border Dispute: A Case Study of the Eastern Sector*, ed. M. L. Sali (New Delhi: A. P. H. Publishing Corporation, 1998), 289–92.

66. See Waheguru Pal Singh Sidhu and Jing-Dong Yuan, "Resolving the Sino-Indian Border Dispute: Building Confidence through Cooperative Monitoring," *Asian Survey* 41, no. 2: 351–76.

67. "Declaration on Principles for Relations and Comprehensive Cooperation between the People's Republic of China and the Republic of India," People's Republic of China and Republic of India (Beijing, June 25, 2003), http://www .fmprc.gov.cn/mfa_eng/wjdt_665385/2649_665393/t22852.shtml.

68. "Joint Statement of the Republic of India and the People's Republic of China," Republic of India and People's Republic of China (New Delhi, April 11, 2005), http://www.mea.gov.in/bilateral-documents.htm?dtl/6577/Joint+Statement+of +the+Republic+of+India+and+the+Peoples+Republic+of+China.

69. "Joint Declaration by the Republic of India and the People's Republic of China," Republic of India and People's Republic of China (New Delhi, November 21, 2006), http://www.mea.gov.in/bilateral-documents.htm?dtl/6363/Joint +Declaration+by+the+Republic+of+India+an.

70. Sumit Ganguly, "India and China: Border Issues, Domestic Integration and International Security," in *The India-China Relationship: What the United States*

Needs to Know, ed. Francine R. Frankel and Harry Harding (New York: Columbia University Press, 2004), 123.

71. "Joint Declaration by the Republic of India and the People's Republic of China," Republic of India and People's Republic of China (New Delhi, November 21, 2006), http://www.mea.gov.in/bilateral-documents.htm?dtl/6363/Joint +Declaration+by+the+Republic+of+India+an; "A Shared Vision for the 21st Century of the People's Republic of China and the Republic of India," People's Republic of China and Republic of India (Beijing, January 15, 2008), http://in .china-embassy.org/eng/zgbd/t399545.htm.

72. Shivshankar Menon, "What China's Rise Means for India," *The Wire*, January 4, 2016, http://thewire.in/18511/what-chinas-rise-means-for-india/.

73. Claude Arpi, "Where Is the LAC?," *India Defence Review*, June 22, 2015, http:// www.indiandefencereview.com/spotlights/where-is-the-lac/.

74. On some of these infrastructural developments, see Iskander Rehman, "A Himalayan Challenge: India's Conventional Deterrent and the Role of Special Operations Forces along the Sino-Indian Border," *Naval War College Review* 70, no. 1 (Winter 2017): 104–42.

75. See Gardiner Harris and Edward Wong, "Where China Meets India in a High-Altitude Desert, Push Comes to Shove," *New York Times*, May 2, 2013, http:// www.nytimes.com/2013/05/03/world/asia/where-china-meets-india-push-comes -to-shove.html?mcubz=0; and Brahma Chellaney, "Ladakh Incursion: China Scores Bloodless Victory over India, More Intrusions May Come," *Economic Times*, May 13, 2013, http://economictimes.indiatimes.com/opinion/ladakh-incursion -china-scores-bloodless-victory-over-india-more-intrusions-may-come/articleshow /20006435.cms.

76. For an overview of the standoff and how it connects to the broader rivalry, see, for instance, Jeff M. Smith, "High Noon in the Himalayas: Behind the China-India Standoff at Doka La," War on the Rocks, July 13, 2017, https://warontherocks .com/2017/07/high-noon-in-the-himalayas-behind-the-china-india-standoff-at -doka-la/.

77. See, e.g., Long Xingchun, "New Delhi Didn't Draw Lesson from 1962 Border War," *Global Times*, July 23, 2017, http://www.globaltimes.cn/content/1057632 .shtml.

78. See Ankit Panda, "What's Driving the India-China Standoff at Doklam?," *The Diplomat*, July 18, 2017, http://thediplomat.com/2017/07/whats-driving-the -india-china-standoff-at-doklam/.

79. "Transgressions, Not Intrusions, Occur along Sino-India Border: Manohar Parrikar," *Economic Times*, December 2, 2014, http://economictimes.indiatimes .com/news/politics-and-nation/transgressions-not-intrusions-occur-along-sino -india-border-manohar-parrikar/articleshow/45349224.cms.

80. Kallol Bhattacherjee, "Doklam De-escalation Based on Mutual Agreement, Says MEA," *The Hindu*, August 28, 2017, http://www.thehindu.com/news/national /india-china-agree-to-disengage-at-doklam/article19575154.ece?homepage= true.

81. Ankit Panda, "What to Expect from India-China Border Talks in the Modi-Xi Era," *The Diplomat*, March 24, 2015, http://thediplomat.com/2015/03/what-to -expect-from-india-china-border-talks-in-the-modi-xi-era/.

82. For a recent book-length take on this relationship, see Sumit Ganguly, *Deadly Impasse: Indo-Pakistani Relations at the Dawn of a New Century* (Cambridge: Cambridge University Press, 2016). Also see T.V. Paul, *The India-Pakistan Conflict: An Enduring Rivalry* (New York: Cambridge University Press, 2005).

83. See Paul, "Why Has the India-Pakistan Rivalry Been So Enduring?"

84. On India's early moves in this direction, see Atul Kohli, "Politics of Economic Growth in India, 1980–2005: Part I; The 1980s," *Economic and Political Weekly* 41, no. 13 (April 1–7, 2006): 1251–59.

85. For an overview of this process and the move from gradual to more rapid reforms, see Barry Naughton, *The Chinese Economy: Transitions and Growth* (Cambridge, MA: MIT Press, 2007), 85–109.

86. See Subhomoy Bhattacharjee, "How WB, IMF Got India to Adopt Reforms in 1991," *Indian Express*, September 17, 2010, http://indianexpress.com/article/news-archive/web/how-wb-imf-got-india-to-adopt-reforms-in-1991.

87. See chapter 10 by Matthew A. Castle in this volume for more details.

88. Gauri Bhatia, "China and India: A Love-Hate Relationship," CNBC, August 11, 2016, http://www.cnbc.com/2016/08/11/china-and-india-a-love-hate-relationship.html.

89. See details in chapter 10.

90. Piyush Pandey, "China to Invest $100 Billion in India over 5 Years," *Times of India*, September 13, 2014, http://timesofindia.indiatimes.com/business/india-business/China-to-invest-100-billion-in-India-over-5-years/articleshow/42386772.cms.

91. See chapter 10.

92. Bhatia, "China and India."

93. See chapter 10.

94. For a comprehensive discussion of the issue of regime legitimacy in China, see Heike Holbig and Bruce Gilley, "Reclaiming Legitimacy in China," *Politics and Policy* 38, no. 3 (2010): 395–422.

95. For a discussion of status as a driver in world politics, see T.V. Paul, Deborah Welch Larson, and William C. Wohlforth, eds., *Status in World Politics* (Cambridge: Cambridge University Press, 2014).

96. Varghese K. George, "India Gets More Voting Rights in IMF Reforms," *The Hindu*, January 29, 2016, http://www.thehindu.com/business/India-gets-more-voting-rights-in-IMF-reforms/article14024758.ece. On the BRICS NDB, see Parag Khanna, "New BRICS Bank a Building Block of Alternative World Order," *New Perspectives Quarterly* 31, no. 4 (2014): 46–48.

97. On the Make in India initiative and its challenges, see Amitabh Dubey, "A Closer Look at Modi's Make in India," *The Wire*, August 30, 2016, https://thewire.in/62808/a-closer-look-at-make-in-india/.

98. For a discussion on some of the lessons of the standoff, see Oriana Skylar Mastro and Arzan Tarapore, "Countering Chinese Coercion: The Case of Doklam," War on the Rocks, August 29, 2017, https://warontherocks.com/2017/08/countering-chinese-coercion-the-case-of-doklam/.

99. Indeed, a common claim in Indian commentaries has been that the Doklam standoff was less a territorial issue and more a Chinese retaliation for Indian and Bhutanese refusal to join the Belt and Road Initiative. See, e.g., Happymon Jacob, "Lessons from Doklam," *The Hindu*, August 29, 2017, http://www.thehindu.com/opinion/lead/lessons-from-doklam/article19582450.ece/amp/.

Chapter 3

Asymmetrical Competitors

Status Concerns and the China-India Rivalry

XIAOYU PU

In 2017, China and India came near the brink of conflict over a remote road in the Himalayas. The standoff began when Bhutan, a close ally of India, discovered Chinese workers trying to extend the road. India responded by sending troops to halt China's construction. China angrily denounced India's move and demanded that India pull back. It was one of the worst border disputes between the two nations in more than thirty years.[1] It took considerable back-channel diplomacy for both sides to agree on a de-escalation agreement in late August 2017. Given the enormous risk of conflict, why was it so difficult for India and China to de-escalate the tensions?

Both China and India were surprised that the other side had taken such a strong stand. China's power advantage did not necessarily increase its leverage to change India's behavior. Meanwhile, the asymmetry of status and the memory of the war in 1962 may have given India a strong resolve to defend its position.[2] Even before the standoff, the Indian side complained that Beijing had ignored Indian concerns about Kashmir by announcing $46 billion in investments in infrastructure projects in Gilgit, Baltistan, and Pakistan-occupied Kashmir as a part of its China-Pakistan Economic Corridor.[3] According to Indian China expert Srikanth Kondapalli, Beijing often expects India to pay attention to China's sensitivity, but why doesn't China show a similar level of sensitivity to India's concerns?[4] C. Raja Mohan, a leading analyst of India's foreign policy, argues that India should rethink whether it really shares global interests with China.[5] From India's perspective, Mohan highlights three of Beijing's actions as being problematic: Beijing has opposed New Delhi's entry into the Nuclear Suppliers Group (NSG) and the United Nations Security Council (UNSC) and has also blocked Indian efforts to get the UNSC to designate Masood Azhar a terrorist. Furthermore, Beijing has not yet recognized India as a legitimate nuclear state.[6]

These episodes reflect the complex and asymmetrical relationship between India and China. In recent years, China has pursued an active economic engagement with India, and the two countries have strengthened their cooperation on various global issues, from climate change to global finance. But economic engagement and global cooperation have largely failed to yield a significant breakthrough in China-India bilateral relations.[7] While China tends to underestimate India's concerns for some issues, a growing number of Indian elites and the general public believe that "China is the only major power that does not accept India as a rising global power that must be accommodated."[8] Given the great potential for cooperation, why could not China and India improve their relationship? Why is China willing to integrate India into only some international institutions but not others? Besides territorial and other disputes, a major hurdle to improving the bilateral relationship is the status concerns of the two countries. However, compared with the India-Pakistan relationship, the China-India relationship is more peaceful and stable.[9] Why isn't the China-India relationship more cooperative despite increasing economic interdependence between the two countries? Why is the China-India relationship still much more stable than the India-Pakistan relationship, despite all the disputes over territory, status, and natural resources? How do the status concerns in particular shape the China-India rivalry?

This chapter aims to address the above questions through the analytical framework of status in world politics. While existing studies often assume status is a driving factor in international rivalry, I argue that the role of status is more nuanced. First of all, status scarcity and status discrepancy do drive international rivalry, but status competition can be mitigated. In particular, emerging powers do not always want to enhance their status, as status is social and is not always scarce. Second, there is a deep asymmetry of status and perceptions between India and China.[10] This asymmetry has both positive and negative effects on China-India relations: On the one hand, the asymmetry makes China less likely to view India as a major source of threat, but it also makes China less sensitive to India's concerns. Finally, while status has been an important source of the China-India rivalry, the bilateral relationship is shaped by many factors, and the China-India rivalry could be managed.

The chapter proceeds as follows. The first section discusses general patterns regarding how status shapes the behavior of emerging powers. The second section presents an analysis of the asymmetry of status and perceptions between India and China. The third section discusses why status is a driving factor in the China-India rivalry. The fourth section explains how status competitions could be mitigated. The conclusion summarizes the key findings and policy implications.

STATUS AND EMERGING POWERS

Status matters both in social life and in international relations. At the individual level, the struggle for status is driven by human beings' psychological need for self-esteem. According to an experimental study, people are willing to trade off a status symbol against immediate material rewards.[11] In international relations, status can be defined as "collective beliefs about a given state's ranking on valued attributes (wealth, coercive capabilities, culture, demographic position, sociopolitical organization, and diplomatic clout)."[12] The existing studies highlight why status often drives competitions in international relations. However, in the contemporary world, the role of status is more nuanced. Status can be a driving factor as well as a mitigating factor in international rivalry. Status scarcity and status discrepancy are two possible explanations for how and why status drives international rivalry.

First of all, status drives international rivalry because it is often viewed as a scarce resource. In particular, if international status is viewed as a positional good, it is a scarce resource that cannot be shared by all nations.[13] In international politics, the struggle for status has been recognized as one of the major sources of conflict.[14] In some contexts, status competition among great powers is even viewed as a zero-sum game.

Second, status often drives international rivalry because nation-states (especially emerging powers) often want to have higher status. Traditionally the status concern of emerging powers is the gap between their desired high status and others' recognition of their status. There are psychological and political motivations to close the gap. Status discrepancy is the core issue of the power transition problem in world politics. According to power transition theory, the onset of war between a dominant and a rising power grows more likely as the gap in relative strength between them narrows and as the latter's grievances with the existing order move beyond any hope of peaceful resolution.[15] In international relations, emerging powers are especially sensitive about their status. For countries such as China and India, historical trauma and national humiliation at the hands of Western colonial powers have constructed a postcolonial ideology that pushes them to strive for more power and status.[16] Historically, an emerging power that sought higher status would act assertively, and this struggle for higher status might lead to conflict during a power transition.[17] Given that emerging powers want to have higher status, the struggle for the change in position can lead to zero-sum competitions, conflicts, and even wars.[18] When global power shifts, the key issue is whether the established powers will accommodate the increasing demands of emerging powers.[19]

The existing arguments of status scarcity and status discrepancy are not necessarily wrong, and they are still valid in some contexts. However, I contend that these two arguments are not always valid. Status competition can be mitigated in a number of ways.

First of all, status is fundamentally social and cultural, which means that it is not always scarce. Scholars conventionally conflate status with class or power, but status is "more fluid, more easily changed than class or power."[20] As status is primarily rooted in social interaction and social context, the standards of status are subject to change. In domestic society, there are various social spheres with different status symbols and status criteria. As sociologist Joel Best suggests, "recognizing the way that new social worlds are constantly being created in our society forces us to rethink some of sociologists' most basic assumptions about status. Their tendency to link status to the enduring edifice of social class ignores the relative ease with which status standards can be created and changed."[21] As people in domestic societies achieve status in various ways, the criteria of status change over time and across societies. Instead of seeing status always as a scarce resource, we have seen an emerging phenomenon of status abundance.[22] Prizes proliferate in every corner of our society, from "Academy Award Winner!" to "Best Neighborhood Pizza!" In international politics, while some institutions such as the UNSC are highly privileged status clubs, we see the proliferation of international clubs, from the Group of Twenty, the World Economic Forum (Davos), and the BRICS countries (Brazil, Russia, India, China, and South Africa) to the Asia-Pacific Economic Forum. Because there are different criteria to rank countries, states that seek to have a distinct positive national identity might choose different strategies to achieve status, including the strategies of competition, emulation, or creativity.[23] An important question in the twenty-first century is whether great powers still regard military capabilities as a major tool for gaining status or international standing.[24] As international cultures change, political actors in different times come to regard different things as status symbols.[25]

Second, even in a competitive context, status politics is not necessarily a zero-sum game. It might be useful to make a distinction between status as a "positional" good and status as a "club good." When status is viewed as a club good, it will not always be scarce. If status is regarded as a positional good in some absolute sense, status competition is a zero-sum game.[26] According to this view, the pursuit of status is inherently competitive because status is relative and scarce. This would imply that great-power competition could be positional, in that as one state gains status, another loses it. This zero-sum view of status competition is qualified by the notion of a club good.[27] A club is "a voluntary collective that derives mutual benefits from sharing one or more of the following: production costs, the members' characteristics, or an impure public good characterized by excludable benefits."[28] Club goods are often partially rival in their benefits owing to congestion or crowding. Crowding means that one user's utilization of the club good decreases the benefits still available to the remaining users.

In social life, as well as in international politics, members of elite groups typically restrict membership to an organization to preserve its status and privileges. If anyone can become a member of the club, then membership is not worth much.[29] In international politics, there are different kinds of power clubs, such as the club of the Western industrialized economies (G-7), the nuclear powers club, the permanent five members on the UNSC, and the emerging power club (the BRICS countries).

Finally, emerging powers do not always want to have higher status. Political actors consider the trade-off between the instrumental value and expressive value of status. People sometimes refuse to take a high-status position because it might be too costly. Similarly, nation-states may not necessarily want to maximize their status. For instance, while most studies assume a rising India will always struggle for more recognition as a great power, India sometimes seems to complain about the overrecognition of its rise in the international system.[30] China is striving for great-power status while trying hard to maintain the image of developing-country status.[31] As a dominant player in South America, Brazil has always been afraid of being viewed as a hegemon. Thus, Brazilian diplomats try to describe their country's position through the notion of "consensual hegemony," meaning Brazil tries to play a leadership role through organizing multilateral dialogues rather than through explicit coercion.[32]

ASYMMETRY OF STATUS AND PERCEPTIONS

There is an asymmetry of status and perceptions between India and China, and this asymmetry has profoundly shaped the relationship. While the two countries initially had similar status as two newly independent Asian countries, they have gradually grown apart as China has become a stronger economic power since the start of its "openness and reform" initiative in the late 1970s.

Admittedly, India has achieved tremendous economic growth in the last two decades, and recently India became the fastest-growing major economy in the world.[33] However, India started its economic reform much later than China, and the power gap between India and China is still wide despite India's rapid rise.[34] For instance, China's gross domestic product (GDP) is nearly four times that of India, and China has a standing military force and nuclear stockpiles that are twice as large as those of India.[35] China's international status is also more established than India's, as China has entered into many "great-power clubs" that India still aspires to join. China has also played a leadership role in creating many new international institutions, such as the Shanghai Cooperation Organization (SCO) and the Asian Infrastructure Investment Bank (AIIB).

Partially due to the material gap between India and China, China does not view India as a major threat. The Chinese public has identified the United States as a top threat even though more than half still has a favorable view of the

United States.[36] In comparison, the Chinese public does not regard India as a major source of threat: It views India's influence on the world as being more positive than negative, and a majority of Chinese people have a favorable view of India.[37] This is in contrast to Indians' opinions of China, as a large majority of the Indian public identifies China as a security threat.[38] To some extent, then, the bilateral relationship is still a "one-sided rivalry," as India sees China as a major rival while China does not share the similar type of threat perception.[39]

From China's perspective, India poses challenges for China only in regard to specific issues such as Tibet, but those challenges can be managed pragmatically. There are still some ignorance and stereotyping characterizing the views of India at the Chinese mass-population level. Such ignorance and stereotyping are reflected in online public opinions, as well as in Chinese nationalistic media such as the *Global Times*. This negative stereotyping is due to two factors. First, some Chinese media outlets attempt to promote Chinese national pride and foster nationalist sentiments by focusing on negative social news of India. Second, sometimes there is a tit-for-tat reaction to the negative coverage of China in India.[40] However, it should be noted that the impact of nationalistic opinion on China's foreign policy is limited. While some might claim rising Chinese nationalism is driving China's foreign policy in a more assertive direction, Alastair Iain Johnston has recently contended that the rising popular nationalism meme is empirically inaccurate. He suggests that there are other factors that may explain China's assertive diplomacy, such as elite opinion, the personal preferences of top leaders, security dilemma dynamics, and organizational interests.[41] There are complicated interactions between public opinions and China's foreign policy. When the Chinese government wants to signal resolve to an international audience, the government will allow or even encourage antiforeign protests to emerge; when the Chinese government wants to signal reassurance in diplomacy, the government suppresses antiforeign protest.[42] In recent years, the United States and Japan have occasionally become major targets of China's antiforeign protests.[43] In comparison, India has only rarely become the target of China's antiforeign protests. China views the United States as the country that could potentially pose a more serious threat to China's security, status, and national interests. While wanting to avoid confronting the United States directly, China prefers an alternative international order where power is more diffused rather than concentrated in the hands of the US. Based on this premise, a rising India, together with other emerging powers, would serve China's long-term interests of shaping the emergence of a multipolar world at a global level. That is why Chinese leaders advocate greater cooperation in multilateral contexts such as BRICS.

While the gap between India and China makes China less likely to see India as a major threat, the asymmetry makes India more sensitive to Chinese actions. It also makes China sometimes less sensitive to India's concerns, about which India often complains. On the other hand, China sometimes complains that India is overly sensitive about China and that India has often overreacted to China's behavior.[44] For instance, regarding India's recent failure to join the NSG, the Chinese saw India's entry as a very complicated situation that might need further deliberation. According to a senior Chinese diplomat, China did not oppose India's entry into the NSG in principle. China's hesitation to support India's entry was at least partially driven by China's concerns about the criteria of the NSG and implications for nonproliferation in a wider context.[45] In contrast, Indians tended to see that China was using the NSG issue to intentionally contain the rise of India.[46] After the Indian government decided to expel three Chinese journalists in 2016, the dispute escalated. Chinese media and experts largely interpreted this as an example of Indian overreaction. In addition, in May 2017, India boycotted Beijing's summit meeting on the Belt and Road Initiative (BRI). India's official explanation emphasized concerns over international norms and transparency, as well as the projects in the disputed Kashmir region.[47] However, the sensitivity over China's rising influence and status in India's neighborhood might be a more important factor in shaping India's thinking and decision.[48] In these cases, asymmetry of status and perceptions did shape their bilateral relationship. However, it should be noted that the asymmetry between China and India involves a far more complex relationship than the hierarchical model can explain.[49] Even if there is asymmetry between India and China, it is not as lopsided as the relationship between a dominant hegemony and its client state.

While India's political attributes, such as a liberal democracy and vibrant civil society, are valuable sources of soft power in front of a Western audience, India receives ambivalent reactions from China. Among Chinese intellectuals, there are lively debates on India that reflect more on China's domestic divides rather than Chinese perceptions of India. In other words, the discussion of India among China's intellectuals and policy advisers is less about India than about China itself.[50]

CHINA-INDIA RIVALRY: STATUS AS A DRIVING FACTOR

Achieving a great-power status for India has always been a long-standing foreign policy goal of India's elites. Even though Prime Minister Jawaharlal Nehru often spoke against great-power politics, underneath his idealism lay a submerged realism about India's struggle for high status.[51] India's current prime minister, Narendra Modi, makes the goal of advancing India's status even more explicit through his active global diplomacy. During his speech at Tsinghua University in Beijing in 2015, Modi said, "China's support for India's permanent membership of a reformed UN Security Council, and for India's membership of export control regimes like Nuclear Suppliers Group will do more than just strengthen our international cooperation. It will take our relationship to a new level. It will give Asia stronger voice in the world."[52] As status aspiration is so important for India, why won't Beijing accommodate New Delhi's great-power aspiration more positively? Why is status a major hurdle between India and China? Regarding status concerns and China's approach to India's status struggle, I argue that status could be both a source of China-India rivalry and a mitigating factor in the bilateral relationship. This section will discuss why status is a driving factor in China-India rivalry.

As discussed before, status scarcity can drive international rivalry, and status politics between India and China is often competitive. While most studies focus on the accommodation between the rising powers and the established powers, status politics among rising powers is relatively understudied. The case of the China-India relationship is an example of how a more powerful rising power half-heartedly engages the rise of another rising power.[53] China's international status is more consolidated compared with India. While China often seeks to engage India as a regional South Asian country, India wants to engage China as an equal rising global power.[54] The China-India competitions over status are not new. Even though China is not always trying to contain India, both countries have been competing for status for decades. During the early period of the Cold War, India and China competed for influence and leadership in the developing world, and their behavior at the 1955 Bandung Conference was one of the earlier examples.[55] In the post–Cold War era, India has often complained that China is still unwilling to accommodate India as an equal rising global power in global institutions such as the UNSC and the NSG. Furthermore, while an early champion of multilateralism, India has been frustrated that it has not been treated fairly by many existing international regimes. For instance, while it actively participated in early negotiations over the Treaty on the Non-Proliferation of Nuclear Weapons, India refused to sign it in 1968 because India saw the dichotomy of five nuclear-weapon states and all other non-nuclear-weapon states as discrimination against India.[56]

Status discrepancy is also a major factor of international rivalry. Given India's historical influence in South Asia and the size of its population, it is natural that India wants to achieve higher international status. According to Nehru's expectations, India would emerge as a power to be counted despite temporary weaknesses.[57] According to a recent public survey, both the Indian and Chinese publics expect that their countries should play a more important role in international affairs.[58] In reality, there is a gap between India's aspiration of great-power status and the extent to which more established powers (including China) are willing to accommodate India. In particular, while India is eager to get China's support for entry into various international institutions, China is ambivalent about accommodating some aspects of India's great-power aspirations. While emphasizing its sources of soft power, India has sped up its steps to achieve great-power status in the twenty-first century. India, together with Brazil, Japan, and Germany, has tried to become a new member in an expanded UNSC. In 1998, India tested nuclear weapons, which generated backlashes from the United States and China but did not change India's resolve to become a legitimate nuclear state.

In all these cases, China's support is often a crucial factor for India to succeed. While China has not completely "blocked" India's entry into these major international organizations, China's attitude has been ambiguous, which has posed challenges for India in advancing its status. For instance, the most authoritative statement of China's position on India's UNSC entry has been consistently positive but not specific, as when President Xi Jinping said, "China supports India in its aspiration to play a bigger role in the United Nations, including in the Security Council."[59] A nonspecific statement such as this is unsatisfactory for many Indian officials, even though Chinese leaders have never used such positive words to describe China's position on Japan's aspiration to the UNSC. Chinese leaders have expressed their positive feelings toward India's great-power aspirations in a general sense. But China's further support for India may be conditional on the overall improvement of the China-India relationship, as well as UNSC reform in a broader context.[60]

Status competition between India and China is further complicated by balance-of-power politics. China has maintained a strong diplomatic and military relationship with Pakistan for decades.[61] China's assistance to Pakistan on economic and nuclear capabilities is viewed in India not simply as traditional balance-of-power politics but also a "status balancing" to keep India as a regional, not global, power. China's alliance with Pakistan is viewed in India as China's status-equalization strategy. India's big complaint during the Cold War was that the West kept India-Pakistan hyphenated and treated the two nations as equal powers. China is keeping the same approach, and the economic and military ties are keeping India on Pakistan's level to compete with its smaller neighbor.[62] On the other hand, India's rise will provide a possible counterweight to China, and this consideration has largely contributed to the US strategic accommodation with India.[63] US accommodation of India is viewed by China not simply as balance-of-power politics but also as an act of balance of status: By upgrading India's international profile, the United States is trying to prevent China from dominating Asia. In recent years, Prime Minister Modi has started active great-power diplomacy, trying to strengthen its security cooperation with the US and Japan.[64] In regional affairs, India has always regarded South Asia as within its sphere of influence and thus has tried to establish a dominant status in the region. India's struggle for regional leadership has complicated implications. India is very sensitive about any presence of the outside great powers in South Asia.[65] Whenever China tries to strengthen its relationship with India's neighboring countries, India views this behavior as threatening. The 2017 standoff between India and China was not so much about territory as the "great game" over Bhutan. India has been treating Bhutan as its "protectorate." As China started to improve its relationship with Bhutan, India felt uneasy about China's direct dealings with Bhutan. By the military intervention in Doklam, India has inserted itself as the proverbial elephant in the room.[66]

In addition, both China and India are expanding their naval power, and there could be more naval competition between the two countries. Many

Chinese elites do perceive India's aspiration to be a great power, but they do not recognize India's rights to exclude China's presence in the Indian Ocean.[67] To some extent, few Chinese analysts appear to have a deep understanding and recognition of the depth of Indian sensitivity about China's presence in South Asia, as well as in the Indian Ocean. In other words, China's strategists do not challenge India's special interests and role in the Indian Ocean, but they believe that the Chinese navy must have the right to share the responsibility of protecting Indian Ocean sea lines of communication.[68] Regarding India's great-power diplomacy, India has strengthened its strategic cooperation with the United States, Japan, and numerous Southeast Asian countries. These activities drive fear into Chinese strategists who see India's strategic direction as a move toward building a potential "anti-China club" in the region. Ironically, this worry does increase the salience and profile of India in the eyes of Chinese strategists. Regarding maritime strategy, India considers itself as the leading Indian Ocean power and feels it should be the natural leader of the Indian Ocean region. The presence of extraregional naval power, particularly China, is viewed as essentially illegitimate. This position also indicates that the military presence of other outside powers in India's neighborhood is viewed as illegitimate by India. Indian elites assume that the regional countries should rely exclusively on India as the predominant security provider.[69] India's positions regarding South Asian leadership are defensive from an Indian perspective, but such beliefs are not necessarily widely shared and recognized by other countries (including China).

CHINA-INDIA RIVALRY: MITIGATING FACTORS

While status has driven the China-India rivalry, the competitive nature of striving for status might be exaggerated in some contexts, and there are important mitigating factors in the bilateral relationship.

While status often drives the China-India rivalry, status itself can sometimes be a mitigating factor in the China-India relationship. China and India share a similar status as large developing countries that are also emerging powers. Deng Xiaoping once said, "No genuine Asia-Pacific century or Asian centenary can come until China, India and other neighboring countries are developed."[70] Both Chinese and Indian leaders have often tried to promote a solidarity narrative of the China-India relationship based on the common ground of China and India as two Asian developing nations.[71] India's solidarity signal of the developing-country status resonates well with Chinese elites. From China's perspective, India's rise is compatible with China's preference for a multipolar world rather than a US-led unipolar system. As President Xi emphasized, "China and India, as two major players in the shaping of a multi-polar world and two vibrant forces driving Asian and global economic growth, have, once again, been brought to the forefront of the times. China-India relations have gone way beyond the bilateral scope and assumed broad regional and global significance."[72] The shared identity and status of India and China have created new space in which to cooperate under a multilateral platform. During the Copenhagen Climate Change Summit in December 2009, India and China coordinated their nego- tiating positions. At the UN, China and India often share similar political posi- tions on a variety of policy issues. In contrast to conventional impressions, India and China share far more common foreign policy behavior than either of them does with the United States.[73]

While India and China sometimes compete for status, India does not neces- sarily always seek a higher status. While India is striving to attain great-power status, it is projecting multiple images on the global stage. According to Kate Sullivan, the ambiguity of India's image projection stems from its need to rec- oncile its quest for great-power status with a desire to maintain solidarity with developing countries.[74] India increasingly seeks great-power status with the accorded special rights and privileges, but it still claims to remain a champion of equality between states and is unwilling to abandon its long-term efforts of developing-country solidarity. While recognized as a rising power and an emerging economy, India sometimes still challenges the mainstream norms and rules championed by established powers.[75] India's dissatisfaction with the Western-dominated international institutions has created some opportunities for China and India to cooperate on global governance issues such as climate change and financial institution reform.[76] Furthermore, striving for higher sta- tus does not always resonate well with the Indian public. The "India Shining" slogan was popularized by the then-ruling Bharatiya Janata Party (BJP) for the Indian general elections in 2004. The slogan was initially developed as part of an Indian government campaign to promote India's positive image interna- tionally. The government spent an estimated $20 million in public funds on advertisements featuring the slogan, but the campaign was one of the causes for the subsequent defeat of the government of Atal Bihari Vajpayee in the parliamentary elections because it appeared to be inappropriate in the eyes of India's poor people.[77]

India does not always seek hard power as a source of its status. Prime Minis- ter Modi's active diplomacy to promote economic cooperation and soft power is well received by the Chinese elites and public. A rising India could choose a variety of strategies to project its preferred status, as there are multiple status criteria in international society. In the early years after their nation's indepen- dence, Indian elites downplayed the role of military power as a symbol of inter- national status. In contrast to China's rapid quest for nuclear weapons, India debated for more than two decades whether it should acquire "the bomb."[78] India demonstrated pride in its distinct status as a large developing country that championed nonviolence, nonalignment, and peaceful coexistence. Given India's attributes, it has tried to position itself as a "synthesizing" power that is at the center of a range of political geographies between the West and the East, between the Global North and the Global South.[79] India has also tried to build an image of an "exemplary power" that is a unique force for global power based on morality, noncoercion, and democracy.[80] Building on the idea of itself as a synthesizing and noncoercive power, India has sought a distinct global role as an "alternative power."[81] In recent years, Modi has pursued a much more active diplomacy effort toward China. Economically, India has actively embraced the development of an economic partnership with China. During Modi's official visit to China in 2015, India signed investment deals worth $20 billion with Chinese companies.[82] Modi has also strengthened his active diplomacy toward Chinese leaders, as well as the Chinese public. He has hosted both President Xi and Premier Li Keqiang, and Xi and Modi visited each other's hometowns as a friendly gesture. During Modi's formal visit to China, Modi also tried to strengthen India's public diplomacy and soft power. As a social media superstar among world leaders, Modi became the first Indian prime minister to open an account on Weibo, a Chinese social media platform. "Hello, China! Looking forward to interacting with Chinese friends," his inaugural post said.[83]

Even though status politics between India and China is sometimes competitive, the struggle for status is not always a zero-sum game. Most China-India competitions over status are not zero-sum games, as they typically involve "club goods" rather than "positional goods."[84] As discussed before, club goods are often partially rivalrous in their benefits, owing to congestion or crowding. In social life as well as in international politics, members of elite groups might restrict membership to preserve their status and privileges. In this sense, status as a club good could be competitive. However, more states joining a club does not make existing member states lose their status, and thus it is not a zero-sum game. India's entry into some great-power clubs might impact the privileges of China as an existing member of these clubs, but India's entry will not eliminate China's privileges. China has no reason to view India's rise as a zero-sum game, and China's ambivalence might be due to the substantial policy disputes instead of intrinsic status competitions. In addition, all BRICS countries have benefited from their membership: This BRICS club provides each member a new rising-power status while excluding others from benefiting from this status attribution. China and India have been two active members within BRICS, and the club dynamics generate incentives for India and China to overcome their differences and to create opportunities for cooperation in global governance.[85]

Finally, economic interdependence plays a mitigating role in the China-India rivalry, which is different from the India-Pakistan relationship.[86] China sees the growing economic power of India as a great opportunity. China enthusiastically invited India to participate in several major economic initiatives, including the AIIB and One Belt One Road (OBOR), and the two sides have also strengthened their cooperation by jointly building the New Development Bank within the BRICS framework. India has become a founding member and the second-largest shareholder of the Beijing-based AIIB, even though India has more reservations regarding OBOR.[87] China also supported India's entry into the SCO in June 2017. India's rise will provide China many opportunities for economic cooperation. In his book *Making Sense of Chindia*, Jairam Ramesh, a member of the Congress Party, has advocated the concept of "Chindia," which denotes synergy and cooperation between the two emerging powers.[88] Chinese leaders have embraced this idea, even though they might not use the term "Chindia." During his first official visit to India in 2013, Premier Li said, "As neighboring countries with the largest populations and greatest market potential, China and India are natural partners of cooperation."[89] Highlighting the potential for China and India to develop a "close partnership for development," President Xi said, "Known respectively as the 'factory' and 'office' of the world, China and India need to enhance cooperation to tap into our mutually complementary advantages."[90] From this perspective, economic cooperation between China and India might be the best way to build trust, leading to a long-lasting peace between the two states. Many Chinese elites see the rise of India and China as a positive force. According to Xi, there is enough space for both nation-states to continue to grow and simultaneously achieve their aspirations of national revival.

The India-China relationship has acquired a multidimensional character. While competition and disputes remain, India and China share common interests on the global stage, including trade, technology transfers, and climate change. Despite the recent diplomatic rifts between India and China, economic ties between them are growing both in strength and importance.

CONCLUSION

As India rises on the world stage, China has pursued an active economic engagement with it, and the two countries have strengthened their cooperation in various global issues. But economic engagement and global cooperation have largely failed to bring any breakthrough in China-India bilateral relations. Status concerns are widely regarded as a significant hurdle for China and India to improve their relationship.

India and China are Asian giants struggling for their status on the world stage. Status is an important source of the China-India rivalry. Great-power status is a scarce resource, and China and India have been competing for power and status in the developing world for decades. As India is striving for great-power status, China is hesitating to accommodate India's great-power aspirations in some contexts. Status competition is also further complicated by traditional balance-of-power politics. As China is building its military and economic relationship with Pakistan, India largely views China's action as a status-balancing behavior against India. The asymmetry of status and perceptions between India and China has additionally complicated the bilateral relationship. China is less sensitive about India's concerns, while India might sometimes overreact to China's behavior and policies. In recent years, India's fast economic growth and Modi's diplomatic activism have attracted increasing attention from Chinese analysts, who no longer look down on India as a lightweight. China has noticed India's growing capabilities and diplomatic activism.

However, there are several ways in which the China-India status rivalry could be mitigated. As two large developing countries, India and China do not necessarily always want to have higher status on the global stage. They both emphasize their developing-country status, which could facilitate their cooperation at the global level. India's solidarity signals about its developing-country status are well received by Chinese elites, as the Chinese leaders have tried to develop China-India cooperation in a broad global context. Meanwhile, economic interdependence also mitigates potential conflicts. Even in a competitive context, status competitions between India and China are not always a zero-sum game. In most cases, status contestations between India and China are related to a club good status rather than a positional good status. India's entry into some great-power clubs might impact the privileges of China as an existing member of these clubs, but India's entry will not eliminate China's membership and its associated rights. Furthermore, the club dynamics generate some new incentives for India and China to strengthen their solidarity and cooperation within BRICS. India and China have an increasingly complex relationship. Yet despite the competitive nature of the relationship, there is room for mutual accommodation and bargaining. While the risks of a territorial standoff like the 2017 Doklam are real, there remains cause for cautious optimism. China and India have accumulated a strong record of peacefully resolving border disputes since 1962, and they have built active diplomatic channels for dialogue and cooperation. Economic and strategic costs of conflict for both sides are extremely high.[91] In the twenty-first century, economic growth, innovation, and domestic governance fundamentally shape balance of power.[92] To revive their nations, Indian and Chinese leaders should wisely focus on domestic growth rather than great-power conflict. It is not in their interest to spark a war over a remote road in the Himalayas.

NOTES

1. Steven Lee Myers, Ellen Barry, and Max Fisher, "How India and China Have Come to the Brink over a Remote Mountain Pass," *New York Times*, July 26, 2017, https://www.nytimes.com/2017/07/26/world/asia/dolam-plateau-china -india-bhutan.html.
2. Devesh Kapur, "Asia's Hierarchies of Humiliations," *Straits Times*, July 15, 2017, http://www.straitstimes.com/opinion/asias-hierarchies-of-humiliations.
3. Srikanth Kondapalli, "India Must Tell China It Is Playing with Fire," Rediff, August 12, 2016, http://www.rediff.com/news/column/india-must-tell-china-it -is-playing-with-fire/20160812.htm.
4. Ibid.
5. C. Raja Mohan, "Raja Mandala: The Myth of a Political Bond," *Indian Express*, January 10, 2017, http://indianexpress.com/article/opinion/columns/the-myth -of-a-political-bond-4467027/.

6. Ibid.
7. Harsh V. Pant, "China's Half-Hearted Engagement and India's Proactive Balancing," in *The Engagement of India: Strategies and Responses*, ed. Ian Hall (Washington, DC: Georgetown University Press, 2014), 111–28.
8. Ibid., 111.
9. For the differences between the China-India rivalry and the India-Pakistan rivalry, see T.V. Paul's chapter 1 in this volume.
10. Various scholars have noted the asymmetrical nature of China-India relations. For instance, see John Garver, "Asymmetrical Indian and Chinese Threat Perceptions," *Journal of Strategic Studies* 25, no. 4 (2002): 109–34; Tien-sze Fang, *Asymmetrical Threat Perceptions in India-China Relations* (New Delhi: Oxford University Press, 2014); and Selina Ho's chapter 7 in this volume.
11. Bernardo A. Huberman, Christoph H. Loch, and Ayse Önçüler, "Status as a Valued Resource," *Social Psychology Quarterly* 67, no. 1 (2004): 103–14.
12. Deborah Welch Larson, T.V. Paul, and William C. Wohlforth, "Status and World Order," in *Status in World Politics*, ed. T.V. Paul, Deborah W. Larson, and William C. Wohlforth (New York: Cambridge University Press, 2014), 7.
13. Randall Schweller, "Realism and the Present Great Power System: Growth and Positional Conflict over Scarce Resources," in *Unipolar Politics: Realism and State Strategies after the Cold War*, ed. Ethan B. Kapstein and Michael Mastanduno (New York: Columbia University Press, 1999), 28–68. For the concept of positional good in a general sense, see Fred Hirsch, *Social Limits to Growth* (Cambridge, MA: Harvard University Press, 1976), 27.
14. Richard Ned Lebow, *A Cultural Theory of International Relations* (Cambridge: Cambridge University Press, 2008).
15. For a comprehensive review of power transition theory, see Jonathan M. DiCicco and Jack S. Levy, "Power Shifts and Problem Shifts: The Evolution of the Power Transition Research Program," *Journal of Conflict Resolution* 43, no. 6 (1999): 675–704. For the application of power transition theory in US-China relations, see Ronald L. Tammen and Jacek Kugler, "Power Transition and China-US Conflicts," *Chinese Journal of International Politics* 1, no. 1 (2006): 35–55.
16. Manjari Chatterjee Miller, *Wronged by Empire: Post-Imperial Ideology and Foreign Policy in India and China* (Stanford, CA: Stanford University Press, 2013).
17. For a comprehensive review of power transition theory, see DiCicco and Levy, "Power Shifts and Problem Shifts."
18. For instance, see Deborah Welch Larson and Alexei Shevchenko, "Status Seekers: Chinese and Russian Responses to US Primacy," *International Security* 34, no. 4 (2010): 63–95; Yong Deng, *China's Struggle for Status: The Realignment of International Relations* (Cambridge: Cambridge University Press, 2008); and Allan Dafoe, Jonathan Renshon, and Paul Huth, "Reputation and Status as Motives for War," *Annual Review of Political Science* 17 (2014): 371–93.
19. Randall L. Schweller and Xiaoyu Pu, "After Unipolarity: China's Visions of International Order in an Era of U.S. Decline," *International Security* 36, no. 1 (2011): 41–72.
20. Joel Best, *Everyone's a Winner: Life in Our Congratulatory Culture* (Berkeley: University of California Press, 2011), 12.
21. Ibid., 11.
22. Ibid.
23. Larson and Shevchenko, "Status Seekers."
24. Lebow, *Cultural Theory*.

25. For the discussion of status markers, see Alastair Iain Johnston, *Social States: China in International Institutions, 1980–2000* (Princeton, NJ: Princeton University Press, 2007), 87.

26. Fred Hirsch, *Social Limits to Growth* (Cambridge, MA: Harvard University Press, 1976), 27.

27. Todd Sandler, *Collective Action: Theory and Applications* (Ann Arbor: University of Michigan Press, 1992).

28. Ibid., 63.

29. For a study of elite club membership in social life, see Lauren Rivera, "Status Distinctions in Interaction: Social Selection and Exclusion at an Elite Nightclub," *Qualitative Sociology* 33, no. 3 (2010): 229–55.

30. Manjari Chatterjee Miller, "India's Feeble Foreign Policy: A Would-Be Great Power Resists Its Own Rise," *Foreign Affairs* 92, no. 3 (2013): 14–19.

31. Xiaoyu Pu and Randall L. Schweller, "Status Signalling, Multiple Audiences, and China's Blue-Water Naval Ambition," in Larson et al., *Status in World Politics*, 141–62.

32. Sean W. Burges, "Consensual Hegemony: Theorizing Brazilian Foreign Policy after the Cold War," *International Relations* 22, no. 1 (2008): 65–84.

33. For instance, in 2015, India's GDP growth rate was 7.6 percent while China's was 6.9 percent. In addition, South Africa had a much lower growth rate of 1.3 percent, while Russia and Brazil had a negative growth rate in that year. World Bank, http://data.worldbank.org/.

34. Swaran Singh, "China and India: Coping with Growing Asymmetry," *Asan Forum*, December 19, 2014, http://www.theasanforum.org/china-and-india-coping-with-growing-asymmetry/.

35. Ibid.

36. Richard Wike and Bruce Stokes, "Chinese Public Sees More Powerful Role in World, Names U.S. as Top Threat," Pew Research Center, October 5, 2016, http://www.pewglobal.org/2016/10/05/1-chinese-views-on-the-economy-and-domestic-challenges/.

37. This pattern is based on analysis of several years of public opinion data in China, including Pew Global Attitudes Project and BBC World Service Polls. For the summary of the analysis, see Yang Lu, *China-India Relations in the Contemporary World: Dynamics of National Identity and Interest* (New York: Routledge, 2016), 91–93.

38. Rory Medcalf, "India Poll 2013," *Lowy Institute for International Policy*, http://www.lowyinstitute.org/publications/india-poll-2013.

39. Susan Shirk, "One-Sided Rivalry: China's Perceptions and Policies toward India," in *The India–China Relationship: What the United States Needs to Know*, ed. Francine R. Frankel and Harry Harding (New York: Columbia University Press, 2004), 75–100.

40. Lu, *China-India Relations*, 91.

41. Alastair Iain Johnston, "Is Chinese Nationalism Rising? Evidence from Beijing," *International Security* 41, no. 3 (2017): 7–43.

42. Jessica Chen Weiss, "Authoritarian Signaling, Mass Audiences, and Nationalist Protest in China," *International Organization* 67, no. 1 (2013): 1–35.

43. Jessica Chen Weiss, *Powerful Patriots: Nationalist Protest in China's Foreign Relations* (New York: Oxford University Press, 2014).

44. John Garver, "Asymmetrical Indian and Chinese Threat Perceptions," *Journal of Strategic Studies* 25, no. 4 (2002): 109–34.

45. Suhasini Haidar, "India's NSG Membership Bid Calls for In-Depth Discussion, Says Beijing Envoy Liu Jinsong," *The Hindu*, July 17, 2016, http://www.thehindu.com/news/national/article8862103.ece.

46. Shubhajit Roy, "No Entry in NSG: India Blames One Country (China), Others Said No Too," *Indian Express*, June 25 2016, http://indianexpress.com /article/india/india-news-india/no-entry-in-nsg-india-blames-one-country -china-others-said-no-too-2874377/.

47. Ministry of External Affairs, Government of India, "Official Spokesperson's Response to a Query on Participation of India in OBOR/BRI Forum," http:// mea.gov.in/media-briefings.htm?dtl/28463/Response_to_a_query_on_participa tion_of_India_in_OBORBRI_Forum.

48. Srikanth Kondapalli, "Why India Is Not Part of the Belt and Road Initiative Summit," *Indian Express*, May 15, 2017, http://indianexpress.com/article/opinion /why-india-is-not-part-of-the-belt-and-road-initiative-summit-4656150/.

49. Brantly Womack, *Asymmetry and International Relationships* (New York: Cambridge University Press, 2016).

50. For a liberal interpretation of India, see Ding Xueliang, "Yingdu zhengzhi fazhang dui zhongg de qishi" [What China could learn from Indian political development], *Lilun Cankao* 9 (2007): 62–63. For a nationalistic/conservative interpretation of India, see Yang Guangbin, "Yizhong meiguoxintiao xia de yiloupiancha: Ping Huang Yasheng de zhongying Jinji bijiao" [Research on "omitted bias" under the "American creed": Comments on Professor Huang Yasheng's economic comparison between China and India], *Xueshuqianyan* 25, no. 5 (2014): 86–95.

51. Baldev Raj Nayar and T.V. Paul, *India in the World Order: Searching for Major-Power Status* (New York: Cambridge University Press, 2002), 27.

52. Narendra Modi, "Speech at Tsinghua University, Beijing," *Times of India*, May 15, 2015, http://timesofindia.indiatimes.com/india/Read-full-text-PM-Modis -speech-at-Tsinghua-University-Beijing/articleshow/47295807.cms.

53. Pant, "China's Half-Hearted Engagement."

54. Ibid.

55. Amitav Acharya, *Bandung Revisited: The Legacy of the 1955 Asian-African Conference for International Order* (Singapore: National University of Singapore Press, 2008).

56. Amrita Narlikar, "India's Role in Global Governance: A Modi-Fication?," *International Affairs* 93, no. 1 (2017): 93–111.

57. Nayar and Paul, *India in the World Order*, 132–33.

58. Wike and Stokes, "Chinese Public."

59. Xi Jinping, "In Joint Pursuit of a Dream of National Renewal," speech, Indian Council of World Affairs, New Delhi, September 18, 2014, Ministry of Foreign Affairs of the People's Republic of China, http://www.fmprc.gov .cn/mfa_eng/topics_665678/zjpcxshzzcygyslshdsschybdtjkstmedfsllkydjxgsfw /t1194300.shtml.

60. According to one Chinese scholar and former diplomat, India's efforts to enter the UNSC as a part of a group with three other countries (Japan, Germany, and Brazil) also poses a challenge for China, as China has clearly opposed Japan's entry. See Zhang Jiadong, "Zhong yin guanxi de wenti yu chaoyue [Tangle and detangle in China-India relations]," *Journal of China's Neighboring Diplomacy* 1 (2016), http://www.cnki.com.cn/Journal/G-G1-ZBWJ-2016-01.htm.

61. Andrew Small, *The China-Pakistan Axis: Asia's New Geopolitics* (Oxford: Oxford University Press, 2015).

62. Harsh V. Pant, "The Pakistan Thorn in China-India-US Relations," *Washington Quarterly* 35, no. 1 (2012): 83–95; Kanti Bajpai, "Narendra Modi's Pakistan and China Policy: Assertive Bilateral Diplomacy, Active Coalition Diplomacy," *International Affairs* 93, no. 1 (January 1, 2017): 69–91.

63. T.V. Paul and Mahesh Shankar, "Status Accommodation through Institutional Means: India's Rise and the Global Order," in Paul et al., *Status in World Politics*, 165–91.

64. Harsh V. Pant and Yogesh Joshi, "Indo-US Relations under Modi: The Strategic Logic Underlying the Embrace," *International Affairs* 93, no. 1 (2017): 133–46.

65. David Brewster, "India and China at Sea: A Contest of Status and Legitimacy in the Indian Ocean," *Asia Policy* 22 (July 2016): 4–10.

66. M. K. Bhadrakumar, "Indian Military Standoff with China Was All about Bhutan," *Asia Times*, July 17, 2017, http://www.atimes.com/article/indian-military-standoff-china-bhutan/.

67. Ji You, "China's Emerging Indo-Pacific Naval Strategy," *Asia Policy* 22 (July 2016): 11–19.

68. Ibid.

69. Brewster, "India and China at Sea."

70. Deng Xiaoping, "A New International Order Should Be Established with the Five Principles of Peaceful Coexistence as Norms," in *Selected Works of Deng Xiaoping* (Beijing: Foreign Languages Press, 1994), 3:182–84.

71. For instance, public speeches of the Chinese leaders emphasize these themes. See Li Keqiang, "Seize the New Opportunities in China-India Strategic Cooperation," speech, Indian Council of World Affairs, New Delhi, May 21, 2013, http://www.fmprc.gov.cn/mfa_eng/topics_665678/lkqipsg_665690/t1051164.shtml; and Xi, "In Joint Pursuit."

72. Xi, "In Joint Pursuit."

73. George J. Gilboy and Eric Heginbotham, "Double Trouble: A Realist View of Chinese and Indian Power," *Washington Quarterly* 36, no. 3 (2013): 125–42.

74. Kate Sullivan, "India's Ambivalent Projection of Self as a Global Power: Between Compliance and Resistance," in *Competing Visions of India in World Politics*, ed. Kate Sullivan (London: Palgrave Macmillan, 2015), 15.

75. Narlikar, "India's Role in Global Governance," 97.

76. See Feng Liu's chapter 11 in this volume.

77. "BJP Admits 'India Shining' Error," BBC, May 28, 2004, http://news.bbc.co.uk/2/hi/south_asia/3756387.stm.

78. Arun Prakash, "Bridging Historical Nuclear Gaps: The View from India," in *The China-India Nuclear Crossroads*, ed. Lora Saalman (Washington, DC: Carnegie Endowment for International Peace, 2012), 16.

79. Sullivan, "India's Ambivalent Projection," 24–25.

80. Ibid., 27.

81. Ibid., 30.

82. "India and China Sign Deals Worth $22bn as Modi Ends Visit," BBC, May 16, 2015, http://www.bbc.com/news/world-asia-china-32762930.

83. Niharika Mandhana, "How India's Narendra Modi Became a Social Media Superstar," *Wall Street Journal*, May 6, 2015, http://www.wsj.com/articles/indias-prime-minister-a-hit-on-social-media-1430905148.

84. Sandler, *Collective Action*.

85. Andrew Cooper and Assif Farooq, "Testing the Club Dynamics of the BRICS: The New Development Bank from Conception to Establishment," *International Organizations Research Journal* 10, no. 2 (2015): 32–44. For the analysis of status motivations of BRICS, see also Oliver Stuenkel, "Emerging Powers and Status: The Case of the First BRICS Summit," *Asian Perspective* 38, no. 1 (2014): 89–109.

86. See Matthew Castle's chapter 10 in this volume.

87. For analysis of the origin and challenges of China's OBOR, see Xiaoyu Pu, "One Belt, One Road: Visions and Challenges of China's Geoeconomic Strategy," *Mainland China Studies* 59, no. 3 (2016): 111–32.

88. Jairam Ramesh, *Making Sense of Chindia: Reflections on China and India* (New Delhi: India Research Press, 2005).

89. Li, "Seize the New Opportunities."

90. Xi, "In Joint Pursuit."

91. Ryan Hass, "Navigating the Current China-India Standoff in Bhutan," Brookings Institution Report, July 28, 2017, https://www.brookings.edu/blog /order-from-chaos/2017/07/28/navigating-the-current-china-india-standoff-in -bhutan/amp/.

92. Randall L. Schweller, "Rational Theory for a Bygone Era," *Security Studies* 20, no. 3 (2011): 460–68.

Chapter 4

China, India, and Their Differing Conceptions of International Order

MANJARI CHATTERJEE MILLER

In 1965, Raymond Aron asked, "Under what conditions would men (divided in so many ways) be able not only to avoid destruction but live relatively well in one planet?"[1] In his understanding, international order constituted the "minimum conditions for co-existence," and states were the principal architects of such conditions.[2] While the particular content of the "conditions" was ambiguous, it was underlined by a premise that would later be elaborated, implicitly, by Hedley Bull, and, explicitly, by Robert Gilpin—the building and destruction of international order are intricately linked with the conflict between states.[3]

Bull, in his seminal work, talked of order as a shared framework of rules and institutions within the anarchical society of states, which existed so states could retain their independence, preserve international society, and regulate war and violence.[4] In Gilpin's view, however, order is the international system that is built after conflict between the status quo and rising states, and world politics consists of a succession of such ordered systems.[5] G. John Ikenberry more comprehensively defined international order as

> the organizing rules and institutions of world politics. It is the governing arrangements that define and guide the relations among states. To speak of international order is to invoke notions of a functioning political system—however rudimentary—among states. International order is not just the crystallization of the distribution of power. It exists in the organizing principles, authority relations, functional roles, shared expectations, and

settled practices through which states do business. It establishes the terms by which states command, follow, benefit and suffer."[6]

These discussions show us that states' perceptions of international order matter for three reasons. First, order is not simply the condition of nonwar. It is the active creation of powerful, usually hegemonic states rather than the passive outcome of an anarchical international society or the distribution of power. Powerful challenger states emerge after war, and they have both the influence and the desire to reorganize the international system.[7] Thus order, rather than being built on the balance of power, is built on an "asymmetry of power" by a powerful state or states and is a deliberate (re)organization of "the rules and arrangements of interstate relations."[8]

Second, much of power transition theory, which has focused on the destruction and rebuilding of international order, sees it as the outcome of "asymmetries of power." That is, new orders are built when "changes in the distribution of power trigger rivalry among states seeking to sit atop a new international hierarchy." Order thus, in this iteration, relies "exclusively on material variables."[9] However, order is also built on norms. To begin with, the challenger's dissatisfaction, which, power transition theory points out, leads to the establishment of new orders, "rests on the premise of the ideas of the challenger about the distribution of goods in the international system rather than the distribution of the goods itself."[10] A change in international order is also thus a "contest among competing norms,"[11] and the term itself bears "normative and ideological connotations."[12] As Andrew Hurrell has pointed out, the challenge facing international society is not simply the need to "manage unequal power" but also the need to emphasize "shared and common interests" and "mediate cultural diversity."[13] Consequently, order is underpinned by norms, rules, and institutions by which states seek to structure and regulate their interactions.[14] This, in turn, can affect whether the transition between orders is peaceful or conflictual. For example, Charles A. Kupchan points to the similarity of ideas and rules between Pax Britannica and Pax Americana, calling it "uniquely peaceful," while the Ottoman order was hugely normatively different from Pax Britannica.[15]

Finally, order rests on "a concert of great powers"[16] or perhaps even more arguably a concert of willing states. If international order is the deliberate and active creation of rules and institutions of world politics that exist not just through functional roles but also through shared norms, values, and expectations, it is reasonable to assume that its creation, while hugely influenced by a hegemon, is not an act of coercion and does not rest on the hegemon alone. Rather, there is acquiescence, as well as, more often than not, active participation by other states that stand to benefit, not just because of shared material interests but also because of shared ideational interests. Different hegemons had different methods of co-opting other states into building their international order. The Ottoman Empire, for example, despite having religious foundations, promoted religious heterodoxy. The Ottomans forged political bonds across religious boundaries, making significant concessions for non-Muslims even while propagating norms derived from Islamic tradition.[17] Similarly, Pax Americana is not simply an imposition of order by the United States but a complex creation of rules and institutions that are underpinned by ideational interests and norms that are shared across many Western and some non-Western states. The United States has a network of alliances, including friendships and "special relationships,"[18] that helps it create and maintain Pax Americana.

Given that order is actively created, is built on both material interests and norms, and needs a network of compliant states to maintain it, the rise of India and China and the possibility of upending the international status quo compel us to thus ask what kind of international order each would seek to create and how their visions would differ.

BUILDING INTERNATIONAL ORDER
AND THE CHINA-INDIA RIVALRY

In 2015, Prime Minister Narendra Modi took the unprecedented step of opening a social media account with Weibo, China's answer to Twitter, with a post that read, "Hello China! Looking forward to interacting with Chinese friends."[19] His post was highly symbolic, showcasing not just a desire to intensify diplomatic efforts toward China but also an acknowledgment by an Indian leader with the reputation of being an economic crusader that the economic relationship between the two countries had come to be the most important commonality in a very complex relationship.[20]

With the 1962 China-India War, a war in which the disastrous loss India suffered spurred it to massively increase its military spending, the hitherto warm relationship between India and China turned frosty and suspicious. This affected every level of the bilateral relationship, including trade. Even in the 1980s and early 1990s, after both countries had enacted open and reform policies, trade between them was around a billion dollars.[21] Today, however, China is India's largest trading partner, and from 2015 to 2016 the trade between them stood at over $70 billion.[22]

Yet their relationship remains complex. On the one hand, trade ties bind them together. On the other, it is often argued that India is paranoid about China, particularly its dealings in the region.[23] India perceives the bilateral relationship as a rivalry and remains extremely wary and suspicious of China. Thus how China would seek to reorganize the rules and arrangements of the international system, what norms it would propagate, and which states would buy into a China-led and designed world order are incredibly important for Indian foreign policy.

China, however, does not currently see India as a major threat. Xiaoyu Pu suggests that this is due to the vast asymmetry of power between them—among other factors, "China's GDP is nearly four times that of India, and its standing army and nuclear stockpiles twice as large as those of India."[24] As a result, Indian perceptions of order are currently unlikely to be a huge factor in China's calculations about the bilateral relationship. Yet India's support or rejection of the international order is important for China to understand as it rises. An Indian perception of world order that is fundamentally different from a Chinese perception of world order has the potential for conflict not just for the bilateral relationship but also for the international system. India may not currently be the focus of China's strategic calculations but neither can it be ignored.

The rest of this chapter examines Chinese and Indian perceptions of international order, how they are different, and how we can observe these differences through some of the speeches of Xi Jinping and Narendra Modi. In China's case, I examine a traditional and explicit notion of order, *tianxia*, that has informed the ideational frameworks of both Chinese scholars and leaders. In India's case I examine postcolonial notions of order—although India, too, had traditional precolonial ideas of order, these, in contrast to China, have not influenced modern Indian frameworks of order. Indeed, as we will see, discussions of order in the Indian context tend to be very implicit and found deeply embedded within other ideologies.[25]

BUILDING A CHINESE INTERNATIONAL ORDER

With the rise of China, one of the most important and pressing questions that is asked by both international relations theorists and policymakers is whether China will accept or reject the existing international order.[26] Evans points out that today the big question of whether China matters has been replaced by the question of what China *thinks*.[27] The assumptions of the literature on international order outlined earlier are paramount in any answer to this question. If order is built on an asymmetry of power, then will China deliberately reorganize the existing rules and arrangements of interstate relations? What are the norms that will shape this order? And will China be able to use its bilateral and trilateral relationships to persuade other states to not just acquiesce but also actively participate in this order? To unpack these questions, scholars have taken two related approaches.

The first approach is to evaluate if there is a Chinese approach to international relations that is distinct from a Western approach. While there is indeed a mission to develop an approach to international relations with Chinese characteristics that can tell us something about China's "international purpose,"[28] there is also acknowledgment that there is no modern Chinese international relations theory to give a unique insight into China's "blueprint for action."[29]

The second approach, however, is more utilitarian in that it looks specifically to China's traditional order (the *tianxia* system, 天下), both to understand its modern conception of international order and to develop a Chinese international relations theory. Briefly, the Chinese world, tianxia ("all-under-Heaven"), consisted of China, or *zhongguo* ("middle kingdom," 中国), at the center and "barbarians" (nonsinicized peoples) at the periphery. The barbarians recognized Chinese suzerainty by paying tribute to the Chinese emperor (*tianzi*, or the "son of Heaven," 天子) and kowtowing before him. In return, the emperor bestowed lavish gifts on them. This system did not have geographical boundaries in the modern Western sense. Rather, it was a web of concentric territories with the nearer territory forming an inner frontier with China and the outmost territory forming an outer frontier with the lands beyond it. This web receded and expanded depending on the fates of the tributary peoples, both with respect to China and the foreigners in the outer territories.[30]

The tianxia system of tributary model was, according to some narratives, based on strong notions of superiority and hierarchy and on ideas about sovereignty, virtue (*de*, 德), and state roles that were starkly distinct from the Westphalian system, and it was strictly dictated by ritual (*li*, 礼) and sinocentricism.

The reality, however, is complex. While tianxia was indeed unique in many ways, some of its important characteristics need to be parsed. First, the notions of Chinese hierarchy and superiority have to be understood within the reality of China's material capabilities. It was often the case that the tributary system was one of seeming control by China. In other words, depending on the historical period invoked, the Chinese emperors retained nominal control over peripheral areas, while the rulers of those peripheries remained mostly autonomous. It was "a tacit acceptance that Chinese authority could not stretch beyond the empire's military capabilities."[31] Notions of superiority had to be "based on strength and were meaningless during periods of weakness and disorder."[32] What this suggested was a flexibility when it came to norms and practices of external relations so long as the correct order and rituals were nominally adhered to.[33] There was thus a sophisticated pragmatism about foreign policy.

Second, China also had foreign relations outside of the tributary system. In various years of the Ming period, the Japanese and Mongols, for example, did not pay tribute to the Ming emperor. This does not mean, however, that they fell outside of the tributary system, because they had no relations with China. Rather, there continued to be "interesting interactions" between them and the Chinese empire.[34] This implies that China's benevolent "rule by virtue" or the idea that peripheral entities paid tribute and stayed within the system because of the cultural and moral example of China was also flexible—non-Chinese entities could and did, at different points in time, perceive their interests to lie outside of the tributary system.

Third, there was an element of responsibility in the tributary system. While, as has been mentioned above, the strength of China's relations with states within the tributary system varied between dynasties, the question naturally arises as to why the tributary states bought into it at all, particularly when China's rule was nominal. The answer lies in the fact that "China would offer assistance and protection when it was approached to do so."[35] Recognition by the Chinese emperor not only conferred status and prestige on the rulers of these states but also implied that, if requested, he would support and protect the rulers on whom he had conferred such honors.[36] It was a system of diplomatic management that was designed to satisfy both the center and the peripheral entities.[37]

Finally, none of this is to suggest that the tributary system was one of equality. Rather, "China was at the center of a set of regional relationships that it could not force but were not transposable."[38] The risks and opportunities of the system were much greater for the peripheral states than for the center, but it conferred a stability that no one actor could provide unilaterally.[39]

Turning now to India, we find ideas of international order that are important but less structured and historical.

BUILDING AN INDIAN INTERNATIONAL ORDER

As a rising power with the potential to challenge the current international order, the case of India too leads us to ask how it would consider reorganizing the rules and arrangements of interstate relations, what norms it would espouse to underpin these rules and institutions, and how it would promote shared ideational interests among states willing to participate in that order. India, too, like China, has struggled to put forth an *Indian* conception of international relations that would answer these questions.

As Behera has pointed out, scholars of Indian foreign policy have "creatively" deployed Western international relations in their specific local contexts but are yet to move from the "particular" to the "universal."[40] There is today no debate about what an Indian order or international relations would look like. Conceptions of international order are instead embedded, sometimes explicitly but more often implicitly, within domestic discussions of the making of Indian foreign policy that draw from different belief systems.

The most explicit work on categorizing Indian conceptions of international order has been undertaken by Kanti Bajpai. Bajpai finds four competing conceptions of international order embedded within four different and well-known articulations of Indian worldviews.[41] Each of these worldviews has also been explored separately and in great detail by other academics, with more implicit connotations of international order.

The first is Gandhism. Although a Gandhian outlook on foreign policy was rejected by the Indian elite, Mahatma Gandhi's philosophy remained the utopian moral ideal that influenced many Indian nationalist leaders, including the first Indian prime minister, Jawaharlal Nehru (who, as detailed below, would articulate his own vision of order). Gandhian philosophy was dubious about the nation-state as the primary political actor and characterized primarily by nonviolence. This played out in two ways. On one hand, Gandhi was accepting of the Western international system in that he did not reject its principles. On the other, he deeply believed that it needed to be reorganized by devolving power from the nation-state to local institutions that would serve the citizens and by adopting nonviolence as its creed. He ventured that the Indian National Congress should consider having postcolonial India respond with nonviolence even when attacked,[42] calculating that "in aggregate this would amount to fewer deaths than if there were armed resistance."[43]

The second, and possibly the most influential, worldview is Nehruvianism. After India's independence from British rule in 1947, Nehru almost completely dominated foreign policy in India. He held the portfolios of both prime minister and minister of external affairs, and his extensive knowledge of and dedication to international affairs meant that foreign affairs expertise was concentrated almost entirely in South Block—the headquarters of the Ministry of External Affairs—and institutionalized.[44] While Nehruvians accept the Western concept of states as the primary political units in the international system with both rights and responsibilities, they add four elements: "ambivalence" about the use of force; *panchashila*, the five principles of coexistence; nonalignment; and economic equality.[45]

Nehruvians believe that the use of force must be defensive, that mutual respect for territorial integrity and sovereignty, nonaggression, and noninterference in internal affairs is paramount, that states must reject bloc membership, abide by international rules and institutions, that the weak must ally against the strong, and that states as a whole must strive for international economic equality.[46] These different tenets all flow from a unified logic, which is that colonialism had ill served the newly independent ex-colonial states and the postcolonial world threatens to again trap these states within the dictates of neoimperialism.[47]

To escape the power politics of the "haves" in the international system, these weakened states must band together, strive for parity (not just economic but also political) with the richer countries, refrain from being turned against each other by the dictates of the two superpowers, and have harmonious interstate relationships governed by the principles of panchashila. In this order, India would be the shining moral example and lead the way. Nehru even used the Indian anticolonial movement to suggest that in political disputes approaching "another country in a friendly way with goodwill and generosity . . . [will be paid back] in the same coin and probably the payment will be in even larger measure."[48] The moralism underpinning Nehruvianism was derided by many as, at best, unpractical and idealistic and, at worst, an excuse for leaning toward the Soviet Union.[49]

The third Indian outlook is that of Hindutva, or Hindu political ideology. Hindutva espoused by Hindu nationalists such as M. S. Golwalkar argues that social cohesion can be achieved on the basis of an essentialist brand of Hinduism.[50] This drive stems from a conviction that disunity in Indian society has been a source of Indian weakness toward the outside world. The aim is to generate a monolithic Hindu nation in order to develop a "martial spirit and social cohesion" to defend India "against external aggression."[51] The international order is one of struggle not just between states but also civilizations, and therefore violence and war are unavoidable.[52] Hindutva sees an essentially Hindu India as a superior civilization that has made great cultural contributions to the world and, as a result, that Hindus are destined for global leadership. India is an example to the world by virtue of its superior culture.[53]

The final Indian conception of order that can be detected within Indian foreign policy thought, according to Bajpai, is neoliberal globalism. Bajpai conceives of this body of thought as a post–Cold War philosophy embraced by a small group of scholars, journalists, and politicians such as C. Raja Mohan, Sanjaya Baru, Shekhar Gupta, and Jaswant Singh.[54] Neoliberal globalists argue that economic interdependence and the end of the Cold War have reorganized interstate relations, leading to a "pragmatism."[55] With this pragmatic outlook, India will resist great-power intervention yet cooperate with the West to ensure stability.[56]

HOW ARE CHINESE AND INDIAN CONCEPTIONS OF ORDER DIFFERENT?

These discussions of Chinese and Indian conceptions of international order are both qualitatively and quantitatively different in terms of the heritage they refer back to, their acceptance or rejection of the Westphalian system, the different strands of thought within, and even in terms of the urgency of the discussions.

Unlike the Chinese search for order, which is also rooted in its ancient precolonial past, Indian conceptions of order are postcolonial.[57] This difference is particularly interesting because not only was the immediate precolonial era in India marked by the conquest and consolidation of the Mughal Empire—one of the greatest dynasties in Indian history, which ruled over a vast expanse of the subcontinent—but also because the Mughals instituted a form of decentralized political sovereignty, the *mansabdari* system, which was in some ways similar to tianxia. Under the emperor Akbar when the Mughal Empire was at the zenith of its power and wealth with control over most of the subcontinent, conquered territories were ruled either by their original king, who swore fealty to the emperor, or through a descendant of the existing ruling family who was instituted as the king by the emperor. Each of these rulers was given a rank, or *mansab*, and a *mansabdar* could have an official rank anywhere from ten to ten thousand. A mansab of ten would denote the command of ten men and so on. These rulers were called on to defend and administer the empire, and other than these tasks were largely autonomous. "The Mughal emperor was *Shah-an-shah*, 'king of kings' rather than king of India. . . . The emperor's power and wealth could be great, but only if he was skilled in extracting money, soldiers and devotion from other kings."[58]

However, possibly because of the very nature of this decentralized sovereignty, which became a factor in the decline of the Mughals,[59] the lack of a distinction between Indian and non-Indian within the mansbdari system (unlike tianxia, where there was a sense of distinction from nonsinicized peoples), and because the decline of the Mughals was then followed by two hundred years of British rule with strongly centralized sovereignty, India experts looked to the postcolonial era for conceptions of order.[60] Even exponents of Hindutva who tout India's ancient Hindu texts and Hindu heritage do not root their ideas of order in ancient India—rather, they seek to recapture what they believe were the glories of Hindu civilization as a whole.

Moreover, tianxia has often, both to its advantage and detriment, been seen as a contrast to the Westphalian West-led system. On the one hand, the "alienness" of its characteristics rooted in their distinction from Western ideas about the international system has been cited as increasing the propensity for China to have conflicts in its bilateral relations and with the international status quo.[61] On the other, these very characteristics have been lauded as the solution to the problems of the Westphalian system. Early debates about tianxia between scholars such as Mark Mancall, John K. Fairbank, Gungwu Wang, and Benjamin Schwartz had focused on the narrower question of continuity or interruption between the traditional and modern Chinese perceptions of world order.[62] Mancall, Fairbank, and Wang all identified persistent patterns in Chinese foreign policy perspectives. For example, they determined that Chinese notions of superiority and hierarchy that were enshrined in the tianxia system persisted in the modern world. Fairbank viewed it as impacting China's strict modern adherence to sovereignty and territorial integrity, with respect, for example, to the One China policy, while Wang saw the notion of superiority becoming more important to Chinese leaders as they looked to learn from the past, particularly the demonstration of majesty and power that embodied the tianxia system.[63] Schwartz, on the other hand, argued that the old order had been so thoroughly undermined in the contemporary era that it bore little relevance for modern perceptions. What mattered, in his view, was power and whether China could adapt to new realities.[64]

But following Deng Xiaoping's *gaige kaifang* policy (the economic reform and opening up of China), this debate proliferated and shifted. The question now became what tianxia could teach China and how it could play a role in the development of a Chinese international relations. Many Chinese intellectuals proposed China's traditional order as both an external and internal framework for the Chinese state.[65] It was felt that harking back to Mao's Marxist-Leninist views of the international system was increasingly irrelevant, while at the same time the "material and spiritual pollution" that had come in from the West was inappropriate.[66] As a result, while some scholars such as Qin Yaqing attributed the modern lack of a Chinese international relations to tianxia,[67] others, notably Zhao Tingyang, elaborated tianxia as an alternative to Western international relations and the ills of the Westphalian order.

Zhao conceives of tianxia as the "ideal of a perfect empire" that implies a world organized by families, then by loyal but autonomous substates (*guo*, 国) and all-under-Heaven.[68] In contrast to the Western system of individuals, nations, and internationals, in tianxia the individual is valued but relevant only within the context of relations, and this relational system is dictated by coexistence. Tianxia thus aims at a good society that keeps order (*zhi*, 秩) and prevents chaos (*luan*,

乱).[69] Tianxia was promoted as realistic in that the system recognized inequality between states yet supposedly lacked constant confrontation. In effect, China's cultural hegemony ensured that non-Chinese entities bought into the structure, understanding that it was in their interests to do so.[70]

Such a conception of tianxia as the ideal system has been roundly critiqued by, among others, William Callahan, who argues that the all-inclusive harmonious tianxia espoused by Zhao in reality excluded and marginalized social groups and led to many violent interactions.[71] June Teufel Dreyer points out Zhao's problematic linking of Confucianism and tianxia.[72] Apart from such criticisms, whether tianxia actually poses a true alternative or indeed is so very different from Westphalia is a debatable question—but the important point here is that it is touted as an *aspirational* alternative *Chinese* model.

In contrast, Indian conceptions of order do not seek to either reject *or* posit an Indian alternative to the Westphalian system. As Bajpai points out, whether Nehruvianism, Hindutva, or neoliberal globalism, these conceptions accept the Westphalian system for the most part while adding mild modifiers. Nehruvianism adds the element of nonalignment leading to a "'Westphalia plus' notion of order."[73] Hindutva does not challenge rules and institutions of Westphalia, including state sovereignty, but predicts the eventual domination of India leading by example of its superior Hindu civilization.[74] Neoliberal globalists accept the primacy of sovereign states but posit that market forces and nonstate actors will play an increasing role in state-driven economic and welfare functions.[75] Even Gandhism, which comes the closest to positing an alternative conception of world order, accepts the Westphalian system but argues that, ideally, small community governments, or *panchayats*, should be empowered by the state because social and political affairs are ultimately localized.[76]

This does not mean that tianxia, even as espoused in its ideal form by Zhao and others, seeks to overthrow the Western order while Indian conceptions seek to maintain it. In many ways, China is extremely accepting of the status quo and subscribes to important norms such as those about responsibility and great power that are a product of the Western system.[77] There is also little doubt that Indian conceptions of order chafe at the Westphalian system. There is a strong sense, for example, that India must resist the dictates of great powers, that the idea of great-power responsibility is a Western stratagem, and that it must pursue independence in foreign policy. Nehruvianism is the most vocal about this. After all, Nehru had once remarked that, in the context of superpower politics, nothing was worse for India than becoming a "camp follower in the hope that some crumbs might fall from their table."[78] Nehruvianism blamed colonialism for the deprivation suffered by the newly independent states and suggested that colonial powers needed to make restitution. Thus the weak states need not only to counter the influence of strong states by remaining nonaligned but also maintain the right to carve their own path.[79]

While neither Hindutva nationalists nor neoliberal globalists suggest nonalignment, they too are very clear that the current order presents a form of domination. Rules and institutions are made and broken by great powers that can and should be resisted. Madhav Sadashiv Golwalkar, an ardent Hindu nationalist, advocated that India needed to build "invincible national strength" as the world is uncaring of the demands of the weak.[80] Neoliberal globalists suggest that it is domestic politics that is prior to and must dictate the international order rather than the other way around. This implies "a shift to global norms and rules over the sovereign rights of states in respect of economics, security, domestic politics and transnational flows."[81] And Gandhism is unambiguous about the flaws of Western order, suggesting it "would be a mistake to imitate Europe."[82]

However, there is an urgency and concerted effort in Chinese discourse, particularly in more recent years, about developing an alternative Chinese model, a Chinese path to international relations, which is lacking in Indian discourse. The tianxia system (as well as Confucianism) has become the subject of study in China and marked for export.[83] Simultaneously, Chinese presidents have espoused concepts that could both, implicitly and explicitly, be linked to tianxia—Hu Jintao's concept of a "harmonious world" (*hexie shijie*, 和谐世界) was related to *tianxia datong* ("world of great harmony," 天下大同), while Xi Jinping's recent articulation of *zhongguo meng* ("China dream," 中国梦) encompasses working for a harmonious world.[84] Such discussions of order, whether among academics or policymakers, are implicit at best in the Indian context. Whether Indian conceptions of order are critical of the Westphalian system or not, the primary question today is whether Nehruvianism and nonalignment still hold sway in India and what the rise of Hindutva means for Indian domestic politics and foreign policy.[85] The question of an *Indian* alternative and aspirational conception of order is yet to be explicitly asked or espoused.

We can see these differences play out in the speeches of the current leadership.

XI, MODI, AND INTERNATIONAL ORDER

From 2013 to 2015, Xi made a number of speeches that were explicitly on foreign policy and for a foreign audience.[86] After Modi's election in 2014, although he did not take over the portfolio of minister of external affairs, he made his interest in foreign affairs very clear and also made a number of speeches to foreign audiences.[87]

Xi's speeches often refer back to concepts that are seen to be enshrined in tianxia. In a speech to the Boao Forum on March 20, 2015, Xi stated that

> China greatly needs a harmonious and stable domestic environment, and a peaceful and calm international environment. Any unrest or conflict is not in China's fundamental interests. Through the ages, the Chinese people have always loved peace; since ancient times [they have] advocated a mindset of "prizing harmony," "living harmoniously with all nations," "within the four seas all men are brothers," etc. In recent times, China has suffered

more than a hundred years of unrest and war and would never inflict such suffering on others. Throughout history countries that have used armed force to serve their development objectives have ultimately failed. China will always unwaveringly insist on independent policies of peaceful diplomacy, an independent path of peaceful development, and mutually beneficial open strategies and uphold justice. [China] will push for and establish a new type of international relations based on cooperation and mutual benefit, will safeguard world peace, and promote common development.[88]

In contrast, Modi, a man whose personal views, party politics, and political leadership are all heavily intertwined with Hindutva,[89] quotes ancient texts (Hindu scriptures) but seldom if at all refers to precolonial views of international society or order. In a speech to the United Nations Educational, Scientific and Cultural Organization (UNESCO), he quoted, "The wealth that increases by giving, that wealth is knowledge and is supreme of all possessions,"[90] to emphasize the domestic programs India has launched to provide skills and education for Indian children.[91] At the Asian Leadership Forum, he stated, "As some of us in Asia become more prosperous, we must be prepared to share our resources and markets with those who need them. . . . This is the principle that guides India's policies. And, it comes from our timeless belief in the world as one family, 'Vasudhaiva Kutumbakam.'"[92]

Xi's speeches express support for key tenets of the Western international order but make clear that there are limits.[93] He declared to a group of Asian and African states,

> We need to abandon the Cold War mentality and old ways of thinking of zero-sum games, propose commonality, band together, and cooperate. We can promote new ideas about security, persist in dialogue and peaceful solutions to differences and disputes, develop common answers to terrorism, public health and Internet safety, climate change, nontraditional security problems, and global challenges. [We need] to construct a common destiny. [We should forge] a new security path of sharing winning and safeguarding our region and world peace and stability.[94]

He often, sometimes in the same speech, repeatedly touts the Chinese way, which is posited as an aspirational alternative. Chinese domestic politics is also linked to the welfare of international society:

> China will always be a constructor of world peace, will firmly walk the path of peaceful development. No matter how the world situation changes or how we develop, China will never seek hegemony or expansion.[95]
>
> To bring about the great rejuvenation of the Chinese people is the fundamental dream of the Chinese nation.[96]
>
> China insists that countries do not distinguish between the big and small, the strong and weak, the poor and rich but rather adhere to equality and justice. China will be a champion of justice and oppose those who bully and oppress the weaker and use wealth to pressure the poor. China will oppose any interference in another country's internal affairs.[97]

Modi rarely, if ever, actively talks of Indian leadership in the world order, and he espouses no *Indian* way to emulate. Rather, he refers to morality,[98] and he speaks repeatedly of the nuts and bolts of India's domestic achievements. The focus is inward—that is, developing India, including sometimes stressing compliance with the international order and attracting foreign investment—rather than both inward and outward—that is, developing India with a view to assuming an international leadership role or shaping the international system:[99]

> Excellencies, we in India don't see development and climate change as competing objectives. This is centered on the belief in the unity of humanity and Nature. We have ambitious plans for addressing the challenges of climate change. This includes additional capacity of 175 GW of renewable energy by 2022; cut in subsidies on fossil fuel and tax on coal; and, National Clean Energy Fund of US$3 billion to promote clean technologies. With our highly ambitious/Intended Nationally Determined Contributions (INDCs), India would remain in step with the world.[100]
>
> I am pleased that elimination of poverty in all forms everywhere is at the top of our goals. Addressing the needs of 1.3 billion poor people in the world is not merely a question of their survival and dignity or our moral responsibility. It is a vital necessity for ensuring a peaceful, sustainable and just world. . . . Today, much of India's development agenda is mirrored in the Sustainable Development Goals. . . . Since Independence, we have pursued the dream of eliminating poverty from India.[101]

CONCLUSION

China and India both have outlined conceptions of international order. Modern Chinese conceptions of order have often drawn on a powerful and ancient ideational heritage, which in recent years has enjoyed a resurgence of popularity as an aspirational model of international order. At the same time, Chinese elites including the leadership are acutely conscious of the need to forge a Chinese path in international relations, and the ideas embedded in tianxia provide one method of thinking about such a path. China seeks to outline the limits of the Westphalian order without rejecting it per se. It is seeking to be a norm shaper if not a norm maker.[102] Indian conceptions of order, on the other hand, are postcolonial. Despite some common chafing at the current international order, these postcolonial conceptions are distinct from each other in significant ways, and none of them overwhelmingly reject or posit any alternative to the Westphalian order. In India there is little sense of urgency that an *Indian* path of development or forging international order is needed. These differing viewpoints are reflected in the speeches of the current leaders Xi and Modi.

China's dual and, to some extent, dueling perspective (accepting some elements of the Westphalian order while also pushing a distinct Chinese path) can be seen in foreign policy initiatives pushed by Xi, such as the One Belt One Road (OBOR, *yi dai yi lu*, 一带一路) policy, which is an infrastructural network of primarily road and rail enterprises and oil and gas pipelines that will eventually connect "65 countries, 4.4 billion people, and 40 per cent of global GDP."[103] OBOR draws on Xi's conception of great "national rejuvenation" (*minzu weida de fuxing*, 民族伟大的复兴) and his effort to develop a "new type of great-power relations" (*xinxing daguo guanxi*, 新型大国关系) while emphasizing openness, inclusivity, and cooperation with other international development initiatives rather than the replacement of them.[104] But this of course means that because it is undoubtedly geared toward increasing China's international influence (even if, from China's point of view, in a nonthreatening way), there is concern that its ultimate effect will be to "marginalize US influence"[105] and thereby de facto contribute to the erosion of the current order.

Indian foreign policy, under the leadership of Modi, was expected by many to undergo a radical shift. Commentators wondered whether he, as a transformational leader, would come to significantly influence his foreign policy.[106] Others argued that while domestic transformation was possible, there were unlikely to be radical shifts in foreign policy.[107] Modi's speeches indicate that currently the focus of the government is on domestic reform. Unlike Xi, Modi has not yet espoused an accompanying explicit international conception of how India could shape or make the existing international order. Yet his election has brought an ardent proponent of Hindutva into mainstream politics. The question, therefore, remains whether Hindutva now can be adapted and reshaped to articulate an active and outward-looking Indian conception of international order.[108]

The literature on international order tells us that order is built on an asymmetry of power and is the deliberate attempt by a powerful state to reorganize the rules, arrangements, and norms of the international system. Moreover, the rearrangement presumes acquiescence and/or active participation on the part of other states. While China is making more of a push to actively outline a Chinese alternative to world order, it remains to be seen, particularly in terms of the bilateral relationship, whether India will acquiesce, even symbolically, to this alternative view.

NOTES

1. Quoted in Stanley Hoffmann, "Conference Report on the Conditions of World Order," *Daedalus* 95, no. 2 (1966): 456.
2. Ibid.
3. Ibid., 457.
4. Hedley Bull, *The Anarchical Society: A Study of Order in World Politics*, 3rd ed. (Basingstoke, UK: Macmillan, 2003).
5. Robert Gilpin, *War and Change in World Politics* (New York: Cambridge University Press, 1981).
6. G. John Ikenberry, "The Rise, Character and Evolution of International Order," in *The Oxford Handbook of Historical Institutionalism*, ed. Orfeo Fioretos, Tulia G. Falleti, and Adam Sheingate (Oxford: Oxford University Press, 2016), 539.
7. Gilpin, *War and Change*.

8. G. John Ikenberry, "Introduction," in *Power, Order and Change in World Politics*, ed. G. John Ikenberry (Cambridge: Cambridge University Press, 2014), 4.

9. Charles A. Kupchan, "Unpacking Hegemony: The Social Foundations of Hierarchical Order," in Ikenberry, *Power, Order and Change*, 19.

10. Manjari Chatterjee Miller, "The Role of Beliefs in Identifying Rising Powers," *Chinese Journal of International Politics* 9, no. 2 (2016): 218–19.

11. Kupchan, "Unpacking Hegemony," 20.

12. John A. Hall and T.V. Paul, "Introduction," in *International Order and the Future of World Politics*, ed. T.V. Paul and John A. Hall (Cambridge: Cambridge University Press, 1999), 2.

13. Andrew Hurrell, *On Global Order: Power, Values, and the Constitution of International Society* (Oxford: Oxford University Press, 2007), 3.

14. Ibid., 4.

15. Kupchan, "Unpacking Hegemony," 21, 30–35.

16. Hall and Paul, "Introduction," 6.

17. Kupchan, "Unpacking Hegemony," 34–35.

18. Special relationships are strong bilateral relationships (e.g., US-UK, Israel-Germany, US-Israel) that share goals of strategic security but also share values and ideological interests. See Janice Bially-Mattern, *Ordering International Politics: Identity, Crisis and Representational Force* (London: Routledge, 2005), and Y. Bar-Simon Tov, "The US and Israel since 1948: A 'Special Relationship'?" *Diplomatic History* 22 (1998): 231–62.

19. Niharika Mandhana, "How India's Narendra Modi Became a Social Media #Superstar," *Wall Street Journal*, May 6, 2015, https://www.wsj.com/articles/indias-prime-minister-a-hit-on-social-media-1430905148.

20. Soutik Biswas, "Will India's Narendra Modi Be a Reformer?," BBC, May 26, 2014, http://www.bbc.com/news/world-asia-india-27534163.

21. Arvind Virmani, "India-China Economic Cooperation," in *China and India: Learning from Each Other*, ed. Eswar S. Prasad, Jahangir Aziz, and Steven Dunaway (Washington, DC: International Monetary Fund 2006), 272.

22. Ministry of Commerce, Government of India, "Export Import Data Bank," http://commerce.nic.in/eidb/iecnttopnq.asp.

23. Biswas Baral, "India's Self-Defeating Paranoia about China in Nepal," *The Diplomat*, May 14, 2016, http://thediplomat.com/2016/05/indias-self-defeating-paranoia-over-china-in-nepal/.

24. Xiaoyu Pu, "Ambivalent Accommodation: Status Signaling of a Rising India and China's Response," in "India's Rise at 70," ed. Manjari Chatterjee Miller and Kate Sullivan de Estrada, special issue, *International Affairs* 93, no. 1 (2017): 155.

25. While China too has had ideologies that have referred to international order (whether Mao's thought, Deng's thought, etc.), the historical concept of *tianxia*, a very explicit and Chinese idea of international order, has been referred to repeatedly by scholars and leaders. In contrast, historical notions of international order rarely, if ever, find mention in modern Indian thought.

26. Gregory Chin and Ramesh Thakur, "Will China Change the Rules of Global Order?," *Washington Quarterly* 33, no. 4 (2010): 119–38.

27. Paul Evans, "Historians and Chinese World Order: Fairbank, Wang, and the Matter of 'Indeterminate Relevance,'" in *China and International Relations: The Chinese View and the Contribution of Wang Gungwu*, ed. Yongnian Zheng (London: Routledge, 2010), 42.

28. Hun Joon Kim, "Will IR Theory with Chinese Characteristics Be a Powerful Alternative?," *Chinese Journal of International Politics* 9, no. 1 (2016): 66.

29. Yaqing Qin, "Why Is There No Chinese International Relations Theory?," in *Non-Western International Relations Theory: Perspectives on and beyond Asia*, ed.

Amitav Acharya and Barry Buzan (London: Routledge, 2010), 26–50. See also Kim, "Will IR Theory," 66.

30. Sarah C. M. Paine, *Imperial Rivals: China, Russia and Their Disputed Frontier* (Armonk, NY: M. E. Sharpe, 1996), 50.

31. Rana Mitter, "An Uneasy Engagement: Chinese Ideas of Global Order and Justice in Historical Perspective," in *Order and Justice in International Relations*, ed. Rosemary Foot, John Gaddis, and Andrew Hurrell (Oxford: Oxford University Press, 2003), 210.

32. Wang Gungwu quoted in Feng Zhang, "Rethinking the 'Tribute System': Broadening the Conceptual Horizon of Historical East Asian Politics," in Zheng, *China and International Relations*, 82.

33. Rana Mitter, "An Uneasy Engagement," 210; and Zhang, "Rethinking the 'Tribute System,'" 83. Although it is also pointed out that sometimes this hierarchy was not even adhered to nominally. For example, there is a letter written by the Yongle emperor in 1418 to the ruler of the Timurid Empire that refers to him as a fellow monarch. See Zhang, "Rethinking the 'Tribute System,'" 86.

34. Zhang, "Rethinking the 'Tribute System,'" 87.

35. Xiao Ren, "Traditional Chinese Theory and Practice of Foreign Relations," in Zheng, *China and International Relations*, 105.

36. Ibid., 108.

37. Brantly Womach, "Traditional China and the Globalization of International Relations Thinking," in Zheng, *China and International Relations*, 123.

38. Ibid., 120.

39. Ibid., 124.

40. Navnita Chadha Behera, "Re-Imagining IR in India," in Acharya and Buzan, *Non-Western International Relations Theory*, 95, 97.

41. Kanti Bajpai, "Indian Conceptions of Order and Justice: Nehruvian, Gandhian, Hindutva, and Neo-Liberal," in Foot, Gaddis, and Hurrell, *Order and Justice*.

42. Rahul Sagar, "State of Mind: What Kind of Power Will India Become?," *International Affairs* 85, no. 4 (2009): 802.

43. Bajpai, "Indian Conceptions," 247.

44. Behera, "Re-imagining IR in India," 94.

45. Bajpai, "Indian Conceptions."

46. Ibid., 240–43.

47. Most evident at the Afro-Asian conference in Bandung, Indonesia in 1955.

48. Quoted in Sagar, "State of Mind," 804.

49. B. R. Nanda, *Jawaharlal Nehru: Rebel and Statesman* (Oxford: Oxford University Press, 1998), 230, 243.

50. Rahul Sagar, "'Jiski lathi uski bhains': The Hindu Nationalist View of International Politics," in *India's Grand Strategy: History, Theory, Cases*, ed. Kanti Bajpai, Saira Basit, and V. Krishnappa (Abingdon, UK: Routledge, 2014), 234–57.

51. Sagar, "Jiski lathi, uski bhains," 237.

52. Bajpai, "Indian Conceptions of Order and Justice," 250.

53. Ibid.

54. Ibid.

55. Ibid., 255.

56. Ibid., 255–56.

57. This is not to suggest that tianxia has been the only conception of order propagated or harked back to but, rather, that it has cropped up regularly in modern China and given different levels of emphasis by different leaders. There are other varying sources of order, ranging from nationalists such as Liang Qichao and Sun Yat-sen to the Maoists, who have dominated the discourse at varying points

of time, but none of them have rejected tianxia per se so much as sidelined some aspects of it while upholding others. For a discussion on nationalism, see Zhimin Chen, "Nationalism, Internationalism, and Chinese Foreign Policy," *Journal of Contemporary China* 14, no. 42 (2005): 35–53.

58. Christopher A. Bayly, *Indian Society and the Making of the British Empire* (New York: Cambridge University Press, 2002), 13.

59. Muzaffar Alam states: "The basis of the empire, in a measure, had been negative; its strength had lain in the inability of the local communities and their systems to mobilize beyond relatively narrow bounds. . . . Political integration in Mughal India was, up to a point, inherently flawed. It was conditional on the coordination of the interests and the political activities of the various social groups led by local magnates." Muzaffar Alam, *The Crisis of Empire in Mughal North India: Awadh and Punjab, 1707–48* (Oxford: Oxford University Press, 2013), 6.

60. This is not to suggest that precolonial Indian nationalists did not expound on international relations. See Rahul Sagar, "Before Midnight: Views on International Relations, 1857–1947," in *The Oxford Handbook of Indian Foreign Policy*, ed. David M. Malone, C. Raja Mohan, and Srinath Raghavan (Oxford: Oxford University Press, 2015). Rather, individual nationalist thinkers eventually aligned with one or other of the postcolonial Indian conceptions of order—unsurprising when one considers that the postcolonial conceptions were also mostly articulated by influential Indian nationalist leaders.

61. Friso M. S. Stevens, "Why Does Japan's Wartime Ghost Keep Reemerging?," China File, May 26, 2016, https://www.chinafile.com/viewpoint/why-does -japans-wartime-ghost-keep-reemerging; and Wataru Sawamura, "Why Japan Misreads China—and What to Do about It," Huffington Post, September 10, 2014, http://www.huffingtonpost.com/2014/09/10/why-japan-misreads-china _n_5788896.html.

62. See Mark Mancall, "The Persistence of Tradition in Chinese Foreign Policy," *Annals of the American Academy of Political and Social Science* 349 (1963): 14–26; John K. Fairbank, ed., *The Chinese World Order: Traditional China's Foreign Relations* (Cambridge, MA: Harvard University Press, 1968); Gungwu Wang, "Early Ming Relations with Southeast Asia: A Background Essay," in Fairbank, *Chinese World Order*; and Benjamin Schwartz, "The Chinese Perception of World Order, Past and Present," in Fairbank, *Chinese World Order*.

63. Evans, "Historians and Chinese World Order," 48–49.

64. Schwartz, "Chinese Perception," 284.

65. June Teufel Dreyer, "The Tianxia Trope: Will China Change the International System?," *Journal of Contemporary China* 24, no. 96 (2015): 2–3.

66. Ibid., 2–3. Note that tianxia was not explicitly a part of the political discourse during the regime of Mao Zedong.

67. In his view, the traditional Chinese understanding of the world took a society of states to be not one of equality and parity but one that reflected the society of individuals. China and the emperor existed at the center and maintained stability—it was "a complete whole where no dichotomous opposites existed. . . . There was only one ego . . . without an opposite alter." See Qin, "Why Is There No Chinese International Relations Theory?," 36. Modeled on the Confucian notion of "state," which in turn was modeled on the Confucian notion of "family," it had no concept of "international-ness" and the corresponding sovereignty or territorial integrity, a bedrock of Western theories about international relations (ibid., 37).

68. Tingyang Zhao, "Rethinking Empire from a Chinese Concept: 'All-under-Heaven,'" *Social Identities* 12, no. 1 (2006): 30; and *Tianxia Tixi: Shijie Zhidu*

Zhexue Daolun [The tianxia system: A philosophy for the world institution] (Nanjing: Jiangsu Jiaoyu Chubanshe, 2005).

69. Zhao, "Rethinking Empire," 33.
70. Dreyer, "Tianxia Trope," 2.
71. William Callahan, "Chinese Visions of World Order: Post-Hegemonic or a New Hegemony?," *International Studies Review* 10, no. 4 (2008): 749–61.
72. Dreyer, "Tianxia Trope," 9.
73. As Bajpai terms it. See Bajpai, "Indian Conceptions of Order and Justice," 243.
74. Ibid., 252–53.
75. Ibid., 256.
76. Ibid., 246.
77. Alastair Iain Johnston, "Is China a Status Quo Power?," *International Security* 27, no. 4 (2003): 5–56.
78. Jawaharlal Nehru, *India's Foreign Policy: Selected Speeches* (New Delhi: Government of India, 1961), 31–32.
79. Bajpai, "Indian Conceptions of Order and Justice."
80. Sagar, "State of Mind," 808.
81. Bajpai, "Indian Conceptions of Order and Justice," 258.
82. Sagar, "Before Midnight," 69.
83. Through, e.g., the network of Confucius Institutes set up in 2005. See Dreyer, "Tianxia Trope."
84. Ibid.
85. Manjari Chatterjee Miller and Kate Sullivan de Estrada, "Introduction: India's Rise at 70," *International Affairs* 93, no. 1 (2017), 3.
86. I collected thirty-seven speeches that were publicly available. He made many more speeches that were internal and restricted (*neibu*).
87. I collected forty-seven speeches from 2015 to 2016.
88. 中国最需要和谐稳定的国内环境与和平安宁的国际环境，任何动荡和战争都不符合中国人民根本利益。中华民族历来爱好和平，自古就崇尚"以和为贵"、"协和万邦"、"四海之内皆兄弟也"等思想。中国近代以后遭遇了100多年的动荡和战火，中国人民绝不会将自己曾经遭受过的悲惨经历强加给其他国家和民族。纵观历史，任何国家试图通过武力实现自己的发展目标，最终都是要失败的。中国将毫不动摇坚持独立自主的和平外交政策，坚持走和平发展道路，坚持互利共赢的开放战略，秉持正确义利观，推动建立以合作共赢为核心的新型国际关系，始终做维护世界和平、促进共同发展的坚定力量。Xi Jinping, speech to the Boao Forum, March 28, 2015.
89. "More than any other leader, including the previous BJP [Bharatiya Janata Party] prime minister, Atal Bihari Vajpayee, Narendra Modi is closely associated with Hindutva as both a personal belief system and a source of domestic political support." Manjari Chatterjee Miller and Kate Sullivan de Estrada, "Pragmatism in Indian Foreign Policy: How Ideas Constrain Modi," *International Affairs* 93, no. 1 (2017): 32.
90. वयये कृते वर्धते एव नतियं, वदिया धनं सरव प्रधानं (Both the Sanskrit phrase and its English translation are within the speech.)
91. Narendra Modi, "Speech to UNESCO," (Paris, April 10, 2015).
92. वसुधैव कुटुम्बकम्, Narendra Modi, "Speech to the Asian Leadership Forum," Seoul, May 19, 2015.
93. E.g., in a 2014 speech, Xi emphasized the seeking of "mutual trust, mutual benefit, equality, consultation, and respect for diverse civilizations, and common development" (坚持互信、互利、平等、协商、尊重多样文明、谋求共同发展). Xi Jinping, speech to the Shanghai Cooperation Organization, July 12, 2014.

94. 要摒弃冷战思维、零和博弈的旧观念，倡导共同、综合、合作、可持续安全的新理念，坚持通过对话协商和平解决分歧争端，共同应对恐怖主义、公共卫生、网络安全、气候变化等非传统安全问题和全球性挑战，建设命运共同体，走出一条共建、共享、共赢的安全新路，共同维护地区和世界和平稳定. Xi Jinping, "Speech to Asian African Summit," Jakarta, April 22, 2015.

95. 中国将始终做世界和平的建设者，坚定走和平发展道路，无论国际形势如何变化，无论自身如何发展，中国永不称霸、永不扩张. Xi Jinping, "Speech to the UN General Assembly," New York, September 29, 2015.

96. 实现中华民族伟大复兴是近代以来中华民族最根本的梦想. Xi Jinping, "Speech to the Mexican Senate," Mexico City, June 6, 2013.

97. 中国坚持国家不分大小、强弱、贫富一律平等，秉持公道、伸张正义，反对以大欺小、以强凌弱、以富压贫，反对干涉别国内政. Xi Jinping, "Speech in Tanzania," Dar es Salaam, March 25, 2013).

98. A theme in both Nehruvianism and Gandhism.

99. One reading of this could assert that it is consistent with the tenets of Hindutva: a showcasing of India as a superior state that the world will eventually emulate without any concrete pathways by which this could happen.

100. Narendra Modi, "Speech to the G20," Antalya, Turkey, November 15, 2015.

101. Narendra Modi, "Speech to the UN," New York, September 25, 2015.

102. Jinghan Zeng and Shaun Breslin, "China's 'New Type of Great Power Relations': A G2 with Chinese Characteristics?," *International Affairs* 92, no. 4 (2016): 773–94.

103. Bert Hofman, "China's One Belt One Road Initiative: What We Know So Far," World Bank, December 4, 2015, http://blogs.worldbank.org/eastasiapacific /china-one-belt-one-road-initiative-what-we-know-thus-far.

104. Michael D. Swaine, "Chinese Views and Commentary on the 'One Belt One Road' Initiative," *China Leadership Monitor* 47, no. 5 (2015): 6, 9, 13.

105. Ibid., 14.

106. Brahma Chellaney, "Narendra Modi's Imprint on Foreign Policy," *LiveMint*, September 2, 2014; Christophe Jaffrelot, "A Modi Doctrine?," *Indian Express*, November 20, 2014; Amitabh Mattoo, "The Modi Foreign Policy Doctrine: India as a Smart Power," *The Conversation*, June 12, 2014; and Harsh Pant, "Out with Non-Alignment, in with a 'Modi Doctrine,'" *The Diplomat*, November 13, 2014.

107. Manjari Chatterjee Miller, "Foreign Policy à la Modi," *Foreign Affairs*, April 3, 2014; Ankit Panda, "Hindu Nationalism and . . . Foreign Policy?," *The Diplomat*, April 4, 2014; Kanti Bajpai, "Continuity—but with Zeal," *Seminar* no. 688, April 2015, 23–27; and Ian Hall, "Is a 'Modi Doctrine' Emerging in Indian Foreign Policy?," *Australian Journal of International Affairs* 69, no. 3 (2015).

108. Some are very pessimistic about the flexibility of ideational tools that Hindutva provides. See Ian Hall, "Narendra Modi and India's Normative Power," *International Affairs* 93, no. 1 (2017): 113–31.

Chapter 5

Balancing Strategies and the China-India Rivalry

ZHEN HAN AND JEAN-FRANÇOIS BÉLANGER

The military standoff on the Doklam Plateau in the summer of 2017 was a small but demonstrative episode in the long-standing rivalry between China and India. What began as a road construction project by China has snowballed into a heated contest involving territorial issues. India perceives the chosen location for the Chinese road project as a potential risk for its national security.[1] This standoff may have larger implications for the balance-of-power competition between the two states. States are often competitors against each other, but not all competitive relations turn into enduring rivalries. When do competitive relationships become enduring rivalries, and why do states often get entrapped into enduring rivalries? How can we explain the rise and decline of a rivalry relationship? William Thompson and David Dreyer identify three necessary attributes of an enduring rivalry: threatening competitive relations, internalized adversarial interactions, and similar military power.[2] How do states that originally have no enemy identity, such as China and India in the early 1950s, develop and internalize hostile identities? How does the rivalry maintain itself and mature over time?

Whether the China-India relationship is an intense rivalry is debated.[3] This chapter adopts a historical view and asks what causes the ups and downs in the China-India rivalry. We argue that the common understanding that territorial disputes lead to the rise of rivalries is a necessary but not sufficient explanation. The strategies both states employ in the initial crisis matter—external hard-balancing strategies stabilize the crisis but lead to the internalization of an enemy identity, which in turn leads to the rise and consolidation of an intense rivalry. There is a vicious causal cycle between hostile rivalry and hard-balancing strategies that rely on arms buildup and alignment. However, different types of balancing strategies could have different impacts on the ups and downs of rivalry relations. In recent years, both countries have adopted more complicated balancing strategies. A mixed strategy combining soft balancing (relying on institutions to balance other countries), external balancing, and limited hard balancing led to the complicated rivalry relationship we see today.

The first two sections of this chapter review theories of rivalry and balancing strategies and suggest that immediately after the war of 1962 both countries used external hard balancing to mitigate their immediate security threats. However, this strategy led to the internalization of a hostile identity and eventually fostered the endurance of the rivalry between China and India. The following two historical sections provide evidence on how the friendly relations in the 1950s evolved into an intense military rivalry in the 1960s and 1970s. The final section reviews the impact of the complex balancing strategies used by both countries in the contemporary era on the China-India rivalry.

RIVALRY RELATIONS AND THE BALANCE OF POWER

What causes the rise, and the escalation, of a relationship to a rivalry? Disputes over territory between states are often the starting point for an enduring rivalry.[4] Rivalries can emerge as part of a power-transition process: rising and declining powers tend to see each other as antagonists.[5] In the contributed volume *The India-Pakistan Conflict: An Enduring Rivalry*, T.V. Paul suggests that "aggregate power" at the national level might not be sufficient to prevent a rivalry. Asymmetrical dyads may also develop into an enduring rivalry when the more powerful party is unwilling or unable to project its power in theater. Last but not the least, competing states may be dragged into rivalries through alliance commitment to a third party, getting "chain-ganged" into conflict.[6]

These factors played an important role in the emergence of the China-India rivalry. However, structural factors alone cannot explain the process of rivalry escalation in this dyad. Territorial disputes existed since the independence of both countries, but the rivalry relationship started in the 1960s. The power-transition competition has become more intense in recent years, but the rivalry has not escalated. Rather, it developed more uncertainties. This chapter suggests that the policies adopted by both countries in the 1960s—that is, hard external balancing—partially explain the rise of the rivalry, and that the complicated balancing strategies adopted in recent years explain the current complexity of the rivalry. Balancing may once again become a source of rivalry maintenance in the future as the Indian Ocean is being touted as the main area of emerging balance-of-power competition involving the United States, India, and China along with small littoral states.

In this chapter, we are interested in the balancing strategies used by all three main protagonists within the context of the India-China rivalry and not whether the structural dimensions of balance of power are responsible for the overall stability of the rivalry. We agree with the distinction that balancing is "a state strategy or foreign policy behavior while *balances of power* are regarded as outcomes at the systemic or subsystemic levels, that is, as conditions of power equilibrium among key states."[7] We focus here on the foreign policy decisions made within the national security apparatus of the state and not strictly the result of systemic incentives.[8] Balancing as a strategy retains the agency element of balance of power at the core of its logic. They are strategies used by national security elites to constrain and curb the power of an adversary to keep the relationship within the status quo. As all bargaining situations within an intense rivalry are zero-sum, whenever the actions of one of the rivals threaten to upset the status quo we should see the employment of balancing strategies.[9]

Three types of balancing are evident in the China-India relationship: hard balancing, limited hard balancing, and soft balancing. Hard balancing relies on internal arms proliferation and/or external formal alignment and alliances (as in the China-Pakistan alignment against India). Limited balancing has the same features as hard balancing but is expected to be less intense in its application. Arms proliferation will be limited in scope and quantity, and external limited balancing will take the form of strategic agreements short of formal alliances but stronger than simple statements (as increasingly in the India-versus-China case).[10] Both rely on military means to balance.

The third option, soft balancing, entails "restraining the power or aggressive policies of a state through international institutions, concerted diplomacy via limited, informal ententes and economic sanctions in order to make its aggressive actions less legitimate in the eyes of the world and hence its strategic goals more difficult to obtain."[11] Soft balancing retains the balance-of-power core logic of curbing aggression and power accumulation, but via means outside the military realm.

The strategy of soft balancing was how weaker states tried to curb the power of the United States.[12] It is now applied more broadly to explain balancing behavior in situations where the US is not involved but where a stronger regional power exists. It has been applied to efforts by Japan and India to constrain China's foreign policy in the Asia-Pacific region and Moldova's effort to reduce Russian encroachment on its security through the European Union.[13] Soft balancing has also been used to explain cases of balancing against the US outside of the unipolar era, such as how states in Latin America resisted aggressive US policies in the late eighteenth and early nineteenth centuries.[14] Finally, soft balancing has also been used by the US against rising powers, particularly as part of Washington's strategy to curb the increase in relative capabilities of China.[15] It also explains US actions toward Japan from 1918 to 1939.[16]

It is important to note that all three balancing strategies presented here are not mutually exclusive. States choose which strategies are more cost-efficient considering context, threat environment, preferences, or recent interactions with an adversary.[17] India and China are constantly moving on the balancing continuum, depending on how intense the rivalry is at the time. More intense periods are marked by hard-balancing strategies, whereas less intense moments tend to see more soft-balancing strategies. This clear distinction is, of course, an analytical device. Both strategies may be used at the same time depending on the situation. Moreover, the cost of using different balancing strategies must be weighed against the benefits of continued limited cooperation between India and China. While balancing, if successful, will reduce the overall threat posed by an aggressive rival, it will also reinforce enmity and increase the divergence in identities. It is a difficult cycle to break. The discussion below shows how various types of balancing in the contemporary era contributed to the maintenance and the uncertainty of the China-India rivalry.

Moreover, balancing may be a complicated process as the fragmented threat environment involving many unstable littoral states of the Indian Ocean region makes it difficult for any of these two states to play an intense balance-of-power game. Regional stability is a common good, and all three players benefit from it. Thus far, the need for the protection of sea-lanes for oil exports and the common threats of "piracy, terrorism, drugs and arms trafficking" have made the Indian Ocean a shared zone of limited cooperation.[18] The smaller regional states, although trying to reap maximum benefits from the China-India competition, are constrained in the security arena because if they offer base facilities to one, that may generate intense hostility from the other. But these dynamics may slowly change as the material capabilities, power aspirations, and threat perceptions of both China and India increase.

Therefore, we argue that balancing behavior within the rivalry is conditioned on threat and not strictly on increases in material capabilities.[19] The existing relationship has positive elements that would make a strict balance-of-power strategy counterproductive to all parties. However, this is not to say that a shift in material capabilities from India or China has no consequences for the relationship. Rivalries do suffer from the security-dilemma problem—that is, whenever one party increases its share of relative material power, in particular military capabilities, it reduces the security of its adversary.[20] But in the absence of threatening, offensive signals, we should not expect to see balancing strategies used, at least not at a significant level.

INITIAL FRIENDSHIP AND SHARED IDENTITIES

When the People's Republic of China (PRC) and India achieved independence in the late 1940s, cooperation, friendship, and shared identities were the themes of their initial foreign relations. Shared identity first developed from a somewhat similar history of anticolonial and anti-imperialist struggle, although one by more peaceful methods than the other. Both India and China were victims of colonialism and imperialism, and they both achieved national liberation through decades of resistance. Even before independence, Indian leader Jawaharlal Nehru welcomed the visit of the Chinese nationalist leader Chiang Kai-shek by arguing, "The [Chinese] manifest sympathy for India's freedom, helped to bring India out of her national shell and increased her awareness of international issues . . . the bond that tied India and China grew stronger, and so did the desire to line up with India and other nations against the common adversary (namely, fascism and imperialism)."[21]

When the PRC was founded in 1949, India was the first nation outside of the communist bloc to recognize its government. Nehru accepted and appreciated the national liberation agenda of the new PRC government, and even its communist ideology was seen as less threatening.[22] The spirit of the slogan "*Hindi-Chini bhai bhai*" (Indians and Chinese are brothers) reached its climax at the 1955 Bandung Conference. Nehru insisted on inviting Premier Zhou Enlai to the conference. The Five Principles of Peaceful Co-existence (*panchashila*), first proposed by Nehru after his visit to Beijing in 1954, were widely appreciated by the leaders of the newly independent developing countries at the Bandung Conference, and both China and India received much respect as leaders of the emerging third world.

Interestingly, territorial disputes between China and India did exist during this honeymoon period. However, at least before 1960, these disputes did not evolve into militarized conflicts or the form of a rivalry. When the People's Liberation Army occupied Tibet in 1950, some members of India's Parliament warned Nehru that communist China's ambition was not limited to Tibet but also included the North-East Frontier Agency (NEFA) region of India and, even more dangerous, the expansion of the communist ideology to the world. Nehru rejected these concerns in one of his speeches to Parliament in 1950 when he stated, "Some hon. Members seem to think that I should issue an ultimatum to China. . . . I do not see how it is going to help anybody if I act in that way."[23] Although China was unhappy with Nehru's decision to give asylum to the Dalai Lama and his Tibetan refugees, there was an effort not to escalate the dispute to a military conflict. The Agreement on Trade and Intercourse between the Tibet Region of China and India (known as the Panchsheel Agreement) was signed on April 29, 1954. In this treaty, India recognized Beijing's control over Tibet and gave up its "extra-territorial rights in Tibet such as military escorts in Gyantse and Tatung, post offices, telegraph and telephone services and 12 rest houses," all built by previous British colonial authorities and left to independent India.[24] The shared idea of peaceful coexistence played an important role in Nehru's decision: He insisted that "the old advantages are of little use for us," the risk of military conflicts was only due to "irritants left by imperialism," and the Panchsheel Agreement should be regarded as a new model of solving these old irritants.[25]

How China and India managed their territorial disputes in the 1950s shows that territorial issues are important, but not sufficient, factors to explain the rise and persistence of rivalries. Shared identities can allow countries to mitigate their disputes on territorial issues. However, China-India relations in the next decades showed that when balancing strategies were adopted to solve immediate crises, shared identities were replaced by hostile identities as a side effect, widening the definitional attributes of rivalry: hostile competition and enemy identity.

POST–1962 WAR BALANCING STRATEGIES AND THEIR IMPACT ON THE RIVALRY

The *Hindi-Chini bhai-bhai* friendship started to decline as Tibet became a focal point of disputes in the late 1950s. As communist China began to exert control and launched land reforms in Tibet, triggering the 1959 uprising, the Dalai Lama and several of his followers escaped to India and received refugee status in Dharamsala in northern India.[26] China complained to India bitterly for intervening in its domestic affairs, and all of a sudden the territorial dispute became more prominent.

On the disputed territories between India and Tibet, the Indian position was to follow the McMahon Line, which was established in the 1914 Simla Accord between the British colonial government and Tibet.[27] China strongly opposed the McMahon Line and argued that it was not approved by any Beijing officials.[28] Furthermore, China viewed this boundary as a heritage of British colonialism; thus when India defended it, China believed that India betrayed their shared anticolonialism identity.[29] On the Indian side, Nehru became doubtful about China's commitment to the principles of peaceful coexistence as he saw in Mao Zedong's efforts at exporting revolution to the whole world, including India, a fundamental discrepancy between India and China.[30] Insurgents and communist parties in India also drew inspiration from Mao and received support from China. China's demands on the India-controlled northeastern territories and the Ladakh region consolidated Nehru's concerns regarding Chinese expansionist goals. Furthermore, India gave additional support to the Dalai Lama and the Tibetan cause.

While tensions started to rise in the late 1950s, there were reasons to believe that had the two states properly managed their crises, they would not have escalated into a hot war that transformed itself into an enduring rivalry. Misperceptions on intents and capabilities clearly contributed to the rise of tensions and the erosion of shared identities.[31] Even after the military conflict broke out, both nations arguably had chances to control the damage and avoid the emergence of an enduring rivalry. However, the balancing policies they adopted during and after the 1962 war deeply consolidated their enemy identification toward each other.

Facing a landslide military defeat on the eastern front, India immediately felt the need to balance the Chinese threat. Arguably, India did not have to automatically go for balancing policies right after the 1962 war. When China declared a unilateral cease-fire and retreated to its original position before the war, those actions signaled an important message to India. The official rhetoric was that China had not adopted unilateral actions to show its "good intentions," but, rather, that China retreated mostly for tactical reasons. Some Indian leaders pointed out how China did not have the logistical capacity to support a large army occupying the eastern frontier known as the NEFA (later the state of Arunachal Pradesh). The international environment was not friendly to China either. China faced much military pressure on its maritime frontier from the United States, and its relations with the Soviet Union in the north were also deteriorating, so it could not afford a three-front conflict.[32] The John F. Kennedy administration showed support to India, and some weapons were transferred, the first sign of limited hard-balancing activity by India.

China faced major problems in 1962. The "Great Leap Forward," which caused significant damage to its economy, had just ended.[33] One could reasonably argue that China did not have the capacity to launch a full-scale war with India in 1962. Nehru's perception of Chinese threats after 1962 could be exaggerated. His decision to rush for arms acquisition from the West might have been driven by a sense of humiliation and domestic pressure from Parliament. But he did not persist in the balancing activity as India-US relations did not advance to an alliance level or even to a serious rapprochement. This period shows the limitations of automatic balancing theories as Nehru stuck with his nonaligned principles and refused to form an outright alignment. Instead, internal balancing by way of increased defense modernization was the route adopted by both Nehru and his successor, Lal Bahadur Shastri.

China's decision to enter a military alliance with Pakistan to balance India, despite the fact it was a US ally, is also a puzzle. In fact, after the 1962 war, China's strategic goal—defending its eastern frontier in the Aksai Chin region—was already achieved. The western Aksai Chin region is strategically more important to China than to India as it connects Xinjiang and Tibet Provinces. Beijing made this strategic goal clear even in 1960, when Premier Zhou visited India to discuss the territorial disputes and offered a plan of giving up the claim on the eastern disputed territory (the NEFA) in exchange for Aksai Chin.[34] While this strategic goal was clearly achieved after the 1962 war, and India did not have the capacity to change the status quo at least in the short term, China did not need help from Pakistan to consolidate this goal. Pakistan's conceding portions of its disputed Kashmir region to China helped the process, but that only aggravated the Indian sense of hostility toward China. However, the formation of the China-Pakistan semialliance did increase India's enemy identification toward China and led to the escalation of the rivalry.

In sum, both sides overestimated the level of threats after the 1962 war. States balance against threats, but states also tend to overestimate the threats they face in an anarchic system. Therefore, balancing becomes the safe strategy in complex decision-making situations. Had China and India properly estimated the threat from the other side, would they still have adopted balancing strategies? Would they still have internalized enemy identity toward each other? Counterfactuals cannot be easily observed in this case. However, this analysis shows a sufficient causal process: balancing strategies aimed at enhancing national security led to stronger enemy identification in both states, and stronger enemy identification led to the rise and persistence of an enduring rivalry.

THE ESCALATION AND DE-ESCALATION OF THE CHINA-INDIA RIVALRY

The USSR-India quasi-alliance was the direct result of the 1962 war, although it took a while to materialize. Facing a landslide defeat, Nehru admitted that the Indian army was not well prepared for the conflict. While internal balancing through an arms buildup would take some time to materialize, India turned to external options to balance China. The United States provided some military support during the 1962 conflict, but it quickly receded in 1963.[35] As figure 5.1 shows, the export of weapons and military supplies from the Soviet Union to India quickly increased from 1960 until the end of the Cold War.[36] For the next four decades, Soviet weapons constituted 70 to 80 percent of India's military systems. However, Soviet military support to India immediately triggered more hostility within China. When Indian delegates visited Moscow after the conflict, a *People's Daily* article published on December 15, 1962, fiercely castigated the Soviet Union's reception of India's delegation, denouncing Moscow having "forgot proletarian internationalism, pretending to be neutral, calling China a brother while actually regarding the India reactionary group as the kinsmen."[37]

Rising hostility against India and India-USSR military relations led China to move closer to Pakistan, India's largest geopolitical competitor. Due to their ideological discrepancies and US-Pakistan relations, China and Pakistan were not close during the 1950s,[38] but rising tensions between China and India after the 1962 war pushed them closer. In 1963, they signed a "border agreement," in which Pakistan offered a small portion of disputed Kashmir to improve its relations with the PRC.[39] During the Second India-Pakistan War in 1965, China issued the following to India, "charged that India had sent patrols into Chinese territories, . . . and constructed military emplacements on the wrong side of the Tibet-Sikkim border . . . , giving India three days to dismantle their constructions or to face 'grave consequences.'"[40] However, no serious actions were taken by Beijing.[41]

While China and Pakistan used balancing strategies to counter India, New Delhi and Moscow were doing the same to restrain Beijing. Besides military aid, the Soviet Union openly condemned China's position and reconfirmed "India's claim on Kashmir."[42] The USSR envoy at the United Nations denounced Beijing for "pursuing a criminal policy of driving the World's people to serve their imperialist and expansionist aims."[43]

FIGURE 5.1. India's Military Imports from 1950 to 1990 (in millions of US dollars)

These limited hard-balancing strategies probably worked in 1965, as evident in both India and Pakistan agreeing to a cease-fire largely due to Soviet mediation under Alexei Kosygin, who managed to bring the parties to an agreement at Tashkent in 1966. However, the India-Pakistan conflict resumed and resulted in a large-scale war in 1971. In early 1971, separatist movements in East Pakistan led to rising tensions. Premier Zhou visited Pakistan in April and openly condemned India's intervention in the East Pakistan issue. Pakistan played an important role in US secretary of state Henry Kissinger's secret visit to Beijing in July 1971. The balancing game became more stretched as the United States got involved, while on the other side India and the Soviet Union signed the Treaty of Friendship and Cooperation in August 1971. In December 1971, the Third India-Pakistan War broke out and quickly ended in two weeks. As a consequence, Bangladesh achieved independence from Pakistan. The US-China rapprochement had a major impact on India's efforts to align with the Soviet Union, while Moscow viewed India as a major opening to the developing world, which it was attempting to court.[44]

Several important themes have emerged since the late 1960s. Often thought of as separate, the balance of power at the systemic level had a significant impact at the regional level. The result of the former constrains the choices of regional states in the latter. The superpowers, the United States and the Soviet Union, had been involved in the China-India rivalry through external balancing. The regional rivalry became part of the global bipolar competitive structure, which became harder to solve at the regional level. This systemic factor helped internalize balancing strategies in the thinking of leaders from both countries.

Another interesting theme is the internalization of the enemy identification, which is a complete reversal of their shared identities in the 1950s. To India, China was no longer a cooperative leader of the third world but, rather, a communist empire aiming to export revolution to the world. The nationalist school of thinking against China, which interpreted Beijing as "an irredentist and expansionist power that presents a 'clear and present' danger to India," gained more influence in New Delhi.[45] China's perception of India's identity changed even more dramatically. Premier Zhou discussed the India-Pakistan War with President Nixon in 1972, and in one of their meetings they discussed their "new" understanding of India's expansionism: "It is also a great pity that the daughter [Mrs. Gandhi] has also taken as her legacy the philosophy of her father embodied in the book *Discovery of India*. . . . He [Nehru] was thinking of a great Indian Empire—Malaysia, Ceylon, etc. It would probably also include Tibet."[46]

Changing from shared identity to hostile identity during the 1960s marked the establishment of the China-India enduring rivalry. Territorial disputes are not sufficient to explain the establishment of this rivalry, as territorial disputes in the 1950s did not lead to the rise of a rivalry. Even when territorial disputes evolved into militarized conflicts, both countries still had the chance to control the damage. However, external balancing strategies aiming at solving immediate security threats consolidated the enemy identity toward each other and led to the rise of an enduring rivalry. Had India not sought Soviet help, China might not have felt threatened by the India-USSR quasi-alliance as India by itself did not have the military capacity to threaten China. Had China not formed a military alliance with Pakistan and had China been less involved in the 1965 and 1971 wars, they would not have had to threaten India with ultimatums. These counterfactuals show how balancing strategies can cause the rise and persistence of an enduring rivalry.

RAPPROCHEMENT AND BALANCING IN THE POST–COLD WAR ERA

The causal relationship between balancing strategies and enduring rivalries is a vicious cycle: A balancing strategy consolidates enemy identification and leads to the rise of enduring rivalry; a rival relationship limits the chance of possible cooperation and shared identity-building as it restrains states to more intense and complicated balancing strategies. However, changing situations from the late 1970s brought new characteristics to the balancing game between China and India. Mitigating factors, such as economic interdependence and international institutions, have restrained the escalation of the rivalry to some extent. Both countries have adopted a mixed-balancing strategy—a combination of limited hard balancing and soft balancing. While more external actors, such as Japan, Australia, and the United States, became involved in India's external balancing strategy, domestic economic growth calculations have also allowed both countries to adopt a combination of internal and external balancing.

Changes in the relationship were already taking place by the mid-1970s following the defeat of the Indian National Congress in the Indian elections and the arrival of a coalition of opposition parties under the Janata Party umbrella organization. The end of the Cultural Revolution in 1976 and the start of reforms in 1978 marked a major change in the foreign policy of China as its strong ideological incentives were replaced by pragmatism. In 1977, India's foreign minister, Atal Bihari Vajpayee, visited China. The two countries reestablished diplomatic relations in 1978 following the visit. During the 1980s, both countries continued to use limited balancing strategies to check each other, and several territorial disputes arose on the India-Tibet border but did not escalate into major armed conflicts. The end of the Cold War and the collapse of the Soviet Union meant that the external balancing strategy of India faced some important changes. Since China had been identified by military and foreign policy pundits as an important threat to India going forward, New Delhi diversified its sources of external balancing and started to connect with other major regional players with shared interests.

India's military cooperation with the Commonwealth of Independent States (later the Russian Federation) significantly weakened after the complete collapse of the Soviet Union. A report written by a former Indian ambassador to Moscow highlights the effect of the 1990s Soviet economic crisis and the failure of Mikhail Gorbachev's reforms: "By 1998, we began feeling these tremors, including unusually erratic defense supplies."[47] In the 1990s, India tended to see Russia as weaker than the USSR, incapable of helping India balance potential threats from China. This does not mean India needed to abandon external balancing strategies but to diversify its sources of external balancing.[48]

The end of the Cold War also brought new potential military suppliers to India. The economic liberalization that started in 1991 allowed India to purchase more weapon systems from a wider global market. Some global suppliers, such as Israel and France, were less concerned about ideological differences and were willing to sell advanced weapon technology. Increased sources of military supplies also boosted India's bargaining capacity with its traditional partner—Russia—as Moscow became more willing to export its advanced military technology to India. One example was Russia's cooperation with India's Defence Research and Development Organisation to engineer the BrahMos cruise missile system, which is considered "India's most successful military project to date."[49]

In recent years, a rising China has caused an increase in tensions in the Asia-Pacific region, which brought some countries usually outside of the China-India rivalry into the game. The rapid expansion of cooperation between India, Japan, Australia, and the United States highlights this new trend in India's external balancing strategy.

With the regime of Junichiro Koizumi, Japan entered a period of increasing geopolitical competition with China. Tokyo has been searching for other major powers to balance in a limited fashion against Beijing as it does not have sufficient means for hard balancing. India was viewed as the perfect candidate. In 2008, Japan and India signed a "joint declaration on security cooperation," according to which the two countries would share information on security and diplomatic issues, conduct joint practices of their coast guards, and combat together terrorism and other security threats.[50] This joint declaration immediately triggered sharp rebuttal from Beijing, which saw the India-Japan security cooperation as a "China containment strategy."[51]

India and Japan have engaged in joint military exercises since 2012 and most recently in 2016 near the coastline of Chennai.[52] Japan has also sold weapons and military vehicles to India, including twelve US-2 aircraft (an amphibious air-sea rescue plane) in a deal estimated to cost India $1.5 billion.[53] The rise of China and increased cooperation between China and Pakistan have provided incentives for both Japan and India to work together closely on security issues—namely, to increase deterrence and to signal it has the appropriate means to engage in serious balancing activities.[54]

India has also deepened its relationship with Australia in a way that is close to soft balancing. In November 2014, Australian prime minister Tony Abbott made a "joint security declaration" with Indian prime minister Narendra Modi, announcing a "strategic partnership between India and Australia based on a shared desire to promote regional and global security, as well as their common commitment to democracy, freedom, human rights and the rule of law."[55]

Among all of India's balancing efforts, the upswing in relations with the United States was the greatest cause for concern for Beijing. The India-US rapprochement raised concern in China as Beijing saw the rapprochement as containment. It will be much harder for Beijing to successfully use balancing strategies when and if necessary if the hegemon is allied with India. Both President Bill Clinton and President George W. Bush visited India, the former in 2000 and the latter in 2006, showing a strategic reorientation toward the country.

This trend was reaffirmed by President Barack Obama while in New Delhi. He "described the relationship between India and the US as the defining partnerships of the 21st century because of common values and interests."[56] At the time, "Obama and Modi also signed a broad framework for expanding cooperation in the Indian Ocean and the Asia-Pacific." Obama also appreciated India's "Look East" policy and encouraged New Delhi to play a more important role in the region.[57]

Other strategic partnerships and programs between Washington and New Delhi are part of a larger balancing strategy by the latter. The 2005 "India-US civil nuclear agreement" has some impact on New Delhi's military, as India could have more uranium and plutonium, which could be used for its nuclear weapons and nuclear submarines.[58] More important, it has significant implications for India's international status. As Yang Xiaoping argues, India's nuclear arsenal is not strictly aimed at mitigating external threats but also "to force the United States to recognize India as a great power," and India at least has partially achieved this recognition of "great-power status" through the nuclear bargain with the US.[59]

Nuclear balance is an important component in the post–Cold War China-India balance-of-power game. India conducted its second nuclear test in May 1998.[60] Pakistan immediately responded, with possible help from China, with five underground nuclear tests in the same month. T.V. Paul argues that balancing India's nuclear threats was the most important reason why Beijing backed Pakistan's nuclear proliferation.[61] In 2012, India tested its Agni-V missile, an intercontinental ballistic missile able to reach most regions in China.[62] The development of the Agni-V is clearly seen as a sign of nuclear balancing against China because if it was meant to balance the Pakistani threat, India would not need a missile with a range of 5,500 kilometers. After the Indian test, Pakistan also tested its Saheen-II ballistic missile in response.

Moreover, India has engaged in a moderate form of limited balancing in the South China Sea. An important region for China's rise and its constant quest for trade access and energy, the South China Sea has been a contested area between various regional actors, including Japan, the United States, Vietnam, the Philippines, Malaysia, and Brunei. Specifically, India has been involved in a deal whereby it would sell the Akash missile and the BrahMos missile to Vietnam.[63] India had previously offered to lend Vietnam $500 million for defense projects as part of an effort to develop a more rigorous security partnership.[64] Vietnam's reason for buying the weapon systems is one of deterrence, and for India it acts as limited balancing against a rival.[65] The news was not received positively by China. The Asia-Pacific has been the theater of many small clashes between the US and China, as well as between Japan and China. The expenditure by Vietnam for missile systems increases the constraints put on China's ambitions in the region.

China has sought to strengthen its external balancing strategy against India by developing closer economic and military relationships with Myanmar, Bangladesh, Nepal, and Sri Lanka. However, due to the fragmented nature of the South Asian state system, China does not have many options for external balancing against India except the China-Pakistan alliance.

China-Pakistan military-to-military cooperation has deepened in recent years, with China providing military technology to modernize Pakistan's arsenal. A short list of these advanced weapon systems includes the "JF-17 thunder fighter, the F-22P frigate with helicopters, K-8 jet trainers, T-85 tanks, F-7 aircrafts, small arms, and ammunition."[66] China is also the donor of Pakistan's nuclear technology.

China's cooperation with Pakistan has extended to the economic sphere, which also has balance-of-power connotations. The China-Pakistan Economic Corridor (CPEC) became an important development in the balancing triangle of China, Pakistan, and India. The CPEC is a large infrastructure and economic investment venture from China toward Pakistan. The overall monetary value attached to the project is now said to be approximately $57 billion.[67] The crux of the initiative are massive infrastructure projects in an attempt at a new "land and maritime Silk Road."[68] The CPEC also involves energy provisions to increase the Pakistani capacity as well as various investments in Pakistani economic sectors. China has extended an invitation to India and other states in the region to become part of the CPEC,[69] but the offer has not been accepted by India because of balance-of-power and security considerations. Increasing Chinese investment in Pakistan could also lead to a higher risk of conflict between India and China, as on the one hand some of these investments, such as Gwadar Port, can be used for military purposes and can increase the Chinese military presence in the Indian Ocean, and on the other hand, many of these investments would be high-value targets in wartime. If India attacks one of these joint venture investments in Pakistan, China would automatically be dragged into direct conflict with India.

Nevertheless, the post–Cold War China-India rivalry did not move toward a full-fledged hard-balancing equation. Moreover, India's good relations with Japan, Australia, and the United States have not evolved into a formal alliance against China. Both countries restrained their balancing behavior to some extent. In India, the "pragmatic school" is prevalent in policymaking toward Beijing.[70] On the Chinese side, even after India tested its Agni-V missile, Beijing restrained its reaction. Hua Chunying, the spokeswoman of the Foreign Ministry of China, said, "India and China are partners, not competitors . . . and we always think maintaining a strategic balance in South Asia is good for the peace and prosperity in the region."[71] In that sense, both countries try to control the intensity of the balancing game by adopting a mixed-balancing strategy, combining internal, external, soft, and hard balancing into a grand strategy.

Interestingly, soft balancing plays an important role in both countries' balancing strategies. When China forged the Asian Infrastructure Investment Bank, which has been seen as a tool for China to increase its economic and geopolitical influence, India was in the first group of nations to join the new institution. India also cooperated with countries of the Association of Southeast Asian Nations (ASEAN) and tried to push forward a free-trade agreement within the institution. This pact is considered an ASEAN-India-Pacific version of the Trans-Pacific Partnership, aimed to balance against the fast-growing economic might of China.[72] India also joined the China-led Shanghai Cooperation Organization (SCO) in 2016. China had been originally reluctant to endorse India's membership in the SCO but eventually accepted it.

But why did China and India adopt a mixed-balancing strategy in the post–Cold War era? Why is the vicious cycle between hard balancing and enduring rivalry somehow controlled in the post–Cold War era? Economic interdependence could be an important reason and will more likely become more important in the future. However, the importance of economic interdependence should not be overstated. As Matthew A. Castle argues in chapter 10 of this volume, China-India trade relations are highly asymmetrical, with a strong export deficit against India. Whether such asymmetrical trade relations can lead to peace and are sustainable over the long term is still questionable. Moreover, economic interdependence between China and India started to increase rapidly only in the past ten years. It still cannot explain why China and India adopted mixed-balancing strategies in the 1990s and early 2000s.

Another normative explanation is that shared identities, such as beliefs in the principle of nonalignment, negative memories of colonial history, resistances to great-power politics, and strong beliefs in sovereignty and national autonomy, still have some noticeable influence in New Delhi and Beijing. According to Annpurna Nautiyal, India wants to maintain the autonomy of its foreign policy, thus it does not want to formally align with external powers to balance against China.[73] Another important reason is that India and China have quite strong shared interests, which leaves them with noticeable space for cooperation. These include common interests to reform the international financial regime (e.g., the reform of the IMF after the 2008 crisis), cooperation in global climate-change negotiations, shared interests in global economic governance, common interests in antiterrorism, and more. Both China and India were leaders of the Group of 77 states at the Copenhagen climate-change conference in 2009.

The mixed-balancing strategies contributed to the inception and resolution of the 2017 Doklam Plateau crisis. India sought help from Japan and the United States to balance China's military threats, while China reminded India of the risk of a two-front conflict in Doklam and Kashmir. Both countries flexed their muscles through military exercises, front deployment, and threatening speeches. The crisis ended when both sides mutually "disengaged." But India's sense of insecurity did not decrease. By increasing its military buildup and shoring up its alliance commitments to contain China, New Delhi sought to improve its security. Interestingly, the crisis was solved just one week before the 2017 BRICS (Brazil, Russia, India, China, and South Africa) summit in China. New Delhi and Beijing both had the promotion of the BRICS institutions at the international level at heart. Moreover, economic benefits from BRICS cooperation also outweigh the significance of a small, disputed, barren territory. Even as military tension was high in the summer of 2017 and nationalistic sentiment in both countries called for tough punishment against each other, China and India did not move into a full-scale, hard-balancing game but instead found solutions through BRICS institutions.

CONCLUSION

Increasing geopolitical competition led to more intense external and hard-balancing strategies in both China and India. However, mitigating factors such as soft-balancing strategies, economic interdependence, and shared identities and interests have restrained the escalation of the rivalry relationship. The future of the India-China rivalry points to many uncertainties. Mitigating factors could continue to repair the damage from the 1960s and 1970s, and eventually shared interests and identity could turn these two foes into friends. Or changing capacity and relative power could ignite more hard-balancing behavior, and hostility could increase over many issues—such as the South China Sea, Pakistan and Kashmir, and the Indian Ocean sea-lanes. The strategies states use in an uncertain environment matter, just as they mattered in the escalation of the rivalry in the 1960s.

Globalization has also affected the magnitude and type of balancing strategies used by both India and China. While the enduring rivalry is unlikely to dissolve in the near future, some innovation in strategic thinking might help to control the damage done. Some top advisers of the Chinese Ministry of Foreign Affairs have proposed an interesting metaphor to describe China's new understanding of the competition between rival states, arguing that although competition is common between major powers, there are different types of competition. Some interstate competitions, such as the Cold War between the Soviet Union and the United States, are like a boxing fight in which two players punch each other with the goal to knock the other out.[74] However, the China-India rivalry in the twenty-first century does not have to be such a zero-sum game. A boxing fight does not capture the complexity of the current relationship, which might be better described as a soccer game: many players competing on different fronts with the goal to win but not necessarily incapacitate opponents.[75]

The relationship remains competitive, but Beijing and New Delhi have found that they have shared interests worth pursuing together. As Feng Liu points out in chapter 11, they both have a stake in reforming the current international order, and they stand a better chance of achieving their goal through a common front. Their common involvement in multilateral diplomacy on the international stage is a testament to common recognition of the issues they face.

There is some cause for concern, however. India and China are among the most active modernizers when it comes to their military arsenals. New Delhi has been improving its ground forces (specifically its artillery and tanks) and, to more adequately dominate at sea with, its maritime forces.[76] India's military budget continues to be on the increase: New Delhi is now among the largest investors on military capabilities, with a projected investment of $56.5 billion by 2018.[77] China has also continued its military modernization, with perhaps the most talked-about feature being its investment in becoming a "blue-water navy" able to contend with the US Navy.[78] While its navy is not as efficient as it could be at the moment, there is no doubt that China will continue to invest heavily in it in the near future. China, the second largest military spender, announced in early 2017 it would invest 7 percent more in its defense budget.[79]

However, hard balancing as a strategy seems to be taking a back seat in the rivalry. While China and India both continue internal arms acquisitions, these procurements seem to now be more asymmetrical in scope and audience. As Manjari Chatterjee Miller points out in chapter 4, China does not have India at the top of its security list at the moment, whereas China and Pakistan are at the center of security concerns for India.

India and China have moved more toward soft balancing and limited hard balancing in their relationship, as we have demonstrated. Under the mixed balancing strategy, the rivalry will continue for a relatively long period of time. We should observe competition not only in the security arena but also in economic and softpower areas.

NOTES

1. Steve George and Anish Gawande, "China and India in War of Words over Bhutan Border Dispute," CNN, August 25, 2017, http://www.cnn.com/2017/07/03/asia/bhutan-india-border-dispute/index.html.
2. William Thompson, and David Dreyer, "Introduction," in *The Handbook of Interstate Rivalries, 1494–2010*, ed. William Thompson and David Dreyer (Washington, DC: CQ Press, 2012), 1.
3. Mohan Malik suggests the rivalry between the two is deeply entrenched: *China and India: Great Power Rivals* (Boulder, CO: First Forum Press, 2011), esp. ch. 2. Some authors in the present volume take a more optimistic view and suggest the rivalry relations have been in decline in recent years.
4. Paul Senese and John A. Vasquez, *The Steps to War: An Empirical Study* (Princeton, NJ: Princeton University Press, 2010); David Dreyer and William R. Thompson, *Handbook of International Rivalries, 1494–2010* (Washington, DC: CQ Press, 2012). Gary Goertz and Paul E. Diehl find that rivalries developed over territories are especially dangerous, as the probabilities of militarized conflicts occurring within them are three times higher than rivalries not based on territorial conflicts. See "The Empirical Importance of Enduring Rivalries," *International Interactions* 18, no. 2 (August 1992): 151–63. Mahesh Shankar makes a similar point in chapter 2 of this volume.
5. Jack S. Levy, *War in Modern Great Power System, 1495–1975* (Lexington: University Press of Kentucky, 1983).
6. Thomas J. Christensen and Jack Snyder, "Chain Gangs and Passed Bucks: Predicting Alliance Patterns in Multipolarity," *International Organization* 44, no. 2 (Spring 1990): 137–68.
7. T.V. Paul, "Introduction," in *Balance of Power: Theory and Practice in the 21st Century* (Stanford, CA: Stanford University Press, 2004), 2 (italics in text).
8. Steven E. Lobell, Norrin M. Ripsman, and Jeffrey W. Taliaferro, eds., *Neoclassical Realism, the State, and Foreign Policy* (Cambridge: Cambridge University Press, 2009); and Norrin M. Ripsman, Jeffrey W. Taliaferro, and Steven E. Lobell, *Neoclassical Realist Theory of International Politics* (New York: Oxford University Press, 2016).
9. Richard Rosecrance, "Is There a Balance of Power?," in *Realism and the Balancing of Power: A New Debate*, ed. John A. Vasquez and Colin Elman (New York: Prentice Hall, 2003), 156–60.
10. We use these categories as developed by T.V. Paul in his *Restraining Great Powers: Soft Balancing from Empires to the Global Era* (New Haven, CT: Yale University Press, 2018).
11. Ibid., chap. 2.
12. Robert A. Pape, "Soft Balancing against the United States," *International Security* 30, no. 1 (Summer 2005), 7–45; and T.V. Paul, "Soft Balancing in the Age of U.S. Primacy," *International Security* 30, no. 1 (Summer 2005): 46–71.
13. For the Asia-Pacific region, see Paul, *Restraining Great Powers*, chap. 6. For Moldova, see Cristian Cantir and Ryan Kennedy, "Balancing on the Shoulders of Giants: Moldova's Foreign Policy toward Russia and the European Union," *Foreign Policy Analysis* 11, no. 4 (2014): 1–20.

14. Max Paul Friedman and Tom Long, "Soft Balancing in the Americas: Latin American Opposition to US Intervention, 1898–1936," *International Security* 40, no. 1 (Summer 2015): 120–56.
15. Kai He and Huiyun Feng, "If Not Soft Balancing, Then What? Reconsidering Soft Balancing and US Policy toward China," *Security Studies* 17, no. 2 (2008): 363–95.
16. Ilai Z. Saltzman, "Soft Balancing as Foreign Policy: Assessing American Strategy toward Japan in the Interwar Period," *Foreign Policy Analysis* 8 (2012): 131–50.
17. Pape, "Soft Balancing against the United States"; Paul, "Soft Balancing in the Age of U.S. Primacy"; and Friedman and Long, "Soft Balancing in the Americas."
18. Chunhao Lou, "US-India-China Relations in the Indian Ocean: A Chinese Perspective," *Strategic Analysis* 36, no. 4 (July/August 2012): 624–39, 633.
19. Stephen M. Walt, "Alliance Formation and the Balance of World Power," *International Security* 9, no. 4 (Spring 1985): 4–6, 8–13.
20. Robert Jervis, "Cooperation under the Security Dilemma," *World Politics* 30, no. 2 (January 1978): 167–214; and Jonathan Holslag, "The Persistent Military Security Dilemma between China and India," *Journal of Strategic Studies* 32, no. 6 (2009): 811–40.
21. Jawaharlal Nehru, quoted in Ramachandra Guha, "Jawaharlal Nehru and China: A Study in Failure?.," Harvard-Yenching Institute Working Paper Series, 2011, 4.
22. Another example of the China-India friendship in the 1950s was when the UN Security Council voted to condemn the invasion of South Korea by North Korea in October 1950 and threatened military intervention under the collective-security provisions of the UN Charter, India supported the PRC's position by being absent at the vote. India actually acted as an intermediary between Washington and Peking.
23. Guha, "Jawaharlal Nehru and China."
24. Claude Arpi, "The Panchsheel Agreement," *India Defence Review*, August 5, 2015, http://www.indiandefencereview.com/spotlights/the-panchsheel-agreement/.
25. Ibid.
26. Warren Smith, "The Nationalities Policies of the Chinese Communist Party and the Socialist Transformation of Tibet," in *Resistance and Reform in Tibet*, ed. Robert Barnett and Shirin Akiner (India: Jainendra Prakash Jain Press, 1996), 58–61.
27. Alastair Lamb, *The McMahon Line: A Study in the Relations between India, China and Tibet, 1904–1914*, vol. 2 (New York: Routledge & Kegan Paul, 1966), 523–28, 530–34.
28. Ibid., 529.
29. This view is widely accepted in Chinese history and international relations writings but less reported in the English world. E.g., see Yanwei Wang, "Analyzing the McMahon Line from the International Law Perspectives," *Academic Journal of China's Politics and Law University* (2009), http://cdmd.cnki.com.cn/Article /CDMD-10053-2009087318.htm, trans. Zhen Han.
30. Steven Levine, "Perception and Ideology in Chinese Foreign Policy," in *China's Foreign Policy: Theory and Practice*, ed. Thomas Robinson and David Shambaugh (Oxford: Clarendon Press, 1997), 37–40.
31. Robert Jervis, *Perception and Misperception in International Politics* (Princeton, NJ: Princeton University Press, 1975).
32. John W. Garyer, "China's Decision for War with India in 1962," in *New Directions in the Study of China's Foreign Policy*, ed. Alastair Iain Johnston and Robert S. Ross (Stanford, CA: Stanford University Press, 2006), 116.
33. Steven A. Hoffmann, *India and the China Crisis* (Berkeley: University of California Press, 1990), 121, 213–24.

34. Oriana S. Mastro, "The Great Divide: Chinese and India Views on Negotiations, 1959–62," *Journal of Defence Studies* 6, no. 4 (2012), http://www.idsa.in /jds/6_4_2012_TheGreatDivide_OrianaSkylarMastro.

35. The United States was concerned that its military support to India could offend Pakistan, an important US ally at that time. Also, the assumed second wave of Chinese incursions in the spring of 1963 didn't happen. Therefore, the US became less interested in supporting India's military buildup. David R. Devereux, "The Sino-Indian War of 1962 in Anglo-American Relations," *Journal of Contemporary History* 44, no. 1 (January 2009): 71–87.

36. Ramesh Thakur and Carlyle A. Thayer, *Soviet Relations with India and Vietnam* (New York: Springer, 1992), 92.

37. *People's Daily*, December 15, 1962. Cited in S. Gopal, "India, China and the Soviet Union," *Australian Journal of Politics and History* 12, no. 2 (1966): 252.

38. In the 1950s, Pakistan was an ally of the United States, and its Islamic ideology was also incompatible with the communist ideology in China. Anwar Hussain Syed, *China and Pakistan: Diplomacy of an Entente Cordiale* (Amherst: University of Massachusetts Press, 1974), 34.

39. Mavra Farooq, "Pakistani-Chinese Relations: An Historical Analysis of the Role of China in the Indo-Pakistani War of 1971," *Pakistaniaat: A Journal of Pakistan Studies* 2, no. 3 (2010): 76.

40. Paul M. McGarr, *The Cold War in South Asia: Britain, the United States and the Indian Subcontinent, 1945–1965* (New York: Cambridge University Press, 2013), 329.

41. T.V. Paul, *Asymmetric Conflicts: War Initiation by Weaker Powers* (New York: Cambridge University Press, 1994), chap. 6.

42. McGarr, *Cold War in South Asia*, 330.

43. Ibid.

44. Raju G. C. Thomas, "Security Relationships in Southern Asia: Differences in the Indian and American Perspectives," *Asian Survey* 21, no. 7 (1981): 703–6.

45. Malik, *China and India*, 54.

46. Ibid., 73.

47. Ambassador Ranendra Sen, *The Evolution of India's Bilateral Relations with Russia*, Aspen Institute India policy paper no. 2 (New Delhi: Aspen Institute India, February 2011), 109, http://www.anantaaspencentre.in/pdf/the _evolution.pdf.

48. Ibid., 14. India also tried internal balancing strategies such as the indigenization of its military supplies; however, due to limited national industrial capacity, Indian weapon-indigenization programs often suffer severe budget overruns and delays. Therefore, internal-balancing strategies are often inefficient and insufficient for India to respond to external threats. Hence, a mixed-balancing strategy is the optimal choice for Indian leaders.

49. Sunil Dasgupta and Stephen P. Cohen, "Arms Sales for India: How Military Trade Could Energize US-Indian Relations," *Foreign Affairs* 90, no. 2 (March/ April 2011): 24.

50. Japanese Ministry of Foreign Affairs, "Joint Declaration on Security and Cooperation between Japan and India," October 22, 2008, http://www.mofa.go.jp /region/asia-paci/india/pmv0810/joint_d.html.

51. See Takenori Horimoto, "Japan-India Rapprochement and Its Future Issues," Japan's Diplomacy Series, Japan Digital Library (2016), 11, https:// www2.jiia.or.jp/en/pdf/digital_library/japan_s_diplomacy/160411_Takenori _Horimoto.pdf.

52. Noboru Yamaguchi and Shutaro Sano, "Japan-India Security Cooperation," in *Poised for Partnership: Deepening India-Japan Relations in the Asian Century*, ed.

Rohan Mukherjee and Anthony Yazaki (New York: Oxford University Press, 2016), 161–62.

53. Reuters Staff, "India to Buy Rescue Aircraft from Japan for $1.5–$1.6 Billion," Reuters, November 5, 2016, http://in.reuters.com/article/japan-india-idINKBN131029; and Reuters Staff, "Japan, India Likely to Ink Pivotal US-2 Aircraft Deal," *Japan Times*, November 6, 2016.

54. C. Raja Mohan and Rishika Chauhan, "India-Japan Strategic Partnership," in Mukherjee and Yazaki, *Poised for Partnership*, 193–94.

55. John Garnaut, "Rising India Is Vital to Allied Hopes to Deter China," *Sydney Morning Herald*, October 23, 2015, http://www.smh.com.au/comment/all-eyes-on-indias-emergence-as-a-global-superpower-20151022-gkfgms.html.

56. Annpurna Nautiyal, "US Security Strategy of Asian Rebalance: India's Role and Concerns," *Strategic Analysis* 41, no. 1 (2017): 22. See also T.V. Paul and Mahesh Shankar, "Status Accommodation through Institutional Means: India's Rise and the Global Order," in T.V. Paul, Deborah W. Larson, and William C. Wolhforth, *Status in World Politics* (New York: Cambridge University Press, 2014), 165–91.

57. Ibid.

58. Amitai Etzioni, "The Darker Side of the US-India Nuclear Deal," *The Diplomat*, February 13, 2015, http://thediplomat.com/2015/02/the-darker-side-of-the-u-s-india-nuclear-deal/.

59. Yang Xiaoping, "China's Perception of India as a Nuclear Weapons Power," Carnegie Endowment of International Peace, June 30, 2016, http://carnegieendowment.org/2016/06/30/china-s-perceptions-of-india-as-nuclear-weapons-power-pub-63970.

60. A numbers of factors, such as domestic politics, the desire for international status, and the external pressure of signing the Comprehensive Test Ban Treaty, could explain India's decision in 1998. However, security threats from Pakistan and China are an important factor that cannot be overlooked.

61. T.V. Paul, "Chinese-Pakistani Nuclear/Missile Ties and Balance of Power Politics," *Nonproliferation Review* 10, no. 2 (2003): 21–22.

62. Harsh Pant and Yogesh Joshi, *The US Pivot and Indian Foreign Policy: Asia's Evolving Balance of Power* (New York: Palgrave Macmillan, 2015), 70.

63. Rajat Panditil, "Wary of China, India Offers Akash Surface-to-Air Missile System to Vietnam," *Times of India*, last updated January 9, 2017, http://timesofindia.indiatimes.com/india/wary-of-china-india-offers-akash-missile-to-vietnam-both-countries-crank-up-their-bilateral-military-relations/articleshow/56410196.cms; and Sanjeev Miglani, "India Plans Expanded Missile Export Drive, with China on Its Mind," Reuters, June 8, 2016, http://www.reuters.com/article/us-india-missiles-idUSKCN0YU2SQ.

64. "India Offers $500 Million Defence Credit as Vietnam Seeks Arms Boost," *Hindustan Times*, last updated September 3, 2016, http://www.hindustantimes.com/india-news/india-offers-500-million-defence-credit-as-vietnam-seeks-arms-boost/story-2cKaf1oMFyNjkNZQX5q8GO.html.

65. Helen Clark, "China Won't 'Sit with Arms Crossed' While India Considers Arms Deal with Vietnam," *South China Morning Post*, Business Insider, January 13, 2017, http://www.businessinsider.com/india-selling-missiles-to-vietnam-china-relations-2017-1.

66. Lisa Curtis and Dean Cheng, "The China Challenge: A Strategic Vision for US-India Relations," Heritage Foundation, July 18, 2011, http://www.heritage.org/asia/report/the china-challenge-strategic-vision-us-india-relations.

67. Saad Sayeed, "Pakistan Army Chief Sells China Investment Deal in Remote Baluchistan," Reuters, January 7, 2017, http://www.reuters.com/article/us-pakistan -cpec-idUSKBN14S01H.

68. Charlie Campbell, "China's Xi Jinping's Talks up 'One Belt, One Road,' as Keynote Project Fizzles," *Time*, August 18, 2016, http://time.com/4457044/xi -jinping-one-belt-one-road-obor-south-china-sea-economic-trade-business/.

69. "Beijing Wants India, Others to Join CPEC Due to Pakistan's Appetite, Says Chinese Media," *Economic Times*, December 30, 2016, http://economictimes .indiatimes.com/news/politics-and-nation/beijing-wants-india-others-to-join -cpec-due-to-pakistans-appetite-says-chinese-media/articleshow/56255676.cms.

70. Malik, *China and India*, 51, 52–53.

71. Wen Xin, "India Launches Agni-V Missile, MOF Responses," *China News*, December 27, 2016, http://news.china.com.cn/world/2016-12/27/content _39993661.htm, trans. the authors.

72. Nautiyal, "US Security Strategy of Asian Rebalance," 19.

73. Ibid., 28.

74. Yan Xuetong and Qi Haixia, "Football Game rather than Boxing Match: China–US Intensifying Rivalry Does Not Amount to Cold War," *Chinese Journal of International Politics* 5, no. 2 (2012): 126–27.

75. Ibid.

76. Gurmeet Kanwal, "India's Military Modernization: Plans and Strategic Underpinnings," National Bureau of Asian Research, September 24, 2012. http://www .nbr.org/research/activity.aspx?id=275.

77. Peggy Hollinger, "India Moves into Top Five Global Defence Spenders," *Financial Times*, December 12, 2016, https://www.ft.com/content/8404e57a-bfa1 -11e6-9bca-2b93a6856354; and Shane Mason, "Military Budgets in India and Pakistan: Trajectories, Priorities, and Risks," Stimson Center (2016), esp. 7–8.

78. Xiaoyu Pu and Randall L. Schweller, "Status Signaling, Multiple Audience, and China's Blue-Water Naval Ambition," in Paul, Larson, and Wohlforth, *Status in World Politics*, 141–64.

79. "China to Increase Military Spending by 7% in 2017," BBC News, March 4, 2017, http://www.bbc.com/news/world-asia-china-39165080.

Chapter 6

China and India's Quest for Resources and Its Impact on the Rivalry

CALVIN CHEN

In October 2015, India hosted representatives from fifty-four African countries at the third India Africa Forum Summit (IAFS). The gathering, considered by some to be the "most spectacular diplomatic exercise hosted by India since the 1983 Non-Aligned Movement (NAM) summit," offered participants an opportunity to reflect on, expand, and deepen their growing partnerships.[1] At the summit, Indian prime minister Narendra Modi announced that "today, we pledge to walk together, with our steps in rhythm and our voices in harmony. This is not a new journey, nor a new beginning. But, this is a new promise of a great future for an ancient relationship."[2] Within two months of the meeting in New Delhi, Chinese president Xi Jinping set off for a summit of the Forum on China-Africa Cooperation (FOCAC) in Johannesburg, South Africa, and subsequently announced $60 billion in funding for a myriad of development, infrastructure, and energy initiatives across the continent. Like India, China sought to enhance its burgeoning relationship with Africa, and such financing, as Kenyan president Uhuru Kenyatta noted, was a "clear indication that China is committed to Africa's development agenda on the basis of a win-win partnership."[3] Echoing the tone and spirit of the 1955 Bandung Conference, such statements suggest that prospects for economic cooperation, solidarity, and mutual benefit are better than ever.

Nevertheless, skeptics point out that contemporary global dynamics are fundamentally different from those in 1955. As Michael Klare observes, not only is the world's economy far larger, more complex, and more integrated than it was six decades ago, but it is also characterized by "an insatiable need for resources of all types: energy for transportation, manufacturing, and electricity generation; minerals for buildings, infrastructure, and consumer products; and food and water to sustain a growing (and increasingly urbanized) global population."[4] With the world's population at over 7.3 billion in 2015, more than 2.5 times the size of the population in 1955, sustaining—let alone improving—living standards for all will be a tall order. Indeed, pessimists see only a bleak future, one increasingly characterized by win-lose rather than win-win outcomes.

The twin challenges of development and resource depletion in an age of scarcity have been further exacerbated by China's transformation into the world's workshop and India's potential to do the same. As the world's largest economy (based on purchasing-power parity), China has become more dependent on international suppliers to meet its energy demands and has used its growing clout to ensure long-term access to those critical inputs. By contrast, India's economic reform policies have yielded less consistent and comparatively modest results overall; however, more recent data suggests that liberalization policies are now propelling more robust growth. In 2015, for instance, the Indian economy grew at a robust 7.5 percent annual rate, surpassing China's 6.9 percent pace. Not surprisingly, this inversion has fueled speculation in some circles that India will become the "next China." With China and India poised to become the world's largest and third-largest energy consumers by 2035, will their competition for resources enflame their "natural" rivalry and result in crisis? Will their competition lead to more aggressive behavior, one that eventually sparks conflict?

The scholarly and policymaking consensus is a simple yes. For proponents of this view, conflict is inevitable because of two fundamental and inescapable points: The leaders in both countries view resource security as central to national interest, and the fulfillment of these objectives is paramount to any other considerations. Some even argue that such considerations have forced Chinese and Indian leaders to view the existing global order in a new, less favorable light; as a result, they now seem to have a "preference for regimes and empires rather than markets and institutions, and this preference seems to be enabling them to obtain energy resources without participating in any international mechanism."[5] In short, China and India will do whatever it takes to achieve their objectives, including bypassing established market mechanisms and even engaging in war.

In this chapter, I examine the China-India rivalry in Africa and Central Asia and, contrary to conventional wisdom, argue that while a future conflict over resources between China and India is certainly possible, it is highly improbable for two reasons.[6] First, while competition between them will persist, and perhaps intensify, petroleum and natural gas remain commodities that China and India can procure only from other countries. The situation with hydrocarbons is fundamentally different from that of water (see Selina Ho's chapter 7); neither party has the ability to restrict the other's access to the commodity. Indeed, given that access to energy can be secured through various markets and partnerships across the globe, both seem to recognize that the strategic use of economic assets and "soft power" can be a more effective (and safer) means of achieving their ultimate goal of energy security. Second, China and India acknowledge that a full-bore competition between them would be counterproductive in the long term. Chinese and Indian officials have established institutionalized channels through which they can regularly share their concerns and discuss potential remedies before a messy situation turns into a crisis. This suggests that while China and India may have asymmetrical capabilities and enjoyed asymmetrical success over the last twenty years, neither considers the broader relationship to be asymmetrical (see Matthew A. Castle's chapter 10 for a contrasting view).[7] Instead, China and India cooperate whenever it is possible and advantageous to do so and compete whenever and wherever else they must but with an eye toward containing, even mitigating, the potential for conflict.

Unlike those who predict a coming clash, I contend that the more fluid and dynamic nature of developments on both the international and domestic fronts have shifted both countries toward a more pragmatic and, ultimately, less confrontational track. Internationally, new energy and mineral sources continue to be discovered and exploited, with the help of Chinese and Indian investment in new sources around the world. Equally important, China and India now recognize that resource scarcity is the "new normal" and that under such circumstances they are more likely to succeed through cooperation rather than confrontation. Moreover, both continue to move forward with their economic-restructuring efforts and have started moving away from energy- and resource-intensive industries. In China, the party-state has already invested heavily in renewable energy, transforming the country into a global leader. In India, a similar process is unfolding and generating promising results. These policy responses represent smart hedges in the face of increasing uncertainty. Taken together, they have brought both countries to a new "tipping point," one that reduces the chances of conflict even as they move forward with efforts to secure their energy future.

RESOURCE DEPLETION
IN HISTORICAL PERSPECTIVE

There is no doubt that we live in a world of finite resources. Nevertheless, there has been considerable debate over when and how quickly the world will actually run out of key inputs. Advocates of the so-called peak oil theory, for example, project that global petroleum reserves will decline precipitously in the near future, although the exact date of the peak is unclear, ranging anywhere from 2005 to 2020. They contend that should current trends persist, our way of life is likely to disintegrate. While apocalyptic, such a view seems plausible as countries are indeed consuming nonrenewable resources at unprecedented rates. Still, it is easy to forget that since the founding of the modern oil industry in the mid-nineteenth century, fears that the world would run out of oil have cropped up regularly, even though the data on oil production from 1946 to 2011 shows fairly consistent output gains.[8] As Daniel Yergin notes, the first expression of alarm occurred in 1885, just twenty-six years after "Colonel" Edwin Drake discovered oil in Titusville, Pennsylvania.[9] At the time, how oil flowed and how much was actually in the ground was not entirely clear to geologists, leading the state geologist of Pennsylvania to describe it as a "temporary and vanishing phenomenon."[10] However, new sources, most notably in Oklahoma and Texas, were discovered, temporarily allaying widespread fears. These wells helped meet the increasing demand for gasoline precipitated by the rise of the automobile and mechanized transport, especially during the first half of the twentieth century. In the post–World War II era, the development of new sources in the Middle East caused an oil glut, at least until the successful reconstruction of Europe and Japan led to higher demand. That, coupled with tensions and instability in the Middle East, eventually led to the oil shocks of the 1970s. This crisis set off, for a fourth time, pronouncements that the end had *really* been reached. Today in the twenty-first century, we are witnessing yet another—the fifth!—installment of these long-running fears.

While the supply of oil is of central importance in the resource equation, it is not the *sole* factor determining prospects for meeting, even overcoming, the resource conundrum. In the previous examples, fears that the end was near actually precipitated a furious search for and the eventual development of new sources, such as Alaska's North Slope and the North Sea, and eventually a return to stability. More recently, the innovative application of hydraulic fracturing, or "fracking," to old wells and new oil fields has resulted in the unanticipated shale oil boom in the United States. This development has not only reduced American dependence on foreign petroleum suppliers, but in 2016 also led the US to become an oil exporter for the first time since 1975. These and other discoveries demonstrate just how little is known about how much oil there *actually* is in the world. All we know, as Yergin observes, is that "the world has produced about 1 trillion barrels of oil since the start of the industry in the nineteenth century. Currently, it is thought that there are at least 5 trillion barrels of petroleum resources, of which 1.4 trillion is sufficiently developed and technically and economically accessible to count as proved plus probable reserves."[11]

Reserves aside, any comprehensive account of resource depletion must consider shifting consumption rates, government policies, and technological advances. When such factors are taken into account, a different picture emerges. Over the last decade, for example, oil consumption has actually decreased, especially in the countries of the Organization for Economic Cooperation and Development. From 2004 to 2014, Europe and the United States experienced a drop in projected consumption of 13 percent and 25 percent, respectively. While high prices and economic stagnation certainly led citizens in these countries to significantly reduce consumption, policies ranging from the required use of ethanol as an additive in gasoline, improved fuel efficiency standards for vehicles, the promotion of renewable energy, and even demographic shifts also contributed to the "petroleum consumption surprise."[12] What this demonstrates is that the process of resource depletion is more dynamic than is often perceived and that accurately gauging future trends requires a more holistic approach. It is in light of these developments that we must evaluate China and India's quest for resources. Like all countries, China and India are not immune from the constraints imposed by a world of finite resources, but neither are they completely at their mercy. Like Europe and the United States, both have undertaken initiatives that will enable them to manage the challenges ahead while also reducing the chances that competition will spiral into conflict.

CHINA AND INDIA "UP THEIR GAME" IN AFRICA

On July 3, 2008, Brent Crude oil prices reached a peak of $143.95 per barrel. On January 3, 2000, at the dawn of the new millennium, the price per barrel had been only $23.95.[13] In that eight-year span, the price of oil went up an astonishing 600 percent, the largest rise the global oil market has experienced in the postwar era. Panic ensued, and many analysts cited China's seemingly insatiable appetite as the cause of this development. For them, it did not matter that the price shock resulted from the unanticipated combination of growing Chinese demand *and* a lower-than-expected expansion in global supplies. As Elizabeth Economy and Michael Levi argue, the buildup in Chinese demand was only a trigger for the paradoxical retrenchment rather than expansion of worldwide oil production. This makes sense given that state-owned companies in oil-producing countries focus on total revenue rather than profit margins. Thus, "since higher prices can allow them to meet their goals even with less production, high prices can actually prompt them to curb production, or at least reduce incentives to boost output, leading prices to climb."[14] Even as prices gradually stabilized, increasing competition and price volatility were seen as part of the "new normal."

By some accounts, the competition between China and India over resources only began in the mid-2000s, although the foundations for growing resource consumption and potential tensions were laid years before when China and India implemented economic reform policies in 1978 and 1991, respectively.[15] As Chinese reform policies prompted unprecedented economic growth and a concomitant spike in energy demand, policymakers were eventually forced to reevaluate the country's long-standing policy of self-reliance. For over three decades, China had met its energy needs without outside assistance by relying on the famed Daqing oil field (among others). By the early 1990s, however, demand had outstripped the ability of domestic producers to keep pace, and in 1993, China became a net oil importer for the first time. China's growing appetite for energy inputs is captured in Economy and Levi's astonishing observation that "between 1980 and 2010, oil and coal consumption both doubled roughly every dozen years."[16] Under these circumstances, the Chinese leadership had little choice but to establish even wider connections with foreign markets and suppliers.[17]

The new approach eventually came to be known as the "going out" strategy. Premier Zhu Rongji first used the term in a 1999 speech in reference to the inability of domestic oil suppliers to meet national demand. He suggested going out as a means of not only overcoming that gap but also helping Chinese enterprises invest abroad and secure development projects as an outlet for excess capacity back home. This strategy, a crystallization of responses to new needs and emerging opportunities, especially in Africa and Central Asia, was formally incorporated into the Tenth Five-Year Plan (2001–5) and has been an integral part of Chinese policy ever since. In many respects, this policy approach is not new. What is unprecedented, though, is the scale and extent of support the Chinese party-state provides to these primarily state-owned enterprises, a level of assistance that appears to exceed even that of the East Asian miracles.[18]

The Chinese government, through organs such as the National Development and Reform Commission, the State-Owned Assets Supervision and Administration Commission, the Ministry of Commerce, and the Ministry of Foreign Affairs, assists enterprises in identifying investment opportunities, making critical contacts, and finalizing agreements. Key elements in these deals consist of foreign aid, infrastructure development projects, and, more controversially, loans for resources. Such assistance helps stabilize relations between Chinese companies and the nations in which they invest, thus protecting assets and Chinese interests beyond the short term. State owned banks, such as the Export-Import Bank of China and the China Development Bank, working together with government officials, are vital to this process too, for they provide the necessary financing for these projects, usually at generous, below-market rates. It certainly seems that, despite the occasional bureaucratic squabble, Chinese officials are executing a "well-orchestrated dance."[19]

This dance has catapulted Chinese oil companies to the forefront of the industry. Three are especially noteworthy: the China National Petroleum Corporation (CNPC), the China National Offshore Oil Corporation (CNOOC), and Sinopec. Although these firms cannot compare to such rivals as ExxonMobil, they are nevertheless becoming increasingly important players; in fact, they are responsible for over 10 percent of oil production in Sudan and Angola and nearly 25 percent of Kazakhstan's oil output.[20] Yet their emergence would not have been possible without the unprecedented game-changing shifts in geopolitics.

In the mid-1990s, China's investment in Africa resulted from what Fantu Cheru and Cyril Obi describe as the "disenchantment with the poor track record of Western development cooperation over the past fifty years, the double standards that Western governments practice in their relations with African states, and the tendency to give aid with one hand and to retrieve it from Africa with the other through unfair trade practices, capital flight and debt structures."[21] They add that many African countries were hopeful that with China and India as potential trade partners, they too could "one day break away from the shackles of poverty, underdevelopment and aid dependency."[22] Rapid Chinese economic growth overlapped not only with this process of soul-searching but also with mounting political instability and the increasing international isolation of so-called pariah states, creating an unexpected opening for China to broaden its ties with the continent. For example, in Nigeria, currently China's largest trading partner in Africa, the 1993 military coup and the execution of Ken Saro-Wiwa and eight other Ogoni activists in 1995 sparked widespread condemnation and subsequent sanctions by the European Union (EU) and the United States. By contrast, China chose to engage Nigeria and signed new cooperation agreements in addition to those already finalized in 1995 and 1996.[23] In May 1997, Nigeria's minister of information, Walter Ofonagoro, went so far as to declare that "the sooner the West reverses the current trend the better for them because we are moving to China and other nations for support."[24] Over the last decade and a half, the relationship has only become more robust: Nigeria recently announced provisional agreements valued at $80 billion to upgrade its aging oil and gas infrastructure. Among the thirty-eight signatories to the deals was Sinopec.[25]

Similarly, China's ties with Sudan, another pariah state, evolved as the country's decades-long civil war, economic chaos, and increasingly strained relationship with the United States unfolded. Following the 1989 military coup carried out by the National Islamic Front under Omar al-Bashir, the US government suspended development assistance and downgraded relations, with the bilateral relationship eventually reaching a nadir with Washington's 1993 designation of Sudan as a state sponsor of terrorism. Under these circumstances, the Chevron Corporation pulled out of Sudan in 1992, relinquishing the oil concession that it had first secured in 1974. Thereafter, non-Western oil firms entered the fray.[26] In 1995, CNPC finalized an agreement with the Sudanese government for oil development and expanded its presence, securing three additional development blocks through an international auction. In less than five years, that project was producing oil, and CNPC had successfully transformed Sudan from an oil importer into an oil exporter.[27] Despite the outbreak of hostilities in Darfur, CNPC continued to work closely with Sudan and even deepened its stake in Sudanese oil production. As Economy and Levi highlight, "by 2009, CNPC held a stake of at least 35 percent in each of five developments, in addition to majority shares in a petroleum refinery and a petrochemical production facility."[28] The Chinese government found itself in an awkward position. On one hand, it supported Sudanese sovereignty and hewed closely to a policy of noninterference; on the other, it recognized that without some resolution to the conflict, a vicious cycle could set in and perhaps undermine Chinese interests and stature in international affairs. Consequently, China slowly shifted to a strategy of "influence without interference," working behind the scenes with Sudanese officials and at the United Nations to effect gradual change.[29]

Although Chinese efforts to partner with African oil producers have been largely successful, it is worth noting that Chinese companies do not always get their way. In 2009, for example, CNOOC sought to acquire twenty-three blocks in Nigeria for which leases to Western oil companies were set to expire. It was unclear whether the bid, rumored to be worth between $30 billion and $50 billion, was rejected for being too low or was used to extract more favorable terms from Western competitors.[30] In that same year, the Angolan state oil firm Sonangol exercised its right of first refusal and blocked a winning bid of $1.3 billion from CNOOC and Sinopec for US-based Marathon Oil's share in offshore oil block 32.[31] This action grew out of not only Angolan concerns for diversifying foreign investors in the industry but also frustration with the terms of an agreement Sonangol and Sinopec signed in 2006.[32] Following this episode, however, Sinopec worked toward reconciliation and has reestablished itself in Angola.

Although Africa poses significant challenges for China, the benefits of deepening ties between the two outweigh the potential perils of doing so. In October 2000, the Chinese government hosted the First Ministerial Conference on FOCAC in Beijing, marking the formal establishment of a regularized mechanism for "the purposes of further strengthening friendly cooperation between China and African states under the new circumstances, jointly meeting the challenges of economic globalization and seeking common development."[33] Since that inaugural meeting, representatives of China and fifty African states have met at three-year intervals to discuss how to solidify a "win-win partnership." Sensitive to accusations that China's behavior has been "neocolonialist" in nature, President Xi announced at the 2015 summit a wide-ranging set of initiatives that not only included investment in infrastructure, agriculture, and trade but also programs targeting poverty reduction, public welfare, and education.[34] The $60 billion aid package, which includes $5 billion in grants and interest-free loans and $35 billion in loans and export credits, represents a near doubling of the assistance that China offered at the Fifth Ministerial Conference of FOCAC held in Beijing in 2012.[35] At the close of the summit, South African president Jacob Zuma lauded President Xi for "his commitment to taking the relationship with Africa to its highest level ever."[36]

By contrast, India's efforts to secure resources in Africa have been overshadowed by China's, despite their obvious similarities in motivation and objectives. Like China, postindependence India has long considered self-reliance, especially in energy, to be a linchpin of its development strategy and security. The desire to achieve self-reliance has only intensified since the 1970s oil shocks, and the refusal of international oil companies to rein in oil prices exposed India's dependence on international suppliers for meeting its domestic energy needs.[37] Moreover, by the 1980s, despite renewed economic growth aided by a major recovery in agriculture, India was mired in persistent and stifling state interference that culminated in "a period of growing fiscal deficits, trade deficits and foreign debt."[38] This crisis forced the adoption of a major structural adjustment program in 1991, followed by additional reforms that allowed market forces, international trade, and foreign direct investment to play a more significant role in the Indian economy. Consequently, India also began to look outward, especially toward Africa, for new economic opportunities.

India's plans, however, were constrained in two ways. First, it was off to a comparatively late start. If China was a latecomer to the resources quest, India was a late latecomer. Although the falling-out between Western nations and Africa in the 1990s created an unanticipated opening for engagement, India, preoccupied with implementing and consolidating its economic reforms, delayed its outreach to Africa by nearly a decade. When Indian oil companies such as the Oil and Natural Gas Corporation Limited (ONGC), its international subsidiary ONGC Videsh Limited (OVL), and Oil India Limited began engaging Africa in the mid-2000s, China had already established a strong presence there, leaving India in a situation of heightened competition for the few remaining prime investment opportunities. Second, Indian oil firms do not enjoy the same kind and level of governmental support that their Chinese counterparts do. Because of the greater mix of private and public firms competing in the sector, as well as the Indian government's more cautious investment approach, Indian oil firms have not benefited from a version of China's "well-orchestrated dance." However, this will soon change as India moves to merge some of its oil companies in a bid to create a "national champion" and better compete against international rivals.[39] To be sure, the Indian government has, at times, tried to make amends. Moreover, at the third IAFS held in 2015, Prime Minister Narendra Modi, conceding that India had been slow in fulfilling its past commitments, announced an initiative for $10 billion in credit and $600 million in grants for Africa, thus laying out India's vision of a "win-win partnership."[40]

Still, observers such as Luke Patey are not convinced that such efforts will bear significant fruit. In fact, he concludes that "the race between China and India for global oil resources was over before it started,"[41] an assessment that aligns more with those of the asymmetry theory approach. Much of this, as Raj Verma observes, has to do with the ability of Chinese firms to outbid Indian oil companies, state-owned and private, if and when they compete for stakes to the same oil-exploration blocks.[42] The first display of China's prowess came in 2004 when Sonangol Sinopec International (SSI), a joint venture between Sinopec and Sonangol, outbid India's OVL for Angola's deepwater block 18. In April of that year, OVL had reached an agreement with Royal Dutch Shell to secure its 50 percent stake in block 18, but its offer of $310 million was soon eclipsed by SSI's offer of $725 million. In 2006, OVL again ran up against SSI as it made an aggressive bid of $1 billion for Angola's deepwater blocks 15(06), 16(06), and 18(06). SSI shocked the global markets by bidding $750 million for block 15(06) alone and a staggering $2.2 billion for blocks 17(06) and 18(06).[43] Its total bid of $2.975 billion was nearly triple that of OVL's.

When Indian firms are competitive and even successful in outbidding competitors, the Indian government's aversion to risk and its inability to match favorable loans by the Chinese state has led to the unraveling of those deals. In

2005, for example, OVL actually outbid CNOOC for control of Nigeria's Akpo field, but the Indian government blocked the agreement, wary of the political risk involved. As a result, CNOOC acquired the Akpo field. In 2010, both OVL and CNOOC offered to join the Ghana National Petroleum Corporation (GNPC) to make a $5 billion bid to secure Kosmos Energy's stake in the Jubilee oil fields, one of the largest oil discoveries in West Africa in the last two decades.[44] GNPC chose to work with CNOOC as a result of $10.4 billion in loans for infrastructure projects and an additional $3 billion in loans for development of Ghana's oil and gas sectors, all backed by Chinese banks.[45] In comparison, the Indian government permits OVL to invest only in projects worth $75 million or less and is unable or perhaps unwilling to offer the kind of comprehensive financial packages that are often attached to Chinese bids.

Despite these well-publicized "failures," India has nevertheless established a presence, albeit a modest one, in Sudan, Nigeria, and Angola. For example, ONGC Mittal Energy Limited, Sterling, and Essar won six oil blocks during 2005–7 Nigeria oil block bids.[46] In 2010, ONGC and Sonangol agreed to work together in oil exploration and refining in Angola.[47] Moreover, the Indian government has increased its outreach to Africa through the India-Africa Hydrocarbon Conference, first held in 2007, and the India-Africa Forum Summit in 2008. Both gatherings give India an opportunity to "look for niches where it can maximize its comparative advantage in relation to Chinese and Western competitors while pragmatically cooperating with them" and, equally important, demonstrate the ways it is Africa's "true friend."[48] These developments, in combination with the 2012 memorandum of understanding between China's CNPC and India's ONGC encouraging joint bidding and investment, underscore a major shift in thinking among policymakers in Beijing and New Delhi. As Rosalind Reischer suggests, "energy cooperation between India and China appears to be increasing. . . . This agreement may also set a precedent and provide a foundation for greater regional integration of the Asian energy market, which will be essential for stabilizing conflicts rooted in energy security concerns."[49] In short, both China and India seem to recognize that they can benefit more from working together rather than competing against each other in every instance.

RENEWING THE "GREAT GAME" IN CENTRAL ASIA

Although the histories of China, India, and Central Asia have been intertwined since the days of the Silk Road, their recent ties, dormant for much of the twentieth century, date to 1991. In that year, the world witnessed the formal dissolution of the Soviet Union, the stunning denouement to the revolutions of 1989, and the last whimper marking the Leninist extinction. In many ways, this unforeseen but tectonic shift in the geopolitical landscape posed an even greater challenge for China and India. Like Africa, Central Asia, comprising the states of Kazakhstan, Kyrgyzstan, Tajikistan, Turkmenistan, and Uzbekistan, offers a tremendous opportunity for both countries to enhance their long-term energy security. Yet those prospects were initially counterbalanced by larger concerns about the region's long-term political stability, the potential danger posed by radical Islamic fundamentalist movements, and the continuing fallout from the war in Afghanistan. Hence, for China and India, the tantalizing notion of access to energy resources from their "extended neighborhood" continues to be tempered by fears that social and political unrest could spill over their borders and further enflame tensions at home.

In the immediate aftermath of the Soviet disintegration, China's primary focus was to prevent the so-called three evil forces of terrorism, separatism, and extremism from filling the political vacuum and potentially undermining security and stability in Xinjiang on China's western flank. Toward this end, China, Russia, Kazakhstan, Kyrgyzstan, and Tajikistan formed the "Shanghai Five" on April 26, 1996. This created for the first time a multilateral mechanism that formally brought China, Russia, and Central Asia together as a group, resulting in the successful resolution of border disputes and increased cooperation in security matters.[50] The latter, as Pan Guang points out, led not only to the signing of the Shanghai Convention on Combating Terrorism, Separatism and Extremism ("the first international document on antiterrorism in the twenty-first century") on June 15, 2001, but also the formation of what is known today as the Shanghai Cooperation Organization (SCO).[51]

It is in this context that Chinese investments in Central Asia must be understood. While the region offers China additional security in the form of nonsea transport routes for oil and gas, it is also, as Li Xin and Xin Daleng argue, "the ultimate way to protect stability and security. [For China], getting rid of poverty is the fundamental solution to the three evil forces."[52] With this in mind, former premier Li Peng stated in 1994 that it is "important [for China] to open up a modern version of the Silk Road."[53] However, it was only in 1997 that China was able to establish a presence in Kazakhstan's hydrocarbon sector with CNPC's acquisition of the Aktobe field. From 1992 to 1997, Western oil firms dominated the scene, facilitated in part by Russia's preoccupation with shoring up its economy, as well as its short-lived pro-West foreign policy. Soon after the Aktobe deal, however, other Chinese oil firms, such as Sinopec and CNOOC, as well as smaller competitors such as Sinochem, joined in, purchasing smaller shares in the industry. Nevertheless, CNPC remains the most active Chinese firm in the country, having claimed a 67 percent share in PetroKazakhstan (a Canadian-based oil producer with significant reserves in Kazakhstan) for $4.2 billion in 2005 and making a joint purchase of MangistauMunaiGas for $2.6 billion in 2009.[54] By 2010, just thirteen years after China made its first winning bid in Kazakhstan, its oil companies "owned a larger share of oil production in Kazakhstan than in any other country."[55] Perhaps even more important than stakes in oil production is the establishment of oil and natural gas pipelines between Kazakhstan and China.

The China-Kazakhstan pipeline connects Atyrau in northwestern Kazakhstan with China's Xinjiang autonomous region, covering nearly two thousand miles and a capacity of four hundred thousand barrels a day, the equivalent of 5 percent of China's oil imports.[56] This development highlights just how central economic growth and regional integration have become to the fulfillment of China's long-term political and strategic goals in the region.

Besides Kazakhstan, China has sizeable investments in Turkmenistan, which possesses the largest reserves of natural gas in Central Asia and the fourth largest in the world. In 2006, looking to reduce its dependence on Russia and diversify its markets, Turkmenistan signed an agreement to sell gas to China through what has become the Central Asia–China Gas Pipeline. Since that initial signing, additional agreements have been reached in quick succession. In July 2007, CNPC inked a deal to develop the gas field at Amu Darya. In 2009, China provided a $4 billion loan to support a partnership between CNPC and Türk-mengaz, the national gas company, for the development of the Galkynysh gas field. This gas runs nearly twelve hundred miles through three parallel lines of the Central Asia–China Gas Pipeline, beginning in Gedaim, Turkmenistan, and passing through Uzbekistan and Kazakhstan before ending in Khorgos, Xinjiang. A fourth line is under construction and will increase capacity from the current fifty-five billion cubic meters (bcm) per year to eighty billion bcm. Once the line is complete, China will solidify its position as Turkmenistan's largest and most significant economic partner, as it moves from consuming 60 percent of Turkmenistan's total gas exports to 76 percent. In so doing, China has become a critical alternative market for Turkmenistan, further solidifying mutual dependence between the two.

Given these ties, President Xi's announcement of the "One Belt One Road" (OBOR) initiative in 2013 is not surprising. Comprising a proposed "Silk Road Economic Belt" and a "Maritime Silk Road," the initiative would not only further solidify China's relationship with Central Asia but also potentially link the economic fortunes of sixty-five countries and 4.4 billion people, who are responsible for 40 percent of global gross domestic product.[57] Backed by a pledge of $40 billion from the Silk Road Fund and up to $1 trillion in loans through the Asian Infrastructure Investment Bank and China Development Bank, the initiative could potentially become the largest pact of its kind.

If such developments distinguish China as a major and increasingly assertive power in the region, India's connections to Central Asia have been comparatively anemic. Despite the new opportunities created by the Soviet collapse, Gulshan Sachdeva argues that "India was never really part of any competition in Central Asia during this period [the 1990s]." He adds, "With no direct road transportation access plus difficult market conditions, the region was not at that time attractive to Indian private companies."[58] To be sure, India was also constrained in ways that China was not. Long-standing tensions with Pakistan and the US-led war in Afghanistan "kept India and Central Asia physically disconnected,"[59] propelling India's discussion with Iran in 2002 on developing

Chabahar on Iran's coast as a gateway to Afghanistan and Central Asia. The project, delayed for over a decade because of international sanctions against Iran, was recently finalized with Prime Minister Modi's announcement that India would contribute $500 million to the port's development.[60] The agreement has the potential to not only counterbalance China's efforts to transform Gwadar (on the coast of Balochistan, Pakistan, and less than forty-five miles from Chabahar) into a deep-water port but also provide India with a critical entry point for its engagement with Central Asia. Indeed, Chabahar could eventually serve as a node for the proposed International North-South Transportation Corridor, as well as additional rail links throughout the region.

These developments could be harbingers of a more sustained Indian presence throughout the region. This would be a significant development, given the limited success Indian firms have enjoyed against their Chinese rivals in bidding for energy stakes, especially over the last decade. In 2005, for instance, ONGC sought to acquire PetroKazakhstan. However, CNPC, also hoping to buy the firm, raised its bid to $4.18 billion and ultimately secured the asset. It was China's largest foreign acquisition to date, double the price Lenovo paid for IBM's personal computer division. In 2013, CNPC secured an 8.33 percent stake (held by ConocoPhillips) in the Kashagan oil project in the Caspian Sea for $5 billion, preempting an earlier agreement to sell that share to India's ONGC. As was the case in Chinese deals with African states, China sweetened the terms of the agreement by promising additional loans totaling $8 billion.[61] Such near misses have undoubtedly been disappointing: Some analyses estimate that India has lost out on $12.5 billion in Central Asian energy deals to China.[62] Not surprisingly, Indian companies have grown increasingly frustrated with the Indian government's inability to devise a clear and coherent strategy for advancing its interests, underscored by the failed "Connect Central Asia" policy devised in 2012.

Still, India is turning a corner. With the announcement of the first exploratory drilling of the Satpayev oil block by India's OVL and Kazakhstan's KazMunai-Gas on July 7, 2015, India has finally gained a toehold in Central Asian energy production.[63] With the field holding an estimated reserve of 1.8 billion barrels of oil, its development, with production projected to begin in 2020, represents a promising breakthrough after years of negotiation. (The initial agreement was signed in 2009.) Furthermore, the announcement coincided with Prime Minister Modi's grand tour of the Central Asian states, signaling a more concerted governmental effort toward supporting and deepening ties. Modi stated, "We see an important place for central Asia in India's future. We can reinforce each other's economic progress." He also noted, "My visit to all five countries in the region demonstrates the importance we attach to a *new* [emphasis added] level of relationship with Central Asia."[64] Moreover, with the start of construction on the Turkmenistan-Afghanistan-Pakistan-India gas pipeline in December 2015 despite ongoing security concerns in Afghanistan and strained India-Pakistan relations, another roadblock to economic partnership and regional integration will have been removed. This could be a boon for GAIL (India) Limited, India's largest state-owned gas company, and help it to build on its other investments in Chinese gas pipeline projects in Kazakhstan.[65]

Additional momentum has been generated through increased direct consultation between China and India, as well as India's recent inclusion in the SCO. In August 2013, the two countries held their first-ever dialogue on Central Asia, with the talks focusing on such topics as regional and energy security. As the Indian embassy in Beijing points out, the talks highlight a "growing engagement" between the two countries and build on "similar comprehensive dialogues on Africa, West Asia, Afghanistan, and counter-terrorism issues."[66] Lan Jianxue observes, "Now, since we have a China-India Central Asia dialogue mechanism, we can share information and share our common ground on energy exploration and energy cooperation. We can unite our efforts, for example, by considering jointly bidding for an oil field or gas field."[67] More important, Lan concludes, the talks "demonstrate that relations are becoming more and more institutionalized and that we have cooperated very well in the international arena."[68] Similarly, India's admission to the SCO in June 2016 may, in fact, produce a win-win situation for all. Despite China's initial reluctance to admit India to the organization and even its opposition, India's inclusion in the group suggests that regular and frequent consultation can help manage and perhaps prevent their competing interests from turning into confrontation.[69] To be sure, some signs of friction have emerged. India's refusal to join the OBOR initiative or attend the May 2017 Belt and Road Forum held in Beijing reflects not only New Delhi's concerns over the strategic ramifications of the China-Pakistan Economic Corridor (which runs through disputed Kashmir) but also deep-seated anxiety that the Maritime Road may ultimately anchor a "string of pearls" strategy aimed at constraining Indian naval power.[70] While these developments are serious, they have nevertheless been tempered by the recognition that a *convergence* of interests, not a conflict of interests, is what will drive the relationship forward.

CONCLUSION: IS THE GAME CHANGING AGAIN?

When China and India first launched their economic reform programs, few observers expected either to experience the spectacular growth that they have. In 1979, China and India were the world's tenth- and twelfth-largest economies, respectively; in 2015, they ranked first and third (based on purchasing-power parity).[71] While scholars expected their growth to precipitate an increase in their overall consumption of natural resources, few anticipated demand in both to grow at seemingly exponential rates. Such developments initially sent shock waves through markets and policymaking circles, sparking fears that a competition for resources between the two giants, especially over hydrocarbons, would ensue and eventually so would a conflict. While a competition between China and India did materialize, it has not become the heated rivalry that some predicted. Leaders in both countries recognized that a fight over resources is in neither country's interest. Since 2012 especially, competition over hydrocarbons has gradually but unmistakably moved away from potential confrontation and more toward consultation and cooperation.

Paradoxically this dynamic seems to have been a positive for global oil markets, at least thus far. The injection of Chinese and Indian investment capital into oil exploration and development over the last decade has increased overall production capacity and actually resulted in a slight increase in global reserves. Nevertheless, others counter that temporary anomalies account for this unusual state of affairs. The great financial crisis of 2008–9, the American shale boom that began in the mid-2000s, and the 2014 decision by the Organization of Petroleum Exporting Countries to fight vigorously for market share—these are the reasons behind the current oil glut and dramatic fall in prices. Some have pointed out that even if China's current economic slowdown leads to a "new normal" and to plateauing resource consumption, India's projected growth over the next quarter century will absorb any available resources China does not. Thus, we will be right back where we started, in a scramble for what remains. Such a scenario would materialize only if the status quo ante were restored.

Yet a potentially game-changing moment may have arrived with the enactment of new energy policies in both countries. Such policies were implemented even as China and India concurrently ramped up their quests for greater access to resources. Recognizing that fossil fuel consumption rates were increasing and ultimately unsustainable and acknowledging the concerns of Chinese citizens regarding the consequences of environmental pollution, the Chinese leadership has moved decisively to promote renewable energy and efficiency over the last decade. With the passage of the 2005 Renewable Energy Law, for instance, China has made unprecedented investments in clean energy; in fact, China pumped nearly $90 billion into the sector in 2014, an amount that exceeded American investment totals by 73 percent.[72] It has reinforced its "bold claim on leadership in the renewable energy industry" with a commitment to invest an additional $360 billion by 2020.[73] As a result, China is now the world's largest producer of clean energy, especially in installed wind and solar capacity. Moreover, as Deborah Seligsohn puts it, "2006 marked a significant change in Chinese environmental policy. In addition to imposing hard targets for the first time, the Chinese government named 'Energy Efficiency and Pollution Abatement' as 'National Policy.'"[74] Efforts to improve efficiency, the so-called fifth fuel, has resulted in, among other things, not only the aggressive closing of some of the most inefficient steel and cement factories but also the continual elevation of fuel economy standards for vehicles, which are now on par with those in the United States and approximating those in the EU. Such actions certainly increase the chances of China attaining its goal of having renewables constitute 20 percent of its total energy consumption by 2030.

Like China, India can also become a leading producer of renewable energy and has laid out a strategy for achieving that objective. With the adoption of the

2003 Electricity Act, India established a comprehensive national framework for renewable power.[75] Despite challenges in building the necessary infrastructure and transmitting the power to the citizens who need it most, India has nevertheless underscored its commitment to renewables by mandating that utilities purchase an increasing amount of renewable energy over time. In addition, by facilitating cooperation and coordination between government, private companies, and international investors, India has achieved impressive breakthroughs, with renewables now amounting to over 13 percent of the country's power-generation capacity. Even more impressive, in April 2016, the power capacity from renewables, led overwhelmingly by wind and solar sources, exceeded the capacity of hydroelectric plants, the "temples of modern India," for the first time.[76] Finally, with India's first fuel-efficiency standards for passenger vehicles set to take effect in 2017, the country's consumption of hydrocarbons is likely to slow even more.

Should these emerging trends take hold and even accelerate, we may come to see that despite the challenges posed by globalization, there are opportunities as well. Indeed, the short-lived competition for resources between China and India might come to be seen as the trigger that set off the broader pursuit of a smarter and more effective approach to energy security. We might also realize that when it comes to resources at least, China and India are more similar than different in their understanding and approach, making a future conflict between them less likely with each passing day.

NOTES

1. Ruchita Beri, "3rd India Africa Forum Summit: Rejuvenating Relations," Institute for Defence Studies and Analyses, October 29, 2015, http://idsa.in /idsacomments/3rd-india-africa-forum-summit_rberi_291015.
2. "India-Africa Summit: Read Full Text of PM Narendra Modi's Speech," *Times of India*, October 29, 2015, http://timesofindia.indiatimes.com/india/India -Africa-summit-Read-full-text-of-PM-Narendra-Modis-speech/articleshowprint /49577890.cms?null.
3. Rene Vollgraff and Amogelang Mbatha, "China Ups Africa Commitment Even as Both Their Fortunes Fade," Bloomberg, December 5, 2015, http://www .bloomberg.com/news/articles/2015-12-05/china-boosts-africa-commitments -even-as-both-their-fortunes-fade.
4. Michael Klare, *The Race for What's Left: The Global Scramble for the World's Last Resources* (New York: Picador, 2012), 23–24.
5. Raja Mohan and Lydia Powell, "Energy Rivalry between China and India: Less Than Meets the Eye?," in *The New Politics of Strategic Resources: Energy and Food Security Challenges in the 21st Century*, ed. David Steven, Emily O'Brien, and Bruce Jones (Washington, DC: Brookings Institution Press, 2015), 145.
6. While China and India compete across the globe for access to energy resources, Africa and Central Asia are the regions where their rivalry has been the most intense and sustained. While Latin America may eventually become a new site of competition, Evan Ellis notes that thus far China holds the upper hand there.

See *Indian and Chinese Engagement in Latin America and the Caribbean: A Comparative Assessment* (Carlisle, PA: Strategic Studies Institute and US Army War College Press, 2017), 17.

7. The term was developed by Brantly Womack to describe China's relationship with states in Southeast Asia but not India. See "Recognition, Deference, and Respect: Generalizing the Lessons of an Asymmetric Asian Order," *Journal of American-East Asian Relations* 16, nos. 1–2 (Spring/Summer 2009): 108.

8. See the graph in Daniel Yergin, *The Quest: Energy, Security, and the Remaking of the Modern World* (New York: Penguin, 2011), 240.

9. Ibid., 229. This part of the discussion draws heavily from Yergin's comprehensive overview in chapter 11.

10. Ibid.

11. Ibid., 239.

12. Executive Office of the President of the United States, *Explaining the U.S. Petroleum Consumption Surprise* (Washington, DC: June 2015), 2–3, https:// obamawhitehouse.archives.gov/sites/default/files/docs/explaining_us_petroleum _consumption_surprise_final.pdf.

13. US Energy Information Administration, "Europe Brent Spot Price FOB," http://www.eia.gov/dnav/pet/hist/LeafHandler.ashx?n=PET&s=rbrte&f=D.

14. Elizabeth Economy and Michael Levi, *By All Means Necessary: How China's Resource Quest Is Changing the World* (New York: Oxford University Press, 2014), 26.

15. See Kanti Bajpai, Huang Jing, and Kishore Mahbubani, eds., *China-India Relations: Cooperation and Conflict* (New York: Routledge, 2016).

16. Economy and Levi, *By All Means*, 22.

17. See the white paper "China's Policy on Mineral Resources (December 2003)," http://english1.english.gov.cn/official/2005-07/28/content_17963.htm.

18. This section draws heavily from the insightful analysis of Economy and Levi, *By All Means*, 49–60.

19. Ibid., 50.

20. Ibid., 58.

21. Fantu Cheru and Cyril Obi, "Chinese and Indian Engagement in Africa: Competitive or Mutually Reinforcing Strategies?," *Journal of International Affairs* 64, no. 2 (Spring/Summer 2011): 96.

22. Ibid.

23. Human Rights Watch, "Nigeria Country Report," 1997, https://www.hrw.org /reports/1997/nigeria/Nigeria-10.htm.

24. Ibid.

25. Maggie Fick, "Nigeria Unveils Energy Infrastructure Deals with China," *Financial Times*, June 30, 2016, http://www.ft.com/cms/s/0/c8130652-3ec8-11e6 -9f2c-36b487ebd80a.html#axzz4J2P6KrZs.

26. Kabbashi M. Suleiman and Ahmed A. A. Badawi, "An Assessment of the Impact of China's Investments in Sudan," African Economic Research Consortium, 2010, https://www.africaportal.org/dspace/articles/assessment-impact-china%E2%80 %99s-investments-sudan.

27. Economy and Levi, *By All Means*, 180.

28. Ibid.

29. Ibid., 181.

30. Cheru and Obi, "Chinese and Indian Engagement," 102. See also Peter Foster, "China Seeks a Sixth of Nigeria's Oil Reserves," *The Telegraph*, September 29, 2009, http://www.telegraph.co.uk/finance/china-business/6241570/China -seeks-a-sixth-of-Nigerias-oil-reserves.html.

31. Marcus Power and Ana Christina Alves, *China and Angola: A Marriage of Convenience?* (Oxford: Pambazuka Press, 2012), 116.
32. Ibid., 117.
33. Forum on China-Africa Cooperation, "FOCAC ABC," April 9, 2013, http://www.focac.org/eng/ltda/ltjj/t933522.htm.
34. Forum on China-Africa Cooperation, "Xi Announces 10 Major China-Africa Cooperation Plans for Coming Three Years," December 8, 2015, http://www.focac.org/eng/ltda/dwjbzjjhys_1/t1322068.htm.
35. Jacapo Prisco, "China Pledges $60 Billion in Funding Support for Africa," CNN, December 4, 2015, http://www.cnn.com/2015/12/04/africa/china-xi-jinping-60-billion-funding/.
36. Forum on China-Africa Cooperation, "Chinese, African Leaders Upgrade Relations as Historic Summit Closes," December 6, 2015, http://www.focac.org/eng/ltda/dwjbzjjhys_1/t1321664.htm.
37. Mohan and Powell, "Energy Rivalry," 148.
38. Jean Drèze and Amartya Sen, *An Uncertain Glory: India and Its Contradictions* (Princeton, NJ: Princeton University Press, 2013), 26–27.
39. See Kiran Stacey, "India Eyes Merger of State-Controlled Oil and Gas Groups," *Financial Times*, February 2, 2017, https://www.ft.com/content/18d1fd5a-e914-11e6-893c-082c54a7f539.
40. Shubhajit Roy, "PM Modi Offers Africa $10-Bn Loan, Says Projects to Be Monitored," *Indian Express*, December 25, 2015, http://indianexpress.com/article/india/india-news-india/india-offers-africa-10-bn-soft-loan-seeks-stronger-ties/.
41. Luke Patey, "An Opportunity to Outmuscle China in Oil," *The Hindu*, December 18, 2014, http://www.thehindu.com/opinion/op-ed/comment-article-an-opportunity-to-outmuscle-china-in-oil/article6701685.ece.
42. Raj Verma, "The Tiger and the Dragon: A Comparison of Indian and Chinese Investments in West Africa's Oil Industry," South Asia at LSE Blog Series, London School of Economics, October 28, 2013, http://blogs.lse.ac.uk/southasia/2013/10/28/the-tiger-and-the-dragon-a-comparison-of-indian-and-chinese-investments-in-west-africas-oil-industry/.
43. Ibid.
44. Aparajita Biswas, "The Importance of Africa in India's Energy Security," in *India and Africa's Partnership: A Vision for a New Future*, ed. Ajay Kumar Dubey and Aparajita Biswas (New Delhi: Springer, 2016), 94–95.
45. Ibid.
46. A. O. Ogoh, M. T. Shaibu, and J. S. Edegbo, "Nigeria-India Economic Relations: Partners in Development," *International Journal of Innovative Social Sciences and Humanities Research* 3, no. 4 (October–December 2015): 14.
47. Cheru and Obi, "Chinese and Indian Engagement," 103.
48. Ibid., 102.
49. Rosalind Reischer, "China and India Unite on Energy," *The Diplomat*, July 11, 2012, http://thediplomat.com/2012/07/china-and-india-unite-on-energy/.
50. Pan Guang, "The Development of the Shanghai Cooperation Organization: The Impact on China-US Relations in Central Asia," in *China, the United States, and the Future of Central Asia*, ed. David B. H. Denoon (New York: New York University Press, 2015), 348.
51. Ibid., 349.
52. Li Xin and Xin Daleng, "Chinese and Russian Economic Interests in Central Asia: Comparative Analysis," in Denoon, *China, the United States*, 136.

53. Cited in Carolyn Kissane, "The Quest for Energy Security in the Central Asian 'Neighborhood,'" in Denoon, *China, the United States*, 378.
54. Economy and Levi, *By All Means*, 151.
55. Ibid., 152.
56. Ibid.
57. Bert Hofman, "China's One Belt One Road Initiative: What We Know Thus Far," World Bank, December 4, 2015, http://blogs.worldbank.org/eastasiapacific /china-one-belt-one-road-initiative-what-we-know-thus-far.
58. Gulshan Sacheva, "India's Objectives in Central Asia," in Denoon, *China, the United States*, 262.
59. Phunchok Stobdan, *Central Asia: India's Northern Exposure* (New Delhi: Institute for Defence Studies and Analyses, 2015), 12.
60. Keith Johnson, "India's $500 Million Bet on Iran," *Foreign Policy*, May 31, 2016, http://foreignpolicy.com/2016/05/31/indias-500-million-bet-on-iran/.
61. "China, Kazakhstan to Ink Deals Worth $30 Billion on Saturday," Reuters, September 13, 2013, http://www.reuters.com/article/us-kazakhstan-china-deals -idUSBRE98608320130907.
62. Sacheva, "India's Objectives," 268–69.
63. "India, Kazakhstan Launch First Drilling at Satpayev Oil Block," *New Indian Express*, July 7, 2015, http://www.newindianexpress.com/world/India -Kazakhstan-Launch-First-Drilling-at-Satpayev-Oil-Block/2015/07/07/article 2907527.ece.
64. James Kilner, "Modi in Unprecedented Grand Tour of Central Asia," *The Telegraph*, July 12, 2015, http://www.telegraph.co.uk/news/worldnews/asia/india /11735255/Modi-tours-Central-Asia-in-Great-Game-move.html.
65. Stobdan, *Central Asia*, 21.
66. Ananth Krishnan, "Amid Energy Competition, India, China Hold First Central Asia Dialogue," *The Hindu*, August 15, 2013, http://www.thehindu.com/news /national/amid-energy-competition-india-china-hold-first-central-asia-dialogue /article5024973.ece.
67. Ibid.
68. Ibid.
69. See Ashok Sajjanhar, "India and the Shanghai Cooperation Organization: What India's Membership Means for the Organization as well as New Delhi," *The Diplomat*, June 19, 2016, http://thediplomat.com/2016/06/india-and-the-shanghai -cooperation-organization/.
70. Suhasini Haidar, "Why Did India Boycott China's Road Summit?," *The Hindu*, May 20, 2017, http://www.thehindu.com/news/national/why-did-india-boycott -chinas-road-summit/article18516163.ece.
71. "GDP Ranking, PPP Based," World Bank, accessed February 1, 2017, http:// data.worldbank.org/data-catalog/GDP-PPP-based-table.
72. Anna Leach, "Race to Renewable: Five Developing Countries Ditching Fossil Fuels," *The Guardian*, September 15, 2015, https://www.theguardian.com /global-development-professionals-network/2015/sep/15/five-developing-countries -ditching-fossil-fuels-china-india-costa-rica-afghanistan-albania.
73. Michael Forsythe, "China Aims to Spend at Least $360 Billion on Renewable Energy by 2020," *New York Times*, January 5, 2017, https://www.nytimes.com /2017/01/05/world/asia/china-renewable-energy-investment.html?_r=0.
74. Deborah Seligsohn, "How China's 13th Five-Year Plan Addresses Energy and the Environment, Testimony before the U.S.-China Economic and Security Review Commission Hearing on China's 13th Five-Year Plan," April 27,

2016, http://www.uscc.gov/sites/default/files/Deborah%20Seligsohn_Written%20Testimony%20042716.pdf.

75. Sun-Joo Ahn and Dagmar Graczyk, *Understanding Energy Challenges in India: Policies, Players, and Issues* (Paris: International Energy Agency, 2012), 73.

76. Kaavya Chandrasekaran, "Capacity for Renewable Energy in India Hits 42,850 mw; Surpasses Capacity of Hydel Projects," *Economic Times*, June 10, 2016, http://economictimes.indiatimes.com/industry/energy/power/capacity-for-renewable-energy-in-india-hits-42850-mw-surpasses-capacity-of-hydel-projects/articleshow/52680042.cms.

of extreme scarcity, violent conflict can result.[12] In addition, water disputes are seldom about water alone but are often part and parcel of the larger political and strategic relations between countries. A serious deterioration of relations can lead to countries' using water as a pretext for war. For instance, in 1980, Saddam Hussein used the dispute over the Shatt al-Arab River as a pretext for invading Iran, even though Saddam's primary motivation was to take advantage of the postrevolution disarray in Tehran to deal the regime a blow.[13]

The first section of this chapter examines the theoretical framework of my argument. I then demonstrate how asymmetry in China-India relations results in misperceptions and differences in attention and how both countries manage their asymmetrical relationship. In the third section, I examine how the asymmetry between China and India has prevented the creation of robust mechanisms for managing the Brahmaputra and why, despite the lack of strong mechanisms, war over water has not occurred. I then examine the conditions that could escalate the water dispute. The conclusion offers suggestions for both sides to strengthen management of their shared water resources so as to reduce the likelihood of violent conflict.

ASYMMETRICAL RELATIONSHIPS AND CONFLICTS

As a starting point for understanding why riparian relations between China and India are relatively stable, it is useful to refer to Brantly Womack's asymmetry framework for understanding the relationship between states of unequal power.[14] Womack argues that differences in power and capabilities lead to asymmetries in perceptions. Because the stronger side could be a threat to its survival and sovereignty, the weaker side tends to perceive slights from the stronger side as more important than they actually are. The stronger side, by contrast, may be less sensitive to the perceptions of the weaker. Even if it perceives unfairness, its response will likely be slow because of the lower priority it accords to relations with the weaker side.

Asymmetrical threat perceptions in turn result in different levels of attention. Because the weaker side is not seen as a threat to the stronger side, issues related to the weaker side are often neglected by the stronger side so that its response to the weaker side is likely to be uncoordinated and its attention is likely to be intermittent and crisis-oriented.[15] As the stronger side is likely to have foreign policy concerns that are of greater concern than managing ties with the weaker side, it may carry out actions that injure the weaker more than it means to because it does not see the degree to which its policies conflict with the other's interests.[16] The weaker side, by contrast, suffers from overattention. It might overestimate its own importance to the stronger side, thus perceiving every action from the stronger side as a response toward itself, even if these actions are carried out by the stronger side independently of its relations with the weaker side.[17] The weaker side may also see the more powerful side's actions as coordinated and sinister and may be paranoid about the other's actions and intentions. Its actions toward the stronger will also be more coordinated.

Misunderstandings are therefore likely to result from these differences in perceptions and attention. It is easy for negative stereotypes of the other to emerge. A vicious cycle results in which the stronger side's slights or unthoughtful behavior reinforce the paranoia of the weaker party, such that the weaker side desperately opposes the stronger side because it feels threatened.[18] In doing so, the weaker side challenges the superiority of the stronger side, leading to the latter demanding deference and respect from the former.

Nevertheless, Womack argues that despite the disparity in capacities between the two sides and the resulting misperceptions and gap in attention, asymmetrical relations are likely to maintain equilibrium in the long run even if tensions are a constant feature. This is because if the stronger side cannot eliminate the weaker and the asymmetrical relationship cannot be resolved through force, both sides must manage it.[19] To minimize hot-button issues, states will seek to create "a neutral zone in the relationship," while to control the escalation of misunderstandings they will strive to create a "sleeve of normalcy."[20]

To create neutral zones in the relationship, both sides would use inclusive rhetoric to formulate their areas of conflict in terms of common interest, instead of in terms of their exclusive interests, such that they are more likely to work together to resolve their differences.[21] Another way to create a neutral zone is to routinize and institutionalize the issues—for example, by creating joint commissions or expert groups on trade, borders, and use of shared rivers to handle common problems.[22] To create normalcy in asymmetrical relations so that issues that crop up will not escalate, states often rely on diplomatic ritual and historical precedents.[23] State visits and summits, for instance, are symbolic of normalcy and mutual respect. States often look at historical precedents to judge whether a present situation is a crisis or not.

Womack's theory does, to a large extent, explain why relations between states of unequal power can be relatively stable. In the next two sections, I show how creating neutral zones and normalcy are strategies that both China and India have adopted to prevent conflict escalation, first at the broader level of relations and then specifically at the river-basin level.

However, Womack's theory does not give a full account of why there are instances of war in asymmetrical dyads. To understand the conditions under which war could break out between China and India over water, it is necessary to consult the works of those who examine asymmetrical wars. In asymmetrical wars, the initiators of wars are usually the stronger state since its superior capabilities will lead it to expect to win the war against the weaker side. However, the more puzzling question for scholars is why a weaker power would initiate war against a stronger one. T.V. Paul has argued that four critical variables—limited political objectives, changes in short-term offensive capability, great-power alliance relationships, and domestic power structures—could lead to the weak precipitating war against the strong.[24] Similarly, Steve Chan has made the point that a weaker state may initiate war against a stronger one because of the expectation of outside intervention.[25] Other works have also shown that a weak state is not always at a disadvantage in negotiations with a stronger state, as there are means for which it could strengthen its position, such as leveraging its relationship with a third party.[26] Moreover, the weak side in asymmetrical conflicts does not always lose to the stronger; there are conditions under which the weak can win wars.[27]

These studies suggest that Womack's framework needs to be modified to give a fuller account of why asymmetrical wars do break out. Later on in this chapter, I will delineate the conditions that may precipitate a war between China and India over water. These conditions can be grouped into those that are endogenous to the river basin itself and those that are exogenous to the river basin, based on the theories in the preceding paragraph.

ASYMMETRY IN CHINA-INDIA RELATIONS

It seems counterintuitive to think of China-India relations as an asymmetrical dyad. Both countries are regional hegemons: China is the economic and military hegemon in the Asia-Pacific and considers East and Southeast Asia as its traditional sphere of influence, while India is the hegemon in the South Asian subcontinent and regards the Indian Ocean as its backyard. Both countries are also ancient civilizations whose influence in historical times spanned large swaths of land and people. In addition, both are experiencing rapid growth, hailed as rising powers, and regarded as competitors for resources and influence around the world. However, a closer examination shows that the relationship between China and India is asymmetrical. Certainly, the power disparity between China and its neighbors in Southeast and Central Asia is larger than the power disparity between China and India. In the event of a war, for instance, it is unlikely that China as the stronger side could eliminate India. Nevertheless, a gap does exist between them economically and militarily. By the end of 2013, China's GDP (PPP) has expanded to nearly four times India's: $13.39 trillion to $4.99 trillion.[28] Its economy is also more developed and sophisticated than India's. The contributions from China's agriculture, industry, and service sectors moved from 40 percent, 33 percent, and 27 percent, respectively, in 1963 to 10 percent, 44 percent, and 46 percent in 2013, compared to India's shift from 41 percent, 20 percent, and 39 percent to 18 percent, 25 percent, and 57 percent in the same period.[29] Trade between them is highly asymmetrical, with India running a large trade deficit with China. China exports ready-made value-added equipment, machinery, and iron and steel to India, while India exports raw materials and primary products to China.[30]

The military gap between China and India has also widened significantly. In 2015, China's defense spending was $145.8 billion, while India's was $47.9 billion.[31] China's investment in power-projection capabilities—such as aircraft carriers, antisatellite and antiship ballistic missiles, cruise missiles, and space missions—has increased significantly. India, by contrast, has neglected investments in its military in the past decade. China has a standing force that is almost twice as large as India's: In 2016, China's active armed forces comprised 2.3 million personnel, while India's had 1.3 million.[32] China has 260 nuclear warheads compared to India's 110.[33]

In terms of population, China's is larger, but India is catching up. From 1963 to 2013, China's population grew from 682 million to 1.357 billion while India's grew from 477 million to 1.25 billion.[34] However, despite projections that India's population will exceed China's by 2022,[35] giving India a "demographic dividend," India's human development index (HDI) consistently remains below China's. In 2014, China's HDI was 0.719 while India's was 0.586, ranking 91 and 135, respectively.[36]

Asymmetrical Threat Perceptions and Attention

The disparity between China's and India's capabilities produces the misperceptions and differences in attention that Womack's asymmetry framework has predicted. China, as the more powerful country, does not perceive India as a serious threat and does not pay as much attention to India as India does to China. India, by contrast, tends to view Chinese actions as more threatening than they are. In China's worldview, the most important countries are the United States, the major European countries, Russia, Japan, and itself. Its focus is on the West and Japan mainly because China has suffered historically from these countries. China's success in the 1962 border war fostered a sense of superiority on China's part, while India's threat perception of China has been colored ever since by its humiliating defeat.

In recent years, China appears to have become India's number-one threat. In this view, Pakistan is a threat because of the assistance and support it gets from China. China's relative success in creating the current structure of power between India and itself is a fundamental factor in explaining the asymmetrical threat perceptions between them.[37] The current status quo is acceptable to China but deeply troubling for India.[38] The loss of a strategic buffer when Beijing sent People's Liberation Army (PLA) troops into Tibet (resulting in China directly administering Tibet from 1959), China's victory in the 1962 border war, and China's alliance with and support for Pakistan during the India-Pakistan Wars of 1965 and 1971, as well as warming ties between China and India's smaller neighbors, increased India's sense of vulnerability and insecurity with respect to China. The perceptual differences between China and India came across starkly during India's nuclear tests in 1998. The threats posed by China and Pakistan were cited by the Indians as the reasons for the tests. By contrast, China's initial reaction was mild, and it ratcheted up the rhetoric only when India started citing the "China threat" as the reason for the tests.

Since India does not rank among the highest in China's threat assessment, it does not pay significant amounts of attention to India. While China figures prominently in India's defense reports, there is barely any mention of India in China's defense white papers.[39] There is general disinterest in China toward India, which is reflected in the lack of reporting on India in the Chinese media. In the foreign policy journals of the two countries, India's show great concern about China, while China's tend to downplay Indian threats to China.[40] The Chinese public's attitude toward India is said to border on "benign neglect."[41]

Because the current status quo in China-India relations is satisfactory for China, its strategy is focused on maintaining the status quo so that it can focus its attention on more pressing issues. Ties with India are important for China's regional context and are critical only when there is a severe downturn in relations.[42] China's policies toward India are thus aimed at ensuring that trouble with India does not erupt. As long as crises do not develop, the stronger side does not need to pay too much attention to the relationship. The asymmetry in perceptions and attention explains why it is difficult for both China and India to agree to a common agenda, thus preventing the formation of a strong cooperative relationship.

Minimizing Hot-Button Issues and Preventing the Escalation of Misperceptions

Both the Chinese and Indian governments have adopted strategies to minimize hot-button issues and prevent the escalation of misperceptions. Chinese leaders tend to take a broad view of China-India relations and use inclusive rhetoric when referring to India. They have stressed the narrative of two great ancient civilizations working together to champion the interests of the third world. For example, Chinese Premier Li Keqiang, during his May 2013 visit to India, remarked that "without the simultaneous development of China and India, there won't be prosperity in Asia."[43] Prior to President Xi Jinping's visit to India in September 2014, in an editorial in *The Hindu*, Xi described China and India as "global partners" and, respectively, as "the world's factory" and "the world's back office."[44]

Indian leaders have also used inclusive rhetoric with reference to China, although they tread a finer line between the need to avoid angering the Chinese and, at the same time, bringing Indian concerns to the Chinese so as to appease domestic constituencies who want a tougher line on China. Prime Minister Narendra Modi declared during his visit to China in October 2015 that "the re-emergence of India and China and their relationship will have a profound impact on the two countries and the course of this century."[45] However, to ensure that he does not come across as being overly effusive toward the Chinese, Modi added, "I stressed the need for China to reconsider its approach on some of the issues that hold us back from realizing full potential of our partnership."[46]

China and India have also routinized their relationship by creating institutions for various aspects of their relationship. Since 2000, both sides have stepped up high-level engagement, with senior policymakers meeting in bilateral, regional, and multilateral forums.[47] Economically, the most important mechanism is the Strategic Economic Dialogue (SED), established in December 2010. Under the umbrella of the SED, five working groups on policy coordination, infrastructure, energy, environmental protection, and high technology were set up.[48] Both sides also have an ongoing defense dialogue, as well as the Joint Working Group on the Boundary Question to seek clarification of the Line of Actual Control (LAC). On the ground, military commanders on both sides of the LAC meet periodically to prevent conflicts from escalating. These institutions and forums are useful for managing relations during the occasional flare-ups between the two countries.

Both sides have also used diplomatic ritual and historical precedents to "create a sleeve of normalcy" during tense periods in their relationship. High-level exchanges between the governments, parliaments, and political parties of the two countries continued even when tensions flared up. For instance, when reports of Chinese border incursions appeared in the Indian media during Xi Jinping's visit to India in 2014, the visit continued as arranged even though the atmosphere was marred by the border tensions. Both sides can also look to historical precedents to ensure normalcy and prevent crises from developing. They have not fought over water even when the water dispute was linked to territorial disputes. On a broader level, both sides have historically kept their relations stable and restored ambassadorial exchanges in 1976, despite their differences on Tibet and Pakistan, as well as the border war in 1962. Such actions helped normalize their interactions even when conflicts have arisen. In addition, because their differences are not new, both sides have gathered enough experience to keep tensions in check.

IMPACT OF ASYMMETRY ON THE MANAGEMENT OF THE BRAHMAPUTRA

China and India are upper and middle riparians, respectively, of the Brahmaputra River, or Yarlung Tsangpo as it is known in Tibet (see map 7.1). The power asymmetry between them at the river-basin level stems not only from China's economic and military superiority but also China's geographical position as the upstream riparian on the Brahmaputra River, which gives it advantages over India. These advantages are in terms of resource utilization and strategic benefits. China can utilize the river according to its needs without worrying about the negative externalities of its actions and the impact on downstream countries India and Bangladesh if it does not wish to. India fears that China's water-diversion plans and dam-building activities would reduce the flow of water to India, resulting in tremendous ecological and economic costs for India. Strategically, since China controls the headwaters of the Brahmaputra in Tibet, it can undertake actions as leverage against India in the event of a conflict between them.

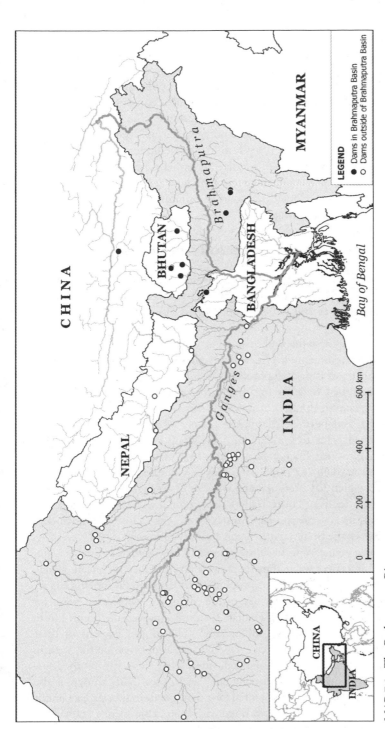

MAP 7.1. The Brahmaputra River

Source: Data from the Food and Agriculture Organization of the United Nations, "AQUASTAT Georeferenced Dams Database" (ESRI shapefile) and "AQUAmaps Regional and Global River Layers"; World Wildlife Fund and the Center for Environmental Systems Research, University of Kassel, "Global Lakes and Wetlands Database" (ESRI shapefile); David T. Sandwell, Joseph J. Becker, and Walter H. F. Smith, The Regents of the University of California, "SRTM15_PLUS: Data Fusion of SRTM Land Topography with Measured and Estimated Seafloor Topography"; Robert J. Hijmans, The Regents of the University of California, "Global Level: A New File with the (2011) Global Country Boundaries"; Bernhard Lehner, Kris Verdin, Andy Jarvis, Conservation Science Program of World Wildlife Fund, in partnership with the US Geological Survey, the International Center for Tropical Agriculture, the Nature Conservancy, and the Center for Environmental Systems Research of the University of Kassel, Germany, "15sec SHAPE: Drainage Basins (Beta)." *Created by National University of Singapore Libraries using QGIS 2.4 as a subset of the original dataset. November 18, 2015. Creative Commons License CC BY 4.0.*

India's downstream position, as well as its military and economic gap with China, increases its insecurity and sense of vulnerability vis-à-vis China. This asymmetry at the river-basin level exerts a strong influence on how China and India manage the Brahmaputra. Differences in perception and attention levels hinder meaningful cooperation and the forging of a common agenda at the river-basin level. Moreover, China has little incentive to step up cooperation with India since it sees little benefit from doing so.[49] It is satisfied with the current status quo at the river-basin level, in a manner similar to its satisfaction with overall bilateral relations with India. Nevertheless, despite the low level of cooperation, riparian relations between them have remained relatively stable because both sides have adopted measures to minimize hot-button issues and prevent conflicts from escalating.

Differences in Perceptions and Attention

Given the asymmetries between China and India, water issues matter more to India than China. India's concerns are driven by China's construction of dams on the Brahmaputra, as well as China's purported plans to divert the Brahmaputra's waters.

China's key interest in the Brahmaputra is to harness its hydropower potential. Hydropower represents a critical renewable source for China's sustainable development and is part of a broader effort to develop its western regions. According to reports, China has already constructed ten dams on the tributaries of the upper reaches of the Brahmaputra, with three more under construction at Dagu, Jiacha, and Jiexu on the middle reaches of the Brahmaputra. China has also indicated plans to build more dams along the Brahmaputra as part of its Twelfth Five-Year Energy Plan (2011–15).[50] China's main project is a large (3,260-meter) dam at Zangmu, less than two hundred kilometers from the Indian border, which has been operational since October 2015.[51] In addition, there is also reportedly a plan to build a dam more than twice as large as the Three Gorges Dam, the 38-gigawatt Motuo Dam, at the Great Bend, which is located just before the Brahmaputra enters Indian territory.[52]

Of even greater concern to India are reported Chinese plans to pursue major interbasin and interriver water-transfer projects on the Tibetan Plateau, which, if realized, may diminish river flows into India and Bangladesh. Indian fears are fueled by perceptions that China has, at the minimum, considered plans for diverting the Yarlung Tsangpo. The State Council approved the South-North Water Diversion Project (SNWDP) in 2002. The project consists of three routes: eastern, central, and western. One of several options for the western route is to divert water at the Great Bend. Initial plans were apparently developed in the 1980s, supported mainly by the PLA.[53] A feasibility study was also conducted in 2003 to assess the potential for a major hydropower project on the Brahmaputra that would divert two hundred billion cubic meters annually to the Yellow River.[54] In addition, reports have also surfaced in India that China intends to divert the waters of the Brahmaputra, not as part of the SNWDP but to Xinjiang instead.[55]

Although China has repeatedly reassured the Indian government that it does not intend to divert water from the Brahmaputra, and it seems unlikely that any diversion would occur anytime soon given the technical, ecological, and financial costs, Indian pundits are not convinced. There is concern among the Indians that through water diversion and dam-building, China will be able to acquire greater power and strategic leverage over India. It fears that China would use threats to withhold water from India to pressure India and extract political and territorial concessions. Indian analysts have suggested that China may use its dams to disrupt the flow of water into India should a conflict arise or use its control of the headwaters as a form of diplomatic leverage.[56] Others in India have also speculated that China will store river water or divert the river at a time when India's water sources are increasingly stressed by population growth and climate change.[57]

China's opaque decision-making structure and belief that it does not need to explain its actions to other riparians create further anxiety for India. It is seen as unilateral in its dam-building activities and unforthcoming in sharing information. For instance, despite the Indian government asking for clarification and Indian intelligence services releasing satellite images of the site of the Zangmu Dam, China was several months into construction before it formally acknowledged the dam's existence.[58] China has also refused to allow Indian experts to visit the sites of its dams, giving the reason that these dams are "run-of-the-river," meaning that the dams do not store or divert water. Due to the lack of information on Chinese plans, Indian officials and experts have speculated about Chinese motives, leading to accusations being hurled at the Chinese. The Indian government has also raised the subject of Chinese plans with Beijing on numerous occasions.

In addition, the water resource dispute between China and India is linked to their territorial disputes. India believes that "water occupies centre stage in China's interest in Tibet."[59] It suspects that China claims Arunachal Pradesh so that it can exploit its abundant water resources. India's perception is fueled by Chinese actions: In 2009, China blocked an Indian request for a loan from the Asian Development Bank because it was earmarked for a watershed development project in Arunachal Pradesh. The mix of territorial and resource disputes have also been a source of concern for China. It worries that India's plans to build dams in Arunachal Pradesh could strengthen India's "actual control" over Arunachal Pradesh and complicate border negotiations between them.[60]

Apart from the strategic advantage that China gains as upper riparian, India also worries about the environmental and ecological implications of Chinese actions in the upper reaches of the Brahmaputra for India's northeastern states.[61] There is, for instance, the common perception among the locals in Assam that China's upstream actions on the Brahmaputra have contributed to the floods downstream in Assam—the locals refer to the frequent floods as "China floods."[62]

In the early 2000s, a major flood killed thirty Indians and left fifty thousand homeless when a natural dam broke due to a landslide on a tributary of the Brahmaputra in Tibet. Many in India asserted that China withheld hydrological data that could have prevented the landslide.[63] The Indians are also worried that a diversion of the Brahmaputra would severely affect agriculture and fishing, as the salinity of water and silting downstream will increase. The impact of climate change on the glaciers in Tibet is also a concern. According to a report by India's Institute of Defence Studies and Analyses, "In spite of the abundance, inadequate water supplies in rural Tibet have led to widespread water-borne diseases and high incidence of hepatitis. The impact of global warming on the glaciers and the melting of permafrost is also alarming. According to the IPCC [Intergovernmental Panel on Climate Change], glaciers in the [Tibetan] plateau are receding at a faster rate than anywhere else in the world."[64]

Whether rightly or wrongly, Indian perception of Chinese actions on the Brahmaputra is filled with suspicion and distrust because of the threat it feels emanating from China's stronger position upstream. To improve its position vis-à-vis China on the Brahmaputra, India is keen to pursue cooperation with China by creating water-management institutions, engaging in joint development of the Brahmaputra, and laying down water-sharing and water-usage principles.

However, China has shown little interest in stepping up cooperation with India. From the Chinese perspective, any significant movement toward joint development and water-sharing is contingent on improvements in other aspects of its relations with India. During my interviews with Chinese experts, it was clear that China is unwilling to give up the strategic advantages it enjoys over India as a result of its upstream position.[65] China will consider significant forward movement in cooperation on India in water management only when there is substantial progress made toward resolving other outstanding issues in their bilateral relations—namely, Tibet, the Dalai Lama, and territorial disputes.[66] This line of thinking conforms to the general Chinese approach to India as discussed earlier: the status quo benefits China, and the Chinese broad policy toward India is to maintain equanimity and the status quo with India and prevent any major conflict or crisis from erupting. China also sees little economic and financial benefit from cooperating with India on the Brahmaputra—for instance, in joint hydroelectric projects—since its dam-building skills are superior to India's and it has greater financial muscle.

Mismatched expectations between China and India with respect to the Brahmaputra make cooperation in managing their shared waters difficult. China does not prioritize relations with India and accordingly does not pay as much attention to the management of the Brahmaputra compared to India. India, by contrast, pays substantial attention to Chinese actions on the Brahmaputra, as a result of which some quarters in India tend to perceive Chinese actions as sinister and conspiratorial. At the same time, it wants increased engagement with China on managing the Brahmaputra, but such initiatives from the Indian side have met with a cool response from the Chinese.

Despite the lack of robust cooperation, however, armed conflict has not happened because both sides are aware of the high costs of war and neither would have the capability to eliminate the other. China wants to maintain the status quo with India so that it can focus on greater threats along its maritime border, while India is wary of escalating the conflict because of its humiliating defeat during the 1962 border war. Moreover, China's rapid economic progress and military buildup puts it ahead of India, and India would not want to overly antagonize China. Thus, even though it is difficult to create a common agenda for both sides to increase transboundary water cooperation because of the differences in their perceptions and attention, they both nevertheless share a common interest in avoiding an escalation of conflict. In the next section, I show how both sides have engaged in strategies to minimize hot-button issues and control the escalation of misperceptions at the river-basin level.

MINIMIZING HOT-BUTTON ISSUES AND CONTROLLING ESCALATION OF MISPERCEPTIONS

Inclusive Rhetoric and Desecuritization of Water Conflicts

Both China's and India's political rhetoric are clearly aimed at desecuritizing the water conflicts between them. Desecuritization is defined as "a moving of issues off the 'security agenda' and back into the realm of public political discourse and 'normal' political dispute and accommodation."[67] This means turning security issues into normal politics, chiefly through the use of rhetoric and forming a narrative around a particular issue that neutralizes or reduces the security implications. Of the three strategies used to desecuritize an issue—namely, to preemptively avoid speaking about certain issues in security terms, to manage securitized issues in ways that do not spawn security dilemmas or vicious cycles, and to transform issues back into the realm of normal politics—the two sides have arguably utilized the first strategy the most.[68]

Both the Chinese and Indian governments have focused on Chinese reassurances that China will not harm India's interest. Official lines from both sides have been consistent; these statements are made periodically and have become routinized and ritualized. China, in the larger interest of ensuring peaceful relations with India, has sought to address Indian concerns. By agreeing to share hydrological data with India, Chinese actions are aimed at assuaging Indian concerns about the floods in northeastern India.[69] China has also tried to quell Indian concerns about its plans to develop the upper reaches of the Brahmaputra by using official rhetoric and media statements. It has time and again reassured the Indians, including in statements by high-level officials, that it has no intention of diverting the water of the Brahmaputra. A *People's Liberation Army Daily* article denies any diversion plans and claims that China took Indian interests into account when it chose not to include the Brahmaputra in the SNWDP.[70] China has also claimed that the dams it is building are run-of-the-river and will not affect the flow of the Brahmaputra. It has propounded a positive view of the impact of its dams, saying that dams may help increase the amount of water during the dry season and provide flood control during the rainy season.[71]

According to Sebastian Biba, the clearest attempts at "assuaging rhetoric" took place in spring 2010, following an official Chinese announcement that the Zangmu Dam was being built after months of denial.[72] Chinese reassurances were quick. The China Huaneng Group, a state-owned hydropower company in charge of the Zangmu Dam, soon stated that, first, "the river will not be stopped during construction" and that, second, "after it [i.e., the dam] comes into operation, the river water will flow downstream through water turbines and sluices. So the water volume downstream will not be reduced."[73] Even more significantly, during a China-India strategic bilateral dialogue around the same time, Chinese vice foreign minister Zhang Zhijun assured the Indian delegation that the project "was not a project designed to divert water" and would not affect "the welfare and availability of water of the population in the lower reaches of the Brahmaputra."[74] Then Chinese premier Wen Jiabao also stated during a visit to India in late 2010 that China takes seriously India's concern about the transborder rivers: "We are ready to further improve the joint working mechanism. . . . I would like to assure our Indian friends that all upstream development activities by China will be based on scientific planning and study and will never harm downstream interests."[75]

The Indian government has also employed rhetoric to desecuritize water conflicts with China. It has avoided inflammatory language and sought to calm incendiary language from other Indian politicians and the Indian media. They have repeated assurances from top Chinese leaders that China has no intention of diverting the waters of the Brahmaputra and that the Chinese would not do anything that would adversely impact India's interests. During a meeting between Prime Minister Manmohan Singh and Xi Jinping in 2013, for instance, Singh told the Indian press that he had raised the idea of a joint mechanism for managing transboundary waters with Xi and that Xi had reassured him that China is conscious of its responsibilities toward the lower riparian states. He added that "as of now, our assessment is that whatever activity that is taking place on the Brahmaputra region in Tibet, it is essentially a run-of-the river project and therefore there is no cause of worry on our part."[76] When news of China's construction of the Zangmu Dam broke in the Indian media, the minister of external affairs issued a statement: "We have ascertained from our own sources that this is a run of the river hydro-electric project, which does not store water and will not adversely impact the downstream areas in India. Therefore, I believe there is no cause for immediate alarm. I would like to share with you the fact that a large proportion of the catchment of the Brahmaputra is within Indian territory."[77]

Top Indian leaders' statements about Chinese reassurances are also supported by positive rhetoric from some retired Indian government officials and academics who downplayed the China water threat. Romesh Bhattacharji, a former bureaucrat, asserted that "India has nothing to worry about" regarding the Zangmu Dam because "the Brahmaputra's waters will continue to flow to India as before, after their brief storage period is over."[78] Bhattacharji also refuted fears that China will divert the waters of the Brahmaputra, given the technical difficulties, and said that even if China does divert the Brahmaputra, its impact on India would not be severe, as the "Brahmaputra gets most of its waters after entering India."[79] An Indian expert, Jayanta Bandyopadhyay, has also said the SNWDP is mostly about damming and diverting China's domestic rivers and would have little impact on the flow of the Brahmaputra as most of the Brahmaputra's flows come from tributaries originating in India: "The Yarlung Tsangpo is a minor contributor to the total flow of the Brahmaputra. Further, snow and glaciers supply about 34 percent of its total flow."[80]

At the same time, the Indian government has consistently raised transborder rivers as an issue of concern to Chinese leaders. The Press Information Bureau of the Indian Ministry of Water Resources stated that "as a lower riparian state with considerable established user rights to the waters of the river, India has conveyed the views and concerns to the Chinese authorities, including at the highest levels of the Government of the People's Republic of China. India has urged China to ensure that the interests of downstream states are not harmed by any activities in the upstream areas."[81] Such diplomatic gestures and rituals ensure that even though Chinese leaders do not prioritize the Brahmaputra issue, the issue is at least not completely neglected due to inattention from the Chinese side. At the minimum, the Chinese are aware that transboundary waters are a concern for the Indians and they must ensure that any misperceptions about Chinese intentions with respect to the Brahmaputra are managed.

As Paul points out in the introduction to this book, India, unlike Pakistan in the India-Pakistan asymmetrical dyad, does not use asymmetrical strategies and coercive bargaining against China. This helps to keep the rivalry between China and India, both on a broader level and at the river-basin level, under control, with both sides working to desecuritize the water issue. In contrast to China and India's management of their water dispute, the India-Pakistan water dispute has been securitized by both sides, even though the Indus Water Treaty has withstood the test of three wars since it was signed in 1960. The official narrative on both sides is that the Indus is an existential security issue that will impact the survival of both nations since it is the major source of water for Pakistan and the northwestern part of India. That the dispute over the Indus is an existential security threat for both countries probably explains why the two sides worked hard to keep the Indus Water Treaty even when wars broke out and bilateral relations were strained. As one scholar notes, "the major credit for the survival of the Indus agreement for so long is a negative one: the high risk involved in its non-compliance."[82] Such a narrative surrounding the Indus probably also enables both governments to account to their people the need for the two rivals to make compromises with the other over water issues. The latest spat over the

Indus Water Treaty as a result of Modi's suspension of water talks in retaliation for the Uri attack in the Indian-administered state of Jammu and Kashmir demonstrates the securitized nature of the Indus waters between India and Pakistan. This stands in sharp contrast to Chinese and Indian rhetoric to downplay their water dispute as a security issue.

Routinization and Historical Precedents

Apart from the use of rhetoric and diplomacy, there are also attempts to institutionalize and routinize management of the Brahmaputra, even though these cooperative efforts are limited. These consist of a series of MOUs on hydrological data-sharing (see table 7.1). Specifically, China agreed to provide India with information about water level, discharge, and rainfall from its three monitoring stations on the Brahmaputra, as well as the Sutlej. An expert-level mechanism was also established in 2006. The expert group meets annually to discuss cooperation and coordination on information-sharing and emergency management.

TABLE 7.1. **Existing China-India Cooperation on Transboundary Rivers**

Date	Frameworks	Details
2002, renewed in 2008 and 2013	MOU on hydrological data-sharing on the Brahmaputra River / Yalu Zangbu River	China agreed in a MOU signed in 2002 to provide hydrological information—namely water level, discharge, and rainfall—from June 1 to October 15 every year. The 2002 MOU expired in 2007 and was renewed in 2008 for another five years. In May 2013, during Premier Li Keqiang's visit to India, the MOU was further extended till 2018. In October 2013, during Prime Minister Manmohan Singh's visit to China, a new MOU on strengthening cooperation on transboundary rivers was signed. China agreed to share data from May 1 instead of June 1. Under the MOU, China and India also agreed to "exchange views on other areas of mutual interest."
2005, renewed in 2010	MOU on hydrological data-sharing on the Sutlej River / Langquin Zangbu River	China agreed to provide hydrological information during flood season. An implementation plan was additionally signed in 2011 for China to provide hydrological information, a data-transmission method, and a cost settlement.
2006	Expert-level mechanism	The expert group made up of representatives from both sides discussed interaction and cooperation on provision of flood-season hydrological data, emergency management, and other issues on an annual basis. The first meeting was held in 2007, and meetings were held every year subsequently.

However, the terms of the MOUs are very limited: China agrees to provide hydrological data for the Brahmaputra and the Sutlej only from May/June to October each year. Implementation of the MOUs has also been piecemeal, they are legally nonbinding, and there is no oversight body that can ensure implementation.

Even though there is limited institutionalization of cooperation between China and India in managing the Brahmaputra, these existing mechanisms nevertheless provide a useful channel of communication between the two sides that helps routinize their interactions and prevents open conflict. The annual meetings of the expert group since 2007, as well as the exchange of information, provide a focal point for discussion and promote better understanding between the two sides.

Both China and India can also look to historical precedents to minimize conflict over water issues. The fact that they have not fought over water can help both sides view water issues between them from the right perspective, despite alarming cries of "water wars" from some quarters in India. Moreover, given the plethora of security issues between them, water is an important issue but does not present any immediate danger of war compared to their differences on the border issue, Tibet, and Pakistan. For instance, the border issue is arguably the most serious dispute between them that could lead to war if not properly managed. However, apart from border incursions and skirmishes, no major clashes have broken out between them since 1962. Both sides can look at these incidents of crisis management as precedents for their management of any water crisis that may arise.

CONDITIONS FOR ESCALATION OF WATER DISPUTE

The current relative stability in the China-India water dispute does not imply that equilibrium will continue indefinitely. An escalation of water issues into armed conflict cannot be ruled out. The conditions that can lead to escalation can be grouped into two broad categories: those that are endogenous to the Brahmaputra River Basin itself and those that pertain to larger issues in China-India relations that could precipitate war, with water acting as a catalyst or a pretext. Should these endogenous and exogenous conditions coincide, war could result.

Changes in the Brahmaputra River Basin

Changes to the physical and environmental conditions of the Brahmaputra River Basin could introduce uncertainties into the water dispute between China and India. In her study of the Jordan River water conflicts between Israel and its Arab neighbors, Miriam Lowi underscores the impact of the physical, human, political, and psychological environments.[83] Severe water conflicts can result as populations grow and climate change continues to manifest.[84] Scholars of river basins have noted that "water resources are subject to change over space and time due to precipitation and temperature cycles, which have become increasingly unpredictable as a result of climate change. . . . Users have altered water resources through various engineering efforts, changing the availability, quantity, or quality of water resources for other users. Such alterations can potentially create conflict."[85]

As these changes to the features of water resources take place, human security will increasingly become an important issue for countries sharing rivers. That large populations in China and India are dependent on water resources will lead to greater conflict in situations of water scarcity and natural disasters, including the effects of climate change and economic development. Earlier in this chapter I mentioned that China and India's economic growth is increasingly affected by water shortages and pollution. Conversely, economic developments in both countries are worsening their water problems. There are also signs that the growing water shortages in China and India pose the largest threat to food security.[86]

Thomas Homer-Dixon has shown that in instances of extreme scarcity, violent conflict is likely. This is because severe environmental scarcity would increase economic deprivation and at the same time disrupt key social institutions, which would in turn lead to violent conflict.[87] In fact, Homer-Dixon's study shows that "the renewable resource most likely to stimulate interstate resource war is river water."[88] As water shortages increase because of population growth and excessive resource consumption, states are bound to increase resource-capture strategies, such as building dams and diverting water supply to their own populations. Resource-capture strategies increase the level of conflict between states. Using examples of the South Africa–Lesotho water conflict and the Egypt-Ethiopia conflict on the Nile River, Homer-Dixon argues that conflict is most probable when a downstream state is highly dependent on river water and believes that it has the military power to rectify the situation.[89] This argument is based on the downstream riparian as the stronger in the asymmetrical dyad. In the China-India water dispute, China is the upstream riparian and the stronger of the two, hence reducing the likelihood of a conflict. However, should India one day believe that it has the capacity to wage war against China, violent conflict over water is a possibility. To make clearer this point, the next subsection examines the changes in the broader relations between China and India that may boost India's belief that it could fight a war with China over water.

Changes in China-India Relations

Water disputes are never about water resources alone. As Paul mentions in the introductory chapter, China-India relations are multidimensional and require resolution on multiple fronts. Water between China and India is interlinked with larger political issues, primarily the territorial conflict. In the limited incidents of water wars in history, more often than not water acts as a catalyst or is used as a pretext for war between countries whose overall relations have deteriorated to the point of hostility.[90] While China-India relations have remained largely stable, it is possible for their relations to deteriorate if they do not carefully manage their rivalry.

There are indications that in recent years India has gained greater significance in Chinese eyes and that the Chinese threat assessment of India has gone up as a result of India's growing strategic relations with the United States, Japan, and Australia, as well as Modi's "Act East" policy.[91] The arena for engagement between China and India has expanded as India becomes more active in Southeast Asia and China's naval presence in the Indian Ocean increases. Clashes may happen unless both sides do more to stabilize their relationship. While opportunities abound when countries form areas of common interest, thus far the overlaps in both countries' spheres of influence have engendered more rivalry than cooperation. Both sides have viewed the other's growing presence in its own backyard with suspicion.

As both China and India grow in power and influence, competition between them seems to be heating up. The standoff between Chinese and Indian troops in the summer of 2017 in Doklam, a disputed territory between China and Bhutan, points to the possibility of a military conflict between the two to occur out of the blue. China-India relations had already soured considerably in the previous year when China blocked India's ascension to the Nuclear Suppliers Group, which denied India recognition of its status, and refused to name the leader of the Pakistan-based group Jaish-e-Mohammed, Masood Azhar, as a terrorist in the United Nations. To the Indians, such Chinese actions are attempts to contain India's rise.[92] China, on its part, has displayed insensitivity to Indian concerns with initiatives such as the China-Pakistan Economic Corridor (CPEC). While China views the CPEC as an economic initiative and as part of its Belt and Road Initiative, it fails to understand Indian views that the CPEC touches on sovereignty issues for India.[93] India is also suspicious of the strategic implications of the Belt and Road Initiative, since it comprises projects around India's periphery but not in India itself.[94]

Adapting from the power transition theory, when the dissatisfied challenger perceives opportunities to change the status quo, it might initiate war against the stronger state. Whatever China's intentions are, if India perceives China to be blocking its rise and denying it its rightful place among the major powers, it might initiate conflict if the conditions are ripe, and water, as well as a host of other issues between them, could act as a catalyst or pretext for war. I have focused on India as the potential initiator of war because it is dissatisfied with the current status quo and would want to change it, either through persuasive or coercive means. So far, it has focused on persuasion, although this might be changing under Modi's more aggressive foreign policy, the insertion of Indian troops in Doklam being a case in point. China is unlikely to be the one initiating war, as I have mentioned earlier, as it is satisfied with the status quo, with its significant leverages over India. The Doklam standoff, however, has shown the possibility of China reconsidering its options when China sees Indian actions as a direct affront and a challenge to its position and status.

Indian perceptions of China as attempting to prevent its rise are necessary but not sufficient conditions for war. There have to be additional factors that strengthen India's resolve for conflict. The conditions that might lead to the weaker side initiating asymmetrical conflicts have been expounded by scholars mentioned earlier in this chapter. Steve Chan makes the point that in asymmetrical dyads, the weaker state may start and escalate a dispute in order to engage foreign attention and recruit outsiders' help.[95] Paul has also shown that changes in alliance structure may result in the weaker state initiating war because it has formed an alliance with a stronger power. It has been the weapon of the weak to leverage on a major power to counter another power. For example, the expectation that the Soviet Union would provide support was one reason that Mao Zedong aided Kim Il-sung in the Korean War. Recurrent conflicts between India and Pakistan also showed that the latter initiated conflict in order to engage outsiders. In recent years, India has stepped up economic and military ties with the United States, Japan, Australia, and Vietnam, countries that seem to be at odds with China. It therefore cannot be ruled out entirely that conflict between China and India may escalate if India feels confident of the support of these countries.

The other three variables identified by Paul seem less likely to trigger a conflict. India's military capability is below that of China's, and it is unlikely that it will be able to gain a sudden increase in short-term capability in the near future. Asymmetrical rivals have taken advantage of domestic troubles of the other to launch war. However, both Modi and Xi enjoy widespread support at home. Even though there are problems with China's economic growth and social stability, it seems unlikely that a rupture of the power structure at home is likely to take place soon. As for a limited-aims strategy to achieve political objectives, China has used such a strategy to forestall India's forward strategy and to teach India a lesson in the 1962 border war. India is unlikely to carry out such a strategy, given the memories of its defeat in 1962. However, it cannot be ruled out that China will not undertake such a strategy again in view of the Doklam standoff. It was feared that if no face-saving withdrawal could be worked out between the two at Doklam, a limited-aims war initiated by China was a possibility.

As the Doklam example has shown, third parties could exacerbate tensions between China and India. Even more complicated than the India-Bhutan-China relationship is the India-Pakistan-China triangular relationship. Historically, as a result of the China-Pakistan alliance, China had sided with Pakistan when conflicts broke out. Although China had sought to delink the relationship and avoided taking sides in India-Pakistan flare-ups when its relations with India became warmer, the possibility of China's using Pakistan as leverage against

India is never far from Indian minds. As mentioned earlier, the blocking of a tributary on the Brahmaputra in September and October 2016 was seen by some in India as China taking retaliatory action against India on Pakistan's behalf. Although this is unlikely to be the case because blocking a tributary is not likely to impact water flows downstream,[96] a convergence of strained ties between China and India and of India's taking action against Pakistan on the Indus River could lead to China exercising its upstream leverage. In such a scenario, it is possible for China to escalate conflict on the Brahmaputra by undertaking actions that disrupt the water flow to India.

CONCLUSION: PROSPECTS FOR THE LONG TERM

Countries with a history of managing the asymmetries in their relationships tend to have relatively stable relations, even if their relations are seldom problem-free. This chapter has demonstrated that the interactions between China and India at the river-basin level fit into the general patterns of interaction between China and India and are in line with the expected interactions between countries with asymmetrical capabilities leading to asymmetrical threat perceptions and differing levels of attention.

Nevertheless, as the above section shows, armed conflict over water is a possibility even if rather remote. China and India could do more to stabilize their riparian relations, which would in turn benefit their overall relationship and reduce the likelihood of an escalation of conflict. For one, both sides could upgrade their current MOU-based cooperation to a higher level of institutionalization. A greater level of institutionalized cooperation would bring greater stability to their riparian relations, as routinization and institutionalization keeps asymmetrical relations stable. Both sides could also enhance mutual exchanges in disaster management. For instance, India is learning flood-control techniques from China: It was reported in June 2016 that flood-prone Assam had set up a team of experts to go to China to study its Yellow River flood-management strategies.[97] Apart from sharing hydrological information for flood control, both sides could move on to the next stage to discuss pollution control and environmental protection. Such exchanges would enhance riparian cooperation and help build confidence on both sides. In addition, both China and India are interested in sustainable economic development, which could serve as a platform for engendering cooperation. For instance, China and India could collaborate on research into the impact of climate change on the Himalayan glaciers. In 2009, China and India signed an MOU ahead of the 2010 UN Climate Conference in Copenhagen to cooperate on climate change issues. Such cooperation could be further extended and given greater substance by bringing in expertise from both sides.

NOTES

1. Jian Xie et al., *Addressing China's Water Scarcity: Recommendations for Selected Water Resource Management Issues* (Washington, DC: World Bank, 2008), xxi.
2. Ministry of Water Resources, People's Republic of China, *2007–2008 Annual Report*, http://www.mwr.gov.cn/english/publs/. Water availability of 1,000–1,700 cubic meters per person is regarded as a situation of water stress, and less than 1,000 cubic meters indicates extreme water stress.
3. Andrea Hart, "Water Demand-Supply Gap Rising at Alarming Rate, Report Shows," Circle of Blue, December 2, 2009, http://www.circleofblue.org/waternews/2009/world/news-waterdemand-supply-gap-rising-at-alarming-rate-report-shows/.
4. 2030 Water Resources Group, *Charting Our Water Future: Economic Frameworks to Inform Decision-Making*, November 2009, 16, http://www.mckinsey.com/business-functions/sustainability-and-resource-productivity/our-insights/charting-our-water-future.
5. Press Information Bureau, Government of India, "Per Capita Water Availability," National Informatics Centre, April 26, 2012, http://pib.nic.in/newsite/erelease.aspx?relid=82676.
6. Sushmi Dey, "80% of India's Water Surface May Be Polluted, Report by International Body Says," *Times of India*, June 25, 2015, http://timesofindia.indiatimes.com/home/environment/pollution/80-of-Indias-surface-water-may-be-polluted-report-by-international-body-says/articleshow/47848532.cms.
7. Brahma Chellaney, *Water: Asia's New Battleground* (Washington, DC: Georgetown University Press, 2011), 152.
8. Institute for Defence Studies and Analyses, *Water Security for India: The External Dynamics* (New Delhi: Institute for Defence Studies and Analyses), 40.
9. There is, however, no strong evidence that the Chinese are using the blocking of a tributary to pressure the Indians. First, the blocking of a tributary is not likely to have a significant impact on water flow into India. Second, there are scholarly works that show that the Chinese government does not have control over the day-to-day activities of Chinese companies. It is likely the blockage had already been planned.
10. Institute for Defence Studies and Analyses, *Water Security*, 44.
11. Brantly Womack, "Asymmetry Theory and China's Concept of Multipolarity," *Journal of Contemporary China* 13, no. 39 (May 2004): 362.
12. Thomas F. Homer-Dixon, "Environmental Scarcities and Violent Conflict: Evidence from Cases," *International Security* 19, no. 1 (Summer 1994): 5–40.
13. Joost Hiltermann, "Water Wars? Lessons from the Middle and North America," International Crisis Group, keynote speech for World Water Week, Stockholm, August 28, 2016, https://www.crisisgroup.org/middle-east-north-africa/gulf-and-arabian-peninsula/iraq/water-wars-lessons-middle-east-north-africa.
14. Brantly Womack, *China and Vietnam: The Politics of Asymmetry* (New York: Cambridge University Press, 2006).
15. Brantly Womack, "Asymmetry and Systemic Misperception: China, Vietnam and Cambodia during the 1970s," *Journal of Strategic Studies* 26, no. 2 (June 2003): 100.
16. Robert Jervis, *Perception and Misperception in International Politics* (Princeton, NJ: Princeton University Press, 1976), 354.
17. Ibid., 344.
18. Womack, "Asymmetry Theory," 361.
19. Womack, *China and Vietnam*, 2.

20. Ibid.
21. Ibid., 90.
22. Ibid.
23. Ibid., 90–91.
24. T.V. Paul, *Asymmetric Conflicts: War Initiation by Weaker Powers* (Cambridge: Cambridge University Press, 1994).
25. Steve Chan, *Enduring Rivalries in the Asia-Pacific* (New York: Cambridge University Press, 2013), 34–38.
26. Jeswald W. Salacuse, "Lessons for Practice," in *Power and Negotiation*, ed. I. William Zartman and Jeffrey Z. Rubin (Ann Arbor: University of Michigan Press, 2000).
27. See arguments that focus on the will of the weak versus the strong in winning war, the vulnerabilities of strong states and democratic states, and the strategic interactions between the weak and the strong: Andrew Mack, "Why Big Nations Lose Small Wars: The Politics of Asymmetric Conflict," *World Politics* 27, no. 2 (January 1975): 175–200; and Ivan Arreguin-Toft, "How the Weak Win Wars: A Theory of Asymmetric Conflict," *International Security* 26, no. 1 (Summer 2001): 93–128.
28. Swaran Singh, "China and India: Coping with Growing Asymmetry," *Asan Forum*, December 19, 2014.
29. Ibid.
30. Hu Shisheng, "Competitive Cooperation in Trade: A Chinese Perspective," in *China-India Relations: Cooperation and Conflict*, ed. Kanti Bajpai, Huang Jing, and Kishore Mahbubani (London and New York: Routledge, 2016), 68.
31. "Chapter Ten: Country Comparisons—Commitments, Force Levels and Economics," *The Military Balance* 116, no. 1 (2016): 486.
32. Ibid.
33. Arms Control Association, *Nuclear Weapons: Who Has What at a Glance*, August 2016, https://www.armscontrol.org/factsheets/Nuclearweaponswhohaswhat.
34. Singh, "China and India."
35. "India 'to Overtake China's Population by 2022'—UN," BBC, July 20, 2015, http://www.bbc.com/news/world-asia-33720723.
36. Data from United Nations Development Programme, *The 2014 Human Development Reports*, accessed May 23, 2015, http://hdr.undp.org/en/data#. The HDI comprises the following components: life expectancy at birth, mean years of schooling, expected years of schooling, and gross national income per capita (PPP).
37. John Garver, "Asymmetrical Indian and Chinese Threat Perceptions," *Journal of Strategic Studies* 24, no. 5 (2002): 122.
38. Ibid.
39. Ibid., 110–14.
40. Ibid., 114–17 and 122.
41. Yang Dali and Zhao Hong, "The Rise of India: China's Perspectives and Responses," in *Socio-Political and Economic Challenges in South Asia*, ed. Tan Tai Yong (New Delhi: SAGE, 2009), 48.
42. Zhao Gancheng, *Status Quo and Prospect: A Study on China-India Relations* [*Zhongyin Guanxi: Xianzhuang, Qushi, Yindui*] (Shanghai: Shishi Chuban She, 2013), 82.
43. Cited in Jeff Smith, *Cold Peace: China-India Rivalry in the Twenty-First Century* (Lanham, MD: Lexington Books, 2014), 8.
44. Xi Jinping, "Towards an Asian Century of Prosperity," *The Hindu*, September 17, 2014, http://www.thehindu.com/opinion/op-ed/towards-an-asian-century-of-prosperity/article6416553.ece.

45. "Prime Minister Narendra Modi's Media Statement in Beijing during His Visit to China," *Indian Express*, May 15, 2015, http://indianexpress.com/article/india/india -others/prime-ministers-media-statement-in-beijing-during-his-visit-to-china/.
46. Ibid.
47. Tanvi Madan, "Indian Prime Minister Modi Visits China," Brookings Institution blog, May 13, 2015, https://www.brookings.edu/blog/up-front/2015/05 /13/indian-prime-minister-modi-visits-china/.
48. Hu, "Competitive Cooperation," 81.
49. See Selina Ho, "A River Flows through It: A Chinese Perspective," in Bajpai et al., *China-India Relations*.
50. Cited in Obja Borah Hazarika, "Riparian Relations between India and China: Exploring Interactions on Transboundary Rivers," *International Journal of China Studies* 6, no. 1 (April 2015): 67.
51. Ministry of Water Resources, Government of India, "Dam on Brahmaputra River by China," National Informatics Centre, December 7, 2015, http://pib .nic.in/newsite/PrintRelease.aspx?relid=132646.
52. Chellaney, *Water*, 144. Chellaney cited a map by HydroChina, a Chinese hydro-power company, as evidence that China intends to build the Motuo Dam.
53. Jonathan Holslag, "Assessing the Sino-Indian Water Dispute," *Journal of International Affairs* 64, no. 2 (Spring/Summer 2011): 24.
54. Elizabeth Economy, "Asia's Water Security Crisis: China, India and the United States," in *Strategic Asia 2008–09: Challenges and Choices*, ed. Ashley Tellis, Mercy Kuo, and Andrew Marble (Seattle: National Bureau of Asian Research, 2008), 384.
55. Sachin Parashar, "Drought-Hit China to Divert Brahmaputra?," *Times of India*, June 13, 2011, http://timesofindia.indiatimes.com/india/Drought-hit-China-to -divert-Brahmaputra/articleshow/8831791.cms.
56. Cited in Joel Wuthnow, "Water Power, Water Worries: China's Goals and Challenges as the Brahmaputra's Uppermost Riparian," in *Water Resource Competition in the Brahmaputra River Basin: China, India, and Bangladesh*, ed. Nilanthi Samaranayake, Satu Limaye, and Joel Wuthnow (Arlington, VA: Center for Strategic Studies, May 2016), 26.
57. Ibid.
58. Holslag, "Sino-Indian Water Dispute," 23.
59. Institute for Defence Studies and Analyses, *Water Security*, 45.
60. Wuthnow, "Water Power, Water Worries," 15.
61. Nimmi Kurian, "China's Dams Bring a Flood of Questions," East Asia Forum, April 14, 2016, http://www.eastasiaforum.org/2016/04/14/chinas-dams-bring -a-flood-of-questions/.
62. Author's interview with locals on the northern bank of the Brahmaputra, Dibrugarh, Assam, April 1, 2016.
63. Wuthnow, "Water Power, Water Worries," 25.
64. Institute for Defence Studies and Analyses, *Water Security*, 47.
65. Author's notes of interview with experts in a Shanghai-based think tank, February 11, 2014.
66. Ibid.
67. Michael C. Williams, "Words, Images, Enemies: Securitization and International Politics," *International Studies Quarterly* 47, no. 4 (2003): 523.
68. Ole Waever, "Securitization and Desecuritization," in *On Security*, ed. Ronnie Lipschutz (New York: Columbia University Press, 1995), 46–87.
69. Wuthnow, "Water Power, Water Worries," 25.
70. Cited ibid., 27.

71. Selina Ho, "River Politics: China's Policies towards the Mekong and the Brahmaputra in Comparative Perspective," *Journal of Contemporary China* 23, no. 85 (2014): 10.
72. Sebastian Biba, "Desecuritization in China's Behavior towards Its Transboundary Rivers: The Mekong River, the Brahmaputra River, and the Irtysh and Ili Rivers," *Journal of Contemporary China* 23, no. 85 (January 2014): 38.
73. Ibid.
74. Ibid.
75. Ibid.
76. Press Trust of India, "'China Seeks Joint Mechanism with India,' Says Prime Minister Manmohan Singh," NDTV, March 29, 2013, http://www.ndtv.com /india-news/china-seeks-joint-mechanism-with-india-says-prime-minister-man mohan-singh-517541.
77. Cited in Satu Limaye, "The Middle Riparian Quandaries: India and the Brahmaputra River Basin," in Samaranayake et al., *Water Resource Competition*, 44.
78. Sudha Ramachandran, "Water Wars: China, India and the Great Dam Rush," *The Diplomat*, April 3, 2015, http://thediplomat.com/2015/04/water-wars -china-india-and-the-great-dam-rush/.
79. Ibid.
80. Cited in Hazarika, "Riparian Relations," 68.
81. Ministry of Water Resources, "Dam on Brahmaputra."
82. Ashok Swain, "The Indus II and Siachen Peace Park: Pushing the India-Pakistan Peace Process Forward," *The Roundtable* 98, no. 404 (2009): 573.
83. Miriam R. Lowi, *Water and Power: The Politics of a Scarce Resource in the Jordan River Basin* (Cambridge: Cambridge University Press, 1993), 19–53.
84. Selina Ho, "Introduction to 'Transboundary River Cooperation: Actors, Strategies and Impact,'" *Water International* 42, no. 2 (February 2017): 100.
85. Jacob D. Petersen-Perlman, Jennifer C. Veilleux, and Aaron T. Wolf, "International Water Conflict and Cooperation: Challenges and Opportunities," *Water International* 42, no. 2 (February 2017): 105.
86. Cited in Uttam Kumar Sinha, "Towards Riparian Rationality: An Indian Perspective," in Bajpai et al., *China-India Relations*, 167.
87. Homer-Dixon, "Environmental Scarcities," 7.
88. Ibid., 19.
89. Ibid.
90. See Aaron T. Wolf, "Conflict and Cooperation along International Waterways," *Water Policy* 1, no. 2 (1998): 251–65.
91. Selina Ho, "Seeing the Forest for the Trees: China's Shifting Perceptions of India," in *Handbook on China and Developing Countries*, ed. Carla P. Freeman (Cheltenham, UK: Edward Elgar, 2015), 445–65.
92. Sentiments expressed by Indian participants in a track-two China-India dialogue organized by the Lee Kuan Yew School of Public Policy at the National University of Singapore, March 10–11, 2017.
93. Ibid.
94. Ibid.
95. Chan, *Enduring Rivalries*, 40.
96. See note 9.
97. Supratim Dey, "Assam to Take a Leaf out of China's Flood Control Measures," *Business Standard*, June 17, 2016, http://www.business-standard.com /article/current-affairs/assam-to-take-a-leaf-out-of-china-s-flood-control-measures -116061700862_1.html.

PART III

STRATEGIES

Chapter 8

Himalayan Standoff

Strategic Culture and the China-India Rivalry

ANDREW SCOBELL

Interstate rivalry is a normal and indeed natural dynamic in international relations. States are inherently competitive and tend to view other states with suspicion, especially major powers that perceive other major powers as threatening or at least as potential threats. But the process by which one state identifies another state as a prime rival is learned because the characteristics of any rivalry lie in the eyes of the beholder. While realism is valuable in understanding and interpreting international relations, other theoretical approaches, notably constructivism, can be useful supplements.

What explains the existence, strength, scope, and longevity of the rivalry between the People's Republic of China (PRC) and the Republic of India? While strategic culture did not trigger the competition, strategic culture has exacerbated its intensity and span and prolonged the rivalry between Beijing and New Delhi. This chapter employs the rubric of strategic culture to illuminate and interpret the contours of the rivalry between the PRC and India. The chapter articulates a "two-faced" conception of strategic culture and discerns a distinctive variant of an extended rivalry that contains elements of both competition and cooperation.[1] It contends that China and India confront each other in a "Himalayan standoff." In contrast to the better-known "Mexican standoff" in a Hollywood Western, Beijing and New Delhi confront a chronic, long-term condition rather than an acute, short-term crisis situation. Unlike gunslingers, the two Asian rivals are not confronting a life-and-death situation requiring an immediate decision on what course of action they should take. According to John Garver, China and India have a "deep and enduring geopolitical rivalry."[2] While gunfighters must swiftly decide whether to escalate (i.e., shoot first) or to de-escalate (i.e., back away slowly without lowering one's weapon), China and India each have the luxury of being able to deliberate on their next move without great urgency. Moreover, instead of being in close proximity with weapons pointed at each other in a tense face-off, China and India have considerable distance between them—being separated by a vast mountain range.

This chapter first outlines the distinctive characteristics of the China-India rivalry by highlighting the elements of a Himalayan standoff through a comparison with a Mexican standoff. Next, the impact of "two faces" of strategic culture is analyzed to illuminate the impact of this dynamic on this enduring rivalry. Lastly, this chapter draws some implications for the future of this ongoing rivalry. While this chapter examines both rivals, the coverage is skewed toward the dominant player in the Himalayan standoff—China.

THE DIMENSIONS OF A "HIMALAYAN STANDOFF"

By "rivalry" I mean an antagonistic relationship between two states embroiled in "long-term hostility" and competition manifested in "multiple disputes, continuing disagreements and the threat of the use of force."[3] A significant interstate rivalry between great powers contains at least four dimensions: identification, intensity, scope, and durability. An examination of each variable in turn highlights the difference between two types of standoffs.

First, a rival must be identified. Unlike in a Mexican standoff, where one's rival is obvious—he has his loaded firearm pointing directly at you—in a Himalayan standoff the identity of one's primary rival or rivals is not always so immediately evident. Typically a state has multiple neighbors and invariably is not on good terms with all of them. Indeed, there is likely to be some level of suspicion, if not tension, involved. Mao Zedong famously observed, "Who are our friends? Who are our enemies? These are questions of first importance."[4] Once one state identifies another as an enemy or a rival, this label tends to stick. While the label can change, assessments of this state and interpretations of its actions are likely to be made in ways that are consistent with its ascribed identity. Thus, the act of identifying a major rival is an important first step.

Second, while the degree of rivalry in a Himalayan standoff is significant, it is of a different kind of intensity than that of a Mexican standoff. In the latter, the intensity is extremely acute; in the former, the intensity is more enduring and chronic.[5] Moreover, the level of intensity can fluctuate across time, just as is the case with multiple flash points in the Asia-Pacific. These flash points are for China and putative rivals the Korean Peninsula, the East China Sea, the Taiwan

Strait, and the South China Sea. Noteworthy is that each of these hot spots is the manifestation of an enduring rivalry.

Third, a Himalayan standoff must have some significant ongoing causes in the real world—a record of discord or conflict, usually on multiple fronts and on an array of contentious issues: a war, a series of wars, ongoing military clashes, or a major unresolved dispute over land or water, for example. Thus the scope is broader than simply a one-off, testosterone-charged Mexican standoff. From New Delhi's perspective, China has not only fought one war directly with India in 1962 but also routinely skirmished along their common disputed frontier and waged war against India on multiple other occasions via a proxy power: Pakistan. Moreover, China provided key inputs that allowed Pakistan to develop a nuclear weapons program. From Beijing's perspective, India has long demonstrated its true colors on a range of issues, including consistently supporting the Tibetan independence movement by granting sanctuary to the Dalai Lama, hosting his Tibetan government-in-exile since 1959, and refusing to engage in good-faith negotiations to resolve territorial disputes.

Fourth, this great-power rivalry has been remarkably durable. While a Mexican standoff is short and sharp—although the situation is often artificially prolonged on film for maximum dramatic effect—a Himalayan standoff is characterized by long-term rivalry. Indeed, there is an extended history of rivalry, which generates considerable amounts of mutual suspicion and distrust. Moreover, while the rivalry is unmistakable, the relationship is marked by elements of both competition and cooperation.[6] Although China and India are rivals, they can and do cooperate on matters of mutual interest, such as trade and commerce. While the rivalry is not diminishing—let alone disappearing—each country recognizes that escalating the rivalry closer to full-blown war is not in anyone's interests.

STRATEGIC CULTURE HAS TWO FACES

I define "strategic culture" as "the set of fundamental and enduring assumptions about the role of collective violence in human affairs and the efficacy of applying force interpreted by a country's political and military elites."[7] Put another way, it is the impact of culture on strategy.

While the principal purveyors of a state's strategic culture narrative are the political and military elites within a country, this narrative can also resonate forcefully with a country's ordinary people who can also serve as keepers or curators of strategic culture. The popular narratives within rising powers such as China and India can be particularly potent, especially when the country has a long history of past glories and rich cultural traditions. These strategic traditions are widely viewed as unique and distinctive. While most countries perceive themselves as peace-loving and defensive-minded, in states such as China and India that are heirs to rich civilizations and great works of philosophy and treatises on statecraft and warfare, these feelings tend to be even stronger. More-over, these self-ascribed traditions are invariably contrasted with those of per-ceived rivals, which are often portrayed as violent and aggressive, with hostile and nefarious intentions. According to the former vice president of the Academy of Military Sciences (AMS) of the People's Liberation Army (PLA), retired lieu-tenant general Li Jijun, "Culture is the root and foundation of strategy. Strategic thinking . . . flows into the mainstream of a country or a nation's culture. Each country or nation's strategic culture cannot but bear the imprint of cultural traditions, which in a subconscious and complex way, prescribes and defines strategy making."[8]

In this conception, culture is part context and part lens—a variable that shapes the menu of options available to an actor in various situations, as well as affecting an actor's perceptions or images of self and others.[9] The presence of strategic cul-ture can be so all-pervasive that its existence is unnoticed and its impact is unrec-ognized. Moreover, an actor's assumptions based on it may be so readily accepted that the stereotypes or biases it produces are not even challenged or questioned.[10] Of course, perceptions may not be consistent with reality. For example, despite firmly held beliefs in Beijing and New Delhi that their countries' respective stra-tegic traditions are distinctive, one objective scholarly comparison of the strategic cultures of China and India reveals no discernible differences.[11]

Strategic culture is a powerful dynamic because it is intimately intertwined with questions of national identities and national myths. Military might and economic clout are important material characteristics of any noteworthy state—indeed, these are defining features of a great power. And yet ideational factors are also important. The influence of a country's perception of its own place in the international system—past, present, and future—on its goals, policies, and actions should not be underestimated. Identities and myths are not formed in isolation. Indeed, identity tends to be shaped and molded not just as a conse-quence of historical experience but also with reference to the experience and interactions with other states. Strategic culture narratives are defined as much by what they are believed to be as by what they are not believed to be. In other words, strategic culture identities and myths are not constructed in a vacuum.

The vast majority of strategic culture analyses have limited their attention to the impact of strategic culture to explain how one country's own strategic culture influences its strategic behavior. In doing so, however, scholars have only grasped half of the story and missed the strategic cultural image that a country's political and military elite hold of a particular adversary or potential adversary. Leaders' perceptions of another country's capabilities, activities, and intentions are filtered through how these elites conceive of the other country's strategic culture. This writer has conducted exploratory research on China's "second face of strategic culture" focused on the United States, Japan, and India.[12]

Strategic culture provides the context within which national leaders make decisions and the lens through which a country's civilian and military elites perceive themselves and their own actions, as well as those of their counterparts in other countries. The former, what I call the "first face of strategic culture," concerns a country's self-image—the perceptions and realities of its own dominant strategic traditions and how these interact and produce outcomes. The latter, what I label the "second face of strategic culture," involves the image constructed in the minds of these leaders regarding another country's dominant strategic traditions. These images are "the preconceived stereotype of the strategic disposition of another nation, state, or people that is derived from a selective interpretation of history, traditions, and self-image."[13]

IDENTIFICATION

Indians and Chinese both tend to consider their respective countries as the rightful hegemon of Asia. While neither New Delhi nor Beijing directly seeks to advance its regional or continental hegemonic ambitions through military conquest, each believes that it is perfectly justified to use force in defense of its vital interests against external threats and to protect putative geographic spheres of influence against encroachments from outsiders. China and India look to each other as rivals and generate "conflicting nationalist narratives that lead patriots of the two sides [i.e., China and India] to look to the same arenas in attempting to realize their nation's modern greatness."[14] Moreover, the elites of each country believe that because of current substantial political, military, and economic clout and past glories—magnificent civilizations and sprawling empires—their particular state is destined to lead. While each country acknowledges the other's storied past, each considers the other to be an unworthy rival in the contemporary era.

India's First Face

The overwhelming majority of Indians perceive their country as the rightful dominant power in the Asian subcontinent, as well as a leader in Asia and the wider world. They also view twenty-first-century India as a peaceful and righteous state that is heir to a glorious and ancient civilization. According to Stephen Cohen, "India sees itself as a civilizationally blessed, responsible, and peaceful state."[15] Hindu nationalism is a potent dynamic in contemporary India that tends to amplify these self-perceptions. While multiple strands of Indian strategic culture have been identified, according to Kanti Bajpai all of them "recognize that interests, power, and violence are staples of international relations" and that a state has the right to protect itself.[16] Moreover, it appears that the adherents of each of the three schools of strategic culture defined by Bajpai—Nehruvianism, neoliberalism, and hyperrealism—would consider themselves to be Indian nationalists.[17] "At the core of India's nationalist narrative," according to Garver, "is the notion that India is a great nation whose radiant influence molded a wide swath of the world beyond its boundaries."[18] Indians perceive their country as a moral exemplar that has not been afforded proper respect and that its efforts on behalf of the developing world have not been fully acknowledged. India sees itself as championing the third world since 1947 and spearheading the Non-Aligned Movement since the Bandung Conference of 1955. Moreover, as one of the largest states in the developing world—second only to China in population—and one of the very few to remain a vibrant democracy, Indians feel they deserve more deference and formal recognition. An appropriate move in the eyes of many Indians would be for their country to become a permanent member of the United Nations Security Council (UNSC).

India's Second Face

Indians naturally compare their country to China and either think of the two as equals or—as India's first prime minister, Jawaharlal Nehru, did—consider China to be India's "younger brother."[19] Consequently, New Delhi firmly believes that it deserves the same treatment—if not better—as Beijing, which after all already has a permanent seat on the UNSC. Moreover, India believes that China has been active behind the scenes to block its efforts to join the body on a permanent basis.[20]

Indians acknowledge that China is the home of another great civilization on the Asian landmass. However, many Indians perceive China to be the home of a very different strategic tradition, an aggressive and conflict-prone culture in stark contrast to what Indians perceive to be their own peace-loving and moralistic one, confirmed in 1962 by China's perceived "betrayal" in an unprovoked and sudden attack and subsequent unwillingness to negotiate in good faith to resolve the two countries' border dispute.[21] According to one scholar of China, a firmly held view in New Delhi—especially prevalent within Indian government civilian and military bureaucracies—is that "China is inherently an aggressive country" that will "show its teeth" once it has accumulated overwhelming power.[22]

Hyperrealism and garden-variety realism are well represented in the Indian national security community. The author's extended—albeit modest—interactions with military and civilian analysts based in New Delhi going back several decades reveal a consistent theme of wariness about China and a perception that China presents a very serious enduring threat to India. If not directly threatening, China is at least viewed as suppressing or sabotaging India's aspirations in subtle or indirect ways. According to one Indian analyst, "While China professes a policy of peace and friendliness towards India, its deeds are clearly aimed at the *strategic encirclement of India* in order to marginalise India in Asia and tie it down to the Indian sub-continent."[23] Of particular note, Indians believe that the strategic rationale undergirding China's long-standing "all-weather relationship" with India's truculent neighbor Pakistan is to check India's efforts to establish a secure and peaceful sphere of influence on the subcontinent.

China's First Face

The image of their own country held by many Chinese elites is of a stirring gentle giant emerging from an extended period of incapacitation. China, they believe, is in the midst of a peaceful rise on an upward trajectory destined to resume its rightful place in Asia and the world. The dominant strategic culture narrative within China is that of a weak and defenseless country exploited and violated by more militarily potent and aggressive Western powers.[24] While China was technologically inferior to these oppressors, many Chinese insist it was morally and ethically more highly evolved. According to the narrative, European states were driven by a culture of violence and materialism, whereby China was governed by a culture that stressed harmony and spiritual fulfillment. The Chinese narrative includes not only European states among the mix of imperialists but also the United States and Japan. While Americans like to think of themselves as qualitatively different from Old World European empire-builders with regard to their interactions with Asia, Chinese tend to lump them all together as unethical and focused on military means to achieve material gains.[25]

China's Second Face

Chinese elites tend to perceive India as an ambitious and pushy pretender to great-power status. Chinese analysts have characterized India disparagingly as having unrealistic pretensions of national greatness. They have used the term "great-power dreams," or "*daguo meng*," in a derogatory manner as a way of demeaning India's sky-high aspirations.[26] Ironically, China under Xi Jinping has now articulated its own "dream" of national rejuvenation. Chinese acknowledge that contemporary India is heir to an ancient and glorious civilization. However, India possesses overly ambitious aspirations of regional and even global hegemony, according to many Chinese elites, which are seen in part as inherited from the country's former British overlords.[27]

While China has ranked its rivalries with other states higher, India's salience shoots up significantly when it appears to be allied or collaborating with these other states against China. During the Cold War, China's main rivals were initially the United States and then the Soviet Union. At the height of the 1971 India-Pakistan War, the PRC ambassador to the United Nations, Huang Hua, expressed alarm to US national security adviser Henry Kissinger that "the Soviet Union and India are now progressing along an extremely dangerous track in the subcontinent. . . . This is a step to encircle China."[28] Since the Cold War, the key Chinese rivals have been the United States and Japan. Yet India's importance as a rival has risen as China has observed improved relations between Washington and New Delhi and between Tokyo and New Delhi; both budding relationships are perceived as emerging coalitions to counter China's rise. Since President Bill Clinton's breakthrough visit to India in 2000, while relations between the United States and India have improved significantly, the warming has fallen far short of an alliance. However, if the Washington–New Delhi relationship were to strengthen even more, then India would become a more prominent rival in China's eyes.[29]

Nevertheless, as India's economy continues to grow steadily and since Prime Minister Narendra Modi—a dynamic and charismatic leader—took office in 2014, Beijing has been taking New Delhi more seriously as a rival. Given the size, population, and growing clout of its southern neighbor, China has begun to view India as a more worthy competitor for influence on the Asian landmass. While India is primarily seen as the hegemon of South Asia, which after all, is New Delhi's own neighborhood, physically separated from China by massive mountain ranges, this is construed with dismay in Beijing.[30] In part this is because China fears that once India has cemented its hold on this area, it will expand its influence into other areas, including Central Asia and Southeast Asia. (Indeed India is already making moves in these directions.)

In sum, realism and geopolitics identify China and India as rivals in Asia and beyond. Yet the rivalry is accentuated by two faces of strategic culture. Subsequent sections will highlight how strategic culture exacerbates bilateral tensions and fortifies negative stereotypes in both countries.

INTENSITY

In countries with thousands of years of history and splendid ancient civilizations, strategic culture narratives can be intense. This is especially true for China and India. The narratives in each country are vivid and impassioned as both contemporary rising powers seek to recapture past glories and status.

India's First Face

India sees itself as the heir to a rich and glorious civilization with splendid monuments and stunning artifacts attesting to a record of remarkable accomplishments and enduring legacies. Symbols of India's past grandeur include numerous lavish temples and palaces, but the most famous is almost certainly the Taj Mahal. The structure, which dates back to the mid-seventeenth century, was built by Mughal emperor Shan Jahan as a memorial for his favorite wife.

India's cultural heritage and scholarship include literary masterpieces, philosophical texts, and religious scriptures. India's sacred traditions include not just Hinduism but also Buddhism and Jainism, as well as Sikhism and Islam. The corpus of writings includes the *Arthashastra*, which dates back some two thousand years. It was reportedly written by Kautilya, an adviser to a South Asian ruler in the fourth century BC. According to two scholars, the treatise is "an inspiration to modern Indian strategic and military thought."[31] The *Arthashastra* stresses adaptability in both politics and conduct on the battlefield rather than a single-minded focus on violence and attrition. Although the text has a hard realpolitik flavor and sociologist Max Weber compared it to Machiavelli's *The Prince*, others have tended to focus on its admonitions to avoid war and emphasis on the importance of moral rulers who look out for the "welfare of the people."[32] Attention to India's religious traditions such as Buddhism and Hinduism, which stress vegetarianism and the sacredness of bovines, respectively, frequently lead observers to stereotypical perceptions of India as a country of mystics, meditators, and pacifists.[33]

Indians themselves emphasize the powerful influence of a Nehruvian strand of strategic culture. While Nehru emphasized principles and dialogue, "he was no pacifist."[34] Moreover, he represents only one, albeit highly influential, school of Indian statecraft. Indeed, the hyperrealism school is also influential and tends to dominate India's national security community. Moreover, the interaction between the three schools is likely to have a combined effect. India has a clear record of the repeated use of military force since 1947. Certainly instability and turmoil on the country's periphery have set the conditions for serial conflicts, crises, and a South Asian rivalry with Pakistan: The partition of British-ruled India produced on the subcontinent an environment prone to tensions. While it would be unfair to assign blame for the use of armed conflict to New Delhi, it is fair to say that India has believed itself to be fully justified in using force to protect its national interests. Moreover, India continues to perceive itself as a righteous, peace-loving, and nonexpansionist state, very consistent with the principles of Nehru and Mohandas K. Gandhi. A logical conclusion, therefore, is that multiple strands are operative, producing a hybrid Indian strategic culture prepared to employ military force, acquire nuclear weapons, and develop a sizeable navy.[35]

India's Second Face

India's perception of the rivalry has been more intense than China's. One scholar has dubbed this a "one-sided rivalry" to underscore that India, as the weaker of the two Asian giants, is far more preoccupied with China than Beijing is with New Delhi (see below).[36] A strong strand of thinking in India views China as "aggressive and expansionist."[37] Indeed, India feels far more threatened by China's actions than vice versa. For example, China's nuclear weapons are of considerable concern to India and have been cited by prominent Indians as a prime justification for New Delhi acquiring its own nuclear capability. In early May 1998, India's minister of defense, George Fernandes, publicly labeled China as his country's "potential threat number one." In addition, the leaked contents of a letter written by Prime Minister Atal Bihari Vajpayee to President Clinton the same year identified China as the primary threat motivating India to acquire nuclear weapons.[38] Chinese responses to this rhetoric from Indian leaders, widely quoted—and misquoted—in China, have reflected more annoyance than alarm.[39] The contrasting commentaries reveal a distinct asymmetry of threat perceptions between India and China.[40]

Many Indians depict China's strategic tradition as violent and/or devious, equating China's strategic culture with one classic of strategy and warfare: Sun Tzu's *Bingfa*, usually translated as *The Art of War*. While China has an array of classic writings on strategy, a focus on *The Art of War* reinforces the stereotype of brutal and deceitful Beijing, which is contrasted with a nonviolent and righteous New Delhi.[41]

China's First Face

For China, culture has long been considered a key dimension in explaining and interpreting security policy and military strategy.[42] Many scholars of history and international politics have emphasized the impact of thousands of years of Chinese civilization and highlighted the pervasive influence of Confucianism on China's foreign and defense policies.[43] Moreover, contemporary Chinese analysts and strategists fervently assert the centrality of culture in guiding the security policy of the PRC since its founding in 1949.[44] The result is a presumption that the PRC possesses a monistic strategic culture that averts war, is predisposed to a defensive military posture, and stands in stark contrast to the bellicose and aggressive strategic cultures of many other countries. Indeed, in contrast to many foreign analysts, who tend to interpret *The Art of War* as exemplifying a Chinese predilection toward deception, Chinese strategists view Sun Tzu as having had a clear aversion to violence and a preference for nonkinetic options in warfare.

The Great Wall is frequently held up as the most striking symbol of the potency of a persistent pacifist, nonexpansionist, defense-minded strategic stance. While the Great Wall is an apt symbol of a romanticized image of Chinese strategic culture, the reality behind the genesis of this impressive fortification and the accompanying pervasive belief in a monistic strategic tradition is that they are figments of the collective contemporary Chinese imagination. Nevertheless, these formidable myths exert real influence on how Chinese leaders and society perceive the policies and actions of the PRC, as well as those of other states. Their effect is especially worrisome because it tends to exacerbate the security dilemma dynamic in the Asia-Pacific region, adversely impacting China's relations with other key countries, including India.[45]

Chinese leaders overwhelmingly tend to view their own strategic tradition as one consistent with the Great Wall strand of strategic culture. But this perception is at odds with the reality that guides Beijing to act offensively and use military force vigorously, all the while rationalizing it as defensive and reluctant acts. Thus, the mantra of "peaceful rise"—or "peaceful development"—is not superficial propaganda but reflects the fervent beliefs of those articulating it.[46] The logic is that China is fundamentally different from other rising powers and that history will not repeat itself. Arguably the most important strategic principle of the PLA is "active defense." According to Chinese strategists, this doctrinal concept in many ways encapsulates the traditional Chinese penchant for fighting only in self-defense. But a more careful analysis reveals that the concept is highly elastic and encompasses all manner of military actions, including preemptive strikes. Indeed, one thoughtful analyst of Chinese strategy contends that "active defense strategy does not acknowledge the difference . . . between defense and offense."[47] The fact is that China labels every use of military force since 1949—including the brief Himalayan border war of 1962—as a "self-defense counter-attack."[48] At the same time, Chinese leaders tend to perceive other states as more disposed to use force than China and more focused on aggressive and nefarious intentions, especially vis-à-vis China.

China's Second Face

China's view of India is of a country hopelessly torn by religious, sectarian, and ethnic divisions that produce a smoldering instability. The country's problems are compounded by what Chinese analysts perceive as India's "immature democracy," as well as "slower growth and continuing economic problems."[49] Consequently, many in China see New Delhi's aspirations to a greater role in Asia and beyond as wildly unrealistic. The tendency toward a dismissiveness of India is vividly captured in a poem Mao wrote in 1974, in which the Chinese leader used the cow as a metaphor for India. According to a Chinese commentary on the poem, a cow "is only food or for people to ride and for pulling carts; it has no particular talents. The cow would starve to death if its master did not give it grass to eat. . . . Even though this cow may have great ambitions, they are futile."[50] This general Chinese lack of great concern for developments in India is exemplified by Beijing's response to New Delhi's demonstration of nuclear capability in May 1998. Chinese elites appeared to take this in stride, even though the timing of India's nuclear test apparently came as a surprise to them.[51]

Despite this, some Chinese believe that India does possess the potential to play the role of spoiler or troublemaker for China. This is based on such things as the challenge New Delhi poses to Tibet and the ongoing border disputes, as well as India's maritime designs on the Indian Ocean and South China Sea (see below). Moreover, Chinese analysts have identified India as one of the primary sources of the so-called China Threat Theory—a paradigm that is much reviled.[52]

An examination of the intensity of the dyadic relationship underscores the asymmetry of this rivalry, whereby India is far more focused on China than vice versa. In Indian eyes, China is the central challenge; yet, for China, India is simply a "mid-level ranking" national security priority.[53] Despite this asymmetry, the timbre of the rivalry is heightened by two faces of strategic culture.

SCOPE

The scope of strategic culture is wide in terms of keepers, artifacts, and manifestations.[54] These keepers include not just elites but also society at large in both India and China. The artifacts include religious texts and epic novels. The manifestations include popular myths and cultural stereotypes. In looking at the writings of influential strategists, scholars have concentrated on what has been called the "great tradition" or "high culture" and all but ignored the arena of popular culture or what has been called the "little tradition." Most societies possess rich and varied folk traditions with graphic depictions of war and violence and are replete with colorful heroes and powerful symbols. These traditions greatly influence members of a society as they develop and imbue them with values, ideals, and images that are likely to remain with them for the rest of their lives.[55]

India's First Face

India has a strong sense of its own national identity and a wide array of symbols and artifacts to reinforce its self-perception of a great civilization and a contemporary narrative of a national project to reclaim its rightful place among the great powers of the twenty-first century. India is justifiably proud of its democratic tradition and the fact that it continues to be a parliamentary system in face of many challenges and despite a significant rate of illiteracy. Moreover, India's military prowess, its nuclear arsenal, and its aircraft carrier program make it a member of an exclusive club. Only a handful of states possess these accoutrements, and New Delhi is justifiably proud of these achievements. In recent decades these accomplishments have been accompanied by a strong and consistent rate of economic growth. Moreover, Indians are proud of their arts, and India possesses a large and vibrant feature film industry. Bollywood has not just an avid following within India but also a wide fan base around the world. Indians tend to believe that "educational and cultural diplomacy—aspects of India's civilizational power— are important ways of persuading other powers of India's inherent strength and the foolishness of trying to confront India in its own region."[56]

India's Second Face

India of course compares itself to China on many fronts. New Delhi views Beijing as a rival for wealth, power, and influence in matters that include industry, trade, foreign direct investment, and information technology (IT). Despite this, there is significant cooperation and interaction. For example, bilateral trade is expanding, and China is now India's most important trading partner.[57] Moreover, there is cooperation between the two states' IT sectors, and Bangalore is widely respected in China as a center of technological excellence and entrepreneurial dynamism.[58] However, New Delhi has publicly rejected participation in Beijing's most ambitious external economic initiative to date, the One Belt One Road (OBOR) project. OBOR is President Xi Jinping's flagship foreign policy effort, formally launched in 2013 with the expressed goal of funding and building a network of massive infrastructure projects across Asia, the Middle East, Africa, and Europe. New Delhi turned down a May 2017 invitation to attend an OBOR summit in Beijing and took the opportunity to issue a critique of the initiative, justified on the bases of principle and national interest.[59] The website of the Ministry of External Affairs criticized the absence of "universally recognized international norms" in the implementation of the initiative and singled out the China-Pakistan Economic Corridor (CPEC) project as one "that ignores . . . [India's] core concerns on sovereignty and territorial integrity."[60] In fact, the CPEC—the largest single commitment of Chinese OBOR funds to date at $46 billion—includes the construction of infrastructure in areas administered by Pakistan that India claims.

Yes, the scope of contested areas where China is encroaching on India is growing. Certainly this is the dominant perception within India's national security community. Beijing continues to challenge New Delhi's territorial claims in the Himalayas. Recent border incidents include one in September 2014, just prior to Xi Jinping's visit to India, and a mid-2017 confrontation between hundreds of Indian and Chinese troops in Doklam on the disputed frontier of China and the lilliputian Himalayan kingdom of Bhutan. What one respected observer described as "one of the most serious standoffs between New Delhi and Beijing in three decades" is further complicated by the fact that Bhutan does not have diplomatic relations with China and looks to India for its defense.[61]

Moreover, China is now starting to contest India's primacy in maritime South Asia. China has taken greater interest in sea lines of communication through the Strait of Malacca across the Indian Ocean to the Middle East, Africa, and Europe, and Beijing is actively engaged in establishing what two Indian participants at a workshop sponsored by an American consulting firm dubbed a "string of pearls" around the rim of the Indian Ocean.[62] India takes umbrage at Chinese efforts to expand its influence within South Asia beyond its long-standing alignment with Pakistan. While China's growing reliance on trade and dependence on imported energy understandably translate into greater attention by Beijing in this body of water, India sounds alarm bells at China's increased security activities and expanded military presence in the region. Chinese efforts to develop port facilities in Myanmar, Sri Lanka, Maldives, and Pakistan have been followed by the establishment of a military logistics facility in Djibouti on the Gulf of Aden.

China's First Face

Political leaders, military brass, and strategic thinkers in academia and research institutes are central players in China's strategic culture narrative—they generate, control, and interpret it. For example, in the post-Mao reform era since the 1980s, the PRC has rediscovered China's rich cultural heritage. But this cultural reawakening was carefully orchestrated by Chinese Communist Party (CCP) leaders as a way to bolster their sagging political legitimacy. Glorifying China's past strongly implied that they were the rightful heirs to a long and distinguished succession of Chinese dynasties. There may be no better symbol of this process than the official rehabilitation of Confucius and revival of Confucianism. During the era of Mao Zedong (1949–1976), the man and his corpus of thought were mercilessly attacked as backward and feudal. Both the philosopher and his philosophy are not only back in favor today but also prominently propagated by CCP leaders.[63] Confucian temples have been refurbished, classes in Confucianism are well subscribed, and Confucius Institutes—funded by the PRC Ministry of Education—are proliferating across the globe.[64] The scope and scale of this state-sponsored revival of Confucianism serves to reinforce the self-image of a peace-loving and righteous China.

The most prominent artifacts of strategic culture are classic works of strategy and statecraft or official doctrine, and it is on these texts that scholars such as Iain Johnston have largely focused. For his study of the Ming dynasty (1368–1644), Johnston looked at the seven military classics, including *The Art of War*, that were combined into a single corpus of work in 1083.[65] For Johnston's later study of strategic culture in Mao's China, he examined Mao's military writings.[66]

Certainly, in post-Mao China official documents and authoritative military writings are quite numerous and readily accessible to scholars and analysts inside and outside of China. One of the most accessible documents is the biannual PRC defense white paper. There have been eight iterations of the white paper, each published in Chinese and English. These are propaganda, of course, but they also represent authentic and authoritative articulations and rationalizations of PRC official policy and PLA doctrine. Indeed, the lead drafters of the official document are researchers at the AMS—China's most important think tank on matters of strategy and doctrine, which answers directly to the Central Military Commission (China's equivalent of the US Joint Chiefs of Staff). The document is also coordinated with high-level civilian entities. Probably the most authentic version of this document was the first white paper issued in 1998. Subsequent iterations become more polished and increasingly steeped in the jargon of international relations theory. Other authoritative writings include volumes and journals published by the AMS Press and the PLA National Defense University Press. Books by PLA strategists such as *The Science of Military Strategy* and *The Science of Campaigns* and articles in journals such as *China Military Science* provide valuable insights into high-level Chinese military discourse and logic.[67] The overarching theme of these documents and texts is of a civilization with an enduring ethical and defensive-minded strategic tradition.

China has a vibrant repertoire of classic dramas, legends, and novels often drawn from ancient Chinese history and well known to most Chinese. One of the most famous of these is the epic *Romance of the Three Kingdoms*, a novel compiled more than six hundred years ago from much older oral accounts. Just as popular but of more recent vintage are wartime films, dramas, and soap operas that seem to play incessantly on Chinese television. Many are set in the era of the so-called Anti-Japanese War during the 1930s and 1940s when Japan invaded and occupied vast areas of China. The cumulative effect of this rich array of cultural artifacts is to highlight a recent history of national victimhood along with a potent narrative of past civilizational glories.

China's Second Face

China's hyperambitious great-power stereotype of India is reinforced by the history of Beijing's relationship with New Delhi since 1949. After initially enjoying good relations with New Delhi, Beijing eventually perceived that its southern neighbor was turning on its erstwhile partner in the Non-Aligned Movement. From China's perspective, treachery was behind New Delhi's reception of the Dalai Lama following the 1959 Tibetan revolt and the subsequent establishment of a government-in-exile in India. New Delhi's goal, as perceived by Beijing, was to split China through a combination of support for Tibetan independence and efforts to aggressively "nibble" away at Chinese territory in the Himalayas.[68] China's response was the 1962 border war with India. Despite multiple rounds of border talks since the 1980s, China's most sizeable and significant unresolved territorial land dispute in the twenty-first century is with India.

In sum, the scope of the China-India rivalry is broad, getting wider, and amplified by two faces of strategic culture.

DURABILITY

The China-India rivalry is enduring. Although it can be managed, the durability of the strategic culture narratives in each country makes the rivalry difficult to dissolve or abandon. These narratives and associated myths are powerful and hard to break. Moreover, the durability of the India-China rivalry is not surprising given the number of contentious issues. A core tension is the border dispute, which continues to simmer despite multiple rounds of on-again, off-again talks that seem to make "glacial progress."[69] And yet despite real cooperation between the two states and growing trade, mutual distrust remains.

India's First Face

India has strong and enduring myths about its national greatness and destiny. These are included in works of strategy such as the *Arthashastra* and Hindu Vedas. These myths highlight moral uprightness and underscore the deviousness of other states. New Delhi's grand strategy focuses on establishing and securing South Asia as India's legitimate sphere of influence and justifies expanded Indian influence in Central and Southeast Asia.[70] Indian strategic thought displays a readiness to use force in defense of these interests, all the while perceived as a last resort, and to build a nuclear arsenal.[71]

India's Second Face

India's enduring myths about China depict its northern neighbor as untrustworthy and threatening. Nevertheless, New Delhi sees outright rivalry and direct conflict as highly undesirable for both countries. Moreover, it is avoidable. While underlying tensions and competition are unavoidable and indeed natural, this does not mean that India and China cannot cooperate for their mutual benefit. New Delhi has permitted China to gain observer status in the South Asia Association for Regional Cooperation and works with Beijing in the BRICS (Brazil, Russia, India, China, South Africa) framework. More recently, India has joined the Asian Infrastructure Investment Bank and the Shanghai Cooperation Organization along with Pakistan in 2017.

According to one Indian official interviewed in 2001, "There will always be a sense of rivalry between China and India. It hasn't gone away regardless of how many centuries we go back. But in ten to fifteen years this rivalry will not degenerate into anything. We don't want it, and they don't want it."[72]

China's First Face

Despite the outstanding research of scholars such as Arthur Waldron and Iain Johnston, which seriously undermines the myths of a single Great Wall and a monistic Confucian strategic tradition extending back more than two thousand years, both myths remain very potent in China. Waldron's work demonstrates that there is no Chinese cultural proclivity to building walls and that what we now call the Great Wall only dates back to the Ming dynasty.[73] Johnston, meanwhile, who focuses on the Ming dynasty, discerns the existence of two strands of Chinese strategic culture: a "*parabellum*" (or realpolitik) one and a "Confucian-Mencian" one. Moreover, he concluded that of these two strands, only one—the realpolitik strand—was operative and that the second one was purely for "idealized discourse."[74] Other research emphasizes the influence of an array of enduring traditions such as legalism and Daoism, as well as popular myths and folk traditions.[75]

This author's own research also discerns the existence of two strands of Chinese strategic culture, but unlike Johnston I argue that *both* the realpolitik and Confucian-Mencian strands are operative. In fact, the two strands interact in a dialectic fashion to produce a distinctive "Chinese cult of defense"—what I have dubbed the Great Wall strand of strategic culture. The outcome is that Chinese elites fervently believe that China is under the sway of a unique peace-loving, nonexpansionist, defensive-minded strategic tradition. Because of the interaction between different strands of strategic culture and the way China's strategists define "defense," virtually any use of force by China is defensive in nature.[76] Thus, paradoxically China is more disposed to use force when confronting a political-military crisis than it might otherwise be. Johnston's research suggests that China is a realpolitik power that historically has not shrunk from using force. This writer's own research has expanded on Johnston's basic findings, suggesting that while China's elites view the world in realpolitik terms, at the same time they perceive China's own strategic culture as Confucian or pacifist and defensive-minded.

China's Second Face

China views India as a long-term rival. But Beijing has tended to view New Delhi less as a peer or even near-peer competitor and more as a spoiler for China's ambitious national goals. According to a 1999 article in a Chinese scholarly journal, India has an extended record of "war adventures" in South Asia against Pakistan, in 1947, 1965, and 1971.[77] During the 1980s, India conducted military interventions in Sri Lanka and the Maldives, and before that, during the 1970s, India annexed the Portuguese colony of Goa and the independent Himalayan kingdom of Sikkim. Since the 1990s, India has embarked on ambitious initiatives in the maritime realm in the Indian Ocean and beyond.[78]

CONCLUSION

Given the respective sizes, national ambitions, and geographic proximity of China and India, it is simply natural that "neither country is entirely comfortable with the rise of the other."[79] But the sentiments Beijing and New Delhi feel are much more than mutual discomfort. The intensity, extensive scope, and extended duration of distrust and suspicion are much more than what would naturally exist between the two Asian giants. Strategic cultural images propagate stereotypes and exacerbate and prolong tensions. And yet "*because* so many sources of dispute exist between China and India, both sides have come to recognize the need to prevent these tensions from leading to costly, overt rivalry."[80] The result is what Mark Frazier labels "quiet competition" or what I call a Himalayan standoff.

China's first face of strategic culture is a Great Wall of the imagination, but its impact is very real. The genesis of the Great Wall is shrouded in the myth of the founding of the first unified Chinese state and inseparable from the myth of a monistic Chinese strategic culture—pacifist, defensive-minded, and non-expansionist. This myth is enormously potent, producing a compelling narrative, and the result is a cult of defense whereby Chinese tend to perceive their own country's military activities as always being defensive and nonthreatening to others—the "first face of strategic culture." Moreover, China tends to view other states, including India, as belligerent and threatening because they are believed to possess violent and aggressive strategic cultures—the "second face of strategic culture." Similar observations can be made about how Indian elites perceive their own strategic traditions and uses of force. As Stephen Cohen observes, "Indian stereotypes concerning the 'inscrutable,' arrogant, and self-centered Chinese abound."[81] Moreover, many of these same Indian leaders and analysts tend to view Chinese traditions and employments of military force in more alarming terms.

The above analysis suggests that the China-India rivalry is destined to persist. Can both sides continue to manage the Himalayan standoff? While this is quite possible, there are also reasons for great pessimism. First, dramatic innovations in weapon technology and qualitative advancements in the strategic capabilities of both India and China have rendered the highest mountains in the world no longer insurmountable barriers.[82] As Paul Bracken notes, "disruptive technologies" have resulted in the "death of distance": long-range ballistic missiles can deliver conventional or nuclear payloads across thousands of miles in a matter of minutes.

Second, the security dilemma may be particularly acute in the China-India rivalry, especially when combined with two virulent and clashing strategic-culture narratives.[83] Indeed, contemporary India and China each possess a strong nostalgia for a glorious distant past and a recent memory of being bullied by stronger powers, and they see themselves as aggrieved underdogs whose time has come to restore national greatness. The outcome is a stark contrast between the first and second faces of strategic culture, and the upshot is a very real inability in New Delhi and Beijing to appreciate the existence of security-dilemma spirals. Consequently there is an increased likelihood of tensions and crises that could escalate into military conflict.[84]

Third, the interactions of each rival with third states can complicate matters. From India's perspective, the complicating third parties are Pakistan and other states in the Asia-Pacific neighborhood. From China's perspective, the complicating third party is likely to be the United States. In conclusion, there is real danger that a series of tactical-level Mexican standoffs (i.e., smaller political-military crises) could escalate into a strategic-level Mexican standoff (i.e., a larger, earthshaking political-military crisis), which could displace the Himalayan standoff that has characterized China-India rivalry for decades.

NOTES

1. For discussion of this conception of "two faces," see Andrew Scobell, "China's Real Strategic Culture: A Great Wall of the Imagination," *Contemporary Security Policy* 35, no. 2 (2014): 211–26.
2. John W. Garver, *Protracted Contest: Sino-Indian Rivalry in the Twentieth Century* (Seattle: University of Washington Press, 2001), 4.
3. William R. Thompson, "Identifying Rivals and Rivalries in World Politics," *International Studies Quarterly* 45, no. 4 (December 2001): 574.
4. Mao Zedong, "Analysis of the Classes in Chinese Society (March 1926)," *Selected Works* (Beijing: Foreign Languages Press, 1967), 1:13.
5. On the important distinction between acute and chronic, see Andrew Scobell, "An Orderly, Pacific Asia or Asia-Pacific Powder Keg?," *Issues and Studies* 41, no. 1 (March 2005): 244–50. The essay is a review of Muthiah Alagappa, ed., *Asian Security Order* (Stanford, CA: Stanford University Press, 2003).
6. See, e.g., T.V. Paul's chapter 1 in this volume.
7. This is a slightly revised definition adapted from Scobell, "China's Real Strategic Culture"; and Alastair Iain Johnston, *Cultural Realism: Strategic Culture and Grand Strategy in Chinese History* (Princeton, NJ: Princeton University Press, 1995).

8. Cited in Andrew Scobell, *China and Strategic Culture* (Carlisle, PA: US Army War College, Strategic Studies Institute, May 2002), 1.

9. On culture as context, see, e.g., the discussion in Jeffrey S. Lantis, "Strategic Culture and National Security Policy," *International Studies Review* 4, no. 3 (December 2002): 87–113. On culture as perception/misperception, see, e.g., Christopher P. Twomey, *The Military Lens: Doctrinal Difference and Deterrence Failure in Sino-American Relations* (Ithaca, NY: Cornell University Press, 2010).

10. This paragraph draws on Scobell, "China's Real Strategic Culture," 213.

11. George J. Gilboy and Eric Heginbotham, *Chinese and Indian Strategic Behavior: Growing Power and Alarm* (New York: Cambridge University Press, 2012), chap. 2.

12. On Chinese perceptions of US and Japanese strategic culture images, see Scobell, *China and Strategic Culture*. On Chinese perceptions of Indian strategic culture images, see Andrew Scobell, "'Cult of Defense' and 'Great Power Dreams': The Influence of Strategic Culture on China's Relationship with India," in *South Asia 2020: Future Strategic Balances and Alliances*, ed. Michael R. Chambers (Carlisle, PA: US Army War College, Strategic Studies Institute, November 2002), 329–59.

13. Scobell, *China and Strategic Culture*, 2.

14. Garver, *Protracted Contest*, 10.

15. Stephen P. Cohen, *India: Emerging Power* (Washington, DC: Brookings Institution Press, 2001), 58.

16. Kanti Bajpai, "Indian Strategic Culture," in Chambers, *South Asia 2020*, 251.

17. Steven Hoffmann also identifies three "grand strategic" schools of thought—"moderate-realism," "Nehruvian idealism," and "ultra-realism," which seem to roughly correlate with Bajpai's three strands. See Hoffmann, "Perception and China Policy in India," in *The India-China Relationship: What the United States Needs to Know*, ed. Francine R. Frankel and Harry Harding (New York: Columbia University Press, 2004). Stephen Cohen also identified three distinct—albeit slightly different—worldviews: "Nehruvian mainstream," "conservative-realist," and "'Hindutva' (or revivalist Hindu) viewpoint." Cohen, *India*, 43.

18. Garver, *Protracted Contest*, 10.

19. Francine R. Frankel, "Introduction," in Frankel and Harding, *India-China Relationship*, 29.

20. Ashley J. Tellis, "China and India in Asia," in Frankel and Harding, *India-China Relationship*, 170–71.

21. Hoffmann, "Perception and China Policy," 148.

22. Giri Deshingkar quoted in Waheguru Pal Singh Sidhu and Jing-dong Yuan, *China and India: Cooperation or Conflict?* (Boulder, CO: Lynne Rienner, 2003), 145.

23. Cited in Tellis, "China and India," 138 (italics in original). See also Hoffmann, "Perception and China Policy," 49.

24. Zheng Wang, *Never Forget National Humiliation: Historical Memory in Chinese Politics and Foreign Relations* (New York: Columbia University Press, 2012).

25. Scobell, "China's Real Strategic Culture," 216–17.

26. Scobell, "Cult of Defense," 341–48.

27. Garver, *Protracted Contest*, 19.

28. Cited in Susan L. Shirk, "One-Sided Rivalry: China's Perceptions and Policies toward India," in Frankel and Harding, *India-China Relationship*, 79.

29. Ibid., 95.

30. Jing-dong Yuan, "China and the Indian Ocean: New Departures in Regional Balance," in *Deep Currents and Rising Tides: The Indian Ocean and International*

Security, ed. John Garofano and Andrea J. Dew (Washington, DC: Georgetown University Press, 2013), 160–61.

31. See the discussion in Gilboy and Heginbotham, *Chinese and Indian Strategic Behavior*, 29.
32. Ibid., 30–31.
33. This point is also made by Stephen Cohen. See *India*, 5.
34. Andrew Bingham Kennedy, *The International Ambitions of Mao and Nehru: National Efficacy Beliefs and the Making of Foreign Policy* (New York: Cambridge University Press, 2012), 159.
35. This is the conclusion of Stephen Cohen. See *India*, 63–65.
36. Shirk, "One-Sided Rivalry."
37. Bajpai, "Indian Strategic Culture," 272.
38. Shirk, "One-Sided Rivalry," 82–83.
39. Scobell, "Cult of Defense," 344.
40. Shirk, "One-Sided Rivalry," 83–89.
41. See, e.g., Hoffmann, "Perception and China Policy," 41.
42. This chapter draws on themes first outlined in Andrew Scobell, "Strategic Culture and China: IR Theory versus the Fortune Cookie?," *Strategic Insights* 4, no. 10 (2005).
43. See, e.g., John K. Fairbank, "Introduction," in John K. Fairbank and Frank Kierman, eds., *Chinese Ways in Warfare* (Cambridge, MA: Harvard University Press, 1965), 1–26; and Mark Mancall, *China at the Center: 300 Years of Chinese Foreign Policy* (New York: Free Press, 1984).
44. See, e.g., Peng Guangqian and Yao Youzhi, eds., *The Science of Military Strategy* (Beijing: Military Science Publishing House, 2005).
45. This paragraph draws from Scobell, "China's Real Strategic Culture," 211–12.
46. Zheng Bijian, *China's Peaceful Rise: Speeches of Zheng Bijian, 1997–2005* (Washington, DC: Brookings Institution Press, 2005).
47. See, e.g., the analysis in Scobell, *China's Use of Military Force: Beyond the Great Wall and the Long March* (Cambridge: Cambridge University Press, 2003), 34–35. These two quotes appear on p. 35.
48. Scobell, *China's Use of Military Force*, 32. The sources referenced are publications of the PLA's AMS.
49. Quotes come from Shirk, "One-Sided Rivalry," 94.
50. Cited in Garver, *Protracted Contest*, 113.
51. Author interviews in Beijing and Shanghai, May 1998.
52. See Deng Yong, "Reputation and the Security Dilemma: China Reacts to the China Threat Theory," in *New Directions in the Study of China's Foreign Policy*, ed. Alastair Iain Johnston and Robert S. Ross (Stanford, CA: Stanford University Press, 2006), 196–97 and table 7.1 on p. 193.
53. Garver, *Protracted Contest*, 381.
54. The following three paragraphs draw from Scobell, "China's Real Strategic Culture," 215–16.
55. Scobell, *China's Use of Military Force*, 23.
56. Cohen, *India: Emerging Power*, 63.
57. T. N. Srinivasan, "Economic Reforms and Global Integration," in Frankel and Harding, *India-China Relationship*, 219–66.
58. Shirk, "One-Sided Rivalry," 94.
59. Alyssa Ayers, "India Objects to China's One Belt and Road Initiative—and It Has a Point," *Forbes*, May 15, 2017, https://www.forbes.com/sites/alyssaayres/2017/05/15/india-objects-to-chinas-one-belt-and-road-initiative-and-it-has-a-point/#449e9db0b262.

60. "Official Spokesperson's Response to a Query on Participation of India in OBOR/ BRI Forum," May 13, 2017, Ministry of External Affairs, Government of India, http://mea.gov.in/media-briefings.htm?dtl/28463/Official_Spokespersons _response_to_a_query_on_participation_of_India_in_OBORBRI_Forum.

61. Ankit Panda, "Explaining the Political Geography at the Center of a Serious India-China Standoff in the Himalayas," *The Diplomat*, July 13, 2017, https:// thediplomat.com/2017/07/the-political-geography-of-the-india-china-crisis-at -doklam/. On the 2014 border incident, see Jason Burke and Tania Brani- gan, "India-China Border Standoff Highlights Tensions before Xi's Visit," *The Guardian*, September 16, 2014, https://www.theguardian.com/world/2014/sep /16/india-china-border-standoff-xi-visit.

62. Juli A. MacDonald, Amy Donahue, and Bethany Danyluk, *Energy Futures in Asia* (McLean, VA: Booz Allen Hamilton, 2004).

63. See, e.g., Zhang Tiejun, "Chinese Strategic Culture: Traditional and Present Fea- tures," *Comparative Strategy* 21, no. 2 (2002): 79–80.

64. For an overview of the revival of Confucianism, see Daniel A. Bell, *China's New Confucianism: Politics and Everyday Life in a Changing Society* (Princeton, NJ: Princeton University Press, 2008). On Confucius Institutes, see James F. Para- dise, "China and International Harmony: The Role of Confucius Institutes in Bolstering Beijing's Soft Power," *Asian Survey* 49, no. 4 (2009): 647–69.

65. Johnston, *Cultural Realism*, 46. All seven works are summarized on pp. 40–44.

66. Ibid.; and Johnston, "Cultural Realism and Grand Strategy in Maoist China," in *The Culture of National Security*, ed. Peter Katzenstein (New York: Columbia University Press, 1996), 216–68.

67. See, e.g., Peng and Yao, *Science of Military Strategy*, which was translated into English from Chinese and is readily accessible.

68. Larry M. Wortzel, "Concentrating Forces and Audacious Action: PLA Lessons for the Sino-Indian Border War," in *The Lessons of History: The Chinese People's Liberation Army at 75*, ed. Laurie Burkitt, Andrew Scobell, and Larry M. Wortzel (Carlisle, PA: Strategic Studies Institute, US Army War College), 327–55. On Tibet as a key issue in the China-India rivalry, see Manjeet S. Pardesi, "Instability in Tibet and the Sino-Indian Rivalry: Do Domestic Politics Matter?," in *Asian Rivalries: Conflict, Escalation, and Limitations on Two-Level Games*, ed. Sumit Ganguly and William R. Thompson (Stanford, CA: Stanford University Press, 2012), 79–117.

69. Sumit Ganguly, "India and China: Border Issues, Domestic Integration and International Security," in Frankel and Harding, *India-China Relationship*, 122–24.

70. Hoffmann, "Perception and China Policy," 50–52; and Ashley Tellis, "China and India in Asia," 134–77.

71. Gilboy and Heginbotham, *Chinese and Indian Strategic Behavior*, chap. 2. See also Cohen, *India: Emerging Power*, chaps. 5 and 6.

72. Mark W. Frazier, "Quiet Competition and the Future of Sino-Indian Relations," in Frankel and Harding, *India-China Relationship*, 317.

73. Arthur Waldron, *The Great Wall of China: From History to Myth* (New York: Cambridge University Press, 1990).

74. Johnston, *Cultural Realism*, 173.

75. Scobell, *China's Use of Military Force*, 19–23. See also Mark Edward Lewis, *Sanctioned Violence in Early China* (Albany: State University of New York Press, 1990).

76. Scobell, *China's Use of Military Force*, chap. 2, esp. 26–39.

77. Cited in Scobell, "'Cult of Defense,'" 344.

78. Ibid.

79. Harry Harding, "The Evolution of the Strategic Triangle: China, India, and the United States," in Frankel and Harding, *India-China Relationship*, 342.

80. Frazier, "Quiet Competition," 295 (italics in original).

81. Cohen, *India: Emerging Power*, 257.

82. Paul Bracken, *Fire in the East: The Rise of Asian Military Power and the Second Nuclear Age* (New York: HarperCollins, 1999), 28.

83. Garver identifies the "two taproots" of the China-India rivalry as the security dilemma and what he characterizes as "conflicting nationalist narratives . . . to realize [a] . . . nation's modern greatness." Essentially Garver is describing strategic culture narratives. See *Protracted Contest*, 11.

84. This is especially the case for China. See, e.g., Andrew Scobell, "Learning to Rise Peacefully: China and the Security Dilemma," *Journal of Contemporary China* 21, no. 76 (2012): 713–21.

Chapter 9

Nuclear Deterrence in the China-India Dyad

VIPIN NARANG

The rise of India and China will mark a tectonic shift in Asian and global power relations. For the first time, the world is witnessing the simultaneous—though largely asymmetrical—rise of two nuclear powers in the global power hierarchy. This volume charts how the competition *between* India and China will affect the character of their joint rise and the implications for regional and global security. This chapter, in particular, focuses on the fact that both India and China possess nuclear weapons. How does that affect their rivalry and the prospect for conflict? What are the likely nuclear developments both will pursue, and will those be stabilizing or destabilizing to nuclear deterrence and regional stability?

Although India's most likely nuclear threat is Pakistan, which continues to expand its nuclear arsenal both in numbers (vertically) and across a diverse array of delivery platforms (horizontally) in support of "full spectrum deterrence," its more difficult strategic threat is undoubtedly China.[1] According to Indian nuclear planners, India needs to develop a force with sufficient survivability, reliability, and reach to threaten China's eastern seaboard in order to credibly deter Chinese nuclear use. It is in the process of doing so, expanding its land-based arsenal and trying to develop a submarine platform that is quiet enough and equipped with long-enough range to be able to survive and to hold major Chinese cities at risk. Much of India's current nuclear efforts are aimed at trying to improve survivability and reach against China in particular. On the other hand, for China, India is almost a nuclear afterthought, since Beijing has to size and deploy a force to deter the nuclear posture of the United States. Any force that can survive and threaten sufficient damage to deter the United States is more than sufficient to meet China's deterrence needs against India, which lacks

America's counterforce and damage-limitation architecture and antisubmarine warfare capabilities and is more proximate. What are the dynamics of the India-China nuclear competition? How does deterrence operate between these two powers, and under what conditions might it break down? These are the driving questions of this chapter.

I argue that both India and China have—with each other—what I term "assured retaliation" nuclear strategies in which both pledge to not be the first to use nuclear weapons in a conflict. This has the major stabilizing benefit that a mechanism to nuclear escalation in the India-China dyad is very difficult to conceive, even leaving aside the perceived veracity of each side's no-first-use (NFU) pledge. It also means that against each other, deterrence requirements are finite since each envisions nuclear use only in retaliation for strategic use by the adversary. Unlike the India-Pakistan nuclear relationship, which seems to have an infinite appetite for expansion because of Pakistan's threat of first use of nuclear weapons, the India-China nuclear relationship does not face major arms race pressures. India still has a way to go in order to achieve a reliable assured retaliation capability against China, as I will show, but China is long past that point with India.

Once India achieves the necessary capability, the relationship ought to settle into a stable, mutually deterrent relationship without much active effort. Barring the development of significant missile defenses by either side—both could saturate limited defenses, but extensive national missile defenses would be a different story—or the development of significant counterforce capabilities that, at the moment, only the United States possesses, there are few threats to the stability of this deterrence relationship. In fact, it is one of the few dyads in the world that meet the requirements of Robert Jervis's "nuclear revolution": mutually accepted second-strike forces. As Jervis and many defensive realists have posited, this is an incredibly stabilizing condition, reducing the risk of major conflict. This is further bolstered by the fact that despite an ongoing border dispute, neither India nor China has significant revisionist objectives against the other. This suggests that although the conditions for a stability-instability paradox may take hold, enabling India and China to fight limited conventional conflicts without escalation to the nuclear level, barring a major domestic political change in either country that may increase either side's revisionism toward the other, the prospect of major conventional war beyond the occasional skirmish is low. This level of nuclear stability is rare, however, and the fact that India and China largely find themselves enjoying the benefits of the nuclear revolution is important. It may be the only dyad in the system that currently does.[2]

INDIA'S NUCLEAR STRATEGY

At its broadest level, India's nuclear strategy is best described as assured retaliation against its primary threats, Pakistan and China. As I have shown elsewhere, India has a security position—enjoying advantageous geography against a potential Chinese invasion and with conventional superiority over Pakistan—in which it does not need to use nuclear weapons to deter or defeat a potential conventional invasion. This enables India to operationalize nuclear weapons purely to deter nuclear use against it. The central pillar of India's declaratory nuclear doctrine is thus its stated NFU pledge.[3] This pledge is backed by the fact that India's force structure consists of no tactical nuclear weapons but solely fission and boosted-fission devices for strategic nuclear retaliation. In the past, India undertook procedures to keep its nuclear forces disassembled and demated, which made a bolt-out-of-the-blue first-use highly improbable. As the technical condition of its forces improves and its command-and-control infrastructure enables the maintenance of forces at higher states of peacetime readiness, such as fully encapsulated (canisterized) systems, India is gradually moving to a force more ready than before. While India is seized with the dilemma of what forces it needs to develop in order to address the threat of early, lower-yield Pakistani nuclear use, the deterrence requirements for China are easier to identify, though harder to develop technologically: reliable and survivable long-range ballistic missiles and a submarine-based nuclear force.

In terms of nuclear warheads, India's most reliable design, which was tested in May 1998, is a simple plutonium-based implosion fission device, with a yield on the order of twenty kilotons, the size of the nuclear weapon used on Nagasaki in World War II. There was a very public debate about whether India has successfully designed a true thermonuclear (or fusion) weapon, after the May 1998 test of a purported such device fizzled.[4] One key scientist, K. Santhanam, publicly stated that the test failed. Another, R. Chidambaram, simply stated that the test met the government's objectives.[5] There are several points to make. First, there is a lot of confusion about whether India's design was a boosted-fission device, which inserts small quantities of fusion material to "boost" the yield to around two hundred kilotons, or whether it was a true thermonuclear device, which has a fission primary that ignites a fusion fuel to generate yields on the order of a megaton. This is important because the larger the yield, the fewer warheads required to threaten unacceptable damage on an adversary such as China, and there are also less stringent requirements on missile accuracy because the larger the blast radius, the less relevant it is where it is precisely delivered. It is almost certainly the case that Indian scientists are referring to boosted-fission devices, not true thermonuclear weapons, due to sheer design complexities of the latter, which would require further testing. Second, even if the May 1998 test of the boosted-fission device failed, the test probably did generate enough data to correct the design. It is thus reasonable to assume that India has a mix of pure-fission devices on the order of twenty-kiloton yields, as well as some boosted-fission devices on the order of two-hundred-kiloton yields, though the reliability of the latter is probably lower. Without further live testing, it is reasonable to assume that the reliability of India's warheads assigned to Pakistani targets are thus higher than those assigned to Chinese targets. Furthermore, as India increasingly moves to sea-based platforms, the warheads for its submarine-launched ballistic missiles may require novel designs and—again without full testing—may not be as reliable as its early simple-fission-device designs.

How does India intend to deliver these warheads against, particularly, China in the event it must retaliate with nuclear weapons? At least two features eliminate the reliance on aircraft as a delivery vector against Chinese strategic targets. First, the range needed to reach them requires multiple refuelings. Second, Chinese air defenses would likely destroy all incoming nuclear-capable aircraft given that they would have to traverse the entirety of Chinese territory (and India does not yet have nuclear-capable aircraft certified for carrier operations). Indeed, India in general is increasingly deemphasizing aircraft as a delivery platform and vector for nuclear weapons, with no more gravity bombs being produced for aircraft. And though there are several "nuclear-capable" and nuclear-certified aircraft in the Indian inventory, none is controlled by the Strategic Forces Command (SFC), the military organization created in 2003 to manage India's nuclear forces. They would have to be tasked to SFC in a crisis or conflict, which may not be the easiest bureaucratic arrangement if India intends to rely on aircraft as a primary nuclear-delivery platform. Even against Pakistan, India is deemphasizing aircraft and instead developing a more robust ballistic and cruise missile capability.

The backbone of the land-based force against China is therefore the Agni missile family, which ranges from eight hundred kilometers for the Agni-I (specifically for Pakistani targets) to three to five thousand kilometers for the Agni-V, which is obviously more China-specific. Indigenous development of solid-fuel, road- and rail-mobile ballistic missiles is not a trivial feat. India's Defence Research and Development Organisation (DRDO) has been able to piggyback off and benefit from the success of the Indian Space Research Organisation (ISRO), which has successfully developed rockets suitable for ballistic missiles. The DRDO, which otherwise has not delivered a major defense capability to the Indian armed forces in half a century of operation, has been able to develop these capabilities with greater success due to ISRO's work.[6] The challenge is that the DRDO faces a limited testing sequence due to the cost of each missile and the provocativeness of major ballistic missile tests. This has hampered the DRDO's ability to develop reliable missiles—the Agni family has suffered from spectacular testing failures. It further hampers full systems tests that include empirical data on the reliability of real warhead separation, fusing, and detonation in addition to delivery. Indeed, it is reasonable for India to worry about the full systems reliability of the China-specific missiles—the probability that an Agni-V would successfully deliver a warhead to its intended target and detonate at the intended altitude. And it would be reasonable today for China to question that reliability. As a reference point, the United States' Trident II submarine-launched ballistic missile (SLBM), one of its most advanced systems, has an estimated systems reliability of 90 to 95 percent after extensive tests. It would be stunning if the full systems reliability of the Agni or its sea-based variants were close to that reliable.[7]

A key ongoing development with particular relevance to India's China strategy is the development of multiple independently targetable reentry vehicles (MIRVs), which are essentially multiple warheads that can be mounted on, for example, the Agni-V. This entails the development of miniaturized warheads with diameters a little less than a quarter of the standard Agni-V warhead. It also entails mastering the design of a "warhead bus" that can reliably deliver multiple warheads—the Indian design is estimated to carry four to six warheads—without so-called fratricide, in which warheads knock each other out. During the Cold War, the development of MIRVs was designed to be a first-strike counterforce weapon, whereby the United States envisioned using a single missile fitted with up to ten warheads to destroy multiple (in theory, ten) Soviet nuclear missiles. MIRVs thus carry the legacy of arms-race instability because it puts pressure on the adversary to build more missiles to avoid being completely disarmed by a "MIRVed" nuclear force. In the India-China context, however, there is a logic for Indian (as well as Chinese) MIRVs that supports an assured-retaliation strategy, meaning that the development of MIRVs should not necessarily be viewed as an offensive or first-strike capability for India. Namely, warheads are much cheaper to build than long-range missiles. And in the contingency where India will have suffered nuclear first-use against it and may have had significant attrition of its Agni-V missiles, having surviving Agnis with multiple warheads enables India to threaten certain retaliation and unacceptable damage with greater credibility.[8] Thus, MIRVs in the India-China context—as far as both India and China are concerned—should not be viewed as supporting a shift to a more aggressive first-use strategy. It is simply a more cost-effective method to ensure significant retaliation given a smallish missile force that might be further attrited following nuclear first-use against India.

Perhaps the more significant long-term development on the Indian side is the move to the sea—that is, the development of a nuclear submarine fitted with nuclear-armed ballistic missiles (also known as an SSBN). In theory, the development of a submarine-based nuclear force imparts a state with a virtually invulnerable and completely survivable platform to deliver nuclear weapons, assuming the submarine is quiet enough to avoid detection by an adversary's antisubmarine warfare capabilities. These assumptions are not trivial, and indeed it may be the case that only the United States has been able to develop stealthy SSBNs that are quiet enough and enjoy enough sanctuary in the deep expanses of the Atlantic and Pacific to avoid detection.[9] India's first SSBN, the *Arihant* is presently undergoing sea trials, and a second larger design, the *Aridhaman*, is under development. The *Arihant*, however, is plagued with several problems that render its survivability questionable. First, it is quite noisy and therefore more easily detectable by both passive and active sonar. Luckily for India, its adversaries—China and Pakistan—have limited antisubmarine warfare (ASW) capabilities now. But that will change, and China will likely develop sufficient ASW capacity to track and destroy the *Arihant* generation in the future. Subsequent generations of Indian SSBNs may be quieter, however, so this is a dynamic assessment. Second, the *Arihant* was originally to be fitted with SLBMs known as K-15s, which had a range of only seven hundred kilometers. In order to hold the Chinese eastern seaboard at risk, the *Arihant* would have to venture out of friendly sanctuaries in the Indian Ocean and Bay of Bengal into the South and East China Seas, where it would be extremely vulnerable to ASW. There are increasing reports that the *Arihant* and subsequent SSBNs will be fitted with K-4 missiles, based on the Agni design and having a range on the order of three thousand kilometers. Future-generation SSBNs are being designed to carry these longer-range missiles and more of them than the *Arihant*. This would allow Indian SSBNs to operate in friendlier deterrent patrol boxes and reach firing positions where they would be less vulnerable.

Over time, subsequent generations of Indian SSBNs will undoubtedly become stealthier and more capable of launching retaliatory strikes from the Indian Ocean, and that will certainly impart to India a more reliable assured-retaliation capability against China. It is not there yet, however, and may be decades away from being so. India's broader submarine force has also been plagued by a series of disasters, including fires that destroyed the INS *Sindhurak-shak* in port and the recent leak of sensitive acoustic data on India's order of *Scorpène*-class submarines from France. None of these directly impacted India's SSBN force, but it suggests how difficult it is to build, operate, and maintain the integrity of modern submarines. The SSBN force should not be viewed as a panacea for survivability in India's nuclear force but rather as a complement to a robust land-based Agni force, which is itself quite survivable given India's large territory.

What does command and control look like in India, and what are the implications for its deterrence relationship with China? India's security managers, most notably the national security adviser and the SFC, have taken significant procedural measures to ensure that India's nuclear forces are operationalized primarily for retaliation.[10] It is important to note that the land-based force is—and will probably continue to be—managed differently than the sea-based force.[11] The land-based force made up primarily of Agni missiles can largely be maintained under assertive control, where arming and/or release codes must be actively transmitted by the national command authority (NCA) to enable nuclear use and retaliation. A growing number of the China-specific missiles, such as the Agni-Vs, are intended to be encapsulated, or "canisterized," where they are placed under hermetic seal to protect them from the extreme heat in India. This has implications for warhead mating to the missile: It is easier to premate the warhead and place the seal and then periodically break the seal to perform warhead maintenance. It also is time-consuming and logistically difficult to mate a one-ton warhead atop a seventeen-meter missile in the field at a limited number of locations where the missiles would also be exposed and highly vulnerable. It may be the case that India intends to mate the warheads only at some higher alert level and accept some risk. But even if India premates the warheads on the Agni-V and beyond, this premated state does not necessarily imply that the system is armed or ready to fire. Certain digital inputs would be necessary either directly from the NCA or from the NCA to the SFC. Therefore, canisterization, although placing the system at a higher state of readiness, has the benefit of protecting the missile's solid fuel from the heat and reducing the vulnerability of the system during the mating process if the warhead is premated. It can still be consistent with a retaliatory strategy. The fact that the land-based communication system between the NCA and the SFC or to the systems directly is more reliable and hardened enables the NCA to maintain sufficient nega-tive and assertive control over the Agni missiles regardless of whether they are canisterized.

The sea-based force is a different story. By definition, an SLBM has to be canisterized since it is emplaced in launch tubes in the submarine. It would also be incredibly impractical to have demated or disassembled nuclear warheads on a submarine for mating during a deterrent patrol. So, one has to assume that the warheads are premated to the SLBMs before they leave port. Furthermore, even though India is erecting very-low-frequency and extremely-low-frequency com-munication systems for its SSBNs, the reliability of these systems is questionable.

Since the SSBN would be India's last line of defense for nuclear retaliation, the question is whether India's security managers would want—in the event that communication to the SSBN force was severed—the system to "fail safe" or "fail deadly." To maintain assertive control over the nuclear force, one can imagine that they are thinking of designing the system to fail safe—that is, if communi-cation were severed and the NCA had not transmitted the appropriate codes, the submarine captain would not be able to physically fire the nuclear weapons. If, however, a severed communication link might suggest that the worst had come to transpire in India and the SSBN was the last platform available to retaliate, one might envision that the system could be designed to fail deadly—that is, the captain could, on his own authority with, for example, the accession of the first officer, fire the nuclear weapons even without codes from the NCA. Failing deadly runs the risk of unauthorized use but increases the credibility of India's retaliatory threat. Failing safe maintains strong assertive control over the force but runs the risk of an adversary such as China targeting communication links to neutralize India's primary retaliatory platform.

It is unknown how India will operationalize the SSBN force in the future. The US SSBN force does not have use controls such as permissive-action links but requires the consent of multiple officers to release weapons, which is envi-sioned to be a check on release procedures. Britain famously has the "letter of last resort" stored in a safe on the submarine with instructions for what to do if the prime minister is unreachable, but that too requires that the onboard officers have the *physical* ability to release British SLBMs without particular inputs or codes from the equivalent NCA.

Another choice India faces with respect to managing the SSBN is its deploy-ment model. The United States and Britain, for example, strive to maintain at least one SSBN (the US strives for multiple) on continuous deterrent patrol so that they are always in a position to use nuclear weapons from their submarines if necessary. The downside to this model, especially for noisier submarines such as India's, is that it makes tracking the submarine force much easier, as it provides ample opportunity for the adversary to acquire the acoustic signature and attempt to determine the deterrent patrol routes, which, for a variety of reasons, are limited. The Soviet Union, on the other hand, employed a bastion model whereby the SSBNs were kept in port until a crisis. The upside to this approach is that it made tracking Soviet SSBNs harder since adversaries had limited exposure to the acoustic signatures. The downside is that there are only a limited number of ports in which to house SSBNs, so an adversary can sit off a port in a crisis and attempt to sink them as they venture out, which increases the vulnerability because there are a limited number of choke points. The other downside is that the bastion model limits the amount of operational experience the SSBN crew has, which can be a real vulnerability in a crisis situation.

Therefore, the two key choices India has to make with its future SSBN force are how to manage the nuclear weapons aboard the submarine and whether it opts for a continuous-deterrent patrol model or a bastion model. These are related in some ways too, as India could opt for a bastion model, for example, and empower the submarine captain to fire weapons after the submarine is flushed out of the base, reducing the strain and dependence on a completely reliable communication link. Because of limited operational experience, however, that may increase the risk of unauthorized or accidental use if negative/assertive control were lost at that point. The fundamental trade-off India faces is that the more credible it makes its SSBN force to retaliate against China—that is, the greater control it delegates to the submarine captain to physically release nuclear weapons on his own accord—the greater the management challenges it faces, as well as different vulnerabilities to the survivability of the SSBN force.

Deterring Chinese nuclear use is an easier conceptual challenge than deterring Pakistan, which is attempting to lower the nuclear threshold and putting pressure on India to "close the deterrence gaps." The Pakistani challenge requires both creative thinking on escalation dominance and the development of a more diverse array of capabilities to be able to retaliate against a variety of contingencies. Against China, however, India's deterrence requirements are both straightforward and finite. They are straightforward because India simply needs to develop survivable land- or sea-based platforms capable of reliably reaching China's main strategic targets on its eastern coast. They are finite because China lacks advanced counterforce capabilities, and thus survivability should come easier than for, say, the Soviet Union during the Cold War. This means that India can calculate its deterrence requirements, assume some level of attrition, determine how much surviving throw weight it believes it needs to credibly achieve substantial retaliation, and size its force accordingly. Even if it leaves a buffer of doubling the force, this is not a massive requirement. However, although China is conceptually easier to deter for India, practically and technologically speaking it is more difficult because of the reach and reliability necessary to hold China's eastern coast at risk. India's missiles are reaching the required ranges but not at the level of full-systems reliability necessary to credibly assure retaliation, particularly when considering the issue of a missile being able to successfully deliver a warhead that correctly detonates. India's SSBN program is still in its relative infancy, though not an outlier compared to other nuclear programs at a similar stage. But it is still a generation of SSBNs away from having the stealthiness and numbers to ensure complete survivability at sea.

CHINA'S NUCLEAR STRATEGY

In many ways, China's nuclear strategy has been an enduring enigma. When China tested nuclear weapons in 1964, it officially and publicly forswore their first use, unlike the superpowers and France and Britain before it.[12] With a conventional force advantage in the Far East over the Soviet Union, China's strategy was to couple a conventional defense in depth with an official NFU policy. (Although it allegedly considered tactical nuclear weapons in the late 1970s, it opted against them and invested in conventional strength to offset the Soviet Union.) There was also a strong preference for centralized and assertive control over the nuclear arsenal, which was managed in a largely demated state for decades.[13] This overwhelmingly pushed China to an assured retaliation strategy, very similar to the one India selected after 1998. The fundamental challenge for China, however, is how to ensure assured retaliation against its primary contemporary adversary, the United States. The US has a growing array of counterforce capabilities—both conventional and nuclear, such as conventional prompt global strike and highly accurate counterforce nuclear weapons[14]—and potentially a game-changing damage-limitation capability if it can ever erect a functional national missile-defense system. Although the US claims its missile defenses are for small arsenals, such as North Korea's, the reality is that if the US leads with its counterforce capabilities, it can make a limited arsenal such as China's look like North Korea's and intercept any residual forces that it misses with missile defenses. This puts incredible pressure on China to modernize its forces to enhance survivability—improving mobility and concealment—and to increase the numbers to present enough forces to be able to saturate any missile defenses following an attempt to disarm it. This is presently where China is with its nuclear modernization effort. It is sizing its force and improving survivability at land and sea to address the American arsenal.

India is a nuclear afterthought for Beijing. This simply reflects the reality that any force structure capable of deterring the United States is more than sufficient to deter Indian nuclear use. In particular, China is improving the mobility and survivability—shifting to mobile solid-fuel missiles[15]—not just for its ICBM force (the DF-31/A and possibly the DF-41) but also for a whole host of intermediate-range missiles, especially the DF-21, that can hold America's regional targets and allied high-value assets at risk. The DF-21 is the primary delivery vehicle that China would use against India as well. Thus, improvements to the DF-21 force to ensure survivability and penetrability against the United States would simultaneously help meet China's deterrence requirements against India, which are relatively finite given India's proximity, limited number of strategic targets, and concentrated population centers. Holding just four major strategic centers at risk would end India as a functioning nation-state: Delhi, Bombay, Kolkata, and Bangalore. Unlike India's missiles, China's mobile solid-fuel missiles are more reliable and, China's nuclear weapons designs having been tested almost fifty times over the decades, their overall systems reliability is certainly credible. Moreover, India lacks any sort of counterforce capability, which means that China's land-based missiles are almost completely survivable in any India contingency. Therefore, China's existing forces are sufficient to inflict unacceptable damage on India.

China largely relies on large megaton-range thermonuclear weapons, whereby a single warhead that reaches its target can largely destroy an entire major city. This reduces the required accuracy of its nuclear delivery systems, since the blast radius of these thermonuclear devices is larger than the error range of the missile. China, like India, is contemplating MIRVing some of its heavier missiles for the same reason India is: so that any surviving missiles that were attrited in an attempted first strike by its larger adversary would carry enough throw weight to inflict unacceptable damage on their envisioned targets. In addition, MIRV buses are important for China as it tries to defeat American midcourse missile defenses, since they can be loaded with multiple warheads or dummy warheads to saturate a missile-defense system, thereby assuring penetration and thus retaliation. But, like India, MIRVs for China can still be consistent with an assured-retaliation strategy and are not necessarily a first-use weapon. Nevertheless, it is unclear whether the medium-range missiles that China would assign to Indian targets would be MIRVed. They do not have to be, because China probably does not fear significant attrition of those forces in the event of a conflict with India.

At sea, China does not necessarily need an SSBN force for assured retaliation against India the way that India requires against China. But like India, China is having significant trouble with its first-generation SSBN, Type 094 (*Jin* class), which succeeds the failed Type 092 (*Xia* class), which never ran a deterrent patrol in its life. The *Jin* SSBN is exceptionally noisy. China has further had some difficulty fitting its SLBM, the Julang-2 (JL-2) on the *Jin*, with reportedly some challenges related to the underwater launch. Because of these vulnerabilities, the *Jin* is being protected in sanctuaries against a very powerful US ASW capability. It may be a while before China is able to develop a stealthy-enough submarine to risk venturing out into the open Pacific where US ASW assets will be waiting for it and certainly before China can consider operating a continuous deterrent patrol. If it does not run one given US ASW capabilities, it will not have a continuous deterrent at sea as far as India is concerned either. But, against India, the development of an SSBN capability is largely unnecessary due to the number and reliability of medium-range ballistic missiles in the Chinese inventory. Given their mobility and the geographic expanse in which they are stored and deployed, China today has a survivable assured retaliatory force against India.

ESCALATION MECHANISMS?

How might India and China find themselves in a position to threaten or use nuclear weapons against each other? Both of their other primary nuclear adversaries—Pakistan and the United States, respectively—explicitly reserve the right to use nuclear weapons first against them, so against those states India and China have clearer contingencies under which they may have to retaliate with nuclear weapons. But against each other, it is difficult to conceive of scenarios where a conflict would escalate to the point where either would consider violating its NFU pledge. There are at least two potential conflict scenarios where India and China could find themselves in a hot war, where the prospect of escalation may loom: on land over the unsettled land border between them and at sea as the maritime competition amplifies.

On land, India and China are engaged in decades-long disputes about the demarcation of their border in two key places: around Aksai Chin, bordering Jammu and Kashmir in the north, and around the so-called McMahon Line, bordering Arunachal Pradesh farther southeast. The 1962 war between India and China was due to disagreements about the delimitation of the international border and China reacting to Prime Minister Jawaharlal Nehru's "forward policy," which augmented the Indian presence in the disputed territory of Aksai Chin. China pushed Indian forces back before adhering to a unilateral cease-fire.[16] Disagreements in the Sikkim sector resurfaced in 2017 with the months-long standoff on the Doklam Plateau, which occurred at the "trijunction" between India, China, and Bhutan.[17] But this was peacefully resolved after three months when India and China agreed to expeditious withdrawal from the standoff. Both India and China have periodically augmented their conventional deterrent presence along their border. On the Indian side, this entails the raising of mountain units, given the terrain. A long-standing proposal—presently an unfunded mandate[18]—is the raising of an offensive mountain strike corps, XVII Corps, to implement its "proactive strategy" concept on the Chinese side to parallel the strategy it has on the Pakistani side. The idea of XVII Corps, if it is ever funded, raised, and operationalized, is to be able to take and hold small pieces of territory across the disputed border as bargaining chips to trade for any Chinese gains on Indian territory. Supporting the ground forces has been a concerted effort to station advanced airpower, particularly the advanced, heavier Su-30MKI fighter aircraft in theater as a stronger conventional deterrent to China.

For its part, China has developed mobile and airborne infantry capabilities and is improving the infrastructure around the disputed border to rapidly deploy and augment its conventional forces in theater. India has watched with consternation as China has modernized the roads and assembly areas that might enable China to surge a significant number of troops to the theater in the event of conflict. However, it is difficult to conceive of how this conflict would escalate significantly, for several reasons. First, both China and India have largely status-quo intentions regarding the disputed border, despite periodic efforts to "push the line." Neither side has an incentive for a shooting war over this. Unlike Pakistan, which seeks fundamental territorial revision in the Jammu and Kashmir sector, India and China largely agree on the contours of what the international border looks like, except for several kilometers in each sector—which both nearly traded to reach a final settlement in 1960. Beyond these several disputed areas, however, neither seeks territorial gains in the other state that would pose an existential threat. Second, while nationalism runs high in the units manning the disputed border, as former Indian national security adviser Shivshankar Menon stated, "frankly, four men and a dog in a tent are no military threat." He added, "This is political and I think we need to look at it as such rather than, oh, it's about to erupt into some form of military conflict."[19] And, finally, even if there is local conventional escalation, it is difficult to envision any escalation to the point where either India or China considers nuclear threats or violating its mutual NFU pledge. Alarmism aside, the conventional deterrent that both sides have erected around the disputed territory—an area that both sides know intimately and have experience managing for over half a century—is the focal point of this dispute. It is difficult to see how nuclear weapons would enter the equation.

The same is true for the maritime competition, which is presently quite limited but which has the potential to intensify, though not to the extent that China faces in the South China Sea. India's navy matches up quite favorably with China's, with a true blue-water surface capability in the Indian Ocean region and a growing attack submarine capability. China's naval capabilities are concentrated to the South and East China Seas, but they too are rapidly modernizing, also with a growing surface and submarine capability. China's energy requirements necessitate traversing from the Persian Gulf and Africa through the Indian Ocean and then the Strait of Malacca. India has long identified the strait as a key choke point. An Indian blockade strategy of it—what Indian naval officers sometimes term "a knife to the throat" strategy—would pose some challenges for China, but one should not overstate the threat since Chinese ships could sail around Indonesia, just at greater fuel costs and with longer shipping times.

For its part, China's strategy, which American management consulting firm Booz Allen Hamilton dubbed the "string of pearls" strategy, to develop bases in friendly ports such as Hambantota in Sri Lanka and Gwadar in Pakistan could pose a long-term threat to Indian naval hegemony in the Indian Ocean. For now, these ports are claimed to be commercial ports, but some of the dredging activity suggests that they could indeed be converted for military purposes in the future. For China, it is entirely rational to develop friendly ports in the Indian Ocean to support its shipping activity from the Persian Gulf and Africa, which provides substantial energy resources to an increasingly thirsty economy.

How these two navies share the commons of the Indian Ocean will be a strong indicator of their general relationship. Some friction is inevitable. The relevant question is whether there are any escalation pathways that might make nuclear weapons salient. It is very hard to envision what those pathways might be. Unlike in the South China Sea, India and China do not have any disputed maritime boundaries or islands in the Indian Ocean. Even in the event of a serious crisis or dispute where India attempts to blockade the Strait of Malacca, it would be less costly for China to run the blockade or circumvent it to the south than to escalate the conflict to the point where the threat of nuclear use becomes relevant. One might worry about China hunting India's SSBNs in the Indian Ocean, but if India adopts a bastion model, which seems more likely now and in the medium term, it is unlikely to expose its SSBNs to Chinese naval assets, particularly Chinese ASW capabilities. So, even though the naval competition is likely to accelerate and intensify in the future, pathways to nuclear escalation are difficult to envision, particularly so long as both states nominally profess and adhere to NFU policies, which seems likely for a host of structural and civil-military (or party-military) reasons.

CONCLUSION

India and China are both modernizing their nuclear forces but largely for their other primary adversaries. Most of the activity in India's new nuclear development and thinking targets Pakistan, which is the more difficult adversary to conceptually deter because of its first-use doctrine. China similarly faces significant theoretical and practical challenges in generating a nuclear force posture that can withstand the pressure of American counterforce and damage-limitation measures. Although India is steadily improving its retaliatory capabilities against China and has some ways to go before they become reliable, the "multipolar nuclear Asia" is quite stable in this dyad. Fundamentally, this stability is driven by the adoption of assured-retaliation nuclear strategies by both India and China, where both pledge NFU; it is the only nuclear dyad in the system where both states declare and operationally support NFU pledges. China already has—and India will one day be confident it has—secure second-strike capabilities against the other. Neither has shown any intention, nor has any incentive, to threaten the survivability of the other's second-strike capability. Thus, India and China find themselves in a unique position: the only nuclear dyad thus far that meets all the requirements of the Jervisian "nuclear revolution" and where neither side wants to escape the revolution. That is, they mutually accept vulnerability to each other's second-strike forces. The United States only briefly accepted vulnerability from any of its adversaries—as the Soviet buildup in the 1960s made a counterforce mission practically impossible—and currently does not accept vulnerability to any of its adversaries, instead seeking nuclear primacy over Russia and China, its closest competitors. Thus, the India-China nuclear relationship looks fundamentally different from the US-Soviet Cold War balance, the contemporary US-China relationship, and the India-Pakistan equation.

What does this mean? It means that India and China are free to engage in competition, as rising great powers do, without real fear of a major conventional war or nuclear exchange. Minor skirmishes should be capped because neither has an incentive to move up the escalation ladder too rapidly or too high. There is high-level stability in the relationship that does not necessarily exist in other dyads. India can therefore seek its primary objective of Asian multipolarity, attempting to deny China its objective of Asian unipolarity. There will certainly be friction in the relationship as both states compete for energy resources and attempt to manage an unsettled border dispute and while China seeks to diplomatically keep India out of the multipolar world order as rising powers are wont to do—as it did with India's attempt to join the Nuclear Suppliers Group in June 2016. But the presence of mutual second-strike forces in the coming years means that the pathways to escalation—for friction to become fire—are difficult to fathom, even if there is localized and contained conflict at land or sea. This nuclear relationship is enviable and is perhaps what defensive realists envisioned with the advent of nuclear weapons. The United States, in particular, with its persistent hunt to escape the "nuclear revolution" by seeking nuclear superiority and rejecting vulnerability, has made this type of stable nuclear relationship elusive. But India and China demonstrate that it is not just a theoretical end to have mutual nuclear stability. It is practically possible so long as both states accept a certain level of vulnerability, so that the broader relationship can enjoy the stabilizing benefits of mutual nuclear possession.

NOTES

1. See Vipin Narang, *Nuclear Strategy in the Modern Era: Regional Powers and International Conflict* (Princeton, NJ: Princeton University Press, 2014), chap. 3; Mahesh Shankar and T.V. Paul, "Nuclear Doctrines and Stable Strategic Relationships: The Case of South Asia," *International Affairs* 92, no. 1 (January 2016): 1–20; and Shashank Joshi, "Pakistan's Tactical Nuclear Nightmare: Déjà Vu?," *Washington Quarterly* 36, no. 3 (Summer 2013): 159–72.

2. Given Pakistani fears that India seeks to threaten the survivability of its nuclear forces, I would not characterize Pakistan and India as enjoying this condition of mutually accepted second-strike forces.

3. See Shivshankar Menon, *Choices: Inside the Making of India's Foreign Policy* (Washington, DC: Brookings Institution Press, 2016), chap. 5.

4. See Jeffrey Lewis, "India's H Bomb Revisited," Arms Control Wonk, August 27, 2009, http://www.armscontrolwonk.com/archive/202445/indias-h-bomb -revisited/.

5. See Pranay Sharma, "Q: Did Our 'H' Bomb?," *Outlook: The Magazine*, September 14, 2009, http://www.outlookindia.com/magazine/story/q-did-our-h-bomb /261655.

6. See Stephen Cohen and Sunil Dasgupta, *Arming without Aiming: India's Military Modernization* (Washington, DC: Brookings Institution Press, 2010), chap. 5.

7. See Charles L. Glaser and Steve Fetter, "Should the United States Reject MAD? Damage Limitation and U.S. Nuclear Strategy toward China," *International Security* 41, no. 1 (Summer 2016): 63n28.

8. See Vipin Narang, "Five Myths about India's Nuclear Posture," *Washington Quarterly* 36, no. 3 (Summer 2013): 143–57.

9. See Austin Long and Brendan Green, "Stalking the Secure Second Strike: Intelligence, Counterforce, and Nuclear Strategy," *Journal of Strategic Studies* 38, nos. 1–2 (2015): 38–73.

10. See Narang, *Nuclear Strategy*, chap. 4.

11. See Gaurav Kampani, "Is the Indian Nuclear Tiger Changing Its Stripes? Data, Interpretation, and Fact," *Nonproliferation Review* 21, nos. 3–4 (2014): 383–98.

12. See M. Taylor Fravel and Evan Medeiros, "China's Search for Assured Retaliation: The Evolution of Chinese Nuclear Strategy and Force Structure," *International Security* 35, no. 2 (Fall 2010): 48–87; M. Taylor Fravel and Fiona S. Cunningham, "Assuring Assured Retaliation: China's Nuclear Posture and U.S.-China Strategic Stability," *International Security* 40, no. 2 (Fall 2015): 7–50; and Narang, *Nuclear Strategy*, chap. 5.

13. See John Lewis and Xue Litai, *China Builds the Bomb* (Stanford, CA: Stanford University Press, 1988).

14. See Long and Green, "Stalking the Secure Second Strike."

15. See Michael S. Chase, Andrew S. Erickson, and Christopher Yeaw, "China's Theater and Strategic Missile Force Modernization and Its Implications for the United States," *Journal of Strategic Studies* 32, no. 1 (2009): 67–114.

16. See Srinath Raghavan, *War and Peace in Modern India* (New Delhi: Permanent Black, 2010), chaps. 7 and 8.

17. Sushant Singh, "Simply Put: Where Things Stand on the Dolam Plateau," *Indian Express*, August 5, 2017, http://indianexpress.com/article/explained/india-china -standoff-sikkim-doka-la-simply-put-where-things-stand-on-the-dolam-plateau -4763892/.

18. Rajat Pandit, "No Budget, Army Struggles to Raise Mountain Strike Corps," *Times of India*, March 7, 2016, http://timesofindia.indiatimes.com/india/No -Budget-Army-struggles-to-raise-mountain-strike-corps/articleshow/51283303 .cms. See also Sushant Singh, "War Game Quells Doubt on New Corps," *Indian Express*, February 8, 2016, http://indianexpress.com/article/india/india-news -india/war-game-quells-doubts-on-new-corps/.

19. Shivshankar Menon, "India's Role in the World: A Conversation," Brookings Institution, October 7, 2014, https://www.brookings.edu/wp-content/uploads /2014/10/20141007_menon_india_transcript.pdf.

PART IV

MITIGATORS

Chapter 10

Globalization's Impact

Trade and Investment in China-India Relations

MATTHEW A. CASTLE

Since the turn of the twenty-first century, economic ties between China and India have increased dramatically. This represents a sharp departure from historical precedent. China is now India's top trading partner, and bilateral investment has also seen a modest increase. These changes speak to shifts in the two countries' engagement with the global economy. In an ascendency hinted at by Beijing's accession to the World Trade Organization (WTO) in 2001, China became the world's largest trading state in 2013, overtaking the United States. India's growth in trade has also increased during this time, and while it is less integrated in manufacturing supply chains than its East Asian neighbor, India is experiencing rapid growth in its exports of services.[1] In short, the two countries have become active participants in a "globalized" economy. In this chapter, I evaluate these developments in light of the historical China-India rivalry. Theory tells us that greater economic interdependence is associated with more peaceful interstate relations. Can economic ties, and the two countries' participation in processes of economic "globalization" more generally, ease the rivalry between China and India?

The evidence suggests that, for now, economic ties are unlikely to act as much of a conflict deterrent. Bilateral investment remains low, and while China has become India's primary trading partner, India remains less significant for China. This asymmetry—a recurring theme noted by others in this volume[2]—means that even if India is deterred from conflict, China is less likely to be. Moreover, the two countries continue to trade at relatively low levels. For the economic relationship between China and India to mitigate the long-standing China-India rivalry, the two countries may need to find ways to further cooperate through international economic institutions. Joint membership in international institutions such as trade agreements creates stable expectations about future economic flows while establishing mechanisms for overcoming commercial disputes. Yet international institutions may be detrimental if they are used as a means of one state gaining status at the expense of the other. Thus, it will be important to find ways that both states can achieve recognition and status, including through leadership roles, in a positive-sum way.

Broader processes of international economic integration (globalization) present both the promise of greater cooperation and the threat of increasing tensions. The two countries share many economic interests. Both desire a greater role for rising powers in multilateral institutions such as the WTO and international financial institutions such as the International Monetary Fund (IMF). Yet it also appears that China is opting to create alternative international institutions in which it plays a more significant role, a reflection of its rising economic status. The Belt and Road Initiative (BRI) illustrates this dynamic. The plan, the centerpiece of Beijing's foreign economic policy, is promoted by China as a framework for infrastructure-development projects that will be of mutual benefit to all countries in the wider Eurasian region. But other countries, including India, have been concerned by the possibility that the BRI legitimizes Chinese expansionism, providing political cover for a more geopolitically assertive China. For the initiative to improve China-India relations, China will need to ease these fears. One possibility would be encouraging cooperation on noneconomic aspects of the plan. It would be particularly valuable to seek cooperation on those aspects that involve the security of trade and investment routes, since these imply an increasing military and naval presence.

In sum, the current China-India economic relationship may deter India from direct confrontation with China but may be insufficient to deter China from aggravating behavior toward India. Worryingly, there is evidence to support this proposition already. The China-Pakistan Economic Corridor (CPEC), which is linked to China's BRI, traverses Pakistan-occupied Kashmir, reinforcing Pakistan's claim on what remains contested territory between Pakistan and India. Citing concerns that the plan undermines sovereignty and may lead to unsustainable debt burdens, New Delhi declined to send official representation to a high-profile May 2017 forum on the BRI. Some observers linked New Delhi's snub to the subsequent military standoff between China and India in the Doklam triborder area, territory that is disputed between China and Bhutan.

I present empirical evidence in two sections. First, I outline the current trade and investment relationship while considering this in the context of both countries' participation in processes of economic globalization. Then, I examine how the BRI may affect the rivalry between the two rising powers. Before examining this empirical evidence, the following section situates this chapter in the wider literature on the relationship between conflict and economic ties.

INTERNATIONAL ECONOMIC INTEGRATION AND PEACE IN THE TWENTY-FIRST CENTURY

Higher levels of trade tend to correlate positively with peaceful relations, although there is ongoing debate about the direction of causality and scope conditions. Economic ties may have a darker side, however. Overdependence, or asymmetrical dependence, may encourage conflict between trading partners. These findings echo in a broader literature on globalization and conflict. Economic globalization is likely to reduce the attractiveness of military aggression as a means of securing resources, but the proliferation of international economic institutions—one aspect of the latest phase of globalization—may also provide a new arena for power politics. Moreover, despite a shift to "preferential" rather than multilateral institutions as the primary means of achieving trade and investment liberalization, there has been relatively little research about how this change in institutional context might affect security dynamics. We also do not yet fully understand the security implications of broader "trade agreements" that cover other issue areas (notably investment and intellectual property rights). These developments create new opportunities for politics by empowering some actors and disempowering others.

Interdependence and Conflict

Liberal scholars have pointed to the pacifying effects of commerce at least since the Enlightenment.[3] This "commercial peace" argument, central to a vast empirical literature since the 1980s, is generally based on one of two mechanisms.[4] The first is rational self-interest: Since war with one's trading partners is unprofitable, countries that have commercial ties with one another have an incentive for peace. The second is a "costly signaling" mechanism: Interdependence provides states with the means of imposing costly barriers to trade, which means they can credibly demonstrate their resolve in a dispute and thereby solve problems nonviolently.[5] While most of this research has focused on the relationship between trade and peace, other forms of interdependence (such as international investment) may also contribute to peaceful relations between states.[6]

There is, however, ongoing debate about the direction of causality. Trade may correlate with peace, but this may reflect higher levels of trade between allies.[7] Furthermore, there appear to be several factors that moderate the link between trade and peace. Some studies have suggested that the relationship between trade and peace may depend on democratic domestic institutions since democracy allows for social interests to be effectively expressed at the state level.[8] States that are more integrated into the world economy may also be less prone to conflict because of third-party influences,[9] although multilateral trade openness may also reduce the pacifying effects of bilateral dependence.[10] Similarly, large states with more trading partners may avoid a dangerous overdependence on trading partners.[11] It also seems that the trade-peace relationship depends on the sort of goods that are traded. Where traded goods are less easily or cheaply produced domestically, increasing trade creates stronger incentives for peace.[12] Finally, there is evidence that the pacifying effects of trade depend on joint membership in commercial agreements, such as preferential trade agreements (PTAs).[13]

Yet, while PTAs may sometimes be pacifying, they may also be used as instruments of domination, especially among countries that are unequal in size and power.[14] For some observers, asymmetrical trade relations are particularly dangerous. Where only one of two states is dependent on the other as a market for its exports as a source of necessary imports or as a source of foreign capital, the constraints on conflict through the prospect of forgone welfare are not felt equally.[15] Such an asymmetry may reduce the pacifying effects of trade,[16] and it may even increase the likelihood of conflict.[17] To some extent, this observation echoes the warnings of Marxists, for whom the spread of capitalist production is deeply intertwined with domination.[18] Indeed, very high levels of interdependence may make dyads *more* conflict-prone, with lower levels more pacifying.[19]

Globalization and Security

The above caveats notwithstanding, economic ties appear in general to be positively associated with peaceful relations between states. These economic ties are situated within the broader framework of an increasingly globalized world economy, in which interstate relations (including security relations) are likely to be recast.[20] I understand economic globalization to be a set of processes that involve increases in transnational flows of the factors of production (capital and labor), increasing multinationalization of production processes (for instance, through the creation of global value chains, or GVCs), increasing trade in intermediate and finished products (goods and services), and increasing transnational communication and flows of ideas and knowledge (including intellectual property). This is a relatively restrictive definition, but a broader focus on other aspects of globalization is simply beyond the scope of this chapter.[21] These processes may be driven by economic actors such as firms, as well as by government actions to promote or deepen economic ties.

Evidence suggests that globalization does not fundamentally change the definition and operation of state security, particularly for major powers and for states engaged in long-standing rivalry.[22] However, the scope conditions for conflict may have been affected by economic globalization in several ways. The creation of GVCs may increase incentives for cooperation since such production processes rely on stable relations between upstream (supplier) and downstream (consumer) components of value chains.[23] To the extent that international commerce becomes an increasing component of gross domestic product (GDP), states may also be less likely to see conflict as a profitable means of acquiring resources.[24] Some observers therefore expect that as states are increasingly integrated into the global economy, they reduce military spending and focus less on offensive capabilities. Similarly, as conflict becomes less profitable, we may see increasing use of "soft balancing" rather than traditional "hard balancing."[25]

This is perhaps an overly rosy view of things. The spread of global and regional institutions may, in fact, encourage competition between states for status and recognition within them. Moreover, while economic globalization may create some incentives to avoid conflict, it may also create the conditions for populist politics if appropriate political institutions do not match the reduction in barriers to markets. Karl Polanyi argued in the mid-twentieth century that the process by which economic markets become "disembedded" from societies may prompt social backlash.[26] If such a backlash breeds intolerance and belligerence, the pains of economic globalization may ultimately sow seeds for conflict.

International Economic Institutions and the Transformation of the Global Trade Regime

The literature on interdependence and conflict has also largely overlooked two institutional transformations of the international trade regime that characterize the current phase of economic globalization. The first is a surge in agreements negotiated between smaller groups of states rather than at the multilateral WTO.[27] The emergence of economic institutions such as China's BRI or the sixteen-member Regional Comprehensive Economic Partnership (RCEP, a "megaregional" agreement with the Association of Southeast Asian Nations at its hub, currently under negotiation) will likely shape the power-political dynamic of the wider region and will be an opportunity for the politics of status-seeking to play out.[28] Being able to influence the design of long-lasting institutions creates additional incentives for membership, as well as scope for membership to become a source of conflict in world politics: Even as the benefits of joint membership in trade and investment institutions increase, the costs of exclusion may increase as well.

The second major shift in the trade regime concerns its scope. As the number of PTAs has increased, so too has their coverage—to contentious issues such as international investment, intellectual property, and services.[29] The increased reach of trade agreements may facilitate greater economic interdependencies, which may well reduce the appeal of military conflict. Yet the erosion of conventional distinctions between domestic and international policy areas through such institutions may contribute to the sort of social backlash noted above, especially where it is perceived that the benefits are not shared equally.

In summary, there is substantial evidence that greater economic interdependence is associated with more peaceful interstate relations, but there are caveats to this observation. This literature also largely overlooks transformations in the governance of the international trade regime, which has become both more exclusive (in its shift from multilateralism toward preferentialism) and more expansive (in its inclusion of more issue areas). One implication of this theoretical literature for the China-India case is that military rivalry between the two is unlikely to be significantly reduced by the increase in economic ties that has taken place until now. The emergence of new international economic institutions may help to reduce tensions, but this is likely to depend on whether both countries can be meaningful stakeholders in them. If new institutions benefit only one party, they may exacerbate tensions.

TRADE AND INVESTMENT
IN THE CHINA-INDIA CASE

This section examines India and China's bilateral trade and investment. It then places China-India economic ties in the wider context of both countries' participation in processes of economic globalization, before evaluating the impact of these developments on bilateral rivalry. Economic growth in India and China has been accompanied by a significant increase in bilateral trade. Following a global trend of increasing South-South investment (between developing countries), foreign direct investment (FDI) between the two states has also risen, although it remains relatively low.[30] These developments have not been symmetrical. China was India's most important trading partner in 2010, a position it has maintained since 2013. India remains less significant for China. This would tend to suggest India is relatively more constrained by the economic relationship than is China. The two countries' participation in regional institutions does give cause for hope, to the extent that they boost economic interdependencies and contribute to a rules-based environment for international commerce in which the benefits are equitably shared.

China-India Trade in Historical Perspective

China and India traded little with one another through the latter part of the last century, but trade has expanded since the turn of the century. In 2001, two-way trade as reported by China amounted to only $3.6 billion. In 2013, it figured at $70.6 billion. Because of the importance of total Chinese exports, figure 10.1 places the latter on a separate axis.

India's share of total Chinese trade remains relatively low. China-India trade peaked in 2010 at slightly over 2 percent of total Chinese trade and in 2014 represented around 1.6 percent. India was China's ninth-largest export market in 2015 (2.6 percent of Chinese exports) and the twenty-seventh-largest source of Chinese imports (0.8 percent).[31] Increasingly, China trades with a wide range of partners, and trade with India remains a small proportion of total trade.

As figure 10.2 shows, the view from India is somewhat different. Since the early 2000s, there has been a secular increase in Indian trade with China. China now accounts for over 10 percent of India's aggregate exports and imports. Trade with China appears to be entering a more accelerated phase of growth

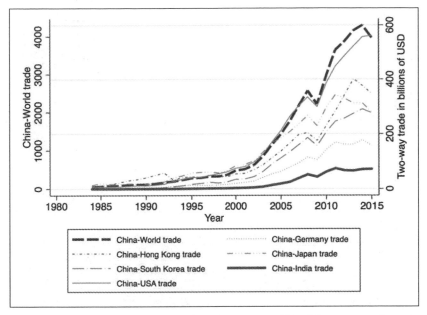

FIGURE 10.1. Chinese Exports to Selected Partners and Total Exports, 1984–2015

Note: Figure shows the absolute growth of Chinese two-way trade (exports plus imports) to selected partners, as well as total trade (China-world). Trade with partners is on the right-hand axis. Trade with the world is on the left-hand axis. Figures are in billions of US dollars.

Source: Data from United Nations, "Comtrade Database," accessed March 23, 2017, https://comtrade.un.org/.

since the mid- to late 2000s, notwithstanding the recent decrease in trade to all of India's top partners.

Yet, as figure 10.3 shows, China-India trade has been driven largely by Indian imports of Chinese products. China accounted for 15.8 percent of Indian imports in 2015. As an export market, China is India's fourth most important market but figures at only 3.6 percent of India's total exports in 2015 (behind the United States at 15.3 percent, the United Arab Emirates, and Hong Kong). In other words, there is an imbalance between Indian imports of Chinese products and Chinese imports of Indian products. This imbalance contributes to India's overall trade deficit, which in turn creates downward pressure on the rupee. This asymmetry may also be a direct source of bilateral conflict. If the availability of imported products becomes an issue of national security (if trade is "securitized"), India is far more vulnerable than China. There may already be evidence of this insecurity: In January 2016, New Delhi reinstated customs duties on pharmaceutical products (disproportionately sourced from China) to curb dependence on imports.[32]

It is also important to understand the composition of products that are imported and exported, as this moderates the extent to which economic

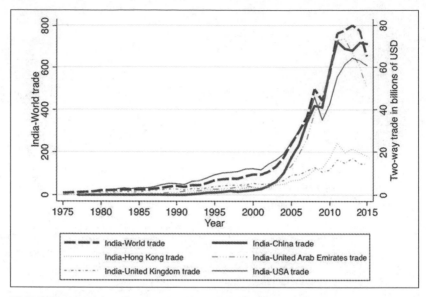

FIGURE 10.2. Indian Two-Way Trade with Selected Partners and World, 1975–2015

Note: Figure shows the absolute growth of Indian two-way trade (exports plus imports) to selected partners, as well as total trade (India-world). Trade with partners is on the right-hand axis. Trade with the world is on the left-hand axis. Figures are in billions of US dollars.

Source: Data from United Nations, "Comtrade Database," accessed March 23, 2017, https://comtrade.un.org/.

interdependence is likely to affect political relations between states.[33] Table 10.1 summarizes this data, noting the relative importance of the two countries' markets. Trade in goods that are more transformed—which require more capital—may be more strongly associated with peace. Such goods are less easy to substitute from another source (such as the domestic market), so they create a stronger incentive to maintain peaceful relations. Given the greater substitutability of primary products, this data further suggests an asymmetry between the two countries: India is more dependent on Chinese imports than the other way around.

Seeing this from a wider perspective, however, we should question whether China-India trade figures make the two countries truly "interdependent." To ascertain this, we can use a trade-intensity index, which indicates whether a given country A exports more, as a proportion of its exports, to a given country B than the world does on average.[34] Values over 100 indicate that a higher than average proportion of A's exports are destined for B. Values less than 100 indicate the contrary. The share of Indian exports to China was low in the 1990s and sat around the global average (100) in the mid- to late 2000s. Since 2010, these figures have been steadily declining, however. In 2015, the figure was around 43. The share of China's exports destined for India, while low up until the early 2000s (ranging from 44 in 1992 to 93 in 2000), is now higher than the global

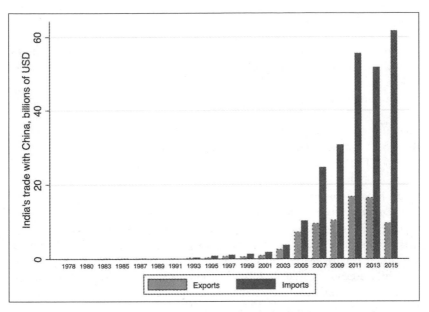

FIGURE 10.3. Indian Exports to and Imports from China, 1978–2015

Note: Figure shows total Indian trade with China, separated into exports to China and imports from China.

Source: Data from United Nations, "Comtrade Database," accessed March 23, 2017, https://comtrade.un.org/.

TABLE 10.1. Top Five Export Categories and Importance of the Export Market (2015)

Indian product imported by China	Rank of Chinese market for India	Chinese product imported by India	Rank of Indian market for China
Cotton	1st largest (26.6% of exports)	Electrical/electronic equipment	9th largest (2.2% of exports)
Pearls, precious stones, etc.	14th largest (0.3% of exports)	Nuclear reactors, boilers, and other machinery	6th largest (2.8% of exports)
Copper and copper products	1st largest (46.5% of exports)	Organic chemicals	1st largest (13.9% of exports)
Organic chemicals	2nd largest (7.7% of exports)	Fertilizers	1st largest (32.5% of exports)
Salt, sulphur, rare-earth minerals, stone, etc.	1st largest (32.0% of exports)	Iron and steel products	3rd largest (4.6% of exports)

Note: The data shows the top five Indian exports to China and top five Chinese exports to India and lists the relative importance of the Chinese and Indian markets for these products.

Source: Data from United Nations, "Comtrade Database," accessed March 23, 2017, https://comtrade.un.org/.

average (a value of 147 in 2015). Yet this is low compared to the figures for trade between China, Japan, and South Korea (which were in the 200s and 300s for much of the same period).[35] Although bilateral trade between China and India is growing, a comparative perspective suggests that this does not amount to significant economic interdependence.

In summary, the China-India trading relationship has grown substantially in the past decade and a half. Bilateral trade has increased from under $200 million during the 1980s to over $70 billion in 2015. This increase has occurred while both countries have undergone huge economic development and market opening. There is reason to believe this will continue as both countries maintain strong economic growth. The relationship is somewhat asymmetrical, however, with China a more important trading partner for India. The dramatic growth of bilateral trade between the two countries has also been largely driven by Chinese exports to India. When we break down the bilateral trade to examine the products that are traded, Indian importers may be more vulnerable to a disruption in Chinese exports, while Indian exporters in key products are more reliant on the Chinese export market and therefore more sensitive to decreases in Chinese demand. In other words, India has a greater disincentive for conflict with China than China does with India.

Bilateral Foreign Direct Investment: Low but Growing

What of FDI? Unfortunately, researchers face several data limitations in this case. The Indian data for the source and destination countries for FDI is skewed because a high proportion of reported FDI flows through Mauritius for tax reasons, so the actual FDI figures for many other countries are greater than reported.[36] A similar distortion for China is due to "round-tripping" from mainland China to Hong Kong and back to take advantage of tax differences.[37] China and India also appear to underreport inward FDI; the Chinese Ministry of Commerce does not report India as a source of inward FDI, and Indian data is very limited in coverage.

What we can take from available figures is that although South-South investment has become increasingly prevalent, bilateral investment flows between China and India remain low. With the caveat about reporting in mind, bilateral FDI constituted less than half a percentage point of total outward FDI for both China and India in 2012.[38] From a reported nil outward FDI flow in 2003, Chinese FDI destined for India increased to roughly $277 million in 2012.[39] Indian FDI to China nearly doubled from 2010 to 2012, increasing from just under $28 million in 2010 to just under $50 million in 2012.[40] Recent reports suggest investment within the BRICS countries (Brazil, Russia, India, China, and South Africa) increased from 3 percent to 10 percent from 2010 to 2015, a figure that remains low, although it is rising.[41] Illustrative cases in 2016 included investment by China's CRRC Corporation in a $63 million joint venture for rail transportation equipment in India and the decision by Huawei Technologies to begin smartphone manufacturing in India.[42]

The Wider International Economic Context

China and India have both become far more integrated into a globalizing economy during the past twenty years. As other chapters in this volume address China and India's strategic and military behavior directly, I focus on how economic globalization may change the incentives for strategic behavior. The most obvious impact of economic globalization is likely to be associated with the increasing proliferation of international economic institutions. As I further illustrate in the following section on the BRI, while government initiatives to promote transnational economic integration may be cooperative, they may also create opportunities to extend new forms of power and influence over other states. With both China and India now active participants in PTAs, and with the emergence of new institutions in several issue areas, there is also increased scope for the politics of status-seeking to play out.

China has undergone a dramatic opening up to the world, signaled by its accession to the WTO in 2001. The increase in Chinese trade during the past decade and a half has been stunning, nearly doubling every five years since 2000. In 2013, this figure topped $4 trillion, leading China to overtake the United States as the world's largest trading nation. In part this has been driven by impressive Chinese economic growth, but even as a proportion of its GDP Chinese trade has been increasing. On China's joining the WTO in 2001, its trade as a proportion of GDP was 38 percent; in 2014, this figure was 45 percent.[43] India has also enjoyed a major increase in its trade figures. India's total trade increased from $94.5 billion in 2001 to $655 billion in 2015, or 26 percent of GDP in 2001 to 49 percent in 2014. This includes a dip in trade values from 2012 to 2015, likely a result of the drop in the world oil market.[44] While in absolute terms India's integration into the world economy remains lower than that of China, as a proportion of GDP trade has become even more important for India than it has for China.[45]

China and India have also become major destinations for foreign investment. China's net FDI inflows for 2016 were recorded at $134 billion—behind only the United States' and the United Kingdom's. India was in ninth place, with a net figure of $44 billion.[46] The major development in the past several years has been the decline in new projects in China since 2011 and the increase in new projects in India, particularly since 2014. In 2015, India overtook China as the leading destination for greenfield investment (i.e., into new projects), with a total sum of $63 billion in announced capital investment for the year 2015, compared with China's $56.6 billion.[47]

China is considered more economically competitive than India, but the latter rose sixteen spots from a fifty-fifth ranking to thirty-ninth in the World Economic Forum's Global Competitiveness Index (against China's twenty-eighth) from 2015 to 2016, an increase that it also achieved from 2014 to 2015. The World Economic Forum attributes this increase to improvements in public institutions, trade and investment liberalization, and increasing transparency in the financial system.[48] The business community has also received Indian prime minister Narendra Modi's progrowth, probusiness, and anticorruption policies favorably. Initiatives such as the "Make in India" campaign to attract investment in manufacturing and industry, coupled with looser FDI regulations, labor law reform, privatization programs, reductions in bureaucratic barriers, and campaigning on the part of the government, have appeared highly effective in promoting India as a destination for FDI.[49]

China and India have also both become much more active participants in international economic institutions. The G-8 (the group of the eight major economies) has been largely superseded by the more inclusive G-20 (which includes both China and India) as the world's preeminent forum to discuss international economic developments. The importance of the G-20 reflects emerging economies' role in the global economic recovery following the 2008 crisis.[50] As greater economic globalization increases states' vulnerabilities to economic downturn, it also encourages greater cooperation.

As rising powers that are increasingly integrated into the global economy, China and India both seek improved representation of their interests in multilateral economic institutions.[51] India was central to organizing the WTO Group of 20 developing countries (not to be confused with the G-20), which enabled developing-country coordination to block developed-country proposals in the Cancun (2003) and Geneva (2008) WTO Ministerial Conferences. Reform of quota and voting share at the IMF implemented in January 2016 means that China, India, Brazil, and Russia are now among the top ten IMF members, although the governance of international financial institutions remains weighted in favor of the advanced Western nations (especially the United States). Yet economic globalization and rapid economic growth have also afforded China and India opportunities to create alternative institutions. This has included a non-Western alternative to the IMF—the New Development Bank, also known as the BRICS bank, which held its inaugural board of governors meeting in July 2015. The major development in recent years, however, has been the creation of the Chinese-led Asian Infrastructure Investment Bank (AIIB), a multilateral lender involved in funding BRI projects.

Finally, China and India have followed the global trend of negotiating PTAs. As of January 2017, China had thirteen bilateral agreements in force or completed. Beijing was currently negotiating eight new agreements and considering a further seven (including a bilateral agreement with India).[52] As of January 2017, India was a member of eighteen trade agreements and negotiating (or upgrading) a further eighteen.[53] China and India share membership in the Asia-Pacific Trade Agreement (APTA, previously the 1975 Bangkok Agreement), but the APTA offers limited liberalization of some goods trade between certain developing countries in the Asia-Pacific; it does not comprehensively reduce tariffs.[54]

More importantly, China and India are negotiating parties to the RCEP, a megaregional agreement in the Asian-Pacific region. Like other megaregional agreements, such as the Trans-Pacific Partnership (TPP) from which the United States withdrew in January 2017, the RCEP regulates a host of nontrade issue areas (services, investment, etc.) in addition to reducing barriers to trade.

Economic Ties and Interstate Conflict

What should we make of the possible impact of bilateral ties and the wider context of globalization as a mitigating factor in China and India's rivalry? Current bilateral economic ties are unlikely to play a significant role in reducing the rivalry. Even if we are to accept the claim that trade can in fact *cause* peace (and is not merely correlated with it), economic ties between China and India are low enough that we could question whether they constitute economic interdependence. Furthermore, recall that trade is particularly likely to be associated with peace when it is relatively symmetrical. It may also be more pacifying when the states in question are both democracies, when these states are well integrated into the global economy, and when they are parties to a PTA (provided they are equal in size). China and India presently satisfy few of these conditions.

What of the wider context? China and India have become active participants in economic globalization. Trade and investment have become major contributors to GDP, and the two countries have begun to take the lead in the establishment of international economic institutions. Both are also actively negotiating trade agreements. How has this greater integration into the world economy affected the scope conditions for conflict? First, greater integration into the global economy has not been accompanied by reduced military spending. Global defense spending declined from 3.42 percent of global GDP in 1988 to 2.27 percent in 2015. Beijing's estimated defense spending also dropped sharply in the early 1990s, from around 2.5 percent in 1992 to 1.7 percent for much of the mid-1990s. Yet in the period since China joined the WTO (after 2001), there has been no clear trend, and spending increased year-to-year from 2011 (1.8 percent) through 2015 (1.95 percent). New Delhi's spending dropped in the early 1990s. It has trended downward from 2009 but since the early 1990s has seen periods of both increased and decreased spending. Spending in 2015 was 2.4 percent of GDP.[55] Given both countries' impressive GDP growth during the past decades, this represents a large increase in absolute terms.[56] The strategic environment in East and South Asia remains tense, and there is no sign of a simple correlation between the importance of trade and reduced military expenditure.

With regard to trade and investment, it is conceivable that the two states may increasingly compete for foreign capital. There is some overlap between the top capital-attracting sectors in the two countries. Transport equipment, information and communication technology, electronics, and environmental technology all figure in the top five sectors for both China and India.[57] Yet the service sector (which accounts for a larger component of GDP and a larger component of exports in India than in China) has historically been a more important recipient of investment in India.[58] By some accounts, there is also little evidence of FDI "diversion." A 2007 study found that increasing FDI in China *increased* FDI in other countries, although the effect was weaker for countries (such as India in 2007) that were less well integrated into the same GVCs as China.[59] With the "Make in India" campaign promoting manufacturing and greater supply-chain integration, India may increasingly participate in regional value chains. In sum, while the two rising powers are both major FDI destinations, this may be a complementary rather than competitive dynamic.

We might expect the two countries to use international economic institutions to "soft balance" in place of traditional hard balancing and to seek advantages over one another in the pursuit of international status.[60] Institutional membership has shown itself to be political in the past. For instance, New Delhi resisted calls for greater Chinese participation in the South Asian Association for Regional Cooperation, in which India has traditionally been the lead power. This is despite considerable overlap in the two states' strategic interests of development in the wider region.[61] Shared membership in the BRICS development bank and in the newly formed AIIB are therefore encouraging, as they point to opportunities for greater cooperation, although economically China dominates both institutions.

Joint membership in the RCEP, currently under negotiation, is also heartening. The RCEP would be the first comprehensive trade agreement between China and India. If negotiations succeed, members will count on an expansion of trade and investment between one another. The RCEP should also facilitate the expansion of GVCs in the wider region, bringing India into production networks in which China already participates; this may reduce India's trade deficit vis-à-vis China. The RCEP's reduction of barriers to services trade will also favor India, whose IT service sector is highly competitive.[62] Taken together, these factors may help to reduce China-India tensions.

In sum, the wider context of economic globalization does offer some hope for reducing political tensions between China and India, especially if the two states can achieve meaningful cooperation through international institutions. Yet, and as outlined in the first section, the wider context of economic globalization also presents challenges. International economic institutions may become a means of one state (likely China, given its greater economic weight) increasing its coercive power over others. To illustrate this concern, the next section examines China's BRI.

THE BELT AND ROAD INITIATIVE

No discussion of the trade and investment relationship between China and India would be complete without assessing China's Silk Road and Maritime Silk Road initiatives, branded One Belt One Road (一带一路) or, more recently, the Belt and Road Initiative. The strategy was announced in 2013 and has become

China's flagship foreign economic policy. Official Chinese pronouncements emphasize the mutual benefits of the project to China and to partner countries. Foreign (and nonofficial Chinese) commentators have been quicker to point to the international political and geostrategic implications of the project. The initiative has the potential to either alleviate or exacerbate existing tensions between China and India. New Delhi's absence from a major summit on the BRI in May 2017, combined with the military standoff that began in June between China and India in the Doklam triborder area, does not bode well. Whether the BRI can contribute to alleviating tensions will likely depend on the extent to which the inevitable noneconomic elements of the project can become a source of cooperation in and of themselves and on the ability of potential participant countries—particularly India—to become stakeholders in the process, including through participation in funding bodies such as the AIIB. The BRI is becoming inseparable from China's efforts to strengthen security and political influence along its borders. The project should be seen not just as an investment initiative but also as a central strategy for China's rise—whether "peaceful" or not.

Evoking the ancient trade routes, the Silk Road and Maritime Silk Road initiatives conceive of a vast infrastructure network including road, rail, and shipping that would extend from China through Eurasia, the Middle East, and East Africa. An overland component (the "Belt"), announced on September 7, 2013, comprises a network of road and rail routes, infrastructure projects, and oil and gas pipelines that will run from Xi'an (central China) through Central Asia to Russia and beyond to Europe.[63] These will follow various paths through Eurasia. Some will run from China's north, to Mongolia, and on to Russia, while others will run from China's south through the Indochina Peninsula.[64]

The twenty-first-century Maritime Silk Road (the "Road," sometimes the "MSR") was announced before the Indonesian Parliament by Xi on October 3, 2013.[65] It involves the establishment of port infrastructure from Quanzhou in China through the South China Sea and the Strait of Malacca to the Indian Ocean (Colombo and Kolkata) and then to East Africa (Nairobi). From there, it will extend through the Suez Canal, before terminating in Europe (Athens and finally Venice), where it will link overland to Rotterdam.[66] The framing document published by the National Development and Reform Commission (NDRC, the Chinese governmental body responsible for the BRI's implementation) notes two additional projects as "closely related to the Belt and Road Initiative": the CPEC and a China-Bangladesh-India-Myanmar route.[67] Most (foreign) observers tend to include these in the list of anticipated Belt projects, however,[68] and while China announced in 2015 that the principal multilateral BRI funding body would not be involved in a $46 billion planned China-Pakistan infrastructure investment,[69] the latter is clearly envisaged as part of the overall initiative.

The potential scope of the BRI is immense. As of 2017, more than nine hundred deals attributed to the BRI are planned or under way, worth collectively around $900 billion. These span more than sixty countries that together account for 4.4 billion people (60 percent of the world's population), with a collective

GDP of around $21 trillion (around 30 percent of the world's total). The funding is also impressive. The Chinese government established a Silk Road Fund, which consists of $40 billion in capital provided by the China Development Bank, the Export-Import Bank of China, the China Investment Corporation, and the State Administration of Foreign Exchange. The AIIB is a second major funding body, a multilateral institution with fifty-seven founding members (including India) and initial total capital of $100 billion. Its voting structure is determined by capital contributions; China, with an initial $29.8 billion contribution, holds the largest vote share—and veto power—at 28.7 percent. India's contribution of $8.4 billion makes it the second-largest shareholder, with 8.3 percent of the vote. In addition to these institutions, China committed in mid-2015 to finance close to $900 billion worth of projects through the China Development Bank.[70]

Many of the slated projects may have proceeded without the initiative (development of Gwadar Port in Pakistan under the auspices of the CPEC is one example), but the project has huge symbolic value. According to Beijing, the project aims to create a "community of interests, a community of development and responsibility, and a community of destiny" in Eurasia.[71] Chinese commentary has dismissed the notion that the BRI is a geostrategic initiative, suggesting instead that it is of a "geoeconomic cooperative design."[72] The NDRC's outline notes, for instance, that the initiative is in line with the purpose and principles of the United Nations Charter and with the "Five Principles of Peaceful Coexistence."[73] Evoking Confucian tenets ("He who wants success should enable others to succeed"), the Chinese ambassador to the United Kingdom has insisted that the project is "an offer of a ride on China's economic express train. It is a public product for the good of the whole world."[74]

Outside commentators are skeptical, noting the wider strategic benefits of the BRI. Economically, the initiative allows China to mitigate the effects of its economic slowdown. Echoing Vladimir Lenin's description of capitalistic imperial expansion (and with no small irony given China's Leninist credentials),[75] China can export overcapacity in steel and construction by building infrastructure throughout Eurasia, strengthen the economies of trading partners (which should improve Chinese exports), and manufacture offshore to counter rising Chinese labor costs.

A second benefit is geopolitical. For one, the plan enables China to improve its trade and energy security. By reducing its vulnerability to interrupted shipping through the Strait of Malacca, through which 80 percent of Chinese energy supplies from the Middle East and Africa pass,[76] China can reduce the relative importance of blue-water naval capabilities and bypass US-dominated sea-lanes. Indeed, Beijing can build political relationships that mitigate its deteriorating relationships with its eastern maritime neighbors and balance against US influence in the Pacific.

Economic integration with the Chinese economy will increase Beijing's influence and soft power in the region. Precedent suggests that weaker, poorer countries stand to benefit from Chinese investment but may find that the jobs that are created will go predominantly to Chinese workers. Those countries may ultimately repay investment by transferring resource rights to China.[77] A greater Chinese presence in Central Asia will fill the vacuum left by the gradual US withdrawal from Afghanistan, and in this there may be some tacit approval from the White House for overland Belt developments to the extent that they secure the wider region and prevent Muslim radicalization, including in China's restive Xinjiang Province, home to the Muslim Chinese Uighurs and the beginning of the overland Belt.[78]

These strategic elements bear directly on India. Most relevant is the CPEC. The initiative was initially envisaged to involve $46 billion in promised Chinese investment (as of mid-2017, this figure sits at $62 billion)[79] in return for which China will have the use of Gwadar Port, now run by the China Overseas Port Holding Company. The project will create a link between the port and Xinjiang Province, traversing Pakistan-controlled Kashmir. Evidently this is a source of tension for India, as the CPEC supports de facto Pakistani control of a territory that India considers occupied. The security risks to Chinese workers on infrastructure projects have also required increased military assistance, and there are Indian concerns that the project will involve a People's Liberation Army presence in contested Kashmir.[80] Military cooperation between China and Pakistan seems inevitable. The Chinese have reportedly requested the Pakistani army to take greater charge of the project's logistics, and a fifteen-thousand-strong army-led security force has been deployed to protect Chinese personnel working on the CPEC.[81]

New Delhi's concerns echo those communicated by Indian officials to the news agency Reuters over the increased Chinese naval presence in Sri Lanka in 2014, which included the docking of a Chinese submarine and warship in Colombo's port (heavily invested in by China) in late October 2014.[82] Chinese commentary stresses that any naval presence would focus on sea-lane security rather than sea-lane control,[83] but Indian commentators have repeated fears of a Chinese "string of pearls" strategy in which India would find itself encircled by China.

Indian apprehensions have triggered countermeasures. New Delhi declined to attend a major forum held May 14–16, 2017, at which Xi Jinping officially launched the BRI, citing concerns about the incursions of the CPEC into contested territory. An official statement from the Indian Ministry of External Affairs explained, "Regarding the so-called 'China-Pakistan Economic Corridor,' which is being projected as the flagship project of the BRI/OBOR, the international community is well aware of India's position. No country can accept a project that ignores its core concerns on sovereignty and territorial integrity."[84] In what is likely to be an effort in contrasting the BRI with its own projects, India has also cautioned about the financial sustainability of servicing the debt from Chinese loans. "Connectivity initiatives," the same document explained, "must follow principles of financial responsibility to avoid projects that would create unsustainable debt burden for communities."[85]

Indeed, India has been making efforts to counter Chinese investment with spending pledges of its own. Just days after the May BRI summit, New Delhi hosted a conference on the International North-South Trade Corridor (INSTC), an initiative launched by India, Iran, and Russia that has long lain dormant but would involve infrastructure investment in order to create a transit corridor from India, through Iran and Central Asia, to Russia. The INSTC was further energized by a subsequent visit by Modi to Russia on June 1–3 for the St. Petersburg International Economic Forum.[86]

New Delhi's efforts to counter Beijing's influence have also been joined by Tokyo. During a May 2016 visit to Iran, Modi pledged $500 million to develop Iran's Chabahar Port, with further goals to extend overland road and rail infrastructure to the Afghan border. The project will help to bolster Indian influence in the Indian Ocean in what has been interpreted as an unambiguous response to the greater Chinese presence in India's maritime backyard.[87] Japan pledged in early 2017 to join the project, a commitment that was reiterated shortly before the May 2017 BRI summit avoided by India.[88] In a May 8 interview with *The Hindu*, the Japanese ambassador to India, Kenji Hiramatsu, explained, "We are interested in connectivity projects and to make sure that this region is free and open and an important port like Chabahar is good for regional connectivity."[89] As part of an initiative to develop a "Freedom Corridor," the two countries have planned further joint infrastructure projects in East Africa, Southeast Asia, and Sri Lanka.[90]

India may also be attempting to limit CPEC progress directly. Pakistan alleges Indian involvement in stoking the Balochistan insurgency—a thorn in the side of infrastructure-development progress for China and Pakistan. This support is denied by New Delhi, but Modi's August 2016 Independence Day address referred to Balochistan while underscoring New Delhi's displeasure at the CPEC and a willingness to hamper its completion.[91]

This competitive atmosphere is only heightened by the military standoff between Indian and Chinese troops in the Doklam triborder area. In June 2017, Indian troops intervened in territory contested by China and Bhutan to prevent Chinese military personnel from building, or improving, a road leading toward the Jampheri Ridge, a strategic point above the foothills of southern Bhutan that ultimately leads to the India-Bhutan border near the Siliguri Corridor. It is difficult to be definitive about the reasons for the standoff,[92] but some commentators have drawn a connection between the road-building and New Delhi's decision not to attend the BRI Forum. A former Indian foreign secretary opined that "in Chinese perceptions . . . India's refusal to join Xi Jinping's signature initiative, the One Belt One Road, is seen as impertinence."[93] If that conclusion goes too far, it is certainly the case that the BRI has so far failed to encourage greater cooperation between China and India.

Much as the bilateral China-India trade relationship has begun to exhibit asymmetries that could leave India vulnerable to China, the new Silk Road will disproportionately increase Chinese investment—and influence—in the wider region. Indian participation in the AIIB goes some way toward alleviating this concern, but China is spearheading this venture, and it is to Beijing that the major political benefits will accrue. If Beijing is serious about the BRI bringing mutual benefits to China and partner countries, Beijing may need to develop cooperative initiatives around the noneconomic aspects of the plan. This might include joint naval patrolling of sea-lanes, particularly in the Indian Ocean, where India will feel most threatened. Unless a meaningful multilateral dimension to the project is fostered, it is likely to remain a source of tension and to encourage countermeasures by threatened countries such as India.

CONCLUSION

A decade and a half into the twenty-first century, international trade has become highly politicized. Attempts to complete the Doha Development Round of multilateral integration at the WTO have all but fallen by the wayside. The world's major powers have turned to negotiating PTAs, including several megaregional agreements. These processes have in part been driven by the rise of new economic powers and their growing integration into the global economy. In this context, it is important to assess how international economic ties between China and India might help—or hinder—the prospects for a resolution of their longstanding rivalry.

This chapter shows that while trade has indeed increased, this has been driven largely by increasing Chinese exports to India, which nevertheless remains a relatively minor export destination for China overall. The relationship is now one of growing asymmetry: China is India's top source of imports and in recent years has been among its most important export markets. India is less significant for China. This asymmetry is compounded by China's BRI, which has become Beijing's flagship foreign policy and in which the "geoeconomic" and the "geostrategic" seem to be increasingly inseparable—despite official pronouncements to the contrary. Bolstered by China's prodigious foreign reserves, the funding for this project is vast, and its scope immense. If it proceeds as planned, the project promises to at once prolong China's economic growth by exporting its overcapacity and to forge political ties with its Western neighbors, mitigating against growing tensions around the South China Sea.

Theory tells us that economic ties such as these are unlikely to improve political relations. Indeed, the asymmetry bodes ill for the China-India rivalry. While it may check aggression on the part of India, it is unlikely to do so for China. There are already signs of this. The CPEC has raised New Delhi's hackles, with fears of Chinese encirclement around its old rival and encroachment into the Indian Ocean.

Moreover, while the literature on the "commercial peace" has been one of the most productive in international relations scholarship, it has not yet caught up with major shifts in the governance of the trade regime. The implications of an expanding network of PTAs and other international economic institutions have yet to be fully realized. In this, there is some hope for the China-India relationship. The two states are both members of the RCEP, the Asian answer to the TPP. Recent signs suggest Indian commitment to integration through the RCEP has increased, with New Delhi willing to accept more ambitious tariff cuts in exchange for greater liberalization of trade in services, where India has a comparative advantage. Successful negotiation of the RCEP will almost certainly boost China-India trade and, hopefully, correct the current trade imbalance to some extent. Crucially, theory and empirical research suggest that such cooperation through a PTA such as the RCEP is also likely to amplify the pacifying effects of trade flows. In addition, India is the second-largest donor to the AIIB, one of the top funding bodies for the BRI.

Yet institutional cooperation cannot be limited to this. It will be important for the BRI to be accompanied by more efforts to create governing institutions than currently exist. This is particularly so since much of the BRI investment is likely to come directly from China, rather than through the AIIB. In this, the literature on interdependence and conflict is unfortunately less helpful a guide. The BRI represents a massive effort to coordinate foreign investment, but how the resulting investment flows will be governed has been given far less attention. Unfortunately, it is precisely the governance of investment flows that has been one of the most contentious areas of international economic law in the past decade. For the BRI to be a promise of peace in Eurasia, it will be important to embed the project in sufficient cooperative institutions in which other states, India most notably, can be afforded a significant stakeholder role and the status that comes with it.

NOTES

1. Indian unilateral liberalization of the services sector has meant that despite China's strict WTO accession, India's services sector is more liberal. As Panagariya notes, the possibility for further liberalization may be stronger in India than in China. See Arvind Panagariya, "India and China," in *Economic Reform in India: Challenges, Prospects and Lessons*, ed. Nicholas C. Hope, Anjini Kochar, Roger Noll, and T. N. Srinivasan (Cambridge: Cambridge University Press, 2012), 96–138.
2. See Selina Ho's chapter 7.
3. Charles de Secondat, Baron de Montesquieu, *The Spirit of Laws* (New York: Cosimo, 2011 [1748]), book 20; and Immanuel Kant, *Toward Perpetual Peace and Other Writings on Politics, Peace and History*, ed. Pauline Kleingard (New Haven, CT: Yale University Press, 2006).
4. Among many others, see Solomon William Polachek, "Conflict and Trade," *Journal of Conflict Resolution* 24, no. 1 (1980): 55–78; John R. Oneal et al., "The Liberal Peace: Interdependence, Democracy, and International Conflict, 1950–85," *Journal of Peace Research* 33, no. 1 (1996): 11–28; and Bruce Russett and John Oneal, *Triangulating Peace: Democracy, Interdependence, and International Organizations* (New York: Norton, 2001).

5. Erik Gartzke, Quan Li, and Charles Boehmer, "Investing in the Peace: Economic Interdependence and International Conflict," *International Organization* 55, no. 2 (April 2001): 391–438.

6. Ibid. See also Solomon Polachek, Carlos Seiglie, and Jun Xiang, "The Impact of Foreign Direct Investment on International Conflict," *Defence and Peace Economics* 18, no. 5 (2007): 415–29; and Margit Bussmann, "Foreign Direct Investment and Militarized International Conflict," *Journal of Peace Research* 47, no. 2 (2010): 143–53.

7. Joanne Gowa, *Allies, Adversaries and International Trade* (Princeton, NJ: Princeton University Press, 1994); Joanne Gowa and Edward D. Mansfield, "Power Politics and International Trade," *American Political Science Review* 87, no. 2 (June 1993): 408–20. This is still debated. See Omar M. G. Keshk, Brian M. Pollins, and Rafael Reuveny, "Trade Still Follows the Flag: The Primacy of Politics in a Simultaneous Model of Interdependence and Armed Conflict," *Journal of Politics* 66, no. 4 (2004): 1155–79; Omar M. G. Keshk, Rafael Reuveny, and Brian M. Pollins, "Trade and Conflict: Proximity, Country Size and Measures," *Conflict Management and Peace Science* 27, no. 1 (2010): 3–27; and Brian M. Pollins, "Does Trade Still Follow the Flag? A Model of International Diplomacy and Commerce," *American Political Science Review* 83, no. 2 (June 1989): 465–80. Against this perspective, see Håvard Hegre, John R. Oneal, and Bruce Russett, "Trade Does Promote Peace: New Simultaneous Estimates of the Reciprocal Effects of Trade and Conflict," *Journal of Peace Research* 47, no. 6 (2010): 763–74.

8. Christopher Gelpi and Joseph M. Grieco, "Economic Interdependence, the Democratic State, and the Liberal Peace," in *Economic Interdependence and International Conflict: New Perspectives on an Enduring Debate*, ed. Edward D. Mansfield and Brian M. Pollins (Ann Arbor: University of Michigan Press, 2003), 44–59. Of course, as Andrew Moravcsik notes in the canonical statement of analytical liberalism, the aggregation of social preferences does not occur solely in democratic regimes. See Moravcsik, "Taking Preferences Seriously: A Liberal Theory of International Politics," *International Organization* 51, no. 4 (Autumn 1997): 518.

9. Brandon J. Kinne, "Multilateral Trade and Militarized Conflict: Centrality, Openness, and Asymmetry in the Global Trade Network," *Journal of Politics* 74, no. 1 (January 2012): 308–22; Katja B. Kleinberg, Gregory Robinson, and Stewart L. French, "Trade Concentration and Interstate Conflict," *Journal of Politics* 74, no. 2 (April 2012): 529–40; Etel Solingen, "Internationalization, Coalitions, and Regional Conflict and Cooperation," in *Economic Interdependence and International Conflict: New Perspectives on an Enduring Debate*, ed. Edward D. Mansfield and Brian M. Pollins (Ann Arbor: University of Michigan Press, 2003), 60–85.

10. Philippe Martin, Thierry Mayer, and Mathias Thoenig, "Make Trade Not War?," *Review of Economic Studies* 75, no. 3 (July 2008): 865–900.

11. Mansfield and Pollins, *Economic Interdependence and International Conflict*, 9.

12. Han Dorussen, "Heterogeneous Trade Interests and Conflict: What You Trade Matters," *Journal of Conflict Resolution* 50, no. 1 (2006): 87–107.

13. Edward D. Mansfield, "Preferential Peace: Why Preferential Trading Arrangements Inhibit Interstate Conflict," in Mansfield and Pollins, *Economic Interdependence and International Conflict*, 222–36.

14. Emilie M. Hafner-Burton and Alexander H. Montgomery, "War, Trade, and Distrust: Why Trade Agreements Don't Always Keep the Peace," *Conflict Management and Peace Science* 29, no. 3 (2012): 257–78.

15. Although from a costly signaling perspective, asymmetry may have little effect. See, for instance, Erik Gartzke and Quan Li, "War, Peace, and the Invisible

Hand: Positive Political Externalities of Economic Globalization," *International Studies Quarterly* 47, no. 4 (December 2003): 561–86.

16. Håvard Hegre, "Size Asymmetry, Trade, and Militarized Conflict," *Journal of Conflict Resolution* 48, no. 3 (2004): 403–29.

17. Albert O. Hirschman, *National Power and the Structure of Foreign Trade* (Berkeley: University of California Press, 1945); and Christopher K. Chase-Dunn, *Global Formation: Structures of the World Economy* (Lanham, MD: Rowman & Littlefield, 1998).

18. John A. Hobson, *Imperialism* (UK: Cosimo, 2005 [1902]); Vladimir Illyovich Lenin, *Imperialism: The Highest Stage of Capitalism; A Popular Outline* (New York: International Publishers, 1939 [1916]); and John Gallagher and Ronald Robinson, "The Imperialism of Free Trade," *Economic History Review* 6, no. 1 (1953): 1–15.

19. Katherine Barbieri, "Economic Interdependence: A Path to Peace or a Source of Interstate Conflict?," *Journal of Peace Research* 33, no. 1 (1996): 29–49.

20. Jonathan Kirshner, "Realist Political Economy: Traditional Themes and Contemporary Challenges," in *Routledge Handbook of International Political Economy: IPE as a Global Conversation*, ed. Mark Blyth (London: Routledge, 2009), 36–47. This is a large literature. See Norrin M. Ripsman and T.V. Paul, *Globalization and the National Security State* (New York: Oxford University Press, 2010), 20–35.

21. For more encompassing definitions, see Ripsman and Paul, *Globalization and the National Security State*, 5–10; and Kirshner, "Realist Political Economy," 41.

22. Ripsman and Paul, *Globalization and the National Security State*.

23. John Ravenhill, "Is Economic Interdependence a Stop-Gap for Regional Conflict in 21st Century Asia?," in *The Asian Century: What International Norms and Practices*, ed. Françoise Nicolas, Céline Paion, and John Seaman (Paris, IFRI, 2014), 75–83.

24. Richard N. Rosecrance, *Rise of the Trading State: Commerce and Conquest in the Modern World* (New York: Basic Books, 1986).

25. Robert Pape, "Soft Balancing against the United States," *International Security* 30, no. 1 (Summer 2005): 7–45; and T.V. Paul, "Soft Balancing in the Age of U.S. Primacy," *International Security* 30, no. 1 (Summer 2005): 46–71.

26. Karl Polanyi, *The Great Transformation: The Political and Economic Origins of Our Time* (New York: Farrar & Rinehart, 1944).

27. Edward D. Mansfield and Helen V. Milner, "The New Wave of Regionalism," *International Organization* 53, no. 3 (July 1999): 589–627; and Caroline Freund and Emanuel Ornelas, "Regional Trade Agreements," *Annual Review of Economics* 2 (2010): 139–66.

28. Deborah W. Larson, T.V. Paul, and William C. Wohlforth, "Status and World Order," in *Status in World Politics*, ed. T.V. Paul, Deborah W. Larson, and William C. Wohlforth (New York: Cambridge University Press, 2014), 3–29.

29. Andreas Dür, Leonardo Baccini, and Manfred Elsig, "The Design of International Trade Agreements: Introducing a New Dataset," *Review of International Organizations* 9, no. 3 (September 2014): 353–75.

30. Karl P. Sauvant, "New Sources of FDI: The BRICs—Outward FDI from Brazil, Russia, India and China," *Journal of World Investment and Trade* 6, no. 5 (2005): 639–710.

31. Ibid.

32. ENS Economic Bureau, "India's Pharma Dependence on China Gets a Cut, via Duties," *Indian Express*, August 16, 2016, http://indianexpress.com/article /business/business-others/indias-pharma-dependence-on-china-gets-a-cut-via -duties-2977713/.

33. Dorussen, "Heterogeneous Trade Interests."
34. For a previous application, see Swapan K. Bhattacharya and Biswa N. Bhattacharyay, "Gains and Losses of India-China Trade Cooperation: A Gravity Model Impact Analysis," CESifo Working Paper Series, no. 1970 (April 2007), https://papers.ssrn.com/sol3/Papers.cfm?abstract_id=985274.
35. World Bank, World Integrated Trade Solution, accessed March 23, 2017, http://wits.worldbank.org/.
36. Sasidaran Gopalan and Ramkishen S. Rajan, "India's FDI Flows: Trying to Make Sense of the Numbers," *United Nations ESCAP: Alerts on Emerging Policy Challenges* 5 (January 2010): 1–8.
37. United Nations Conference on Trade and Development (UNCTAD), *World Investment Report 2006: FDI from Developing and Transition Economies; Implications for Development* (New York and Geneva: United Nations, 2006), 12, http://unctad.org/en/docs/wir2006_en.pdf; and Wenhui Wei, "China and India: Any Difference in Their FDI Performances?," *Journal of Asian Economics* 16, no. 4 (August 2005): 722–23.
38. For comparison, total outward Chinese FDI in 2012 was $87.80 billion, and the Indian figure was $10.97 billion.
39. United Nations Conference on Trade and Development (UNCTAD), FDI/TNC Database, based on data from the Chinese Ministry of Commerce, accessed July 30, 2017, http://unctad.org/Sections/dite_fdistat/docs/webdiaeia2014d3_CHN.pdf.
40. UNCTAD, FDI/TNC Database, based on data from the Reserve Bank of India, accessed July 30, 2017, http://unctad.org/Sections/dite_fdistat/docs/webdiaeia2014d3_IND.pdf.
41. UNCTAD, *World Investment Report 2017: Investment and the Digital Economy* (Geneva: United Nations, 2017), 16, http://unctad.org/en/PublicationsLibrary/wir2017_en.pdf.
42. Ibid., 19.
43. World Bank, World Integrated Trade Solution, accessed June 10, 2016, http://wits.worldbank.org/.
44. Imports and exports of petroleum products accounted for $149 billion and $53 billion, respectively, in 2012 and $72 billion and $30 billion, respectively, in 2015.
45. For a historical overview of China and India's experience with liberalization until the first decade of the 2000s, see Panagariya, "India and China."
46. UNCTAD, *World Investment Report 2017*, 12.
47. fDiIntelligence, *The FDI Report 2016: Global Greenfields Investment Trends* (London: Financial Times, 2016), https://www.fdiintelligence.com/Landing-Pages/fDi-Report-2016/The-fDi-Report-2016. Greenfield FDI and net FDI figures can differ substantially as greenfield figures refer to planned expenditure, while FDI inflows refer to actual flows.
48. Klaus Schwab and Xavier Sala i Martin, *The Global Competitiveness Report 2016–2017* (Geneva: World Economic Forum, 2016), 29.
49. fDiIntelligence, *FDI Report 2016*, 7.
50. Andrew F. Cooper, "The G20 as an Improvised Crisis Committee and/or a Contested 'Steering Committee' for the World," *International Affairs* 86, no. 3 (May 2010): 741–57.
51. G. John Ikenberry, "The Future of the Liberal World Order: Internationalism after America," *Foreign Affairs* 90, no. 3 (May/June 2011): 56–68.
52. Chinese Ministry of Commerce, "China FTA Network," accessed January 20, 2017, http://fta.mofcom.gov.cn/english/fta_qianshu.shtml.

53. Indian Ministry of Commerce, "International Trade," accessed January 20, 2017, http://commerce.nic.in/trade/international_ta.asp?id=2&trade=i.
54. Observers tend not to include the APTA in China's list of trade agreements. For instance, John Whalley and Chunding Li, "China's Regional and Bilateral Trade Agreements," VoxEU, March 5, 2014, http://voxeu.org/article/china-s-regional -and-bilateral-trade-agreements.
55. World Bank, "Military Expenditure (% of GDP)," accessed December 5, 2016, http://data.worldbank.org/indicator/MS.MIL.XPND.GD.ZS?name_desc= false.
56. Stockholm International Peace Research Institute, "Military Expenditure Database," accessed December 10, 2016, https://www.sipri.org/databases/milex.
57. Ibid.
58. Panagariya, "India and China," 118–20; and Rafiq Dossani and Martin Kenney, "The Next Wave of Globalization: Relocating Service Provision to India," *World Development* 35, no. 5 (May 2007): 772–91.
59. Barry Eichengreen and Hui Tong, "Is China's FDI Coming at the Expense of Other Countries?," *Journal of the Japanese and International Economies* 21, no. 2 (2007): 153–72.
60. Pape, "Soft Balancing"; and Paul, "Soft Balancing."
61. Bhoj Raj Poudel and Kawsu Walter Ceesay, "A Zero-Sum Game in South Asia Benefits Nobody," *The Diplomat*, December 4, 2014.
62. Kavaljit Singh, "India Changes Tack on RCEP Negotiations," *Mainstream Weekly*, October 29, 2016, http://www.mainstreamweekly.net/article6783.html.
63. Wu Jiao and Zhang Yunbi, "Xi Proposes a 'New Silk Road' with Central Asia," *China Daily USA*, September 8, 2013, accessed January 16, 2016, http://usa .chinadaily.com.cn/china/2013-09/08/content_16952304.htm.
64. Bert Hofman, "China's One Belt One Road Initiative: What We Know Thus Far," World Bank, April 12, 2015, http://blogs.worldbank.org/eastasiapacific /china-one-belt-one-road-initiative-what-we-know-thus-far.
65. Wu Jiao and Zhang Yunbi, "Xi in Call for Building of New 'Maritime Silk Road,'" *China Daily USA*, October 4, 2013, http://usa.chinadaily.com.cn/china /2013-10/04/content_17008940.htm.
66. Xinhua Net, "Chronology of China's Belt and Road Initiative," June 24, 2016, http://news.xinhuanet.com/english/2016-06/24/c_135464233.htm.
67. People's Republic of China, Ministry of Foreign Affairs and Ministry of Commerce, National Development and Reform Commission, "Vision and Actions on Jointly Building Silk Road Economic Belt and 21st-Century Maritime Silk Road," March 28, 2015, http://en.ndrc.gov.cn/newsrelease/201503/t20150330 _669367.html.
68. Hofman, "China's One Belt One Road Initiative."
69. Ben Blanchard, "China Says AIIB Won't Be Used for $46 Billion Pakistan Deal," Reuters, April 17, 2015, http://in.reuters.com/article/china-pakistan -idINKBN0N80RQ20150417.
70. He Yini, "China to Invest $900 Billion in Belt and Road Initiative," *The Telegraph*, June 10, 2015, http://www.telegraph.co.uk/sponsored/china-watch /business/11663881/china-billion-dollar-belt-road-initiatve.html.
71. Michael D. Swaine, "Chinese Views and Commentary on the 'One Belt, One Road,'" *China Leadership Monitor*, no. 47 (Summer 2015): 1–24.
72. Liu Zongyi, "India's Political Goals Hinder Cooperation with China on 'Belt, Road,'" *Global Times*, July 3, 2016, http://www.globaltimes.cn/content/992047 .shtml.
73. People's Republic of China, "Vision and Actions."

74. Liu Xiaoming, "New Silk Road Is an Opportunity Not a Threat," *Financial Times*, May 24, 2015, https://www.ft.com/content/c8f58a7c-ffd6-11e4-bc30 -00144feabdc0.

75. Charles Clover and Lucy Hornby, "China's Great Game: Road to a New Empire," *Financial Times*, October 12, 2015, https://www.ft.com/content/6e098274 -587a-11e5-a28b-50226830d644; Lenin, *Imperialism*.

76. Nadège Rolland, "China's New Silk Road," *National Bureau of Asian Research Commentary*, February 12, 2015, 3.

77. Sarah Lain, "China's Silk Road in Central Asia: Transformative or Exploitative?," *Beyond BRICS* (blog), *Financial Times*, April 27, 2016, http://blogs.ft.com /beyond-brics/2016/04/27/chinas-silk-road-in-central-asia-transformative-or -exploitative/.

78. Younkyoo Kim and Fabio Indeo, "The New Great Game in Central Asia Post 2014: The US 'New Silk Road' Strategy and Sino-Russian Rivalry," *Communist and Post-Communist Studies* 46, no. 2 (2013): 280.

79. Shailaja Neelakantan, "China Hikes Investment in CPEC to $62bn from $55bn," *Times of India*, April 16, 2017, http://timesofindia.indiatimes.com /world/pakistan/china-hikes-investment-in-cpec-to-62bn-from-55bn/articleshow /58206829.cms.

80. Amy Kazmin, "India Watches Anxiously as Chinese Influence Grows," *Financial Times*, May 9, 2016, https://www.ft.com/content/e9baebee-0bd8-11e6-9456 -444ab5211a2f.

81. Farhan Bokhari, Lucy Hornby, and Christian Shepherd, "China Urges Pakistan to Give Army Lead Role in Silk Road Project," *Financial Times*, July 21, 2016, https://www.ft.com/content/5eea66c0-4ef9-11e6-8172-e39ecd3b86fc.

82. Shihar Aneez and Ranga Sirilal, "Chinese Submarine Docks in Sri Lanka Despite Indian Concerns," Reuters, November 2, 2014, http://in.reuters.com/article/sri -lanka-china-submarine-idINKBN0IM0LU20141102.

83. Morgan Clemens, "The Maritime Silk Road and the PLA: Part One," *China Brief* 15, no. 6 (2015): 6–9; and Morgan Clemens, "The Maritime Silk Road and the PLA: Part Two," *China Brief* 15, no. 7 (2015): 10–13.

84. Ministry of External Affairs, Government of India, "Official Spokes- person's Response to a Query on Participation of India in OBOR/BRI Forum," May 13, 2017, http://mea.gov.in/media-briefings.htm?dtl/28463 /Official+Spokespersons+response+to+a+query+on+participation+of+India+in +OBORBRI+Forum.

85. Ibid.

86. Roshan Iyer, "Good News for India as North-South Trade Corridor Takes Shape," *The Diplomat*, June 10, 2017, http://thediplomat.com/2017/06/good -news-for-india-as-north-south-trade-corridor-takes-shape/.

87. "India and Iran Sign 'Historic' Chabahar Port Deal," BBC, May 23, 2016, http://www.bbc.com/news/world-asia-india-36356163.

88. Sachin Parashar, "India Focused on Chabahar as Japan Reiterates Commitment to Port Project," *Times of India*, January 19, 2017, http://timesofindia.indiatimes .com/india/india-focused-on-chabahar-as-japan-reiterates-commitment-to-port -project/articleshow/56655214.cms.

89. Suhasini Haidar, "Japan Pitches for Chabahar Port," *The Hindu*, May 8, 2017, http://www.thehindu.com/todays-paper/tp-national/japan-pitches-for -chabahar-port/article18405900.ece.

90. Dipanjan Roy Chaudhury, "Pushing Back against China's One Belt One Road, India, Japan Build Strategic Great Wall," *Economic Times*, May 16, 2017, http://economictimes.indiatimes.com/news/economy/infrastructure/pushing

-back-against-chinas-one-belt-one-road-india-japan-build-strategic-great-wall
/articleshow/58689033.cms.

91. Iain Marlow, "Modi Sends Warning Shot to China, Pakistan on Territory Spat,"
Bloomberg, August 17, 2016, https://www.bloomberg.com/news/articles/2016
-08-16/modi-toughens-up-on-territory-spats-as-china-pakistan-ties-grow.

92. See Ankit Panda, "What's Driving the India-China Standoff at Doklam?," *The
Diplomat*, July 18, 2017, http://thediplomat.com/2017/07/whats-driving-the
-india-china-standoff-at-doklam/.

93. Shyam Saran "The Standoff in Doklam," *The Tribune*, July 4, 2017, http://www
.tribuneindia.com/news/comment/the-standoff-in-doklam/431243.html.

Chapter 11

China-India Engagement in Institutions

Convergence and Divergence on Global Governance Reforms

FENG LIU

Effective global governance in the twenty-first century will inevitably be determined by the interests and willingness of great powers to share their responsibilities for providing public goods and addressing challenges in the international system. Global governance has traditionally been dominated by the established powers of the Group of Seven—Canada, France, Germany, Italy, Japan, the United Kingdom, and the United States—especially by the latter. Recently, however, emerging powers such as China and India are attempting to play a greater role in international affairs. This chapter explores how these attempts cause both their competition and cooperation in multilateral institutions.

China and India are leading emerging powers in the current international system. In recent years, the two countries have not only expressed their desire to have a more prominent role in global governance but also have taken concrete actions to reform the current international order. As a result, whether the emerging powers will challenge the existing international order has emerged as a topic of concern among students of international relations.[1] As the world's two most populous and fastest-developing nations, China and India have many shared interests. They both seek the elevation of developing countries in international institutions, contend for greater ability to create international norms, and generally wish to see a more multipolar world order.[2]

China and India have used these shared interests as platforms to strengthen their cooperation in international institutions. Although China-India relations have been often characterized by mutual rivalry and distrust,[3] their cooperation in multilateral institutions, at both global and regional levels, is one of the most promising aspects of, and an important mitigating factor for, bilateral relations. However, in some cases, China and India have divergent interests that constrain their ability to collaborate and thereby intensify rivalry and competition between the two nations.

This chapter proceeds as follows: The first section provides a theoretical framework for understanding how emerging powers influence global governance through international institutions. The second section summarizes the current status of China-India cooperation in major global and regional institutions and analyzes the causes of the discrepancy in their cooperation under the different multilateral institutions. The third section provides an empirical study of China-India cooperation in two important issue areas, international economic governance and climate change, to reveal their appeal for cooperation and the specific results of their cooperation. The fourth section deals with two cases—membership on the United Nations Security Council (UNSC) and in the Nuclear Suppliers Group (NSG)—where divergent interests lead to competition between China and India within international institutions. The chapter concludes with further discussion of the effect that China-India cooperation is having in international institutions.

CHINA-INDIA COOPERATION IN INTERNATIONAL INSTITUTIONS

Emerging powers constantly seek to shape the international system to better conform to their interests. However, the tools that emerging powers have at their disposal for influencing global affairs are limited when accounted individually. Still, it should be noted that emerging powers on the whole benefit from the current international system and do not seek its removal but rather its reform. Emerging powers primarily wish for an international system that better represents the distribution of power between developed and developing nations. In recognition of their limited power individually, emerging powers have taken to forming coalitions with other developing countries within international institutions in order to influence global affairs. This process involves intraorganizational bargaining between emerging powers as they try to reach consensus.

China and India are key players in the modern world economy and global governance, and they try to reshape the architecture and rules of global governance by their own strength. Global governance involves both formal and informal arrangements. Within those multilateral organizations such as the United Nations (UN), the World Trade Organization (WTO), the International

Monetary Fund (IMF), and the World Bank, China and India are seeking to use their positions to bring large change to the international economic order. They are both dedicated to the establishment of an open, fair, just, and transparent multilateral trading system. In addition, China and India both claim that the international community should make efforts to eliminate poverty and narrow the prosperity gap between the Global North and the Global South. Their ultimate vision is a global order of common prosperity achieved through dialogue and cooperation. To this end, they have enhanced cooperation in multilateral organizations such as the WTO and are striving to maintain the stability and growth of the global economy.

Beyond economics, however, China and India also share interests in confronting climate change and human rights. For example, both sides oppose Western countries' use of human rights issues to interfere with the internal affairs of developing countries. For China and India, human rights have too often been used as a hypocritical precursor to outside interference. Both countries advocate building up a multipolar world and in general oppose US hegemony and power politics. Both also stress respecting the right of each country to choose its own political system and development model.

Multilateral institutions provide platforms for China and India to cooperate in numerous fields. In practice, China and India have begun to intensify multilateral interactions with such major international economic institutions as the World Bank, the IMF, and the WTO, enhancing cooperation with regional organizations such as the Association of Southeast Asian Nations, the European Union, and the African Union. They are also partners in some multilateral forums, including the G-20 and the global climate negotiations. Cooperation between China and India in these international institutions is not only conducive to their national interests but also enhances their mutual trust, which would become an important tie to safeguard friendly relations between the two countries.

The deepening cooperation between the two Asian powers in international institutions is driven by their shared expectations of reforming the existing international order, improving their position and status in the current international system, and increasing their barging power vis-à-vis traditional dominant powers. Leaders in Beijing and New Delhi clearly recognize the importance of multilateral cooperation for mitigating their rivalry. On September 19, 2014, China and India issued a joint statement on building a closer developmental partnership, which stated that "as developing countries, India and China have common interests on several issues of global importance like climate change, Doha Development Round of WTO, energy and food security, reform of the international financial institutions and global governance. This is reflected in close cooperation and coordination between the two sides within the BRICS [bloc or grouping Brazil, Russia, India, China, and South Africa], G-20 and other fora."[4]

China-India cooperation in multilateral institutions is of great significance for both sides. Cooperative interactions in multilateral institutions facilitate the settlement of bilateral issues. Both sides may cooperate in extensive fields to enhance strategic mutual trust through multiple channels. Enhancing trust starts with multilateral diplomacy; therefore, China and India have been active partners on multilateral issues such as climate change, reforming financial institutions, and WTO negotiations.[5]

Furthermore, as China and India are faced with similar multilateral challenges, coordination and cooperation may relieve the external pressure. For example, in the field of economics, China and India are challenged by developed countries when it comes to trade, exchange rates, and monetary policies. In terms of reform of the international economic order, the voting rights of countries such as China and India in the IMF and the World Bank have increased to some extent, but the decision-making power of developed countries has not been weakened. Instead, they still maintain outsized influence in these two organizations. These same dominant powers request China and India to assume more obligations, despite their unwillingness to share power. On climate change, developed countries require developing countries to take more responsibility for dealing with the challenge. Against this backdrop, China and India conduct active cooperation in many multilateral institutions in the form of "issue-specific coalitions," which is conducive for them to jointly coping with the external challenges.[6]

Though the two countries strive for playing a bigger role in international institutions, it does not mean that they have the same pursuits on all-important issues. Nor does it mean that they will always satisfy each other's interests. Due to the different preferences and demands, the extent of China-India cooperation in multilateral arenas has also been constrained. For example, both seek to elevate the roles of developing countries in the World Bank, but they disagree on the priorities of this institution. Specifically, China holds that the World Bank should give priority to the construction of a clean and honest administration, transparency, and sustainable development. By contrast, India thinks that the World Bank should put financial development high on its agenda and that it should focus on the least-developed countries.

Both countries also have different opinions on how to coordinate establishing an open external economic order and maintaining the government's control over the economy. China thinks that the reform of state-owned enterprises does not conflict with the existing international economic rules. In contrast, India holds that because the free-trade order is established on the premise of private enterprises, the contradiction between the external free economic order and the realization of state control cannot be settled just through the reform of state-owned enterprises. Furthermore, the two countries have obviously conflicting views on UNSC expansion. India holds that because the current structure of the UN is inefficient and unrepresentative, the UNSC should be reformed and new members should be added. In contrast, China thinks that if the UNSC expands its permanent membership, more developing countries should be added. China does not support India's alignment with Japan, Germany, and Brazil to press for a permanent seat on an expanded council.

Measured in terms of either material capabilities or social status, emerging powers are placed at a disadvantageous position in the current international system. Ideally, therefore, coalition-building in international institutions is the best option for those powers to increase their bargaining power vis-à-vis that of dominant powers.[7] However, emerging powers also face many difficulties in forming close negotiation coalitions in international institutions. Some may choose to follow or support dominant powers in some circumstances, leaving other emerging powers in a difficult position.[8]

Having observed how China and India have interacted under multilateral institutions, we may find there are four modes of cooperation/noncooperation: (1) collective action, (2) policy coordination, (3) unilateral action, and (4) opposition. *Collective action* means that two countries enter into a temporary or permanent coalition for achieving the same objectives and setting the policy agenda in the institutions so that they can take joint actions and bargain with other actors or coalitions. For example, in WTO negotiations and UN climate-change conferences, China and India have frequently formed issue-specific coalitions.[9] *Policy coordination* means that though both sides cannot take joint actions due to policy preferences that diverge to varying degrees, they are willing to take the other side's stances and interests into consideration in bargaining so as to minimize their differences in standpoints under the multilateral framework. In promoting the reform of the IMF and the World Bank in the wake of the global financial crisis, China and India have clearly coordinated their positions, emphasizing the importance of increasing the inclusion of developing countries in international financial institutions.[10] *Unilateral action* means that one side strives for its interests and influence in specific institutions without conducting any policy negotiation and coordination with the other side but does not conflict with the other side. *Opposition* means thwarting the efforts of the other side by not supporting its policy stance. Under such circumstances, the two sides can hardly negotiate over a specific issue, nor can they reach any compromise through bargaining. For example, at the NSG's plenary session in June 2016, China set up a barrier to, in effect, prevent India from joining the group by not putting this topic on the agenda of the meeting. In this case, China implicitly vetoed India's bid.

Evidently, collective action and opposition are two extremes in the continuum of cooperation and competition. From a standard realist perspective, in a unipolar world emerging powers should combine their forces to balance against a real hegemon in the international system. However, in practice, these powers also find some competing interests among them, which prevent them from forging a counterbalancing alliance. At the regional level, their relationship is more complicated than what a classical realist account would provide.

COOPERATION CASES:
FINANCE AND CLIMATE CHANGE

China and India have achieved higher levels of cooperation in the fields of global finance and climate change. But the process toward a final resolution has not often been easy because they also have competing interests and different expectations on specific issues. Overall, the establishment of the BRICS Development Bank and the recent Paris climate-change agreement appear to provide ample information related to the issue under study.

The BRICS Bank

In the past few decades, reform of the international financial system has been a point of contention between emerging and dominant powers. Emerging powers desire increased influence in major international financial institutions, such as the IMF and the World Bank, in addition to a fair and reasonable international financial order. Simultaneously, developing nations endeavor to establish a new, "non-Western model" of financial institutions, such as the New Development Bank (also referred to as the BRICS Development Bank) and the Asian Infrastructure Investment Bank (AIIB). China and India cooperate closely on BRICS matters, and their consultations reveal how these two powers work together to increase their influence by developing new and complementary institutions apart from the current international financial system.

Since 2009, the BRICS grouping has developed from an abstract concept into an important cooperation mechanism for major emerging powers.[11] BRICS nations continue to support the organization's development as a mechanism that allows emerging economies to share positions and views on shared challenges, consolidate their policies on key international issues, and gain rule-setting power for new economies. Internally, BRICS member nations desire to use the organization to promote mutually beneficial economic and trade policies. The BRICS mechanism provides a platform for its member states to have close communication and take coordinated steps.

BRICS countries do more than hold summits. On July 16, 2014, China, Brazil, Russia, India, and South Africa signed an agreement in Fortaleza, Brazil, to establish the aforementioned New Development Bank. Its initial assessed capital was $100 billion, and the initial subscribed capital was $50 billion, which was shared equally by the founding member states.[12] The bank is an organization of practical significance and has served as an important platform for member states to assume their rightful roles in global economic governance.

The concept of the New Development Bank was put forward as early as 2012. In March 2013, the Fifth BRICS Summit was held at Durban, South Africa. The summit decided to establish the New Development Bank, hoping to use it to simplify settlements and loan transactions among BRICS countries and reduce their reliance on the US dollar and the euro. The primary motive for establishing the BRICS bank was to provide funding for infrastructure and construction within its member states. BRICS countries' departments of finance officially launched negotiations on the establishment of the BRICS bank in August 2013. Seven rounds of talks were held; throughout 2013, there was broad media coverage of the China-India negotiations in particular. Some Indian media reported that China suggested the headquarters of the BRICS bank be located in Shanghai and that China intended to make a larger ratio of contributions in order to gain greater control over issues related to bank business. In reaction, India listed as a prerequisite the equal division of stock rights, directly limiting the ability of one country to dominate the bank's affairs. Initially China did not agree to the equal division of stocks but eventually conceded. In the end, the five member states provided an equal amount of funding to the bank.[13]

Despite their consensus on contribution of capital, China and India still greatly differed over the appointment of candidates for the management of the BRICS Development Bank and the location of its headquarters. The two sides finally reached an agreement, and Shanghai was chosen as the location. However, as a concession, China removed its nominee for bank president, clearing the way for the Indian nominee to take the post. In addition, the three other BRICS nations assumed their own roles. The bank's African regional center would be located in South Africa, the first chairman of the bank's council was provided by Russia, and the first chairman of its board was provided by Brazil. The presidency would be held in rotation by India, Brazil, Russia, South Africa, and China, and the president would be elected every five years. This was a win-win solution achieved through mutual concession, compromise, and bargaining between the member states.

Established alongside the New Development Bank was the BRICS Contingent Reserve Arrangement (CRA), which was modeled after the IMF. The CRA reached the promised swap amount of $100 billion when China contributed $41 billion; Brazil, India, and Russia each contributed $18 billion; and South Africa contributed $5 billion. However, the $100 billion was placed in the reserve accounts of the central banks of member states and could be accessed only when urgent capital was needed. Many believe that the establishment of these two institutions challenges the existing international financial system dominated by the World Bank and the IMF.[14] The largest stockholder of both the World Bank and the IMF is the United States. The presidency of the World Bank has long been held by Americans, and the United States has the only right to veto. BRICS countries have positioned the BRICS bank and the CRA as "a supplement" instead of a "challenge" to the existing international monetary system. These two new institutions are not only smaller than the World Bank and the IMF but also limited in scope. Both the New Development Bank and the CRA are necessary, timely, and useful supplements to existing financial platforms.[15] As Leslie Elliott Armijo and Cynthia Roberts observe, "BRICS' preferences, singly and jointly, for global governance turn on reform and evolution, not revolution."[16]

China and India need platforms such as the BRICS cooperation mechanism to broaden their consensus, improve their international influence, and ensure the conformity of their self-interests within the international order. BRICS also assists in indirectly developing China-India relations. China hopes to strengthen its ties with other developing countries through BRICS and promote the internationalization of the renminbi as well as upgrade its bilateral relations with other BRICS countries. India aims to use BRICS membership to foster domestic economic development, create conditions for the nation to become a UNSC member, and promote world multipolarization. Therefore, China and India both attach great importance to BRICS summits and hold the institution in high esteem. Moreover, both sides view it as a strategic goal to continue to improve BRICS, and any achievements secured at the summits deepen mutual trust between the two countries.

Climate Change

When it comes to global negotiations on climate change, China and India share nearly identical interests. As the two largest developing countries and greenhouse gas emitters, China and India have similar interests in coping with climate change due to both internal and external pressures.[17] Externally, faced with pressure from developing nations, China and India need to coordinate their positions to ensure that developed countries assume more responsibilities in dealing with climate change. Internally, both countries simply need to improve their people's livelihood and make their industries greener. Statistics from the World Health Organization in 2016 show that among the twenty most seriously polluted cities worldwide, ten are in India and four are in China.[18] Therefore, China and India both have long-standing mutual interests in dealing with climate change and reducing emissions.

China and India have laid a foundation for cooperative action on combating climate change. In October 2009, the two sides signed the Agreement on Cooperation on Addressing Climate Change between China and India and established the China-India Working Group on Climate Change. In 2010, the two countries signed a memorandum of understanding on cooperation on green technologies. During multilateral negotiations, China and India have, within the framework of the BASIC countries (Brazil, South Africa, India, and China) and "the Group of 77 plus China," maintained close consultations. China and India use similar rhetoric during international negotiations on climate change and actively work toward reaching an agreement based on the principles established by the UN Framework Convention on Climate Change. These principles include equity, common but differentiated responsibilities, respective capacity, and developed countries honoring their commitment to aid developing countries in funding and technology. In addition, China and India insist that the framework's intended nationally determined contributions (INDCs) submitted by nations should be based on an objective, balanced consideration of factors such as emissions reduction, adaptability, capital, technology transfer, capacity-building, and transparency. Finally, both China and India oppose the establishment of a review mechanism by developed countries for fear that such a mechanism would constrain the growth of developing nations.[19]

On November 26 and 27, 2009, prior to the Copenhagen Climate Change Summit, climate negotiators from the BASIC countries gathered in Beijing to discuss their fundamental positions on climate change. The establishment of BASIC illuminates the need for major developing countries to take the initiative to unite on certain issues in order to safeguard their interests from dominant powers in the international system.

Although China actively coped with climate change before 2009, the Chinese government changed its way of thinking after the Copenhagen Summit. China no longer views emissions reduction as a constraint on economic growth but now sees the long-term economic incentives in promoting domestic industrial remodeling, raising energy efficiency, and diversifying energy sources in order to completely modernize China's economic structure. Instead of passively safeguarding its own interests and stressing its position as a developing country, as it did in the past, China is taking the initiative to participate in coping with global climate change as a responsible international stakeholder.

From November 30 to December 11, 2015, the twenty-first United Nations Climate Change Conference was held in Paris. A major aim of the conference was to generate the financial support needed to cut greenhouse emissions. In addition to developed countries, emerging powers, including China, were expected to make concessions and become fund bearers. How to differentiate between developed and developing nations in regard to measuring their respective contributions and making evaluation criteria became a pending issue. At the following ministerial plenary session, representatives from participating countries expressed their dissatisfaction one after another. For example, the Indian minister of the environment, Prakash Javadekar, said, "On finance, it is deeply disappointing that on the one hand developed countries are not fulfilling their obligations and on the other hand, they are trying to shift their responsibilities to developing countries."[20]

From Copenhagen to Paris, the two climate-change conferences produced changes in the roles played by China and India. The world hopefully expected a climate-change agreement to be reached at the conclusion of the Copenhagen Conference. Unfortunately, the conference ended with a bitter squabble between developed and developing nations, with no substantial agreement being reached. The failure of the Copenhagen Conference to produce any deliverables ensured subsequent conferences would be low-key and pragmatic. Both China and the United States were blamed for the failure to conclude an agreement. Western countries laid all the culpability on China, while developing countries blamed the US for its insincerity. Ultimately, the Copenhagen Conference simply became a tit-for-tat battle between China and the US, staining the public's memory of the conference.[21]

On June 30, 2015, China proposed a highly constructive idea in the form of INDCs. Fixed emission targets were proposed in China's INDC: Compared to its 2005 emissions, China would by 2030 slash its carbon dioxide emission per unit of gross domestic product (GDP) by 60 to 65 percent, nonfossil fuels would occupy approximately 20 percent of energy consumption, forest reserves would increase by 4.5 billion cubic meters, and carbon dioxide emissions would peak. China would also strive for earlier fulfillment of stated targets. India's INDC was weaker. Apart from adding the requisite statement "with the support of the international community," India's INDC mentioned only that India's share of nonfossil fuels out of its total energy capacity would increase from 30 percent in 2015 to about 40 percent in 2030 and vaguely asserted a renewable-power target of 175 gigawatts by 2022. However, it did set a deadline for peak carbon dioxide emissions.

India lags behind China economically. As China did years ago, India is sacrificing the environment for its GDP growth. Before this summit, Indian premier Narendra Modi wrote in the *Financial Times* that "advanced countries powered their way to prosperity on fossil fuel," intimating that developed nations should assume more responsibility. Modi further stated that "the principle of common but differentiated responsibilities should be the bedrock of our collective enterprise. Anything else would be morally wrong."[22] During the summit, Modi further explained that "to understand India's position, you must realize that 300 million people live on under $1 a day and have no electricity, and that 700 million people depend on climate-sensitive monsoon-pattern agriculture."[23] So, in dealing with climate change, a distinction should be made between developed and developing countries. There is no one-size-fits-all criterion.

The remarks and actions of the Indian government were reminiscent of those of the Chinese government during the Copenhagen Conference. On December 3, 2015, Xie Zhenhua, China's special representative for climate change, convened a press conference to report on the progress of negotiations. According to Xie, China understood India's predicament, as China had undergone the same process of industrialization. India still has many internal problems to fix, he said, while also facing international pressure to combat climate change. Xie also acknowledged that China and India have cooperated very well on climate change. China, India, and other BASIC countries took the same stance on climate change. On the whole, developing countries, including the Group of 77 plus China, were of the same mind on climate change, although they might be divided on specific solutions. In terms of equality, India hoped that differentiated responsibilities could be acknowledged at the Paris Conference and be represented in all aspects, including reduction, adaptability, and capital. India also hoped that developed countries would raise their target emission reductions. India expected that developed countries would increase their capital commitments as well. After arduous negotiations, an agreement involving the participation of nearly two hundred countries and regions on global emission reduction was concluded on December 12, 2015. It was the first of its kind in history.

From the final text of the agreement, we can clearly see the result of international compromise. First, the goal to limit rising temperatures to 1.5 degrees centigrade, a target mainly supported by small island countries and the European Union, is confirmed but without a specific target and review mechanism for its implementation. Second, developing countries have written into the resolution measures to prevent the commitment of developed countries from becoming a mere formality and to ensure that developed countries provide developing countries with $100 billion per year before the year 2020 to tackle climate change. In addition, the regular inventory mechanism, a concern among the UN and developed countries, will be launched in 2023. It will be reinitiated once every five years to help all countries to make greater efforts to combat climate change. It also reflects concessions made by emerging powers.

It should be noted that India and China are not formal allies but simply have political aims that align when dealing with climate change. These two countries often can reach consensus in principle, but they have remarkably different positions on key issues concerning specific obligations. On the whole, however, China and India have played a leading role in promoting the principle of common but differentiated responsibilities. Moreover, the two countries have worked together to push forward the topic of climate change. Their commitments not only represent the wisdom of Asia but also conform to the interests of developing and developed countries. Global climate governance requires China and India to adjust their development models in order to be seen as active partners in the effort against climate change.

DIVERGENT INTERESTS AND COMPETITION: THE UNSC AND THE NSG

Mistrust is increasingly a defining aspect of China-India relations. As each nation grows in power, it seeks to insulate itself from the other's influence. This process involves a low-intensity but high-stakes competition whereby China and India each vie for influence and status in international institutions. This competition is deeply layered and driven in part by the similarities between the two nations. Similar national narratives centered on postcolonial rejuvenation and territorial integrity have given their populaces a strong national identity, framing conflicting views on their territorial disputes. Efforts at military modernization create a security dilemma that leaves both nations wary of each other's intent. By the very nature of geography, it was always likely that China and India, having risen in the same era, would experience some level of competition.

However, it is important to understand that while China and India are similar, key differences influence competition between the two powers in international institutions. While World Bank data reveals that India's annual GDP growth in early 2017 outpaced China's by 7.1 percent, the data also shows that China's economy is at least four times the size of India's.[24] This disparity in wealth between the two nations can be seen in the amount of funds dedicated to military spending. In 2014, China's military expenditures totaled $214 billion, while India's were only $50 billion.[25] That year China maintained this massive lead while keeping military expenditures at around 2 percent of GDP, while India's were approximately 2.5 percent.[26] India has many security concerns, from safeguarding itself from its perennial rival Pakistan, to expanding its influence over the Indian Ocean. However, China is better able to finance its military and at a lower cost. Furthermore, China is already an established power in many of the international institutions that India wishes to be a part of, such as the UNSC and the NSG. In many aspects, India is fighting an uphill battle against China for power and influence and seeks to offset its disadvantages with closer partnerships with China's rivals, particularly the United States.

The United Nations Security Council

India's quest to become a permanent member of the UNSC remains an important area of China-India competition. China seeks to preserve its status as the sole Asian power represented on the council, while paying lip service to the need for reform. For India, permanent membership represents its "legitimate" right as a major power that cannot be ignored in world affairs.

Decoupled from the lens of great-power politics, it is easy to see why many states (including China and India) would genuinely want to see reform brought to the UNSC. Established in the immediate aftermath of World War II, the UNSC was tasked with providing a platform for nations to secure international peace and stability while promoting cooperation among nations. However, this platform was never intended to be equal, as permanent membership and veto rights were granted exclusively to the victorious nations: the United States, the United Kingdom, France, the Soviet Union, and China. Any proposal put forward by the council can be vetoed by a permanent member, forcing proposals to be politically amenable to permanent members. Decades of politicking by permanent members have called into question the wisdom of allowing the council to continue to be run by the World War II victors. The world has changed greatly since 1945, and new powers are emerging that have compelling arguments for having more say in how the international order is run. After all, the UNSC's perceived failure to rise above the interests of its permanent members harms the legitimacy of the organization and encourages unilateralism in issues of security. Yet when it comes to the interactions between China and India in the UN, it is unlikely that anything is bound to change anytime soon.

By examining then secretary-general Kofi Annan's proposed reforms of the UNSC in 2005, China's views on permanent membership gain clarity. Two reform routes were proposed to the council. Option A would add six permanent members and three nonpermanent members with two-year tenures. Option B would add a new class of ten semipermanent members elected to ten-year terms. Neither option was implemented, and the reforms ultimately failed, but it is important to note that the most likely candidates for permanent membership were India, Germany, Japan, and Brazil.[27] The mutual support of this group of nations for each other's bid earned them the moniker the "Group of Four (G-4)."[28]

China was potentially amenable to Brazil and Germany, as each had shown some independence from US foreign policy. Germany's opposition to the United States' war in Iraq and Brazil's explicit calls for a more independent foreign policy indicated to China that these nations would bolster China's interests on the council.[29] Their ascension to the council would also lend credibility to China's critique of the council's lack of geographic representation, particularly from developing countries. With China supporting reform if it limited the veto to the current permanent members, there was very little risk to having Brazil and Germany become permanent members.

Japan and India, however, were seen as inherently inimical to Chinese interests. With the historical enmity still plaguing China-Japan relations, along with Japan's alliance with the United States, it was almost a foregone conclusion that China would not cede any ground to Japan in a multilateral institution. India, however, represented a more complex issue. While there are many common interests between the two states, the uncertainty of India's foreign policy leads China to respond with ambiguity. Furthermore, the political issues of Tibet, the Dalai Lama, and the lingering border dispute give China pause when dealing with the issue of India's joining the UNSC.

Officially China's stance on India's bid for permanent membership on the UNSC has been ambiguous but consistent. When making official statements, Chinese officials most often say that China "understands and supports India's desire to play a greater role in the United Nations."[30] This phrase has been used at least since 2005 and was restated as recently as 2014 by President Xi Jinping during a state visit to India, where he declared that China "understands and supports India's aspiration to play a greater role in the United Nations including in the Security Council."[31] Through these vague public statements, China is not giving India the open support that it desires, yet neither is China outrightly rejecting India's bid.

The reason for China's apparent ambiguity is that it has a number of strategic interests to evaluate when considering India's UNSC bid. Foremost among them is the power that would be lost by having another veto-wielding state join the council. China is privileged as the only Asian power to be a permanent member on the UNSC, making it the de facto representative of the region. China has mainly used its permanent membership to maintain its support of nonmilitary intervention, with China's abstention from the 2011 UN resolution to place a no-fly zone over Libya being a notable exception. While China and Russia are clear in their attempts to use their position on the UNSC to further their own interests while checking the United States' hegemony, India's intentions and policies remain too ambiguous for China to offer its unconditional support for UNSC permanent membership. While India prides itself on its nonalignment, it has recently taken steps to increase its military cooperation with the United States in what could be seen as an attempt to hedge against China's military power. Most recent is the 2016 signing of the Logistics Exchange Memorandum of Agreement between India and the United States.[32] The agreement allows for increased military cooperation through logistics-sharing and represents a concrete step toward deeper India-US military cooperation. So long as India remains a potential challenger to China, as well a strategic partner for the United States, China has more to gain from remaining ambiguous in its support of Indian ascension to the UNSC, despite China's long-term goal of reforming the council.

Another important factor to consider is China's relationship with Pakistan. Beijing has used its relationship with Islamabad as a leverage against New Delhi. Pakistan remains thoroughly opposed to India joining the UNSC, and China has no incentive to upset its relationship with Pakistan over India. China engages closely with Pakistan, seeking to secure its international interests mainly through economic initiatives. The China-Pakistan Economic Corridor, announced in 2015, represents over $45 billion worth of China's investment in Pakistan and is often touted as being a precursor to the One Belt One Road Project.[33] No other nation would be willing to place such a large amount of capital in Pakistan due to its many security issues and political challenges, meaning that China's investment represents friendly relations between the two countries, as well as economic interests. Within the realm of security, Pakistan is a hedge against India, securing China's long-term interests in a stable but strong Pakistan.

Nuclear Suppliers Group

China's opposition to India's joining the NSG has evolved into a competition for status and legitimacy. China remains the sole major power unwilling to engage India as a legitimate nuclear-weapon state.[34] This stance is not without credibility, as it is true that NSG members have a precedent of being signatories to the Treaty on the Non-Proliferation of Nuclear Weapons (NPT). Furthermore, the NSG was founded in direct response to India's first nuclear detonation in 1974.[35] India further pushed itself into nuclear isolation by breaking international norms and conducting underground nuclear tests in 1998. This move represented a low point in India's relations with the international community, including the United States and China. Given these facts, it may seem surprising how quickly India has managed to ingratiate itself to the international community as a responsible nuclear power. In China's eyes, the answer lies in the balancing efforts led by the United States to contain China, and events within the last two decades lend credence to this position.

To start with, as early as the Bill Clinton administration, the Third Taiwan Strait Crisis and the Chinese embassy bombing in Belgrade highlighted the potential for China to become a serious challenger to US interests in the future. These events in turn cast a spotlight on India's rising capabilities to be an effective counter to China and a military partner to the United States. The basic premise of the world's most powerful and the world's largest democracies jointly working together to ensure international security was simply too attractive to ignore. The biggest obstacle, however, remained the nuclear issue. The Clinton administration had already begun to engage India economically during the late 1990s, and while the nuclear test in 1998 was certainly a setback in US-India relations, it did not completely derail them. As early as 1999, the Clinton administration was trying to delicately balance relations with India and the announcement of the Next Step in the Strategic Partnership.[36] The United States was not at all enthused by India's nascent nuclear capabilities, but it would not be deterred from the strategic assets that India provided.

It was not until the George W. Bush administration, however, that the US view of India as a valuable asset against China became an explicit goal of US-India relations. Secretary of State Condoleezza Rice was quoted as calling India "a rising global power that could be a pillar of stability in a rapidly changing Asia."[37] It was becoming clear that the United States was looking to India to be a potential partner in East Asia, where China's rise was projected to challenge US power. This sentiment was given further credence when the Bush administration unilaterally negotiated the US-India Civil Nuclear Agreement in 2005, which ultimately resulted in India being granted a waiver by the NSG for the trade of nuclear material, essentially recognizing India as a de facto nuclear power.[38] This waiver simultaneously removed the biggest obstacle in US-India relations while it also isolated China as the major challenger to India's formally joining the NSG.

Much like in the UNSC case, China has crafted a public rhetoric that seems rather benign, mainly emphasizing India's need to sign the NPT before joining the NSG. Every member of the NSG has signed the NPT, and not being a signatory calls into question India's dedication to ensuring the careful management of nuclear materials. Furthermore, while India maintains nuclear weapons for deterrence, it remains secretive about the extent of its nuclear weapons capability.[39] It is this ambiguity that belies the severity with which China is willing to oppose India's ascension to the NSG.

As India strives to improve its nuclear weapons capability, China fears that India's participation in the NSG will make obtaining ballistic nuclear-missile technology easier. Therefore, China's main concern is the potential challenge to the balance of power in East Asia that India could pose as a more potent nuclear power. In addition, China fears that should India join the NSG, it would seek to oppose Pakistan's ascension. Therefore, China's public declarations that it opposes India's joining the NSG on the grounds of it not being a NPT member belies its greater concern over the challenge India poses as a potential rival.

For now, India's options remain limited. While it has the support of the United States, Russia, and the United Kingdom, the NSG is consensus-based, and as long as China stands in its way India will not be an NSG member. While

China's opposition may cause it to be an outlier among the great powers, it forces India to be willing to make concessions to China or face a political stalemate in the NSG. This stalemate benefits China by showing India that if it wishes to succeed in international institutions, it cannot ignore China's interests. As put by the government-backed *Global Times*, China aims to show India that "the US is not the whole world. Its endorsement does not mean it has won the backing of the whole world."[40] However, the long-term outlook is favorable to India, which is steadily gaining ground in the nonproliferation regime. Once blocked by Italy in 2015, India finally gained membership to the Missile Technology and Control Regime in 2016.[41] If India continues to strengthen its participation in the nonproliferation regime and reaches an understanding with China, it will remove the barriers against joining the NSG.

CONCLUSION

As major emerging powers, China and India have strengthened their cooperation in coordinating their positions on a series of regional and global issues and enhancing the influences of the emerging powers and their ability to formulate the international rules in those established international institutions. In a recent development that has been gaining increasing attention, they have also combined their efforts to set up alternative international institutions, such as the BRICS Bank and the AIIB.

While some enduring conflicts and contradictions between China and India are irreconcilable in the short term, cooperation based on common interests is still a dominant aspect of China-India relations. The two Asian powers share common interests in improving their status and influence in the post-American world order, and they are willing to take similar positions to achieve that objective.[42] Active cooperation in multilateral institutions has three positive effects. First, it strengthens China and India's bargaining leverage vis-à-vis dominant powers in existing international institutions. China and India, along with other emerging powers, are like-minded actors in the current international system. As latecomers to many multilateral institutions, they are naturally placed in a disadvantageous position. The best option for them is not acting individually but cooperatively. Coordination between emerging nations is why we have witnessed the emergence of BRICS as an important actor in contemporary international relations. Though differences exist on many issues, similar needs are sufficient to generate cooperation among these emerging powers.

Second, cooperation at both the global and regional levels has the effect of diverting the attention of leaders in Beijing and New Delhi from long-standing problems. Through close interaction and coordination in multilateral institutions, cooperation rather than confrontation has become a prevailing feature of contemporary China-India relations. Therefore, China and India's active coordination in existing international institutions, including the IMF, the World

Bank, and the WTO, and efforts to create new institutions such as BRICS and AIIB play a significant role in mitigating conflicting interests between them.

Finally, China and India's active participation and coordination helps to address the current failures or inadequacies of the global governance system in economics, security, and environmental preservation. An international system dominated by Western powers is unfit to solve the global problems of the twenty-first century; therefore, active participation from all major global stakeholders is necessary for the creation of an effective and modern global governance system.

It is impossible to have cooperation without compromise, and while China-India cooperation has much potential, unresolved issues constrain bilateral relations. These issues are diverse and range from long-standing historical conflicts to differences in global vision and ambition. All of the aforementioned factors have impacted bilateral and multilateral relations. Against the backdrop of geopolitical change in the Asia-Pacific region, how will China and India effectively use their strategic partnership to strengthen their roles there? How can they achieve mutually beneficial arrangements within various international institutions? These are important questions for the two major emerging powers. Although historical disputes are unlikely to be resolved in the near future, immediate interests incentivize China and India to temporarily set aside their historical disagreements in order to further their positions in the international system.

NOTES

For valuable comments and discussions on previous versions of this chapter, I would like to thank T.V. Paul and other participants of the workshop "The Himalayan Contest: Sino-Indian Rivalry in the Globalization Era." I also appreciate Antonio Douglas for his excellent assistance.

1. Miles Kahler, "Rising Powers and Global Governance: Negotiating Change in a Resilient Status Quo," *International Affairs* 89, no. 3 (2013): 711–29; and T.V. Paul, ed., *Accommodating Rising Powers: Past, Present, and Future* (Cambridge: Cambridge University Press, 2016).

2. John Humphrey and Dirk Messner, "China and India as Emerging Global Governance Actors: Challenges for Developing and Developed Countries," *IDS Bulletin* 37, no. 1 (January 2006): 107–14; Muthucumaraswamy Sornarajah and Jiangyu Wang, *China, India and the International Economic Order* (Cambridge: Cambridge University Press, 2010); and Ashley J. Tellis and Sean Mirski, eds., *Crux of Asia: China, India, and the Emerging Global Order* (Washington, DC: Carnegie Endowment for International Peace, 2013).

3. Jagannath P. Panda, "Competing Realities in China-India Multilateral Discourse: Asia's Enduring Power Rivalry," *Journal of Contemporary China* 22, no. 82 (2013): 669–90; and Jeff M. Smith, *Cold Peace: China-India Rivalry in the Twenty-First Century* (Lanham, MD: Lexington Books, 2014).

4. Ministry of External Affairs, Government of India, "Joint Statement between the Republic of India and the People's Republic of China on Building a Closer Developmental Partnership," New Delhi, September 19, 2014, http://mea.gov .in/bilateral-documents.htm?dtl/24022.

5. Kanti Bajpai, Jing Huang, and Kishore Mahbubani, eds., *China-India Relations: Cooperation and Conflict* (New York: Routledge, 2015).

6. Building issue-specific coalitions is a very common strategy for developing countries in international negotiation, especially on economic issues. See Amrita Narlikar, *International Trade and Developing Countries: Bargaining Coalitions in the GATT and WTO* (New York: Routledge, 2003).

7. Miles Kahler, "Asia and the Reform of Global Governance," *Asian Economic Policy Review* 5, no. 2 (December 2010): 178–93.

8. Randall Schweller identifies three roles for emerging powers: spoiler, supporter, or shirker. See Randall L. Schweller, *Maxwell's Demon and the Golden Apple: Global Discord in the New Millennium* (Baltimore: Johns Hopkins University Press, 2014), chap. 4.

9. Amrita Narlikar, "Is India a Responsible Great Power?," *Third World Quarterly* 32, no. 9 (2011): 1607–21; Amrita Narlikar, "New Powers in the Club: The Challenges of Global Trade Governance," *International Affairs* 86, no. 3 (May 2010): 717–28; and Larry Crump and S. Javed Maswood, eds., *Developing Countries and Global Trade Negotiations* (New York: Routledge, 2007).

10. Robert H. Wade, "Emerging World Order? From Multipolarity to Multilateralism in the G20, the World Bank, and the IMF," *Politics and Society* 39, no. 3 (2011): 347–78.

11. Leslie Elliott Armijo and Cynthia Roberts, "The Emerging Powers and Global Governance: Why the BRICS Matter," in *Handbook of Emerging Economies*, ed. Robert E. Looney (New York: Routledge, 2014), 503–24.

12. "Agreement on the New Development Bank: Fortaleza, July 15," New Development Bank, http://www.ndb.int/wp-content/themes/ndb/pdf/Agreement-on-the-New-Development-Bank.pdf.

13. P. Vaidyanathan Iyer and Surabhi, "BRICS Summit: PM Modi to Push for New Development Bank in New Delhi," *Indian Express*, July 14, 2014, http://indianexpress.com/article/india/politics/brics-summit-pm-modi-to-push-for-new-development-bank-in-new-delhi/.

14. Donna E. Danns and George K. Danns, "Challenging the Dominance of the World Bank and the IMF: The Role of the BRICS Countries and Their New Development Bank in Latin American and the Caribbean," *Journal of Business and Economic Policy* 2, no. 3 (2015): 125–34.

15. Oliver Stuenkel, *The BRICS and the Future of Global Order* (Lanham, MD: Lexington Books, 2015).

16. Armijo and Roberts, "Emerging Powers," 520.

17. Carl Dahlman, *The World under Pressure: How China and India Are Influencing the Global Economy and Environment* (Stanford, CA: Stanford University Press, 2012).

18. World Health Organization, "WHO Global Urban Ambient Air Pollution Database (Update 2016)," accessed October 10, 2016, http://www.who.int/phe/health_topics/outdoorair/databases/cities/en/.

19. Simon Schunz and David Belis, "China, India and Global Environmental Governance: The Case of the Climate Change," Policy Brief no. 15 (March 2011), Leuven Centre for Global Governance Studies, https://ghum.kuleuven.be/ggs/publications/policy_briefs/pb15.pdf; and Gerald Chan, Pak K. Lee, and Lai-Ha Chan, *China Engages Global Governance: A New World Order in the Making?* (New York: Routledge, 2012), chap. 6.

20. "Developed Countries Not Fulfilling Their Obligations on Climate Change: India," NDTV, December 10, 2015, http://www.ndtv.com/india-news/developed-countries-not-fulfilling-their-obligations-on-climate-change-india-1253159.

21. John Vidal, Allegra Stratton, and Suzanne Goldenberg, "Low Targets, Goals Dropped: Copenhagen Ends in Failure," *The Guardian*, December 19, 2009, https://www.theguardian.com/environment/2009/dec/18/copenhagen-deal; and Radoslav S. Dimitrov, "Inside Copenhagen: The State of Climate Governance," *Global Environmental Politics* 10, no. 2 (2010): 18–24.

22. Narendra Modi, "The Rich World Must Take Greater Responsibility for Climate Change," *Financial Times*, November 29, 2015, http://www.ft.com/cms/s /0/03a251c6-95f7-11e5-9228-87e603d47bdc.html#axzz4J0dXRPoX.

23. John Vidal, "India Pushes Rich Countries to Boost Their Climate Pledges at Paris," *The Guardian*, December 1, 2015, https://www.theguardian.com /environment/2015/dec/02/india-takes-leading-role-for-global-south-nations -in-climate-talks.

24. World Bank, "Country Profile: China," accessed August 7, 2017, http://data .worldbank.org/country/china; and World Bank, "Country Profile: India," accessed August 7, 2017, http://data.worldbank.org/country/india.

25. "India's Defence Budget Compared to Other Countries," *Hindustan Times*, February 29, 2016, http://www.hindustantimes.com/union-budget/india-s-defence -budget-compared-to-other-countries/story-EijOIOiLKA4AmzfTs80IdJ.html.

26. World Bank, "Military Expenditure (% GDP)," accessed August 7, 2017, http://data.worldbank.org/indicator/MS.MIL.XPND.GD.ZS?locations=CN-IN &page=2.

27. J. Mohan Malik, "Security Council Reform: China Signals Its Veto," *World Policy Journal* 22, no. 1 (Spring 2005): 19–29.

28. Ibid., 20.

29. Ibid., 25.

30. "Joint Declaration by the Republic of India and the People's Republic of China," Indian Ministry of External Affairs, New Delhi, November 21, 2006, http:// www.mea.gov.in/bilateral-documents.htm?dtl/6363/Joint+Declaration+by+the +Repjublic+of+India+an.

31. "Joint Statement between the Republic of India and the People's Republic of China on Building a Closer Developmental Partnership," PM India, September 19, 2014, http://www.pmindia.gov.in/en/news_updates/joint-statement -between-the-republic-of-india-and-the-peoples-republic-of-china-on-building -a-closer-developmental-partnership/.

32. Ankit Panda, "India, US Sign Logistics Exchange Agreement: What You Need to Know," *The Diplomat*, August 30, 2016, http://thediplomat.com/2016/08 /india-us-sign-logistics-exchange-agreement-what-you-need-to-know/.

33. Deloitte Consulting, "How Will CPEC Boost Pakistan's Economy?," accessed October 15, 2016, https://www2.deloitte.com/content/dam/Deloitte/pk/Docu ments/risk/pak-china-eco-corridor-deloittepk-noexp.pdf.

34. Harsh V. Pant, "India in the Asia–Pacific: Rising Ambitions with an Eye on China," *Asia-Pacific Review* 14, no. 1 (2007): 54–71.

35. Rajeswari Pillai Rajagopalan and Arka Biswas, "India's Membership to the Nuclear Suppliers Group," ORF Issue Brief, no. 141 (May 2016), http://www .orfonline.org/wp-content/uploads/2016/05/ORF_Issue_Brief_141.pdf.

36. Pant, "India in the Asia-Pacific," 62.

37. Ibid., 63.

38. Ibid.

39. "Draft Report of National Security Advisory Board on Indian Nuclear Doctrine," Indian Ministry of External Affairs, August 17, 1999, http://mea.gov .in/in-focus-article.htm?18916/Draft+Report+of+National+Security+Advisory +Board+on+Indian+Nuclear+Doctrine.

40. "Delhi's NSG Bid Upset by Rules, Not Beijing," *Global Times*, June 28, 2016, http://www.globaltimes.cn/content/990889.shtml.

41. Kallol Bhattacherjee, "India Joins Missile Technology Control Regime," *The Hindu*, June 27, 2016, http://www.thehindu.com/news/national/%E2%80 %8BIndia-joins-Missile-Technology-Control-Regime.-Top-5-things-to-know /article14405165.ece.

42. Undeniably, for both China and India the pursuit of major-power status is a significant determinant for their external behavior. There is an emerging trend of studying status in the field of international relations. See Thomas J. Volgy, Renato Corbetta, Keith A. Grant, and Ryan G. Baird, eds., *Major Powers and the Quest for Status in International Politics: Global and Regional Perspectives* (New York: Palgrave Macmillan, 2011); and T.V. Paul, Deborah Welch Larson, and William C. Wohlforth, eds., *Status in World Politics* (Cambridge: Cambridge University Press, 2014).

PART V

CONCLUSIONS

Chapter 12

Whither Rivalry or Withered Rivalry?

PAUL F. DIEHL

There is little disagreement that China and India were at one time intense rivals. Almost from the birth of the People's Republic of China (PRC), the two states have engaged in multiple military confrontations. In 1950, the two states clashed over the location of the Aksai Chin border based on disputed interpretations of the McMahon Line drawn by the British. Despite a nonaggression pact in 1954, China and India would engage in twenty-one more "militarized disputes" in the next thirty-plus years,[1] with at least one side threatening, displaying, or using military force. The most notable of these was the 1962 border war that ultimately did little to resolve the disputed border and other issues between the two countries.

Despite the history of animosity, the twenty-first century is a notably different context, both globally and with respect to China-India relations. The Cold War, which served as a backdrop for this rivalry even as both of these states were usually more closely aligned with the Soviet Union than with the United States, is over. Globalization and economic growth in both countries have made them important players in the world economy—China more so than India. China's outward-looking strategy has changed its orientation from a narrow regional power to one concerned with global interests, as opposed to merely concerns surrounding bordering states such as Vietnam. The India-Pakistan rivalry, to which the China-India rivalry is linked, remains as intractable as ever, and China's ties with Pakistan have strengthened in recent years.

In light of all these changes, what is the status of the rivalry between China and India? Has it evolved to be less dangerous than in earlier eras? The other contributors to this volume have examined the rivalry in detail along a variety of different dimensions and with various characterizations. For example, in his introductory chapter to this volume, T.V. Paul sees this as a "limited" rivalry now, even as he finds the competition continuous. In chapter 5, Zhen Han and Jean-François Bélanger still refer to this as an "enduring rivalry," as much for its duration as its severity. In this concluding essay, my goal is not to summarize all those efforts but rather to take some of their findings and integrate them with what we know from the extensive scholarly literature about the dynamics of rivalries. I begin with the role of issues in rivalries, as in order to be enemies, states must be fighting over something. Similarly, resolving the underlying issues in dispute often leads to the end of rivalries.

RIVALRY OVER WHAT?

For states to be in a rivalry, there needs to be one or more issues that are in dispute, and the two need to regard military force as a viable option in order to resolve those differences.[2] In this section, I look at a number of issues that typically underlie rivalries and the degree to which they are found in the China-India context.

Territory

Territorial disputes are at the heart of many rivalries, either as the primary or exclusive basis for dispute (e.g., Greece-Turkey) or one significant issue among many others (e.g., North Korea–United States). Indeed, one study found that 81 percent of enduring rivalries had a substantial territorial component.[3] Of particular concern are territorial disputes having certain types of tangible and intangible value. With respect to tangible value, some disputed territories are critical for the security of one or both states (e.g., the Golan Heights for Israel). This presents a "chicken and egg" problem in that the land dispute cannot be resolved until security fears are assuaged, but the territorial dispute is, in part, driving those fears. Intangibly valued territorial disputes occur when one or both states desire control over an area because of historical, religious, ethnic, or linguistic connections to the state(s) rather than its material value; disputes over Kashmir (India versus Pakistan) and Jerusalem (Israel versus her neighbors) are indicative. These are notoriously difficult to resolve, as the stakes are viewed as indivisible, and therefore compromise solutions in which each side receives part of the territory are unacceptable to the parties.[4] Domestic political concerns also make it difficult for leaders to make concessions in such circumstances.

China and India have engaged in a series of confrontations over territory and one full-scale war. As Mahesh Shankar points out in chapter 2, territorial disputes were central to the origins of the rivalry, particularly the northern border between the two countries. Competing claims for those and other areas remain unresolved at this writing. Domestic political pressures likely preclude concessions by either side that would result in a peace settlement. On the one hand, this might be enough to declare the rivalry as ongoing and likely to be sustained well into the future, but such an unqualified conclusion is misleading.

There are several elements that suggest that although the territorial dispute formally persists, its salience has diminished and most of the territories in question do not have the characteristics that are most conducive to another war. First, the tangible value of the territories in questions is limited. Aksai Chin, for example, is an uninhabited desert area with little or no strategic value, much less any economic resources or other worth that merit fighting over. With respect to intangible value, most of the disputed areas have little historical or other value for either of the parties. On value alone, the prospects for extensive violent conflict are low and have diminished over time.

Claims involving Tibet, however, might be the exception, as these are tied to Chinese concerns about Tibetan nationalism and the Dalai Lama. The area of Arunachal Pradesh (formerly the North-East Frontier Agency), controlled by India, is important to China for security reasons, largely because of its attachment to Tibet, an especially sensitive political and security concern to the Chinese.[5] This is perhaps the only aspect of the territorial disagreements that suggests sensitivity and willingness to fight, but the concern is more asymmetrical and therefore less likely to prompt substantial military action than were it the case if both states attached high salience to the land in question.

More important than territorial value has been the conflict management of the dispute by both sides. One might argue that the border dispute has been effectively settled even as a formal agreement has been elusive. The Line of Actual Control (LAC) over time has become the established border around which both sides have converged in terms of expectations and behavior. Multiple Chinese offers for settlement, although not accepted, have been very close to this status quo. In addition, several agreements between the two sides in the 1990s signaled that they are not interested in using military force in this dispute. The agreements, described by Shankar, indicate a commitment to settlement by peaceful means and a framework for a negotiated settlement.[6] Furthermore, confidence-building measures enacted through the agreements assist in preventing engagements that could escalate and indicate a desire to avoid confrontations.

How does the 2017 confrontation over Doklam fit into the territorial disputes between China and India? Technically the Chinese road construction involves territory that the Chinese dispute with Bhutan, not India. Nevertheless, beyond involving its close friend Bhutan, India was concerned about strategic location of the road near what is called the "Chicken's Neck," a narrow passage connecting parts of India to one another.[7] On the one hand, this illustrates how territorial concerns and the risk of escalation can arise even when the LAC status quo is stable; states fully at peace and devoid of rivalry do not react to roadbuilding plans the way that India and China did. That said, the end of the standoff without violence suggests that the two sides are still able to manage their disagreements without the use of military force.

Overall, the territorial basis of the rivalry still exists to some degree in that competing claims continue and other territorial concerns such as Doklam can arise. Nevertheless, the salience of the disputes is relatively low, except for those involving Tibet, and indeed patterns of violent conflict have significantly diminished (see below) since the 1950s and 1960s. A majority of territorial claims exist between friendly states (e.g., the United Kingdom and Spain over Gibraltar, Canada and the United States over maritime boundaries and islands), and thus territorial disputes are not necessarily barriers to better relations between states. Indeed, the majority of territorial claims are latent in that they have not been withdrawn by the parties, but neither are they actively asserted so that they complicate other relations between them.[8] If China and India's territorial disputes have not reached this stage, they have the potential to approach it. Nevertheless, periodic incursions across the declared lines by patrolling troops of both sides tend to reignite tensions and raise the disputed issues, thereby preventing the claims from moving to a latent phase.

Resources and Water

Other sources of rivalrous contention could be competition over natural resources, especially water, an issue that is addressed by Calvin Chen and Selina Ho in chapters 6 and 7, respectively. With respect to resources, there is no doubt that both China and India have experienced tremendous economic growth in the past decades and are major players in the global market. This has resulted in substantial increases in resource demand to fuel this growth. At first view, one might expect that this would lead to competition for resources, possibly prompting military and political clashes in areas where those resources are found. There are instances in which resource competition can prompt violent conflict, but too often the risk is greatly overstated.[9] One only had to recall the predictions in the 1990s that a war between the United States and Japan over resources was likely in the coming decades to see the folly in many of these expectations.[10]

Chen cautions that we must begin an analysis of China-India competition with a realistic assessment that considers not only projected shortages (the purported stimulus for the competition) but also government policies and rates of consumption.[11] In his analysis, there might have been a brief moment of resource competition between the two states, but this proved fleeting. China's investments in Africa have received great attention for the attempt to curry favor with suppliers of energy resources and raw materials. Yet India's presence there is modest and does not overlap with China's to the extent that there is a competitive and zero-sum relationship. Furthermore, new energy policies in both countries—emphasizing renewable sources—should lessen any projected shortages and remove direct competition for external resources. Finally, India and China have engaged in a number of cooperative ventures with respect to consultation and energy investment. Thus energy concerns have been more likely to drive the two states together rather than toward rivalry. In sum, there is little basis at this time to declare resources, especially those connected to energy, as a basis for rivalry between these states.

The concern that water might be a source of conflict between India and China parallels similar alarmist projections about water's role in the India-Pakistan rivalry (specifically the Indus River Basin) and Middle East rivalries, most notably involving Israel. Nevertheless, analysts have a hard time identifying a prior war between any states that was fought over water.[12] Most often, wars over water are projected to occur in the coming years, but such claims fall into the fallacy of "using the future as evidence."[13] Thus there is reason to be skeptical that water rights and usage are a primary or even significant issue in driving armed conflict in rivalries, although they certainly add to the tensions in the India-China context.

Ho's analysis confirms that water is not likely to be a major source of competition between China and India.[14] There are potential sources of disagreement, and this is not surprising between upstream (China) and downstream (India) neighbors. Still, both states have toned down their rhetoric and indeed emphasized cooperation on water issues. This suggests that neither is willing to allow water issues to rise to the level of military clashes or to complicate other aspects of their interactions.

Ho cites examples of cooperation on water concerns.[15] These offer some basis for assuring that any disagreements will be managed peacefully. Nevertheless, there is still less institutionalized cooperation between China and India than other pairs of riparian states.[16] China and India are part of four river-basin systems: Ganges-Brahmaputra-Meghna, Indus, Irrawaddy, and Tarim.[17] There are no international agreements on the latter two. For the Ganges and related tributaries, India is party to a series of bilateral treaties but none with China. With respect to the Indus, India is party to nine of eleven international agreements, including some with its rival Pakistan; none involve China. China and India are both signatories to a few multilateral, non-basin-specific, water-related treaties, but a few of these date to the prerivalry period and in any case deal with concerns such as wetlands that are not likely to be the subject of military confrontation.

Despite limited institutionalized mechanisms, neither India nor China seems poised to fight over water concerns. The salience of competing claims and other disagreements does not rise to the level that primarily defines or exacerbates a rivalry.

Status

Rivalries stem not only from competition over some of the material resources above but also as a result of ideational struggles in the context of relative gains. Most notable are competitions over power status, whether on a regional or global basis.[18] Unlike tangible stakes, status is subjective and dependent more on perceptions than material capabilities, although the latter are not irrelevant in gauging progress toward status goals.[19] Competitions between the United States and the Soviet Union were not fought to acquire or retain territory but rather for power, status, and allies. They are often viewed in zero-sum terms, in that gains made by one state come at the expense of its enemy. William R. Thompson and his colleagues refer to these as "strategic rivalries."[20]

One prominent theoretical lens through which to view rivalry and the competition for status is the power transition model.[21] In that formulation, a hegemon is the system leader, and there is a rising challenger state with different preferences for international order than the leader. The gap in power narrows over time between the leading state and its rival, and ultimately the latter overtakes the former; rivalry is present throughout the transition process, but war is thought to be most likely just after the transition point, with the challenger state coming out on top. German ascendancy vis-à-vis France in the nineteenth century is the prototypical case cited. Nevertheless, power transitions do not inevitably result in war; the transition between the United States and the United Kingdom for global leadership in the early twentieth century is an example. Most power transition model applications refer to international system leadership, but battles for regional status and influence using the model have been considered as well.[22]

Another theoretical lens is social identity theory, in which states have a "reference state" that is "similar in culture, region, or size."[23] In this conception, a state aspires to catch up or become superior to another country along several dimensions. Unlike power transition theory, however, there are two potential differences. First, the competition does not necessarily have to occur between states that are equal or prospectively equal in power; a rivalry in this conception can still occur between states with disparate capabilities. Second, any competition can be asymmetrical, with one state regarding the other as more of a rival than vice versa. The latter might well be the case with respect to India's views toward China rather than the opposite.

Although India might have aspirations for a greater global role, evidenced by its desire for a permanent seat on the United Nations Security Council, there is little reason to regard it as a contender for international system leadership anytime in the near future.[24] Its overall capabilities pale in the face of system leader the United States, as well as Russia, Japan, and China; India doesn't reach or approach the threshold requirements for being a major power and is unlikely to do so anytime soon.[25] Indeed, it is China that is often seen as a prospective global leader in the coming decades, but its role is as a challenger to the United States. As Manjari Chatterjee Miller notes in chapter 4, China and India do not necessarily share some ideational commonalities on the future global order, but neither do they reject the Westphalian order in full.

Although not a direct competitor for global leadership, India has a role in the US-China competition and one that will increase tensions in the region. The United States has given India a key part in the "pivot" of American strategy to the Asian region; the military-to-military contacts and the cooperation in the Indian and Pacific Oceans suggest India fits into the broader competition. One of the last acts of the Barack Obama administration was to sign an agreement allowing US naval vessels to enter Indian ports for berthing and repair, a major change in Indian policy; it is not clear, however, whether successor US administrations will continue with moves in this direction. China's major concern is that India is tilting toward the US. In that sense, rivalry between the Chinese and the Indians in their relationship will be partly a function of the US-China rivalry, and that has turned more hostile in the past decade.

If a global-level struggle for status between China and India is hard to conceive, a regional rivalry for influence is far more plausible, albeit with some qualifications. Both states have sought to enhance their influence in the South Asian region and can be seen as the leading states in that geographic area. There are significant disagreements between the states over Tibet, and China has historically tilted toward Pakistan in the India-Pakistan rivalry. More recently, Chinese ties with Pakistan have been enhanced and are viewed as threatening by India. There is the $53 billion China-Pakistan Economic Corridor being built, connecting Gwadar with Xinxiang and passing through Pakistani-held Kashmir. The port itself is now managed by the Chinese, and there is a plan to bring Chinese naval forces there. China has also increased its arms sales to India's neighbors and explored potential basing arrangements in the region.[26] In the naval realm, China is expanding to the Indian Ocean, having just acquired a base in Djibouti, and India is gradually moving into the western Pacific with Vietnam as its partner.[27] Even the Doklam confrontation can be viewed in terms of regional competition as China has sought to expand its influence in Bhutan, a close friend of India. As Xiaoyu Pu points out, therefore, in chapter 3 of this volume, there are good reasons to see the China-India relationship as competitive in the region.

Another view, however, is that the two states have been engaged in regional competitions but not always against one another. In an analysis through 1990, Douglas Lemke identifies a series of local hierarchies around the world; these are geography-based competitions in which there are a leading state and several other challengers.[28] He has China as the leading state in East Asia, with several other states that cluster (Japan, Mongolia, North Korea, South Korea, and Taiwan). India is placed as the leader in South Asia, with other states listed as Pakistan, Bangladesh, and Bhutan. Notably, there is no overlap between these two regional hierarchies, suggesting that the regional competition in a power transition framework does not directly pit China against India. It might be that Lemke's "regions" are too narrowly drawn, but it does offer the perspective that regional competitions are not necessarily confined to just the two countries under scrutiny here.

Although the China-India relationship might be conceptualized as a rivalry for status, there are a number of points that mitigate the severity of this competition and therefore the expectation of serious militarized conflict. First, India has not challenged China directly and militarily on key regional issues in several decades (see the analysis of militarized confrontations below). Nor have the two sides sought to build formal alliances or ties with states in the region in any ways similar to the US and Soviet scramble for friendly regimes during the height of the Cold War. Neither China nor India has signed alliance agreements anywhere, much less with neighboring states. One tangible indicator of the lack of competition on the ground is that of the forty-six militarized disputes between India and Pakistan since 1947, *all* have remained bilateral—that is, China has not intervened to support Pakistan militarily.[29] Thus the rivalry over status has not manifested itself in the traditional ways that these kinds of struggles do.

Second, India has been isolated from the major attempts by China to assert hegemony in the Asian region. Confrontations have occurred over sovereignty in the South China Sea and Spratly Islands, but these are geographically distant from India. Incidents of fishing boat seizures, drone seizures, and International Court of Justice rulings have pitted China against the United States and many countries in the area but not India. Third, India might be too far behind economically and militarily to be considered a rising challenger with respect to material capabilities, at least in the next few decades. Pu correctly documents the asymmetry of the power competition, and there is reason to anticipate that the gap could widen rather than narrow over time.[30] Perception is an important component of rivalry as well, and Pu argues that China does not necessarily view India as a major threat at either the global or regional level. Finally, Pu indicates an "ambivalent accommodation" strategy pursued by China toward India.[31] This might be an indicator that India poses some threat to China as a rival, but it also suggests that such a strategy is designed to mitigate the worst of rivalry manifestations, especially those dealing with direct military conflict.

THE IMPACT OF POWER ASYMMETRY

Some scholars have defined rivalries as those occurring between states of equal capability. John Vasquez has most clearly stated this position, going so far as to argue that "relative equality is a prerequisite of rivalries."[32] Thompson does not take a direct position that a measure of power symmetry should be included in the concept of rivalry. Nevertheless, he does state that "other things being equal, symmetrical capabilities should be expected to make rivalry more likely and more enduring."[33] The position of others is that rivalries can occur between states that have disparate abilities (e.g., United States versus Cuba or even India versus Pakistan), and over the long term that characterize some rivalries, power distributions can change dramatically even if the rivalry does not dissipate.[34] Thus it would be a mistake to characterize the China-India relationship as a rivalry or not based only on the capability distribution. Nevertheless, it might be equally erroneous to claim the distribution is irrelevant in understanding the dynamics of the relationship.

How much has the China-India ratio of capability distribution changed over time, and where does it stand now? One conventional measure is the Correlates

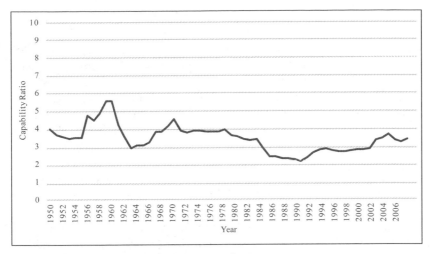

FIGURE 12.1. China-India Capability Distribution, 1950–2007

of War Project's Composite Index of National Capability (CINC).[35] This approach considers six equally weighted indicators of national power across three dimensions: economic (iron/steel production and energy consumption), military (military expenditures and military personnel), and demographic (total population and urban population). Per the CINC measure, I take the ratio of Chinese to Indian values for each of the six indicators and then average them. Data for the two states are available from 1950 to 2007. The results are plotted over time and given in figure 12.1.

Over the period of study, the Chinese superiority has not changed, even as the magnitude of that superiority has wavered. The Chinese dominance peaked in the early 1960s in terms of a 5:1 ratio advantage. Some single-year peculiarities in the data led to apparent anomalous fluctuations thereafter, but the Chinese advantage dissipated in the 1980s, although never falling below the 2:1 ratio. The narrowing gap between China and India, characteristic of the power transition, was actually reversed at the turn of the century, and at the end of the data China had an approximately 3.4:1 advantage.

One can draw at least three conclusions from these data. First, power asymmetry, with a substantial Chinese advantage, is a persistent characteristic of the India-China relationship. This might account for why weaker India regards China as more of a threat or rival than the other way around. Second, there is no evidence that there is a meaningful narrowing of the gap between the two states, and indeed recent trends suggest an expansion of Chinese relative power. Third, given the consistent power asymmetry over time, this characteristic of the relationship cannot be used to account for variations in the hostility or cooperation levels between the two states over time. Accordingly, any understanding of hostile or rivalrous behavior in this pair of states is better accounted for by social identity formulations than those based on material capabilities.

CONFLICT BEHAVIOR

One of the central components of a rivalry is militarized competition. That is, rivals pose a serious and ongoing threat to one another's security. Military acquisition, planning, and deployment are reflective of a state's concern with its enemy. Early definitions required that military confrontations occur with some frequency over a confined time period to be called rivalries or at least "enduring" rivalries. This is no longer a prerequisite for the two most prominent definitions and data sets concerning rivalry research.[36] States can still be rivals even if they do not clash directly in war or lesser military skirmishes because of deterrence or other reasons. Nevertheless, such confrontations can serve as barometers for the severity of rivalries, and patterns over time can signal changes in the rivalry relationship.

To gauge possible changes, I look at the incidence of militarized interstate disputes, or MIDs, between India and China from 1947 to the end of available data (2010). Militarized disputes are "united historical cases of conflict in which the threat, display or use of military force short of war by one member state is explicitly directed towards the government, official representatives, official forces, property, or territory of another state. Disputes are composed of single or multiple incidents that range in intensity from threats to use force to actual combat short of war."[37] Other chapters in this collection suggest that there has been a diminution of hostilities in the India-China relationship. Is this reflected in one element of rivalry—MID frequency and conflict behavior?

In the period 1947–87, there were twenty-two MIDs between the two states, more than one every two years. The most notable of these was the 1962 border war, but there were a variety of lesser confrontations between them. This frequency puts India and China near the top of a list of "enduring" rivalries for the period under scrutiny.[38] Nevertheless, in the time frame 1988–2002, almost two and half decades, there were *no* militarized disputes between India and China. Such a change is stunning.

There have been three MIDs during the 2003–9 period. In 2003, Chinese soldiers crossed over the border into Arunachal Pradesh and briefly detained and interrogated some Indian border patrol guards. Four years later, following local reports that Chinese troops had crossed into Indian territory, India placed its border military forces on heightened alert against future incursions. In 2009, India moved six thousand troops to its border with China after local reports of Chinese troop incursions into Bhutan. Although India stated that it could not confirm the accuracy of such reports, it nonetheless deployed the additional troops as a safeguard against future incursions. These confrontations have all been minor in several ways. First, none involved the use of military force or even the explicit threat per se to use force. Rather, they are regarded as simple "displays of force" and involved no direct action between the two sides' militaries. Indeed, the last dispute might have been a case of mistaken reports, but it does show that some tension remains between India and China; otherwise, the former would not have redeployed troops. Second, each of the disputes lasted a single day. That is, there was a single incident that did not prompt retaliation or escalation, and the matter did not complicate the overall relationship between India and China. Single-day MIDs are not uncommon in the world, but they are best seen as bumps in the road rather than indicative of deep-seated animosities or very hostile rivalry behavior.[39]

Short of overt military confrontations, there are a number of hostile actions that could represent competitive behavior. These include the substantial increases in military spending by both states and the expansion of military bases. India's deployment of several new military divisions might be particularly worrisome to China as these could be directed against that state or its ally Pakistan. This is consistent with Andrew Scobell's analysis in chapter 8 of a "Himalayan standoff," in which hostile, rivalrous behavior persists but at a level that is capable of management and short of direct armed conflict. The "assured retaliation" capabilities of the two states reinforce this situation and restrict competition to that short of major war, as Vipin Narang says in chapter 9.

In light of these changes in conflict behavior, how do rivalry compilations treat the India-China relationship? The results are mixed. Thompson and his colleagues have the pair as rivals starting in 1948 and continuing uninterrupted until at least 2014.[40] They regard this as both a "positional" and a "strategic" rivalry, indicating that the competition is both over territory more narrowly and regional hegemony more broadly. The rivalry is also classified as an asymmetrical one, reflecting Chinese capability superiority over India. The brief description of the rivalry concludes with a decidedly pessimistic assessment: "The prospects for a significant and permanent de-escalation of this rivalry in the near future are not promising. The two states are predisposed by their size and improving economic development to compete for leadership of an expanded Asia in the generations to come."[41]

Gary Goertz and his colleagues offer a more nuanced view of the India-China relationship.[42] They code all state relationships in the international system according to a five-point "peace scale": severe rivalry, lesser rivalry, negative peace, warm peace, and security community; the latter two are considered to be the "positive peace" realm. With respect to India and China, they code the relationship as negative peace for the 1947–50 period, in which the new governments of both states were neither close friends nor enemies. This is followed by a period of severe rivalry starting in 1950. This is based on the frequency of MIDs noted above, as well as the contentious issues and competition cited by Thompson and his team.

Nevertheless, Goertz and his colleagues place 1987 as a breakpoint in relations, and code that the relationship entered a period of transition lasting until late 1991. In late 1988, India's Prime Minister Rajiv Gandhi visited Beijing, the first leader to do so since Prime Minister Jawaharlal Nehru in 1954. China's Prime Minister Li Peng reciprocated in 1991. The initial period of change was also characterized by a joint working group to settle the border dispute. The authors see an improvement in relations occurring gradually in that period, and for 1991 they reclassify the relationship as a lesser rivalry; there was still hostility and disputed issues, but direct military confrontations were absent, and the risk of war was considerably less. The two countries signed a series of agreements to cooperate on trade, diplomatic representation, and science. For 1996 to the end of 2006,[43] Goertz et alia code the relationship as negative peace, signaling the view that the rivalry had ended, even as unresolved issues persisted and the two states did not necessarily have identical preferences for regional and global order.

ACCOUNTING FOR THE DECLINE OF RIVALRY

There is a consensus based on the analysis above and the other contributors to this collection that there has been a diminution of hostility between the two sides in the last two or three decades based on a number of indicators. Much of this decline began somewhere in the late 1980s and early 1990s if one goes solely by militarized conflict incidence. In this section, I address some of the theoretical and empirical explanations for rivalry decline and termination and apply those to the China-India context.

Other Rivalries

A common element across several rivalry studies is the emergence of other rivals for one or both of the original rivals, which can lead to a reevaluation and often de-escalation of hostilities in the extant competition. Scott D. Bennett suggests that states might need to end one competition in order to concentrate on a new enemy.[44] His analysis of rivalry termination also indicates that some rivalries end when the rivals begin to have common external security threats; in effect, the advent of new rivalries with negative links to extant rivalries causes the latter to end. Similarly, Charles Kupchan sees the end of rivalries and the formation of peaceful relationships as a process involving a series of steps.[45] Prompting these steps is a "strategic predicament," which can arise from multiple simultaneous rivals. A state might need to choose to accommodate one enemy in order to effectively deal with another. Eric Cox emphasizes the resource pressures that stem from multiple rivalries.[46] He argues that resource strains emanating from multiple rivalries produce domestic policy failures as the government spends more on external concerns rather than domestic needs.

This account does not have much resonance in the India-China relationship. China does not regard India as its primary rival and perhaps never did. Currently it is likely that China sees the United States as its leading rival. This might suggest that the Chinese place Indian relations secondary to other relationships, except as they intersect with the US-China rivalry. Nevertheless, the timing of changes does not correspond to alterations in the dynamics of the China-India relationship and in some cases run opposite of the theoretical expectations. Over time, and particularly surrounding the transition points in the relationship, China was actually shedding existing rivalries or de-escalating them rather than adding new rivalries.[47] Among major states, China largely resolved its disputes with the United Kingdom via an agreement to return Hong Kong to China in 1997. Rivalry with the Soviet Union / Russia, which started in the 1960s, dissipated in the late twentieth century and ended early in the new millennium. Relations also improved with the United States and Japan prior to 2000. In addition, in the 1990s or thereabouts, hostile relationships diminished between China and South Korea, Myanmar, and Mongolia. Thus, rather than *new* rivalries taking the place of the China-India one, there have been fewer or diminished rivalries for China at the time that its competition with India became less hostile. Conflict over the South China Sea has heated up in recent years, but this comes well after the change in China-India relations, and in any case there does not seem to be solid logic in arguing that the maritime conflict would prompt China to direct its resources away from its interests on the Indian subcontinent.

Considering the rivalries of the other state in the pair—India—leads to similar conclusions about the disutility of multiple rivalries to explain shifts in the China-India relationship. India's primary rivalry is with Pakistan, and that has been persistent since both states gained independence. Any fluctuations in that relationship were not correlated with changes in the India-China relationship and vice versa. Similarly, the changes in and dynamics of lesser rivalries with Sri Lanka and Bangladesh were not temporally or substantively connected to the India-China rivalry.

Overall, the emergence of other rivalries for either China or India does not correspond to changes in their relationship. Neither does the rise of a common enemy that would improve relations between the two. Although multiple rivals as a trigger for improved relations for rivals represent general patterns, it does not apply to this case. We need to look elsewhere for keys to the rivalry transformation.

Shocks or Perturbations

Another factor associated with changes in rivalry, most notably with rivalry termination, is political shocks. These are reflected in the punctuated-equilibrium model of rivalries, which begins with the expectation that once established, rivalry processes are difficult to alter.[48] If rivalries are the result of well-entrenched causes, then alterations in the dynamics or terminations of rivalry should be associated with some dramatic change that disrupts established patterns of behavior. Goertz and I argue that political shocks are virtually necessary conditions for the end of rivalries.[49] These can occur at the system level, with world wars and major shifts in the power distribution among those shocks believed to have those effects. Shocks might also occur within either of the rival states, with civil wars and regime change thought to open the possibilities for rivalry termination.

Domestic-level shocks can make ending rivalries a necessity to deal with internal problems or substantially change the policy preferences of the regime. Cox sees domestic policy failure as the instigator of the rivalry-termination process.[50] Failures in policy prompt changes in preferences and domestic realignment that comes from a regime change or a new government within existing regime structures. The direction of the regime change is as critical as the domestic realignment itself. If one hawkish leader replaces another, then there is likely to be little impact on the rivalry. There must be a movement toward leadership that is "moderate" or "dovish," leaders who are more willing to make concessions and reach compromise with an enemy. Cox also argues that domestic realignment that leads to rivalry termination is less likely to produce changes in rivalry dynamics unless it is accompanied by foreign policy failure; domestic policy failure alone is not sufficient to alter rivalry dynamics, and foreign policy failures might not lead to changes in government if the domestic economy is healthy.[51] The combined domestic and foreign failures are said to produce a greater willingness to accept rivalry concessions, thereby opening up the bargaining space with a rival and making some kind of accommodation possible.

Domestic explanations, including those coming from political shocks, seem to fit imperfectly with changes in the dynamics of the India-China rivalry. Some argue that domestic political considerations played no role in rivalry dynamics at least through the 1980s and with respect to Tibet.[52] China did undergo a significant government change when Deng Xiaoping assumed power in 1978. He introduced dramatic economic reforms and transformed Chinese policy in the direction of greater engagement with the world. Leadership change is associated with changes in Chinese foreign policy generally. China is said to no longer adhere to the Maoist worldview of its role as revolutionary challenger but rather has become more integrated into the world and has adopted a less coercive and more restrained posture; Chinese military behavior generally reflects this new orientation.[53] Nevertheless, the change in Chinese government did not perfectly coincide with the alteration in rivalry dynamics that occurred a decade later. It is also not clear that the impetus for economic and global reorientation from China came from significant policy failures or that the changes can be directly tied to subsequent improvement in relations with India in particular.

With respect to India, the key period of change in rivalry dynamics is marked by instability in the governing coalitions there. Beginning with the Rajiv Gandhi–led Congress Party government from 1984 to 1989, India went through four leadership transitions among four political coalitions in the next seven years. Changes in foreign policy from such shifts are not clear, and in any case there were multiple shifts in power in the period during which China-India rivalry behavior changed.[54]

Unlike other rivalry changes and terminations, there were no civil wars or other dramatic domestic events in either China or India to account for the diminution of the rivalry. In general then, domestic political shocks cannot account for changes here. Might changes in the international system be responsible?

Some possibilities from previous research can be dismissed immediately.[55] There was no world war that realigned alliances or political order in the international system. Neither were there massive territorial changes that were characteristic of the colonization and decolonization processes in earlier historical eras.

The one political shock that does correspond to changes in the India-China relationship is the end of the Cold War between the United States and the Soviet Union. This is conventionally designated as occurring during the late 1980s and solidified with the breakup of the Soviet Union in late December 1991. Although the timing is coincidental to rivalry de-escalation here, are there substantive connections between the two phenomena? India pursued closer relations with the United States during this period, but nuclear and other cooperation would come more than a decade later. Chinese relations with the United States improved during the 1970s, and the rivalry did not move from "severe" to "lesser" until after the turn of the century, according to one compilation.[56]

The net result is that explanations for rivalry de-escalation or termination based on political shocks do not comport well with what we know about the China-India rivalry. This is evident from both the perspective of timing and substance. There are, however, several other factors that merit examination.

Other Factors

Within scholarly studies of rivalry, there are several other factors associated with the decline or the end of rivalries. I do not discuss the limited literature on transitions to positive peace, as no analyst would regard the present China-India relationship as similar to those between European Union members or between the United States and Canada. Andrew Owsiak and his colleagues argue that "stable borders" increase the likelihood that rivals will transition to negative peace (neither friends nor enemies).[57] Stable borders also consolidate that relationship once negative peace has occurred (i.e., they are less likely to revert back to rivalry). The authors cite two sources of stable borders. One is the settlement of past disputed borders. The territorial disputes between China and India were discussed above. On the one hand, we know that the border dispute between those two states has not been formally settled. On the other hand, based on the analysis above and that by Shankar, one could argue that they are effectively settled in that the LAC is firmly established and no change is likely in the near future.[58] Whether this has been the result of decreased tensions, the cause of hostility reduction, or a recursive relationship is unclear.

The other source of stable borders is said to be the absence of civil wars.[59] Three specific civil war activities breed border instability and unpredictability: cross-border rebel movements, rebel military support, and refugee flows. First, rebels attacking a government might seek shelter in a neighboring state, thereby receiving protection by virtue of international sovereignty norms. Second, rebels attacking a government might receive military support from neighboring states. Finally, civil wars can generate refugee problems that transcend borders, creating a humanitarian crisis for neighboring states. These dynamics are often sources of rivalry between neighbors or exacerbate existing competitions. Nevertheless, none of these seems to apply well to the India-China rivalry. Each state has significant internal unrest in selected provinces, but these do not tend to be near the border areas of the two countries. Nor is there strong evidence that either neighbor is actively supporting rebel groups in the other state. Perhaps only India's support for indigenous groups in Tibet qualifies, but there is no civil war there and no militarized confrontations between India and China over cross-border incursions in the area. India, however, has moderated its policy over time with respect to Chinese occupation, so there is some minor effect on improved relations from this issue.[60]

Global and regional forces are also thought to play a role in moderating rivalries. Such organizations channel disagreements between members into the institutions and processes that promote peaceful conflict management and resolution. Asia generally lacks strong regional institutions for conflict management. East Asia does not have a general-purpose organization with strong norms and processes; instead, it relies on traditional alliances and deterrence to keep the peace.[61] The South Asian Association for Regional Cooperation exists for that region but is restricted in terms of the degree to which security matters can be managed, and China is not a member in any case.[62] Nevertheless, in chapter 11, Feng Liu documents expanding cooperation between India and China in global and regional institutions. This has facilitated pursuit of common interests between the two sides, something Liu calls the "dominant aspect of China-India relations."[63]

Trade is sometimes cited as a generator of improved relations between hostile states. In chapter 10, Matthew Castle deftly explores this possibility in the China-India context. Although there has been a significant expansion in trade between the countries over time, he notes that this is largely asymmetrical—much of the expansion has been in the form of Chinese exports to India. These patterns and other aspects of the trade relationship are not necessarily the types that promote peace between rivals.

CONCLUSION

The China-India relationship once was among the more hostile rivalries in the international system. Since at least the late 1980s, however, the competition has diminished, although several issues remain unresolved. At this writing, the competition seems to be as much over status and regional influence as it is over substantive concerns, even as territorial disputes linger in the background.

Although the China-India rivalry is not as severe as it once was, this does not mean that relations will continue to improve or that the decline in hostility is permanent. So-called interrupted rivalries are those that end or dissipate at one point in time only to reoccur after a latent period. Gennady Rudkevich and his colleagues have determined that the chances of rivalry recurrence were greatest when the original rivalry involved frequent and serious confrontations and resulted in one side being victorious and the "settlement" was not imposed (indicating an overwhelming victory).[64] The former was characteristic of the India-China rivalry, but with respect to the second part there is no clear "winner" in the competition.

What would it take for a renewal of the most severe form of rivalry between these states? A change in political leadership to ones that have more hawkish orientations is associated with the onset or renewal of enduring rivalries. To some extent, this has already occurred with the ascension of more nationalist leaders in both China (Xi Jinping) and India (Narendra Modi). As the Doklam confrontation demonstrates, minor incidents along the border have the potential to escalate and become part of a broader regional struggle for influence. Thus the potential for rivalry enhancement is ever present, and Paul is correct in seeing no end in sight to this competition.[65] Nevertheless, the two states have shown an ability to manage their conflict short of the use of military force, and Doklam is a recent example. Neither side would benefit from an escalation, and heightened rivalry would threaten many of the economic benefits that both sides enjoy in their relationship. Deterrence, both nuclear and conventional, might also be sufficient to prevent any escalation.

Although a major military encounter might not be on the horizon, there are other forms of conflict that could characterize the China-India relationship. With each country developing advanced cyber capabilities, there could be the frequent use of cyberattacks and probes that is increasingly common among rival states.[66] It has yet to be demonstrated that deterrence can work in the same way for these kinds of attacks as they do for nuclear or conventional military threats. There is also the expectation of gray-zone conflict in which each side conducts military exercises, weapons acquisition, and other activities that will be viewed as threatening by the other side. In this way, any China-India rivalry henceforth might represent a change of tactics away from traditional military confrontation toward new forms of competition as many of the sources of the conflict persist.

NOTES

1. Glenn Palmer, Vito D'Orazio, Michael Kenwick, and Matthew Lane, "The MID4 Data Set: Procedures, Coding Rules, and Description," *Conflict Management and Peace Science* 32, no. 2 (2015): 222–42, http://correlatesofwar.org/data-sets/MIDs.

2. Sara M. Mitchell and Cameron G. Thies, "Issue Rivalries," *Conflict Management and Peace Science* 28, no. 3 (2011): 230–60.

3. Jaroslav Tir and Paul F. Diehl, "Geographic Dimensions of Enduring Rivalries," *Political Geography* 21, no. 2 (2002): 263–86. See also Michael Colaresi, Karen Rasler, and William Thompson, *Strategic Rivalries in World Politics: Position, Space and Conflict Escalation* (Cambridge: Cambridge University Press, 2008).

4. Paul Hensel and Sara McLaughlin Mitchell, "Issue Indivisibility and Territorial Claims," *GeoJournal* 64, no. 4 (2005): 275–85.

5. This area is now called Arunachal Pradesh by India and South Tibet (Zangnan) by China.
6. See Mahesh Shankar's chapter 2 in this volume.
7. A cogent analysis is given in Jeff M. Smith, "High Noon in the Himalayas: Beyond the China-India Standoff at Doka La," *War on the Rocks*, July 13, 2017, https://warontherocks.com/2017/07/high-noon-in-the-himalayas-behind-the -china-india-standoff-at-doka-la/.
8. Bryan A. Frederick, Paul R. Hensel, and Christopher Macaulay, "The Issue Correlates of War Territorial Claims Data, 1816–2001," *Journal of Peace Research* 54, no. 1 (2017): 99–108, http://www.paulhensel.org/icow.html.
9. Jeff D. Colgan, *Petro-Aggression: When Oil Causes War* (Cambridge: Cambridge University Press, 2013).
10. George Friedman and Meredith Lebard, *The Coming War with Japan* (New York: St. Martin's, 1991).
11. See Calvin Chen's chapter 6 in this volume.
12. Steve C. Lonergan, "Water and Conflict: Rhetoric and Reality," in *Environmental Conflict*, ed. Paul F. Diehl and Nils Petter Gleditsch (Boulder, CO: Westview, 2001), 109–24.
13. Nils Petter Gleditsch, "Armed Conflict and the Environment: A Critique of the Literature," *Journal of Peace Research* 35, no. 3 (1998): 381–400.
14. See Selina Ho's chapter 7 in this volume.
15. Ibid.
16. I would like to thank Alisha Kim for the information that follows.
17. The last is actually disputed, as China controls the area that India claims.
18. See Anne Clunan, "Why Status Matters in World Politics," in *Status in World Politics*, ed. T.V. Paul, Deborah Welch Larson, and William Wohlforth (Cambridge: Cambridge University Press, 2014), 273–96. See also Xiaoyu Pu's chapter in this volume for a discussion of relevant regional status politics.
19. Deborah Welch Larson, T.V. Paul, and William Wohlforth, "Status and World Order," in Paul, Larson, and Wohlforth, *Status in World Politics*, 3–29.
20. Colaresi et al., *Strategic Rivalries*; and David R. Dreyer and William R. Thompson, *Handbook of International Rivalries, 1494–2010* (Washington, DC: Congressional Quarterly Press, 2011).
21. A. F. K. Organski and Jacek Kugler, *The War Ledger* (Chicago: University of Chicago Press, 1981); and Jonathan M. DiCicco and Jack S. Levy, "Power Shifts and Problem Shifts: The Evolution of the Power Transition Research Program," *Journal of Conflict Resolution* 43, no. 6 (1999): 675–704.
22. Douglas Lemke, *Regions of War and Peace* (Cambridge: Cambridge University Press, 2002).
23. Deborah Welch Larson and Alexei Shevchenko, "Managing Rising Powers: The Role of Status Concerns," in Paul, Larson, and Wohlforth, *Status in World Politics*, 37.
24. This is something that China opposes, and because of its Security Council veto it can block India from achieving it.
25. Thomas Volgy, Renato Corbetta, J. Patrick Rhamey, Ryan Baird, and Keith Grant, "Status Considerations in International Politics and the Rise of Regional Powers," in Paul, Larson, and Wohlforth, *Status in World Politics*, 58–84.
26. C. Raja Mohan, "Neighbourhood Defence: New Delhi Is Waking Up to China's Growing Relations with India's Neighbours," *Indian Express*, March 28, 2017.
27. For additional examples of hostile interaction and accompanying discussion, see T.V. Paul and Mahesh Shankar, "Status Accommodation through Institutional Means: India's Rise and the Global Order," in Paul, Larson, and Wohlforth, *Status in World Politics*, 165–91.

28. Lemke, *Regions of War*.

29. Palmer et al., "MID4 Data Set."

30. See Xiaoyu Pu's chapter 3 in this volume.

31. Xiaoyu Pu, "Ambivalent Accommodation: Status Signaling of a Rising India and China's Response," *International Affairs* 93, no. 1 (2017): 147–63. See also Pu's chapter 3 in this volume.

32. John A. Vasquez, "Distinguishing Rivals That Go to War from Those That Do Not: A Quantitative Comparative Case Study of the Two Paths to War," *International Studies Quarterly* 40, no. 4 (1996): 533.

33. William R. Thompson, "Identifying Rivals and Rivalries in World Politics," *International Studies Quarterly* 45, no. 4 (2001): 573.

34. James P. Klein, Gary Goertz, and Paul F. Diehl, "The New Rivalry Dataset: Procedures and Patterns," *Journal of Peace Research* 43, no. 3 (2006): 331–48.

35. J. David Singer, Stuart Bremer, and John Stuckey, "Capability Distribution, Uncertainty, and Major Power War, 1820–1965," in *Peace, War, and Numbers*, ed. Bruce Russett (Beverly Hills, CA: SAGE, 1972), 19–48, accessible online at http://www.correlatesofwar.org/data-sets/national-material-capabilities.

36. Colaresi et al., *Strategic Rivalries*; Dreyer and Thompson, *Handbook*; Klein, Goertz, and Diehl, "New Rivalry Dataset"; and Gary Goertz, Paul F. Diehl, and Alexandru Balas, *The Puzzle of Peace: The Evolution of Peace in the International System* (Oxford: Oxford University Press, 2016).

37. Daniel M. Jones, Stuart A. Bremer, and J. David Singer, "Militarized Interstate Disputes, 1816–1992: Rationale, Coding Rules, and Empirical Patterns," *Conflict Management and Peace Science* 15, no. 2 (1996): 163–213.

38. Paul F. Diehl and Gary Goertz, *War and Peace in International Rivalry* (Ann Arbor: University of Michigan Press, 2000).

39. Based on the coding rules, the Doklam confrontation is very likely to be classified as an MID when the data set is updated.

40. Dreyer and Thompson, *Handbook*.

41. Ibid.

42. Goertz, Diehl, and Balas, *Puzzle of Peace*.

43. Now updated through 2015.

44. Scott D. Bennett, "Security, Bargaining, and the End of Interstate Rivalry," *International Studies Quarterly* 40, no. 2 (1996): 157–83.

45. Charles A. Kupchan, *How Enemies Become Friends: The Sources of Stable Peace* (Princeton, NJ: Princeton University Press, 2010).

46. Eric W. Cox, *Why Enduring Rivalries Do—or Don't—End* (Boulder, CO: First Forum Press, 2010).

47. All the analysis below comes from the relationship and peace-scale data from Goertz, Diehl, and Balas, *Puzzle of Peace*.

48. Diehl and Goertz, *War and Peace*.

49. Ibid.

50. Cox, *Why Enduring Rivalries Do—or Don't—End*.

51. Ibid.

52. Manjeet S. Pardesi, "Instability in Tibet and the Sino-Indian Strategic Rivalry: Do Domestic Politics Matter?," in *Asian Rivalries: Conflict, Escalation, and Limitations on Two-Level Games*, ed. Sumit Ganguly and William Thompson (Stanford, CA: Stanford University Press, 2011), 79–117.

53. Xiaoting Li, "The Taming of the Red Dragon: The Militarized Worldview and China's Use of Force, 1949–2001," *Foreign Policy Analysis* 9, no. 4 (2013): 387–407.

54. Pardesi, "Instability in Tibet," rejects an explanation based on party coalitions for changes in Indian policy toward Tibet.

55. Diehl and Goertz, *War and Peace*.
56. Goertz, Diehl, and Balas, *Puzzle of Peace*.
57. Andrew P. Owsiak, Paul F. Diehl, and Gary Goertz, "Border Settlement and the Movement toward and from Negative Peace," *Conflict Management and Peace Science* 34, no. 2 (2017): 176–93.
58. See Mahesh Shankar's chapter 2 in this volume.
59. Owsiak, Diehl, and Goertz, "Border Settlement."
60. See Pardesi, "Instability in Tibet," 20.
61. Victor Cha, "The Dilemma of Regional Security in East Asia: Multilateralism versus Bilateralism," in *Regional Conflict Management*, ed. Paul F. Diehl and Joseph Lepgold (Lanham, MD: Rowman & Littlefield, 2003), 104–22.
62. Kanti Bajpai, "Managing Conflict in South Asia," in Diehl and Lepgold, *Regional Conflict Management*, 209–38.
63. Ibid.
64. Gennady Rudkevich, Konstantinos Travlos, and Paul F. Diehl, "Terminated or Just Interrupted? How the End of a Rivalry Plants the Seeds for Future Conflict," *Social Science Quarterly* 94, no. 1 (2013): 158–74.
65. See T.V. Paul's chapter 1 in this volume.
66. See Brandon Valeriano and Ryan Maness, *Cyber War versus Cyber Realities* (Oxford: Oxford University Press, 2015).

CONTRIBUTORS

Jean-François Bélanger is a PhD candidate in the Department of Political Science and a research fellow with the Centre for International Peace and Security Studies (CIPSS) at McGill University. He specializes in nuclear proliferation, coercive diplomacy, and the role of reputation in international relations. His doctoral research examines the importance of deterrence as a norm and as a creator of reputation and its impact on nonproliferation efforts. He has coedited two books with David Beitelman, *Rise of the Rest? Opportunities and Implications* and *Weapons of Mass Destruction and the New Strategic Environment*.

Matthew A. Castle is a PhD candidate in the Department of Political Science, McGill University, and a research fellow at CIPSS. His research interests include international and comparative political economy, with a particular focus on processes of international economic integration in the international trade and investment regime. Castle's doctoral project examines the politics of international economic rule-making in areas of the international trade and investment regime in which regulatory regimes are relatively undeveloped. He has published in the *Review of International Studies* and the *Journal of European Integration*.

Calvin Chen is an associate professor of politics at Mount Holyoke College. His specializations include the political economy of East Asia, Chinese politics, comparative politics, work and labor politics, rural economic development, and public administration. His writings include "Communist Legacies, Postcommunist Transformations, and the Fate of Organized Labor in Russia and China" (with Rudra Sil), "Made in Italy (by the Chinese): Migration and the Rebirth of Textiles and Apparel," and a book, *Some Assembly Required: Work, Community, and Politics in China's Rural Enterprises*. His current research focuses on Chinese migration to Italy and Spain.

Paul F. Diehl is Ashbel Smith Professor of Political Science at the University of Texas at Dallas. He joined its School of Economic, Political and Policy Sciences in 2015 and helped establish the Center for Teaching and Learning at the university. His areas of expertise include the causes of war, United Nations peacekeeping, and international law. Some of his books include *The Puzzle of Peace: The Evolution of Peace in the International System* (with Gary Goertz and Alexandru Balas), *International Mediation* (with J. Michael Greig), *The Dynamics of International Law* (with Charlotte Ku), *Evaluating Peace Operations* (with Daniel Druckman), *The Scourge of War: New Extensions on an Old Problem*, and *Territorial Changes and International Conflict* (with Gary Goertz). He is the editor of thirteen other books and the author of over 150 journal articles and book chapters on international security matters. He is past president of the Peace Science Society (International) and the International Studies Association (ISA).

Zhen Han is a PhD candidate in the Department of Political Science at McGill University and a research fellow with CIPSS. His doctoral dissertation studies the microfoundations of the commercial peace theory and examines to what extent economic interdependence has changed the internal structure of a rising state, using China as the case. He has published in the *Journal of Social Sciences* and the *Journal of World Economy and Politics*. He specializes in international political economy and security studies, with a focus on economic interdependence and conflict.

Selina Ho is an assistant professor at the Lee Kuan Yew School of Public Policy at the National University of Singapore. She specializes in Chinese politics and foreign policy, with a focus on resources and infrastructure projects. Her book, *Thirsty Cities: Social Contracts and Public Goods Provision in China and India*, is expected to be published in 2018. She is also working on another book project, examining China's plans to construct high-speed railways in Southeast Asia. She has published journal articles and book chapters on China's transboundary rivers, including "Big Brother, Little Brothers: Comparing China's and India's Transboundary River Policies," "A River Flows through It: Transboundary Waters in China-India Relations," and "River Politics: China's Policies in the Mekong and the Brahmaputra in Comparative Perspective."

Feng Liu is a professor and an associate dean of the Zhou Enlai School of Government at Nankai University. His research interests include international relations theory, international security, and the international relations of East Asia. Liu has published more than sixty journal articles in both English and Chinese, including "China's Security Strategy towards East Asia" and "China, the United States, and the East Asian Security Order," as well as a book, *The Logic of Balancing: Structural Pressure, Hegemonic Legitimacy and Great-Power Behavior*. He has served as a research fellow at the Institute of International Relations at Tsinghua University, as an editor of the *Chinese Journal of International Politics*, and as a member on the editorial board of *Foreign Affairs Review*.

Manjari Chatterjee Miller is an associate professor of international relations at the Pardee School of Global Studies at Boston University. Miller works on ideas, security, and foreign policy in international relations, with a focus on South and East Asia. She specializes in the foreign policy of rising powers India and China and is the author of *Wronged by Empire: Post-Imperial Ideology and Foreign Policy in India and China*. In addition to academic journals, Miller has published in policy and media outlets that include *Foreign Affairs*, the *New York Times*, *The Diplomat*, *The Hindu*, and the *Christian Science Monitor*. She is currently working on her second book on historical and contemporary rising powers. For more, see http://blogs.bu.edu/manjarim/.

Vipin Narang is an associate professor of political science at the Massachusetts Institute of Technology and a member of MIT's Security Studies Program. His research interests include nuclear proliferation and strategy, South Asian security, and general security studies. His first book, *Nuclear Strategy in the Modern Era*, on the deterrence strategies of regional nuclear powers, won the 2015 ISA International Security Studies Section's Best Book Award. He is currently working on his second book, *Strategies of Nuclear Proliferation*, which explores how states pursue nuclear weapons. His work has been published in several journals, including *International Security*, the *Journal of Conflict Resolution*, the *Washington Quarterly*, and *International Organization*.

T. V. Paul is James McGill Professor of International Relations in the Department of Political Science at McGill University. He served as president of the International Studies Association (ISA) during 2016–2017. Paul is the author or editor of eighteen books and over sixty scholarly articles or book chapters in the fields of international relations, international security, and South Asia studies. His books include *Restraining Great Powers: Soft Balancing from Empires to the Global Era* (forthcoming), *The Warrior State: Pakistan in the Contemporary World*, *Globalization and the National Security State* (with N. Ripsman), *The Tradition of Non-Use of Nuclear Weapons*, *India in the World Order: Searching for Major Power Status* (with B. R. Nayar), *Power versus Prudence: Why Nations Forgo Nuclear Weapons*, and *Asymmetric Conflicts: War Initiation by Weaker Powers*. Paul currently serves as the editor of the Georgetown University Press book series South Asia in World Affairs. For more, see www.tvpaul.com.

Xiaoyu Pu is an assistant professor of political science at University of Nevada, Reno. His research has appeared in *International Security*, *International Affairs*, the *China Quarterly*, the *Chinese Journal of International Politics*, *Asian Affairs*, *Mainland China Studies*, and *Foreign Affairs Review*. He is a coeditor of the *Chinese Journal of International Politics* and an editorial board member of *Foreign Affairs Review* (Beijing). His commentaries have appeared on BBC and Phoenix Satellite Television and in the *South China Morning Post*. He is the author of a forthcoming book titled *Rebranding China: Contested Status Signaling in the Changing Global Order*.

Andrew Scobell is a senior political scientist at the RAND Corporation and adjunct professor at Georgetown University's Edmund A. Walsh School of Foreign Service. Prior to this, he was an associate professor of international affairs at the George H. W. Bush School of Government and Public Service and director of the China certificate program at Texas A&M University. His publications include *China's Search for Security, China's Use of Military Force: Beyond the Great Wall and the Long March*, and more than a dozen monographs and reports, as well as dozens of journal articles and book chapters. He has also edited or coedited more than twelve volumes on various aspects of security in the Asia-Pacific region, including *PLA Influence on China's National Security Policymaking*.

Mahesh Shankar is an assistant professor of international affairs at Skidmore College. His research focuses on Indian security and foreign policies and the rise of India and China, as well as sociopsychological theories of state behavior in international politics. Shankar's forthcoming book *The Reputational Imperative: Understanding Nehru's India in Territorial Conflict* will provide a reputational explanation for Indian policy in its territorial disputes with Pakistan and China during the Jawaharlal Nehru era. His other published works have appeared in such journals as *International Affairs, Asian Security*, and *India Review*, as well as in several edited volumes.

INDEX

Abbott, Tony, 106
Afghanistan, 127, 128, 130, 221; and
    India, 9, 129
Africa, 117, 121–26, 132n6
African Union, 233
Agni-V missiles, 13, 107, 190–91, 192
Agreement on Confidence Building Mea-
    sures in the Military Field along the
    Line of Actual Control in the India-
    China Border Areas (1996), 40
Agreement on Cooperation on Address-
    ing Climate Change between China
    and India (2009), 238
Agreement on the Maintenance of Peace
    and Tranquility along the Line of
    Actual Control in the India-China
    Border Areas (1993), 40
Aksai Chin, 7, 197, 253, 255; China's
    claims and interests in, 29, 31,
    33–34, 101; India's claims and inter-
    ests in, 29, 33, 34, 35, 36
Amu Darya gas field, 128
Angola, 122, 124, 125, 126
Annan, Kofi, 242
antisubmarine warfare (ASW), 188, 191
Ardagh-Johnson Line, 29
Arihant, 191–92
Armijo, Leslie Elliott, 237
Aron, Raymond, 75
Arthashastra (Kautilya), 172, 179
Arunachal Pradesh: China's interests in,
    29, 37, 138, 147, 255; Indian hydro-
    power development in, 7–8, 147;
    India's position on, 5, 7, 29, 38, 147;
    militarized dispute in, 101, 262
ASEAN Regional Forum (ARF), 5, 14
Asia-Africa Growth Corridor, 4
Asian Development Bank, 147

Asian Infrastructure Investment Bank
    (AIIB), 220, 236; China-India
    interaction in, 5, 218, 247; China's
    creation of, 59, 108, 216; India
    membership in, 15, 66, 180, 223
Asia-Pacific Economic Forum, 58
Asia-Pacific Trade Agreement (APTA),
    216
Assam, 147, 157
Association of Southeast Asian Nations
    (ASEAN), 108, 209, 233; Regional
    Forum of, 5, 14
asymmetrical relationships, 133n7, 139–
    40, 208, 260
asymmetry (China-India), 5, 55–56,
    141–42; in economics and wealth,
    45, 59, 141, 241; military, 13–14,
    37–38, 141–42, 263; and power, 15,
    260–61, 263; of status and percep-
    tion, 55–56, 59–61, 67–68, 142–43;
    in trade, 3, 46, 108, 141, 222–23
Australia, 4, 104, 105, 106, 108, 155, 156
Azhar, Masood, 155

Bajpai, Kanti, 80, 81, 84, 169
balancing strategies, 9–10, 95–111; during
    1960s and '70s, 102–4; following
    1962 war, 100–102; in globalizing
    world, 108–10; hard balancing, 10,
    96, 97, 106, 108, 110, 209, 218;
    internal, 101, 102, 113n48; limited
    hard balancing, 9–10, 17, 96, 97,
    104, 110; and nuclear weapons, 107;
    in post–Cold War era, 104–9; and
    rivalry relations, 95–98; soft balanc-
    ing, 10, 17, 96, 97, 104, 106, 108,
    209, 218; and status competition,
    63; types of, 97–98